DATE DUE

Cross-Border Banking
Regulatory Challenges

World Scientific Studies in International Economics
(ISSN: 1793-3641)

1 World Scientific
Studies in
International
Economics

Cross-Border Banking

Regulatory Challenges

Editors

Gerard Caprio, Jr
Williams College, USA

Douglas D Evanoff
Federal Reserve Bank of Chicago, USA

George G Kaufman
Loyola University Chicago, USA

World Scientific

NEW JERSEY • LONDON • SINGAPORE • BEIJING • SHANGHAI • HONG KONG • TAIPEI • CHENNAI

Published by

World Scientific Publishing Co. Pte. Ltd.

5 Toh Tuck Link, Singapore 596224

USA office: 27 Warren Street, Suite 401-402, Hackensack, NJ 07601

UK office: 57 Shelton Street, Covent Garden, London WC2H 9HE

Library of Congress Cataloging-in-Publication Data
Cross-border banking : regulatory challenges / edited by Gerard Caprio, Jr., Douglas D.
  Evanoff, George G. Kaufman.
    p. cm.
  ISBN 981-256-829-8
    1. Banks and banking, International. 2. Banks and banking, International--Law and
  legislation. 3. International business enterprises--Finance. I. Caprio, Gerard. II. Evanoff,
  Douglas Darrell, 1951– III. Kaufman, George G.

  HG3881.C6956 2006
  332.1'5--dc22

                                                                        2006044622

British Library Cataloguing-in-Publication Data
A catalogue record for this book is available from the British Library.

Typeset by Stallion Press
Email: enquiries@stallionpress.com

Printed in Singapore by World Scientific Printers (S) Pte Ltd

Acknowledgements

Both the conference and this resulting volume represent a joint effort of the Federal Reserve Bank of Chicago and The World Bank. Numerous people at both organizations aided in their preparation and successful execution. The three editors served as the principal organizers of the conference program and are indebted to the assistance of many people who contributed at various stages of the endeavor. At the risk of omitting some, they wish to thank John Dixon, Ella Dukes, Jennie Krzystof, Hala Leddy, Loretta Novak, Elizabeth Taylor, Silvina Vatnick, Demet Cabbar, Julia Baker, and Wempy (Ping) Homeric.

Special mention must be accorded Regina Langston and Pam Suarez who shared primary responsibility for administrative duties, and Kathryn Moran who compiled the information for both the program and this conference volume.

Preface

Cross-border banking in the form of direct investment in physical facilities is increasing rapidly. Advances in telecommunication and computer technology permit more efficient operation of offices both in greater numbers and at greater distances as countries dismantle their regulatory and legal barriers to such banking in order to enhance the competitive environment. But cross-border banking introduces a number of challenges. Cross-border facilities are often subject to legislation and regulation both in the home and host countries. This not only increases the complexity and costs of such operations, but introduces the potential for conflicts between the home and host countries in areas such as maximizing the efficiency of the banking organizations as a whole and resolving liquidity or solvencies problems. For example, it may be that cross-border banking in the form of branches maximizes operating efficiency, but that such banking in the form of subsidiaries enhances failure resolution efficiency. Similarly, growth in cross-border banking has important implications for competition in banking and financial markers as well as for the design and conduct of both prudential regulation and the provision of any safety net, such as deposit insurance and central bank lender of last resort operations.

These and similar issues were explored by the participants at a conference cosponsored by the Federal Reserve Bank of Chicago and the World Bank at the Chicago Reserve Bank on October 6–7, 2005. That exploration resulted in the papers published in this volume. The conference was the eighth in an annual series of international finance conferences at the Federal Reserve Bank of Chicago, focusing on important current issues in global economics and finance. As at past conferences, the speakers and audience reflected the international flavor of the title and represented some 25 countries. By publishing the papers in this book, the important analyses and policy recommendations discussed at the conference will be able to reach a far larger and even more diverse audience.

The authors represent a wide array of affiliations, including policymakers, bankers, and academics, from a broad spectrum of countries and official multinational organizations. Although all the authors are well-recognized experts in their respective areas, the four keynote speakers bring particular expertise as they are either current or recent leading policymakers who helped to shape both the current and future form of cross-border banking. Most of the presenters agree that cross-border banking will only increase in importance in coming years and the challenges that it represents for financial stability and prudential regulation will grow in importance and complexity. Thus, the intent of the conference was to identify and publicize these conditions while they are still relatively small and easier to deal with from the point of view of public policy. To the extent that it was successful in doing so, these papers will make an important and positive contribution to enhancing the safety and efficiency of banking around the globe.

Gerard Caprio, Jr.
Douglas D. Evanoff
George G. Kaufman

Contents

SAFETY NET ISSUES

INSOLVENCY RESOLUTION ISSUES

POLICY PANEL: WHERE TO FROM HERE?

Special Addresses

Cross-Border Banking: Forces Driving Change and Resulting Regulatory Challenges

Michael H. Moskow*
Federal Reserve Bank of Chicago

I would like to welcome you to Chicago and thank the World Bank for cosponsoring this conference. Our partnerships with the World Bank, the International Monetary Fund, and the Bank for International Settlements have enabled us in recent years to discuss some very topical and timely issues affecting the international financial markets. We've been at this for nearly a decade now, and the conferences seem to get better and more policy relevant each year.

The topic for our current discussion is cross-border banking, and to initiate the discussion I'd like to address several basic questions in my opening remarks. First, why is cross-border banking suddenly such an important issue? What is driving the activity? Why do we need to be careful in the way that it progresses? What lessons can we draw from U.S. banking history? And finally, what are the relevant regulatory issues that we will hopefully begin to resolve over the next few days? While I won't cover all of these issues in detail, I will provide some general insights and hopefully set the stage for the discussion to follow.

First, why are we seeing such an increased push for cross-border banking? The answers are not all that surprising, and they align closely with the explanations for the recent consolidation of domestic banking sectors. The typical reason given for this expansion is financial liberation, or deregulation. Suddenly banks are not constrained and have the ability to expand beyond their previous borders. In the U.S., this evolved through a patchwork of state and federal laws and court decisions allowing states to give their banks the right to do business outside of their local areas. Over time there was a gradual relaxation of restrictions, allowing expansion first only at the local level, then to the state level. State legislators then agreed to

3

introduce regional compacts which allowed banks limited expansion across state lines. Years of fragmented, partial deregulation culminated in the passage of the Riegle–Neal Act of 1994, which eliminated almost all barriers to interstate banking in the U.S.

In the European Union (EU), cross-border banking evolved through a number of legislative acts, summarily referred to as the "Single Market Program." The First Banking Coordination Directive, the Single European Act of 1986, and the Second Banking Directive of 1989 created a single banking market restricted only by constraints imposed by a bank's home-country regulator. Since regulators did not want to place their own banks at a competitive disadvantage, the program essentially makes the EU a single market characterized by universal banks.

So deregulation is always given, and appropriately so, as a driving force behind geographic expansion in banking. But deregulation is endogenous. It doesn't occur in a vacuum, but rather as a result of forces that caused the regulatory restrictions to increasingly bind firm behavior. In fact, these forces themselves are not independent of one another, but rather evolve as the others change.

Perhaps the single most important of these forces is technological change. Advances in technology have changed the bank production process, enabled banks to search out new markets, and provided new means by which they can service those markets. I think another factor affecting the progress of cross-border banking is a general realization by regulatory and legislative authorities that protected markets, and the associated market power created by that protection, is simply too costly for the local economies. There is a growing tendency to favor market mechanisms or regulatory liberalization to reap the associated efficiency gains. There is also a realization that the resource misallocation resulting from directed financing or state-controlled banks is simply too inefficient and costly to continue.

With these forces at work, the potential benefits from deregulation and the resulting cross-border activity are numerous. Economies of scale, economies of scope, and technical advances create efficiency gains that can then be passed on to consumers. A greater array of financial services becomes available, with better pricing, higher quality, and greater availability. Bank portfolios become more diverse, leading to decreased risk or a shift of the risk–return trade-off for banks. This diversification can lead to less volatile lending over the local business cycle, since the international presence allows banks to better withstand variability in local country business conditions over time. Credit allocation decisions improve and credit becomes more available. Finally, new entrants into local markets bring in new risk management processes, new methods for delivering services, and new service offerings, creating demonstration effects that allow local firms to replicate them.

But does the research evidence indicate that any of these gains have been realized? While there is a wealth of research in these areas, I'll only highlight evidence concerning a few of the potential benefits.

Using quarterly data from Argentina and Mexico, Goldberg (2002) found that foreign banks exhibited lower loan volatility than domestic banks, resulting in more stability overall in the local credit markets. This is consistent with the position that foreign-owned banks have access to a more diversified, and therefore more stable, supply of funds. This can also result in an additional benefit as it serves as a countervailing force to the local business cycle.

Staff at the World Bank, using a sample of 80 countries, found that foreign bank entry reduced the profitability and improved the efficiency of domestic banks.[1] This is similar to the finding by staff here at the Chicago Fed, evaluating the impact of consolidation within the U.S., where local banks in the affected market respond aggressively to a new entrant by improving their technical efficiency.[2] For both studies, the findings are consistent with the expected beneficial response to a new competitive entrant.

But while the efficiency of other market participants has been shown to increase with a new entrant, there is less evidence concerning the efficiency gains for the parties involved in the merger. Studies using U.S. data have shown that, while mergers appear to have potential efficiency gains, since the acquiring firm is typically found to be more efficient than the acquired firm, these gains are frequently not realized. In fact, even using a more comprehensive measure of the impact of the merger, the stock price reaction, the findings are not consistent with gains being realized for the merging parties, as U.S. bank mergers are often met with a negative market reaction.[3] However, a recent study by DeLong and DeYoung (2006) suggests that things may be changing. Using a "learning-by-observing" model, the authors argue that acquisitions of large complex banking organizations were a relatively new phenomenon in the U.S. when cross-state acquisitions were first allowed. During this period there were no best-practices to enable bank

---

[1] See Claessens, Demirgüç-Kunt, and Huizinga (2000, 2001).
[2] See Evanoff and Örs (2005).
[3] See Evanoff and Örs (2005) for a summary of this literature.

managers to distinguish value-creating acquisitions. Through time, though, this has changed, and the authors find more recent mergers of large complex banking organizations to be value creating with a corresponding positive stock market reaction.

Similar changes may be occurring that could affect the attractiveness of cross-border acquisitions. Berger and DeYoung (2001) analyzed the extent to which parent bank companies were able to exert efficiency control over their affiliates as the distance between the head office and affiliate increases. They found that the parent exerted some control over the efficiency of the affiliate, although it dissipated with distance to the affiliate. A follow-up study,[4] however, found that parental control over affiliates had increased over time, and the role of distance to the affiliate had declined. Thus, technological progress, and perhaps "learning-by-observing," has facilitated geographic expansion in banking. Again, this could have implications for the viability of future cross-border banking activity.

So while there appear to be significant potential benefits from cross-border banking, there is also a realization that there may also be greater supervisory or regulatory problems associated with them, particularly during times of crisis. These potential problems increase as the role of the foreign-owned bank in the local domestic financial market increases, and there are numerous countries where the role of foreign banks in the industry structure is quite significant.

One major issue of concern is the role of the home- and host-country supervisory agencies and central banks. While the Basel Concordat lays out the framework for host/home-country cooperation, there may be times when their goals conflict and their interests diverge.[5] The fear is that this divergence could be greater during crises.

At last year's international conference, Alan Bollard, Governor of the Reserve Bank of New Zealand, spoke about why these conflicts can occur.[6] This was particularly important to him given the dominant role of foreign banks in New Zealand. He argued that conflicts are most likely to arise:

- When home- and host-country authorities have different statutory objectives, such as depositor protection versus protection of the deposit insurance fund;

---

[4] See Berger and DeYoung (2001, 2006).
[5] For example, see Kane (2006) in this volume.
[6] See Bollard (2005).

- When in times of stress, the host authority requests that the parent bank inject additional capital into the bank subsidiary; the home country authority may typically be more concerned about the viability of the parent organization than the sub; and finally,
- When home and host authorities disagree about whether a crisis actually exists. What is considered a major crisis by the host authority may be viewed less seriously by the home-country authority.

In addition to these potential conflicts between home- and host-country authorities, there is an array of issues that could lead to additional complexities in addressing cross-border banking problems. How do the problems differ if the distressed bank is a branch versus an affiliate of a foreign bank? How and by whom are liquidity needs met? How should safety nets be structured? While the Basel Concordat emphasizes the importance of efficient information exchange between the home and host countries, it does little to lay out a framework for the coordination of intervention during a crisis. Should it? Or would this generate moral hazard and create additional costly distortions in private banking markets? Are there payments system issues associated with the increased cross-border activity? Will the increased activity help solve or exacerbate multicurrency settlement concerns? Finally, how will the eventual introduction of Basel II affect the supervision and regulation of active cross-border banks? These are the relevant questions going forward, and I'm sure we'll hear much about these and related issues during this conference.

I should emphasize that attempts to stifle this natural cross-border evolution can generate significant banking and financial market distortions. One only needs to look at the U.S. markets to see the evidence. Due to geographic regulation that precluded or significantly limited new entry into banking markets, the U.S. has one of the most unique industry structures in the world, with more banks, banks per capita, and banks per area than any other country. When we began relaxing the cross-state restrictions, we did it via the regional compacts that I mentioned earlier. As a result, we had money centers developing in areas that would not typically be thought to be prime candidates as financial giants. However, consolidation was allowed to occur in these areas, and it generated a rather unique and unexpected industry structure.

A final example of attempting to stifle natural industry evolution concerns the State of Illinois, which always had rather restrictive geographic expansion laws and waited years before allowing cross-state acquisitions.

In fact, when Continental Illinois Bank got into financial difficulties in the 1980s, the state legislature passed a bill that would have allowed a bank from outside of Illinois to acquire Illinois banks with certain characteristics. Those characteristics described Continental Illinois, and only Continental Illinois. It was an attempt by the legislature to continue to protect local markets, while at the same time realizing the realities of the marketplace.

Again, the goal was to keep "foreign"-owned banks out of the state. But the evolution of banking markets continued, and when industry consolidation did occur, Chicago's larger banks were more apt to be acquisition targets instead of acquirers. As a result, today there are very few money center banks headquartered in Chicago.[7] My point is that the evolution of banking markets is going to continue. Attempts to choose a local champion and artificially slow that natural evolution process will only serve to generate market distortions and inefficiencies for customers in those protected markets. And it will change the starting point for the inevitable industry consolidation. As regulators and supervisors, we need to figure out how best to address the safety net concerns and resolution processes and move forward. I'm interested in hearing your views during this conference on precisely how that can best be done.

References

Berger, Alan N., and Robert DeYoung, 2006, "Technological Progress and the Geographic Expansion of Commercial Banks," *Journal of Money, Credit, and Banking*, forthcoming.

Berger, Alan N., and Robert DeYoung, 2001, "The Effects of Geographic Expansion on Bank Efficiency," *Journal of Financial Services Research*, 19, pp. 163–184.

Bollard, Alan, 2005, "Being a responsible host: Supervising foreign-owned banks," in *Systemic Financial Crises: Resolving Large Bank Insolvencies*, Douglas Evanoff and George Kaufman (eds.), New Jersey: World Scientific Publishing Company, pp. 3–16.

Claessens, Stijn, Asli Demirgüç-Kunt, and Harry Huizinga, 2001, "How Does Foreign Entry Affect Domestic Banking Markets?," *Journal of Banking and Finance*, 25, pp. 891–911.

---

[7]See DeYoung and Klier (2004) and DeYoung, Klier, and McMillen (2004) for a more detailed discussion of the evolution of U.S. banking markets in general, and Chicago markets more specifically.

Claessens, Stijn, Asli Demirgüç-Kunt, and Harry Huizinga, 2000, "The role of foreign banks in domestic banking systems," in *The Internationalization of Financial Services: Issues and Lessons for Developing Countries*, Stijn Claessens and Marion Jansen (eds.), Boston: Kluwer Academic Press.

DeLong, Gayle and Robert DeYoung, 2006, "Learning by Observing: Information Spillovers in the Execution and Valuation of Commercial Bank M&As," *Journal of Finance*, forthcoming.

DeYoung, Robert and Thomas Klier, 2004, "Why Bank One left Chicago: One piece in a bigger puzzle," *Chicago Fed Letter*, Federal Reserve Bank of Chicago, April #201.

DeYoung, Robert, Thomas Klier, and Daniel L. McMillen, 2004, "The Changing Geography of the U.S. Banking Industry," *The Industrial Geographer*, 2, pp. 29–48.

Evanoff, Douglas and Evren Örs, 2005, "The Competitive Dynamics of Geographic Deregulation in Banking: The Implications for Productive Efficiency" manuscript, Federal Reserve Bank of Chicago.

Goldberg, Linda, 2002, "When Is Foreign Bank Lending to Emerging Markets Volatile?" in *Preventing Currency Crises in Emerging Markets*, Sebastian Edwards and Jeffrey Frankel (eds.), Chicago: University of Chicago Press.

Kane, Edward J., 2006, "Confronting divergent interests in cross-country regulatory arrangements," in *Cross-Border Banking: Regulatory Challenges*, Douglas Evanoff and George Kaufman (eds.), New Jersey: World Scientific Publishing Company.

Michael H. Moskow is president and chief executive officer of the Federal Reserve Bank of Chicago.

Cross-Border Banking and the Challenges Faced by Host Country Authorities

Guillermo Ortiz*
Banco de México

1. The Evolution of Cross-Border Banking

Cross-border banking has evolved over time from the cross-border offering of products to the purchase or establishment of subsidiaries abroad. I have had the privilege of witnessing this phenomenon very closely during my professional career as a public official over the course of the last 30 years. My early experiences with cross-border banking had to do with the simplest form: cross-border lending. The oil price increases of the 1970s brought a windfall of foreign lending to Mexico, primarily to the public sector, which — to put it mildly — was unwisely spent. At the beginning of the 1980s, our "fiesta" ended abruptly when oil prices fell and dollar interest rates increased. In the aftermath, the Mexican government declared a moratorium on foreign debt service and expropriated all of the private banks triggering the Latin American debt crisis of the 1980s. We thought we had learned our lesson, and so did the foreign banks.

In the 1990s, Mexico undertook a review of the public sector's participation in the economy. During this period, as was the case in many other emerging-market economies, Mexico deregulated and privatized its banking sector. At that time, we also started removing restrictions on foreign ownership within the banking system, and foreign lending resumed. Some of these foreign-lending funds were diverted into government securities.

In the mid-1990s, we were confronted with what Michael Camdessus, then of the International Monetary Fund, labeled "the first financial crisis of the twenty-first century." The banking crisis that ensued paved the way for full foreign ownership of Mexico's larger banks. Today, our banking system is dominated by foreign institutions. These developments coincided

11

with a global trend whereby many international banks moved from cross-border lending to setting up branches and subsidiaries abroad. This obviously changed the nature of the risks they assumed.

2. What's New in Cross-Border Banking?

The provision of financial services across legal borders, either directly or through the establishment or purchase of local entities, has been around for centuries. What is new is (1) The size and scope of the financial institutions involved, which not only transcends national boundaries, but also goes beyond traditionally defined business lines; (2) The speed with which shocks are transmitted across markets and business lines. In other words, the way in which global financial institutions react to events taking place in one particular country or market speeds up the transmission of shocks across other markets and/or regions; and (3) The potential impact that a disorderly failure of a global financial institution could have on other institutions, markets, and payment systems. These factors increasingly are becoming a concern for financial authorities everywhere. Therefore, I would like to talk about the specific challenges that host financial authorities face when, for whatever reason, their countries' financial sectors become important recipients of foreign direct investment.

3. Why Have So Many Foreign Banks Entered Emerging Markets?

There are several explanations as to why large banks are increasingly interested in expanding their operations through the acquisition of subsidiaries rather than by lending across borders. These include: First, a preference for avoiding cross-border and exchange-rate risks. The foreign-exchange crises and sovereign defaults of the 1980s made banks seek to attenuate these risks by funding overseas loans in the same currency and country where they are exposed to them. Second, the emphasis on developing a consumer banking industry which requires a retail base in order to offer credit cards, mortgage loans or insurance products. Banks therefore have an interest in establishing subsidiaries in order to begin capturing clients to whom these types of products can later be sold. Third, the recognition of the advantages of economies of scale as well as the importance of replicating successful home-grown business lines and products abroad. Fourth, the need to increase size to avoid unfriendly takeovers. And finally, the opportunities brought about by global financial liberalization, including the removal of restrictions on foreign direct investment in financial sectors. For any of these reasons, the presence of global banks, through the acquisition of overseas subsidiaries, has been growing fast in recent years. From 1994 to 2004 foreign participation increased from 10 percent to 54 percent in Latin America and from 14 percent to 84 percent in Central and Eastern Europe. In the emerging-market countries of East Asia (excluding Hong Kong and Singapore) the entry has not been as rapid, but it nevertheless changed from 7 percent to 24 percent in the same period.[1]

In the case of Mexico, the opening of the banking system to foreign investment took place as part of the privatization of the banking sector in the early 1990s. However, at that time, Mexican banks had to be widely held. No individual was allowed to own more than 10 percent of ordinary bank shares, and foreign investment was limited to 30 percent of each bank. With the negotiations of the North American Free Trade Agreement, we allowed the entry of wholly owned foreign subsidiaries. But we set very strict individual and aggregate limits to the market share of foreign subsidiaries. The banking crisis of 1995 forced the authorities to remove the remaining restrictions to foreign investment in order to attract enough resources to recapitalize the banks. Less than five years after the remaining restrictions were removed (1999), foreign banks controlled five out of Mexico's seven larger banks and 80 percent of total Mexican banking assets.

I recognize the benefits that foreign banks have brought to Mexico's financial sector. However, I certainly would have preferred a more balanced combination between foreign-owned and domestically owned banks. As things stand now, we need a more competitive financial system. We also need to recover some of the benefits derived from having widely held ownership bank structures through the participation of minority shareholders in subsidiaries' boards.

4. Benefits Derived from Attracting Foreign Direct Investment to the Financial Sector

The entry of foreign banks has brought about a substantial improvement in efficiency. In Mexico, just to mention a figure, bank efficiency, measured as

---

[1]The *Bankers' Almanac* and publications by national central banks.

the ratio of operational expenses to total income, decreased from 70 percent in 2000 to 53 percent in 2005. Foreign banks established in Mexico have contributed to a greater level of competition in many financial products and services. For example, transaction costs for money transfers from Mexican immigrants in the U.S. to their relatives in Mexico have been cut in half in recent years. We are also witnessing lower prices and better conditions for mortgages. In other segments, such as credit cards and basic banking services, competition has translated into a wider variety of products without a significant impact yet on prices.

Finally, the entry of foreign banks enhances the capacity of subsidiaries to absorb shocks. It is well documented that foreign banks have access to the deep pockets of their parent companies and, therefore, may be reliable and stable sources of funding during economic downturns. There is no doubt that foreign investment can benefit local markets. Nevertheless, it also creates new challenges that have to be addressed by financial authorities.

5. Challenges for Host-Country Financial Authorities

The first challenge is confronting the adverse impact that *regulatory differences* in home and host countries could have on host-countries' markets. The second is the *conflicts of interest* that could arise among different stakeholders of subsidiaries. The third is the adverse effect on *market discipline* and host-countries' capital markets when subsidiaries de-list from local stock exchanges. And the fourth is the need to devise new mechanisms to improve information flows and *coordination efforts* among home and host supervisory authorities and central banks.

5.1. *Differences in regulation between home and host countries*

As I mentioned earlier, differences in the regulation in home and host countries could have adverse effects on host-country markets. We know that all banks established in a particular jurisdiction have to comply with the laws and regulations of that jurisdiction. However, when a bank is a subsidiary of a foreign bank, it also has to observe the guidelines put forth by the parent company and the regulations of the jurisdiction where the foreign bank is established. In general, we would expect the stricter regulation to prevail. Nevertheless, subsidiaries have to consolidate their books with those of their parent banks. In fact, parent bank shareholders follow the consolidated balances, not those of the local subsidiaries. This means that the subsidiaries' business and trading decisions are taken with a careful consideration of their impacts on the parent banks' balance sheets. This situation can have important adverse effects on host country markets. For example, capital adequacy rules usually establish a zero risk weight on local sovereign claims denominated and funded in domestic currency. Nevertheless, the new Basel Capital Accord establishes risk weights on sovereign claims based on ratings provided by external credit assessment institutions or by internal rating methodologies. Although the accord gives national supervisors discretion to apply lower risk weights to their domestic banks, it is very likely that subsidiaries of foreign banks will apply the capital weights established by their parent banks and by their home countries. Should this happen, it will increase the financing cost of host-countries' sovereign debt denominated and funded in domestic currency.

5.2. *Conflicts of interest among banks' different stakeholders*

Global banks tend to centralize their strategic decision-making processes and risk-management practices across global business segments. The centralization of decision-making and the possibility of allocating their capital and business lines across subsidiaries on a portfolio basis facilitates the maximization of expected profits. For example, it is already a common practice to book some transactions where their funding costs are lower and not where the business is originated. Often, subsidiaries close deals in the name of a parent bank. There is also a growing trend to register derivatives and foreign-exchange operations at special off-shore hubs. While these approaches increase the potential of global banks to attain higher risk-adjusted rates of return, they also deprive subsidiaries of some potential sources of income. In other words, the allocation of capital, business lines, and risk among subsidiaries could have adverse effects on some subsidiaries while benefiting others.

It is clear that any profit-maximizing entrepreneur has the right to make decisions to improve his global risk–reward profile. However, when a private firm is a large bank, any business decision that benefits the controlling shareholders but diminishes the ability of the bank to generate value should be a matter of concern for the local financial authorities, the deposit insurance agency, the depositors, and the tax authority. The existence of a series of laws, rules, and regulations to address the conflicts of interest among parent firms and subsidiaries highlights the importance given by authorities in many countries to this issue. I am referring to the extensive legislation on tax issues (and transfer pricing), source-of-strength principles, and the doctrine of the corporate veil, among other things. In the case of large banks, financial authorities must be especially careful to preserve their soundness. The soundness of a bank does not depend solely on its compliance with capitalization rules. A bank's soundness depends also on its liquidity, proper management and ability to generate profits on an ongoing basis. The question, then, is, how can we create the incentives to entice managers of large subsidiaries to put the subsidiaries' interests before the controlling shareholders'? As we are well aware, the soundness of banks cannot be assured only by regulations and strict supervision. What we need are the right incentives in place. One answer is to strengthen market discipline at the local level.

5.3. *Market discipline*

Market discipline refers to the ways in which economic agents can influence the behavior of financial entities as well as the way in which market prices send signals to financial authorities regarding investors' perceptions of these institutions' performance. The acquisition of local banks by global financial entities often results in the de-listing of subsidiaries from local stock exchanges. When financial institutions are not listed on stock exchanges or when they do not have a reasonable amount of subordinated outstanding debt, market participants are deprived of market information. The obvious regulatory response would be to require subsidiaries to disclose the same amount of information as if they were listed. However, the publication of information in itself will not lead to greater market discipline. Market participants need signals — in the form of prices — that reflect market perceptions, instruments to exert their discipline, and the research carried out by independent analysts. The latter play an important role in markets, given that financial information is not always easy for the common investor to understand.

It is true that the shares of the most important global financial institutions are widely held and are thus subject to market discipline. However, the relevant question is whether or not de-listed subsidiaries reap the benefits of having a market-disciplined parent bank. If you are a financial authority in a country where most of its important banks are subsidiaries of foreign banks, you would like to have the right incentives in place to entice local bank managers to look after the interests of the subsidiaries under their management and not exclusively those of the individual shareholders. There are some measures that would be useful to address these challenges. One, which I have already proposed, is to require large local banks to list a percentage of their equity, say 25 percent, on local stock markets. This proposal has a double advantage: First, the presence of minority shareholders in the capital structure and on the boards of large subsidiaries will help to deter controlling shareholders from making decisions that may go against the best interests of the subsidiary. The existence of minority shareholders will also give relevance to the work of independent board members. Second, it would bring subsidiaries close to the eyes of equity markets' scrutiny and thus, increase market discipline.

5.4. *Cross-border crisis management*

Finally, I would like to talk about the conflicts of interest that arise when a global bank fails. This issue was covered extensively at last year's Chicago Fed conference. In the event that a large cross-border bank finds itself in a crisis, the situation could lead to conflicts of interest among the various parties. A similar situation could arise if a systemically important subsidiary gets into trouble. Another situation that could lead to conflicts of interest is if a parent bank tries to prop up the capital of a troubled entity by transferring resources from one of its subsidiaries to the ailing unit or units or between the parent and the problematic subsidiary. Still other conflicts could occur if emergency liquidity assistance is provided. In principle, liquidity assistance has to be provided by the central bank of the country where the troubled entity is legally established. However, when business and risk-management decisions are centralized at the parent level, host-country authorities will naturally be more reluctant to provide liquidity assistance.

The conflicts among home- and host-country authorities will be particularly significant if the relative sizes of the parent bank and its subsidiaries are substantially different. For example, home-country authorities will not be very keen on supporting failed small subsidiaries overseas, even if they are relatively important in their respective host countries. On the other hand, host-country authorities will face serious political difficulties if they attempt to use public resources to resolve a foreign-owned bank. The lack of a standardized set of rules and criteria to deal with troubled global institutions as well as problems arising from the lack of a common or supranational jurisdiction complicates the attainment of reasonable solutions. Therefore, it is very important to devote more efforts to devise ways to improve existing frameworks so that cooperation among supervisors and central banks is encouraged. These frameworks should include full and equal access to relevant and timely information on both a subsidiary's and a parent bank's global position as well as each one's risks. Home-country authorities should not have informational advantages over host regulators unless they are willing to accept more responsibilities in terms of the resolution processes.

European countries, particularly those in Scandinavia, are arranging nonlegally binding memoranda of understanding (MoUs) to facilitate exchange of information and coordinate actions of supervisory authorities and central banks. I consider this to be a very positive step. In order to prove the effectiveness of cross-border MoUs and coordination arrangements to deal with a crisis, countries have started to conduct crisis simulation exercises in Europe and the Trans-Tasman region. It is very important that European and American supervisors, central banks, and ministries of finance start to conduct simulation exercises with their counterparts in Latin American countries where the presence of European and American banks is of great importance. Needless to say, no simulation will ever reproduce the precise features of a real crisis. However, these simulations, involving supervisors, central banks, and finance ministries from home and host countries, constitute, in my view, a necessary step towards the future orderly resolution of a troubled global bank.

6. Final Remarks

The increasing globalization of markets and institutions offers many potential benefits to the users of financial services. However, we cannot ignore the trade-offs of the new global environment and the particular challenges that the new situation presents to host-country financial authorities, especially in countries where systemically important banks are owned by foreign global financial institutions. I have argued that countries whose banking systems are dominated by foreign banks face important challenges to fostering the safe and sound development of their financial systems.

There are no simple solutions to these challenges. However, financial authorities should continue to dedicate their efforts to accommodate the inherent conflicting interests that arise when global financial institutions operate across different jurisdictions. The ultimate objectives are to maintain the efficient operation of global institutions and also to procure the soundness of domestic financial sectors and the orderly resolution of troubled financial firms with due regard to the interests of bank stakeholders (shareholders, depositors, taxpayers) in every jurisdiction.

*Guillermo Ortiz is Governor of Banco de Mèxico.

Remarks on Cross Border Banking: Regulatory Challenges

Eugene A. Ludwig*
Promontory Financial Group

Like Marshall McLuhan who, in 1964 coined the phrase, "The medium is the message," Thomas Friedman has captured a truth about the modern world in his thoughtful aphorism, "The world is flat." What Friedman means by this is that a variety of forces — including technology — have conspired in a way to make the world more homogenous than it has been in previous decades. Friedman's focus is on virtual labor mobility, where workers can be located anywhere and still offer competent and effective service by telephone or Internet.

This insight about a flattening world can certainly be applied to cross-border bank regulation. Bank regulation is becoming more homogeneous. For example, most countries in the world now employ some version of risk-based capital standards, which were originally developed by the Basel Committee for the Group of Ten (G10) countries. Regulators in Asia and Europe have shown an interest in applying bank governance standards of a type akin to those of the Sarbanes–Oxley Act, even though they are not required to do so by international treaty. A similar international interest has also emerged in respect of compliance standards.

Bank regulation is flattening for five principal reasons: First, the fundamental economics of banking are essentially the same from nation to nation and people to people. Second, it is in the interest of virtually all nations to provide for global regulation in order to keep local banking crises from becoming international disruptions. Third, the Basel Committee and other international bodies, such as the International Organization of Securities Commissions and the Joint Forum on Financial Conglomerates, have shown themselves remarkably able to set complicated standards that are readily adopted worldwide. Fourth, international commerce has greatly enhanced the multinational nature of banking. Finally, the fact that large institutions desire, no matter where they are domiciled, to list on the U.S. and London exchanges, means that multinational financial institutions need to comply with the rules of those two exchanges.

However, practitioners in the fields of either regulation or banking know that Thomas Friedman is only partially right when it comes to international banking. Yes, the world is flattening, but it remains quite lumpy. The fact is that for all the harmonization of banking law and regulation, there remain important differences in national laws, supervisory standards and customs. Further, there remains a keen interest on the part of local regulators to enforce even international standards their own way and with their own supervisory teams.

Dealing with this regulatory world that is both flat and lumpy at the same time is an enormous challenge for both banks and regulators. While the Basel Committee and other groups have made great strides, and expended no small effort, to establish global standards that level out the playing field, these efforts have not been fully successful. I would like to focus today on a set of issues that causes considerable concern for both the regulator and the regulated. These issues pertain to the relationship between host- and home-country oversight and, in particular, host-country bank organizational requirements.

1. The Traditional Pyramid Structure

Host-country bank organizational structure has become an increasingly important topic as banks have expanded their product lines abroad. From the bank's perspective, the preferred organizational format is one that allows the enterprise to most efficiently and effectively prosecute its business. Traditionally, many banks favored a structure with a reasonably strong country head who understood the customs and laws of the host country. The country head was essentially the top of a local pyramid, and it was he or she who was a key point of contact between the host-country and home-country bank officers and employees.

This model worked fairly well where banks had a limited product set and the mores and customs of the host country were distinct. The ability of the bank to be successful in the host country depended upon local knowledge and contacts. Accordingly, country heads were frequently local nationals with a considerable local rolodex and ties by way of social and professional friendships with the host-country government.

This pyramidal structure also was acceptable from the regulators' perspective, provided that two things remained true: First, that the local enterprise had enough local liquidity and capital to see it through a crisis. Second, that the local institution had enough financial support from the home country to be operated safely. Organizational structure and personnel remained secondary.

2. The Shift to a Business-Line Structure

In more recent years, at least for larger global banks, the pyramidal organizational structure has worked less and less well from a commercial perspective. Bank products have expanded both in numbers of items offered and in complexity, and they are continuously changing. A local generalist banker in a host country is less and less able to successfully handle all products. And, banks have found that they gain reasonable, if not considerable, operational efficiencies if they do not have to duplicate the same structure of product experts and sales staffs in each country. Further, the product-line organizational structure is believed to markedly improve the level and sophistication of sales. Accordingly, many banks have shifted to a business-line structure, including for their overseas operations, which arguably makes for effective and efficient worldwide distribution of complex and dynamic financial products.

However, this shift to a business-line structure has not been a panacea for banks' risk-management and compliance problems. There are several reasons for this. One reason is that the compliance and risk-management related problems for banking organizations have become increasingly complex, just as operating full-service modern integrated financial institutions over multiple geographies with multiple product lines has become more complex. One way to conceptualize this complexity is to consider it in a formulaic fashion. Irrespective of how the formula is constructed, just contemplating the elements of such a formula is daunting. For example: multinational control complexity = [number of geographies + number of different languages] × [number of relevant laws + number of regulators in those geographies] × [number of product lines] × [number of people selling and/or managing those product lines].

3. The Host-Country Regulators' Perspective

Theoretically, at least, the business-line structure could be compatible with the supervisory concerns of a host country. Yet, from the regulators' perspective, the modern multi-line, multi-national financial institution presents significant supervisory challenges. The host-country regulator often has to adapt rules, regulations and supervisory techniques to new products and product lines. The regulator has to have the specialists who understand, and can thus effectively supervise, new, complex financial products. The host-country regulator also has to determine what impact the parent institution, often located very far away, has on the local operation. And the host-country regulator may well have challenges from a language perspective. For even if the host-country regulator demands that documents and interaction with the institution be in the language of the host country, frequently, useful documents and communications from the home country are only available in the language of the home country. The emergence of a trend toward stricter compliance with the laws and regulations has further complicated matters.

In the face of this complexity there has been a tendency on the part of host-country regulators in some countries to favor, if not insist upon, a return to the pyramidal structure with local control personnel in order to facilitate supervision. This predilection runs somewhat counter to the worldwide trend toward independent control organizations (risk management, internal audit, compliance, etc.) within financial institutions that are controlled from corporate centers so that one can have an enterprise-wide view of risk. I have myself been somewhat partisan in favor of some degree of centralization of risk and control functions in financial institutions. For a variety of risk — (including avoiding concentrations, reputation damage and the coherent deployment of specialty risk experts) and governance-related reasons (including legal obligations of holding company executives and boards), a considerable degree of centralization of a bank's control infrastructure makes sense.

Where both countries try to resolve the tension between host- and home-country supervisory activities by doing the maximum job of supervision with respect to activities of that portion of the financial enterprise that each has the jurisdictional right to supervise (in the case of the home country, typically 100 percent of the bank and its affiliates) — the burden on banks can be heavy. For the bank, it almost certainly means a considerable amount of duplication and often contradictory prescriptions.

The direction of Basel Committee guidance, as well as regulatory comity among the developed world, has tried to deal with the excessive burden, contradictory dictates and occasional conflicts between supervisors by emphasizing the importance and primacy of the home-country supervisor. In theory, where a bank has "comprehensive consolidated supervision" from the home country, there is to be considerable deference paid to that supervisor's decisions and assessments.

In practice, deference to the home-country supervisor under these agreements has turned out to be less robust than many regulators had hoped. So, for example, one large multi-national bank headquartered in the United States, that has made great strides in fulfilling its Basel II requirements worldwide under the careful and watchful eye of its primary U.S. regulator, has found that in at least one major foreign jurisdiction, it is going to have to have all of its Basel work reexamined and re-approved, and it is going to have to pay the foreign supervisor for this pleasure.

These costs and discontinuities discourage multilateral activities by financial services companies, making markets less fluid, less efficient, and perhaps, less competitive. That means that desirable banking products will not necessarily be offered in all jurisdictions. It also raises the risk that banks lose business to less regulated competitors, leaving banks less profitable and less safe and sound, and leaving consumers less protected. And, harkening back to Tom Friedman's flat world, these costs and discontinuities can result in banks concentrating their operations in areas of friendly regulation, and dealing with global customers electronically.

4. Supervising Global Institutions — New Initiatives

The basic architecture of global supervision that the Basel Committee, the Joint Forum, and others have espoused is excellent — including deference to an enterprise-wide consolidated supervisor from a country that adheres to the Basel standards. However, more needs to be done for multi-national financial institutions to avoid the complications that come from multiple regulators, and to strengthen regulation and supervision so that it deals in a more effective way with the internationalization of finance.

I would suggest in this regard that two steps be taken: First, the establishment of an international forum to raise practical problems with multi-lateral supervision. And, second, the elaboration, in more granular detail than in the past, of multi-lateral supervisory principles.

4.1. *New forum*

I would propose that a forum be established, perhaps under the auspices of the Basel Committee, whose mission is to identify and consider the practical problems associated with the current set of international supervisory rules and their implementation. I would not suggest this forum be a decision-making body. Too often, national interests impede the effectiveness of attempts at deciding about individual cases. Rather, it should have the purpose of listening both to industry and government representatives to identify the difficulties in attempting to operate or supervise financial institutions in multiple jurisdictions. Since many of these difficulties are often unintended and problematic consequences of attempts at international harmonization of supervisory standards, the forum would also assist the Basel Committee and other bodies in refining and clarifying standards in ways that improve their efficiency and effectiveness.

4.2. *Principles for multinational organizational structure*

An elaboration of principles applicable to multi-lateral banking should be an ongoing activity. Among those that most need addressing at the moment are principles applicable to the appropriate form of organization with which to operate in a host country. My own suggestions as to principles that should be adopted in this area are the following:

- Supervisory goals should be achieved in the least burdensome and most efficient fashion;
- Home- and host-country supervisors and the Basel Committee should focus on substantive national needs and outcomes from a safety and soundness and compliance standpoint, and much less on form;
- Organizational approach and form used by a financial institution to achieve these needs and outcomes should be left as much as possible to the individual financial institution and to the marketplace;
- Where a particular form of organization is prescribed, it should, wherever possible, be left to the home-country supervisor to determine. There will be, for the foreseeable future, many instances

where banks face local national requirements in host countries that differ markedly from those of their home countries. In these instances, host countries should be encouraged to achieve adherence to these rules through enforcement mechanisms, ideally in conjunction with a home-country supervisor;

- Supervisors should make every effort to avoid duplication;
- Supervisors should make every effort to streamline rules on an international basis so that efficiencies can be achieved. For example, supervisors should emphasize a minimal number of offices where information needs to be filed by a financial institution. Forms of filing and information required should be standardized worldwide as much as possible; and,
- Wherever possible, there should be empirical evidence that a rule or supervisory approach in fact achieves the substantive goal required before the rule or approach is adopted.

5. Conclusion

Finance will become ever more complex. These forces will press for an ever-flatter financial services marketplace, and for more uniform international rules and supervisory practices to deal effectively with that marketplace. But, for the foreseeable future, national norms and needs will stand in the way of total uniformity, keeping the financial world a rather lumpy place. Financial firms must respond to this lumpiness of practice, or they proceed at considerable peril.

It is in the interest of a safe and sound international marketplace that regulators work toward more efficiency and uniformity where that can be accomplished. In this regard, host-country regulators should shift their focus away from rigid forms of governance and organization within their countries and toward substantive compliance with national laws.

Eugene Ludwig is founder and chief executive officer of Promontory Financial Group.

Regulatory Challenges: The Road Ahead

Nicholas Le Pan*
*Office of the Superintendent of Financial Institutions Canada;
Basel Accord Implementation Group; and
Basel Committee on Banking Supervision*

1. Introduction

The topic of this conference is Cross-Border Banking: Regulatory Challenges. I like the word "challenge". The author John Ford had a great line. "We are not lost. We're locationally challenged." "Locationally challenged." That says a lot about cross-border banking both for banks *and* for regulators. If only governance and control systems everywhere could be seamlessly doing their job. If only regulators could be as well.

Many of the more prominent, serious failures in banking organizations have been due to the challenges of overseeing foreign operations. These sometimes have been safety and soundness problems, while at other times they have concerned reputation lapses and were costly. So, while I will focus on regulatory and supervisory challenges and what regulators are doing, I will also say a few words about the banks themselves.

I do not think we will totally tame the challenge of regulation or effective oversight in a cross-border world. Progress is occurring, though more is possible. The aim is to have a greater understanding of real risks, a greater ability to deal with inevitable mistakes and surprises, a greater comparability (the ubiquitous more level playing field), and more financial resiliency and financial stability.

A few caveats. I am going to be talking mainly about subsidiaries, not about branches. However, some branches can be systemically important and some subsidiaries are run much like branches. Again, we must recognize that the stylized assumption of which countries are "homes" and which are "hosts" is not accurate. The biggest homes are also often the biggest hosts.

In addition, I will not be focusing on cooperation in a crisis. However, I think that continuing to build enhanced communication and cooperation in meeting more day-to-day regulation and supervision challenges will also pay off when serious problems arise.

I intend to use Basel II as an example, as it is a main driver of enhanced cooperation among prudential regulators. The Accord Implementation Group (AIG), which I chair, does not have a strong harmonization mandate from the Basel Committee countries. I do not think we are going to see major changes in international regulatory architecture or fundamental changes in responsibilities over the next few years, yet progress in enhanced cooperation and communication is essential. So I think the more bottom-up approach we are following through the AIG is important.

2. Background

While any discussion of challenges must focus a fair amount on the development of policy and rules, we must still recognize that regulation, supervision and risk management in a cross-border context are about people and relationships and behaviors.

Over the past 24 months there have been approximately 191 Basel Committee and subgroup meetings about Basel II. I do not know how many dinners and lunches that is, but it is a lot.

Some would look at the trips and dinners as a frivolous waste. Some of the participants may (privately) see them as an inevitable and inescapable round of challenges to their personal desire to remain fit. For me they are an investment in relations, trust and understanding. These elements are hugely important in building more effective cross-border regulation and supervision. One of my colleagues has referred to this as supporting "the community of regulators and central bankers." When we cannot be everywhere and do everything ourselves, we are in the world of reliance. And reliance on someone you do not feel you know, understand and trust is pretty unlikely. If forced, it can be downright risky. And not every regulator is up to the challenge, nor will everyone meet challenges in ways that are easily recognizable to other regulators. So informal contact is also a key part of building reliance.

There are several trends that are changing the dynamics of the cross-border banking challenge.

2.1. *The changing nature of banks*

It is now trite to recognize that banks are no longer run on jurisdictional lines and there is often no concurrence between legal entities and business lines. So there is a mismatch between the way banks operate and national prudential and insolvency regimes and responsibilities to legislatures. Economies of scale in risk measurement and modeling exacerbate that mismatch. Banks also want to capture the economic or regulatory benefits of cross-correlations between risks at the enterprise-wide level. Certain risk-management methodologies really only make economic sense at a group-wide level. These trends lead to more centralized operations of oversight and risk-management functions. Marketplace success, however, demands material local autonomy and local knowledge for some businesses, and local input into risk assessment. So we have a stronger push–pull between group-wide oversight and local oversight. Bank governance, control functions, and regulators have to understand how well this tension is being managed within the bank.

Many aspects of what banks do are getting a lot more complex. A good deal of this complexity of instruments, hedging and risk-management transactions, netting, and risk transfer, happens as risks are aggregated up from separate business units, legal entities, and countries within the banking group and are dealt with closer to the group-wide level. Much of the bank's funding strategy is at a group level. Tax issues can also have a major impact on how certain parts of a bank's operations are structured from a legal and business perspective.

The good news is that the number of significant subsidiaries is not large for many of the large internationally active banking groups. The bad news is that even previously insignificant operations can create costly surprises.

2.2. *The changing nature of risk and risk management*

I also believe that the relative importance of risks may be changing. I emphasize the word *relative*. Credit risk is still generally the most important, but the rise of operational risk relative to credit and market risk is a key development. In the market risk area more focus is needed on things like liquidity risk (the fact that in stressful times marketability is not liquidity) and more extreme event scenarios. These are raised in the "Corrigan" report and are also dealt with in part in the Basel Committee's recent changes to the framework for market risk capital. Many of these risks are less well understood and lend themselves less to standard analysis techniques. The demands on expertise, in banks and in home and host regulators, are rising.

We also have the risks related to the use of the banking system for criminal and terrorist acts. And we have outsourcing of activities that are outside of the regulatory oversight net in some cases.

How is risk management changing? All of us know that Basel II is much more than a compliance exercise. The same is true for other aspects of safety and soundness regulations and market conduct regulations (including suitability rules, know your customer, and anti-money laundering/counter-terrorism financing). Simply enacting new rules and checking periodically to ensure they are being respected is not enough. Behaviors matter. Basel II, as an example, puts the onus on banks' boards and managements to better focus on the measurement and management of risks and to better relate risks to capital. While the modeling aspect of risk management has definitely increased, risk management is not just a quantitative exercise. Banking is not just about arithmetic and higher mathematics. Neither is bank supervision. For risk managers and regulators, the challenge is assessing how the judgments are being made.

The rise of reputation risk is part of the relative changing nature of risks. This includes the risks arising from the more aggressive expectations of consumers, investors and the legal system as to how they should be treated. These risks can be large and can arise even in parts of a bank's operations that previously would not have been thought of as material to its safety and soundness.

There is also a move to expect banks to be more vigilant in "policing" the behaviors of third parties with whom they are dealing. These trends can add to cross-border challenges — they can bring conflict of law and conflict of enforcement challenges. They bring in new participant regulators to the cross-border arena.

2.3. *The changing nature of bank regulation and supervision*

Partly in response to these challenges, bank supervision and regulation is becoming more judgmental, more reliance based — relying in a 'trust but verify' approach on bank oversight and control systems. I think this trend is generally accelerating, and I think it is a good thing for more effective and more efficient bank regulation. Pillar 2 in the new Basel II framework is supporting and pushing this development in many countries. More commonality here allows more supervisors to more easily share, cross border, information on how they view a bank's risks.

There are also more integrated supervisors, which can affect the ease of home–host relations. We are seeing more peer assessments of regulators against agreed core principles. More *basic* commonality of approaches is occurring, with appropriate variation for national circumstances. Again this makes enhanced cross-border cooperation more feasible.

Basel II is not a compliance exercise for supervisors. Basel II puts the onus on supervisors to focus their supervisory efforts and react to a bank's processes and assessments. Effective supervision is a matter of knowledge and expertise, and we too cannot rely on models to the point where we fail to assess the qualitative aspects of banks' risk-management practices and exercise prudent discretion.

Also, many, including myself, would like rules to be more in the form of principles. One implication, however, is that how principles-based rules are interpreted in different jurisdictions matters more than if the rules were detailed. The judgment issue again.

2.4. *Penetration in foreign markets*

The penetration of foreign banks in countries where financial liberalization has taken place over the past 15 years has become significant. In several countries, the largest retail bank is a foreign-owned subsidiary and foreign-owned banks may dominate the banking market. This situation raises legitimate host-country concerns with respect to their ability to safeguard the stability of their financial systems. It puts pressure on them to understand more about the group-wide bank and the quality of its oversight and controls. To avoid duplication, they must implicitly or explicitly rely on processes in part occurring outside their borders.

Those four changes in banks — risk, risk management, bank regulation, and supervision — exacerbate the cross-border challenge. Host-country supervisors want to better understand what is happening on a consolidated basis that can affect them. Home countries want to better understand how centralized control systems are working in practice in significant offshore operations. Supervisors (and banks) in different countries need to understand more thoroughly how principles-based rules are being interpreted and applied by their counterparts. And the less-well-defined nature of risks that are rising in importance makes for more cross-border challenges. Regulators also have incentives to cooperate and share more information in order to economize on scarce resources.

Remember, effective cross-border regulation and supervision is a lot about trust and communication. You cannot communicate effectively with, much less trust, someone who operates a system not even remotely close to your own.

3. What to Do — Some Suggestions

I have four suggestions on what to do in the short term to make progress.

First, international organizations involved in rule making and standard setting need to make sure their governance and processes are adapted to the world I have just described. Involvement and effective consultation with the range of regulators and industry participants affected is important. In the past, these organizations focused mostly on their contribution to the standard-setting process and much less on their contribution to the implementation process. This must change.

In the case of Basel II, the Basel Committee on Banking Supervision (BCBS) created the Accord Implementation Group, which was a 'first' for the committee. Its mandate is not to force harmonization but to share information and experiences, and thereby promote consistency in the implementation of the Accord. We have strong feedback loops to industry and involve non-Basel countries in a good deal of our work.

Second, we must explicitly consider cross-border issues in rules processes. In the case of Basel II, the BCBS has explicitly recognized that cross-border cooperation has to be enhanced for effective implementation of Basel II. The Basel Committee has set out some principles for enhanced cooperation in implementation of the new framework (high-level principles for the cross-border implementation of the new accord).

While attention is, understandably, now on Quantitative Impact Study 4 (QIS4) in this country and QIS5 in other countries, with the possibility of changes, specific implementation challenges, and timetable issues, I think enhanced cooperation in cross-border implementation is essential if the Basel II framework is to be implemented well. I have been emphasizing the need to not take our eyes off that ball. The principles deserve repeating.

Principle 1

The new accord will not change the legal responsibilities of national supervisors for the regulation of their domestic institutions or the arrangements for consolidated supervision already put in place by the Basel Committee on Banking Supervision.

Principle 2

The home-country supervisor is responsible for the oversight of the implementation of the new accord for a banking group on a consolidated basis.

Principle 3

Host-country supervisors, particularly where banks operate in subsidiary form, have requirements that need to be understood and recognized.

Principle 4

There will need to be enhanced and pragmatic cooperation among supervisors with legitimate interests. The home-country supervisor should lead this coordination effort.

There are implications for all if this does not work well enough. Banks would face unacceptably high implementation costs, and they may react in ways that would reduce the benefits, to home and host countries, of the new framework (for example, by not adopting more sophisticated approaches in local markets or by shifting from subsidiaries to branches). Both home- and host-country regulators could lose out on obtaining the quality of information that they would ideally like to receive to meet their mandates.

Principle 5

Wherever possible, supervisors should avoid performing redundant and uncoordinated approval and validation work in order to reduce the implementation burden on the banks, and conserve supervisory resources.

Principle 6

In implementing the new accord, supervisors should communicate the respective roles of home-country and host-country supervisors as clearly as possible to banking groups with significant cross-border operations in multiple jurisdictions. The home-country supervisor would lead this coordination effort in cooperation with the host-country supervisors. We are making progress in this area.

At this time, many internationally active banks have started their discussions on implementation plans. We are seeing a variety of communication approaches being used. Some jurisdictions have initiated informal discussions that take place on a bi-lateral or tri-lateral basis, depending on the complexity and the nature of the relationships. Others have organized "colleges" of supervisors where the home supervisor for each bank arranges meetings with key host supervisors and with bank management. During the meetings they discuss the bank's plans for the implementation of Basel II, what the bank needs from the supervisors in terms of direction, and what the supervisors want from the banks and from each other. Indeed, AIG members are clearly moving from case studies into actual, tangible implementation planning. However, given the Basel II timetable, this work needs to be accelerated. Not all the work happens in these groups, but they can foster closer cooperation that pays benefits in other enhanced relations.

I believe this approach, strongly grounded in practicality and bottom-up not top-down, is the most effective way to promote better cross-border implementation of Basel II. The AIG started these efforts because we believe that enhanced trust and communication is not built solely by talking, but also by doing. The AIG monitors progress against the principles at every AIG meeting. Going forward, this has to be done by regulators, not by any form of central control.

Third, avoid simplistic changes in "grand design" that are not achievable. Ideally, for example, major internationally active banks would like to deal with only one lead supervisor. This is understandable — but unrealistic. It may be efficient from the banks' point of view, but I know it is unacceptable from the host supervisors' point of view. And many Group of 10 (G-10) countries are both home and significant host supervisors, so I doubt it would be acceptable to them as well.

Let us remember that while regulators and supervisors can do a better job to reduce duplicative work, banks have a role as well. Sometimes local management of certain subsidiaries has virtually no knowledge of the Basel II implementation approach to be adopted by the parent bank. Banks need to recognize that to implement Basel II efficiently, they must invest time in keeping local management and host jurisdictions adequately informed.

Banks should understand that subsidiaries with a significant share of total banking assets or operations in a given market — not just those that are significant in the context of the overall banking group — merit special attention.

Fourth, we must continue to foster practical effective communication. Implementing an initiative like Basel II well does not mean home-country control and host countries blindly accepting in all cases capital calculations done elsewhere (no matter how much some banks would like that approach). Nor does implementing Basel II well mean a free-for-all, with host countries acting totally independently in their jurisdiction regardless of how the bank is organized or regardless of what work is being done by the home supervisor. Neither of these extremes will work, in my view.

I am encouraging home-country supervisors to pay particular attention to the information needs of host-country supervisors especially in situations where the bank is systemically important in the host market. Similarly, I am encouraging host countries to focus on what they *really* need from the home country or the bank about group-wide operations in order to increase reliance and do their job. They may not need everything.

4. Some Next Steps re: Basel II Home–Host Cooperation

In this regard, the BCBS, in association with the Core Principles Liaison Group (CPLG), a BCBS working group which includes representatives from sixteen non G-10 jurisdictions, is in the process of finalizing a further paper addressing the question of information-sharing between home and host supervisors under Basel II. The paper is confined to Basel II implementation and does not address wider information-sharing issues. However, if considered desirable, work undertaken in the context of Basel II may help prepare the way for broader guidance in the future that addresses additional aspects of home–host cooperation.

The focus of this paper is on significant foreign subsidiaries. It covers general principles to guide the information-sharing process and examples of the types of information that supervisors should consider sharing. It suggests how to reduce the chance of uncoordinated requests by different banking groups.

The paper also covers the key role of banks in supporting effective home–host cooperation. It is a fundamental element of corporate governance that local management should understand and manage a banking subsidiary's risk profile and ensure that the subsidiary is adequately capitalized in light of that profile. Subsidiaries therefore need to have or have ready access to Basel II implementation information that is directly relevant to their operations (this information may reside in part in the subsidiary or in part in the parent depending on the methodologies being used).

The paper therefore envisages a menu of options from which pragmatic choices can be made. I think the process of developing this paper, which I hope will be released soon for consultation, has, by itself, built lines of trust and communication.

5. Conclusion

Since dealing successfully with being "locationally challenged" is a lot about trust and reliance, I want to close by reminding all of us of four things.

1. It is good to trust but also to verify;
2. The only way to make people trustworthy is to trust them;
3. When you really trust someone, you have to be comfortable with not understanding some things; and
4. A person who trusts no one cannot be trusted.

Thank you.

*Nicholas Le Pan is Superintendent, Office of the Superintendent of Financial Institutions Canada; Chairman of the Basel Accord Implementation Group; and Vice Chairman of the Basel Committee on Banking Supervision.

Comments on Cross-Border Banking:
Regulatory Challenges

Howard Davies*

London School of Economics

I am grateful to the Chicago Fed, and to Mike Moskow, for inviting me to speak to you at this important conference. I also congratulate the Fed on the choice of topic. It is perhaps the most important issue faced by banking supervisors today. It is also one of the most complex, as economic problems, regulatory issues, legal issues, and politics interact in a potentially combustible way.

The problems are especially acute in the European Union, as a number of the papers prepared for this conference amply demonstrate. It is interesting that it should be in Chicago that the most comprehensive set of analyses of the European regulatory problem should have been assembled. Maybe this is yet another example of the new world attempting to redress the balance of the old. (As long as it does not result in an attempt by the administration to engineer a comprehensive regime change in Europe, this should be a constructive exercise).

A number of those who have contributed to the excellent set of papers submitted have described the problem very well. There are many countries, not only in Europe, where a large proportion of the domestic banking system is foreign owned. There are some places, notably New Zealand, where that has been the case for some time. Perhaps the New Zealanders did not worry about it since their banks were owned by benevolent friendly nations like Australia and the UK (in the past). And of course the New Zealanders have adopted the practice of requiring banks to operate there as subsidiaries.

But in other countries, the problem looks more difficult. In some cases the foreign-owned banks are very large, and potentially systemically significant in the host country, but may still be a very small part of the total global institution. That is clearly the case in some Eastern European countries where banks like Citi and some of the Scandinavians are very active. There is also the particular case of GE Capital which owns banks in some Eastern European countries. Supervisors in those countries reasonably ask whether there is not a risk that, in the event of serious liquidity or solvency problems in the parent, their subsidiaries might not be cast adrift.

A related, albeit slightly different point is that some banks with large operations overseas may have their head offices in countries where the capacity to supervise and conceivably provide financial support to the whole may be in doubt. One extreme example of that occurred in relation to Bank of Credit and Commerce International (BCCI), which was notionally located in Luxembourg.

These problems are accentuated within the European Union where banks have an entitlement to operate in third countries through branches, making it impossible to impose the New Zealand solution. Some of those branches may be of considerable significance in the domestic banking system. That is even the case in London, where Deutschebank, for example, is often the largest participant in the London Stock Exchange from day to day, yet it operates through a branch for which the German Financial Services Authority (BaFin) is responsible, and over which the Financial Services Authority (FSA) has very little formal authority.

A further complicating factor is that bankruptcy and deposit protection schemes are not well aligned internationally, not even in the European Union, where there are remarkable differences in coverage and scope. It is also notable that in some countries, notably the U.S. and Australia, there are differences in the way depositors in country and elsewhere are protected. The FSA has had to draw attention to the fact that UK depositors in a U.S. institution will certainly rank below depositors in the U.S. in the event of a wind-up. That point had some very sharp practical significance in one case I had to handle.

If you take all these points together, they would certainly point towards an argument that host supervisors need considerable powers and responsibilities in relation to institutions located on their patch. My successor at the FSA has made the point that politicians would certainly expect the host supervisor to be able to answer questions about the failure of an institution supervised elsewhere. And, indeed, I wonder whether politicians in many European countries are aware of the limited responsibilities their domestic supervisors now have. When I explained to members of the British Parliament my lack of responsibility for branch operations of other European banks in London, they looked rather blankly at me.

All of these considerations, taken together, lead supervisors to think that, while of course they are in favor of consolidated supervision, and of course they recognize that the lead supervisor of the parent institution has particular responsibilities, they are highly reluctant to see further powers pass away from them to that consolidated supervisor. Indeed, in Europe some have argued that the traffic in power and responsibility should be moving in the opposite direction.

But it is equally important to recognize that, from the perspective of internationally active banks, the problem looks very different altogether. What they see is a multiplicity of different regulatory authorities, all over them — like a rash — in the vivid Australian phase. I spoke at a session on regulatory overload at the Institute of International Finance in Washington two weeks ago. The session was introduced by Cees Maas, the chairman of ING, who began by trying to put the regulators on the back foot by saying that his institution was overseen by 250 different regulatory bodies around the world. This may be a debating point, but it is one which attracts attention. And there are some signs that the regulatory pendulum, which has been moving away from banks in recent years, given the well-publicized scandals and problems, may be beginning to swing back a little. Certainly that is true in the UK, where even Prime Minister Blair has gone on record saying that financial regulators are getting in the way of wealth creation.

The frustration felt by the major firms, combined with the analysis of academics who have pointed to weaknesses in our defenses against systemic crises, have led some to argue for radical institutional change. There have even been cases presented for a world financial authority. John Eatwell of Cambridge has argued for a strong form of world financial authority (WFA), able to intervene in the event of systemic crises, which would be a solution to one part of the problem. But I cannot see the likelihood of support emerging in the international community for such an authority in the foreseeable future.

More realistically, perhaps, some firms have agued for a pan-European financial supervisor. Some have seen this as a separate entity, with a brand new constitution and a brand new office block or three in Brussels. Others have seen it as an addition to the powers and responsibilities of the European Central Bank (ECB). Under Wim Duisenberg and Tommaso Padoa-Schioppa the ECB for a time agued that it could fulfill the role of a pan-European banking supervisor, or indeed be a kind of pan-European FSA, as well as maintaining its monetary policy responsibilities.

I have to say that I see little or no prospect of a creation of a new financial regulatory authority in Europe in the near future. The key point is that there is no current treaty basis for it, so new primary European legislation would be needed. In the run up to the debate on the constitution there were some who argued for enabling provisions to allow the creation of such an authority in the future. Those arguments did not find favor at the time and now that the constitution is now effectively dead, killed off by the no votes in France and the Netherlands, we can forget about it.

There are many interpretations of the meaning of the votes in France and Holland. Certainly they were not manifestations of straightforward euro-skepticism, as we in Britain would call it. To some extent they reflected hostility to the kind of liberal free market Europe which we, on the whole, would support. But the net effect of the no votes is to create, at the very least, a hiatus in European decision-making. The optimists think that this may simply be what the Germans call a Denkpause. Others say it is much more fundamental and that Europe's political elites have become so distant from their populations that the whole future of the European project is now in question.

If the Chicago Fed wishes to continue to solve the problems of Europe, then perhaps next year's conference can be devoted to that more fundamental question. But, for now, we can simply note that the climate for the creation of a new regulatory authority at the centre of the European Union is simply not present.

But what of the role of the ECB, which does have a somewhat vague prescription in its treaty base, which allows it to contribute to the smooth functioning of the financial system?

In fact this treaty provision has not formally been triggered, and on a number of occasions European finance ministers have rejected the possibility of doing so. They also rejected an attempt by the European Central Bank to strengthen the role of its banking supervision committee to take on a more clearly coordinating and leading function. Instead, a committee of European banking supervisors was established, based in London.

Why did that happen? Essentially, I think, because finance ministers were concerned about accountability and control. While, for monetary policy purposes, the high degree of independence given to the ECB is consistent with international good practice (even though a number of politicians, notably in Italy and Germany, seem now to regret having giving such autonomy to the bank), it is not at all clear that the same kind of independence is appropriate for an institution making the decisions which a financial supervisor is required to make.

Finance ministers in Europe, certainly including Gordon Brown of the UK, note that any solvency support for a troubled bank in the end comes from taxpayers, and are therefore concerned to ensure that the central bank, which effectively pre-commit such support, are properly accountable to them.

So I see little prospect at present of the ECB being given a significantly stronger role in banking supervision than it currently has. Indeed if you look country by country, the trend is towards separating banking supervision from the central bank. Not everywhere, or course, but in more than half the countries of the European Union the central bank is not the principal, or indeed even a banking supervisor. That makes the ECB's role even more problematic. Subordination of the FSA or the BaFin to the ECB Governing Council through the Banking Supervision Committee just doesn't work.

It is also clear that, for the foreseeable future again, the European Union and the EuroZone will not be coterminous. At the moment, 12 of the 25 members of the European Union use the euro as their currency. Perhaps 10 of the others have an ambition to do so, though it may take some time for all of them to meet the criteria. But in 3, Denmark, Sweden and the UK, membership is a long way off. I can speak with authority only of the United Kingdom, but I see almost zero probability of our joining the EuroZone in the next decade.

I say this with no pleasure, since I am one of the few supporters of the euro in London still at liberty. Support for the euro in London these days is "the love that dare not speak its name." I simply note that it is hard to see the combination of circumstances which would lead to our membership — unless Mervyn King were to make catastrophic errors at the Bank of England, and I would not bet my shirt on that possibility.

So in Europe we must operate on the basis that there will not be a pan-European banking supervisor, or a Euro Securities and Exchange Commission, or a Euro FSA, anytime soon. So we need to work with the existing constellation of financial authorities.

Within that constraint, what can be done?

Firstly, I have to say that I do not think the problem is as serious as some make out. For example, I am doubtful about the proposition that major global banks might walk away from branches or subsidiaries in smaller countries.

There is very little evidence of that ever happening. Perhaps Argentina is the nearest we have to a case, but the Argentine government did behave in an aggressive way to foreign institutions, and even then the banks were reluctant to cut bait. The reputational damage which would be done to a Citigroup or an HSBC if it washed its hands of an underperforming subsidiary, and thereby created financial difficulties in a small country, would be extremely severe. And I cannot easily see a consolidated supervisor allowing it to get away with that, unless the viability of the whole institution was at stake.

Nonetheless, I do accept that there is an issue about the distribution of responsibilities between home and host supervisors. And the development of what my successor has called "a distinctly hard edged concept of the lead supervisor" in some EC documents is somewhat problematic. Under this hard edged concept host supervisors throughout Europe would cede to the home supervisor any responsibility for assessing the financial soundness, management, controls, or governance in a subsidiary in their jurisdiction. Like Callum McCarthy, I think this is unrealistic. I cannot see that, in the case of a British bank, supervisors across Europe would simply be able to refer all potential questions to the FSA in all circumstances. Any approach to home regulatory powers — or to supervisory consolidation — has to take into account the democratic accountability of host supervisors.

So while it would make sense to try to consolidate and harmonize the regulatory powers available to regulators in different member states, I think it is necessary to ensure that host regulators retain some powers in respect of some subsidiaries, and indeed in respect of branches.

How does one achieve that, and to which institutions would this apply?

It is surely not necessary for host supervisors to duplicate all the actions of the consolidated supervisor. Financial firms have some justified complaints at present about duplication and overlap, which we should take into account.

Here I think part of the answer may lie in the approach the FSA takes to classifying the institutions within its care. From about 2000 onwards, the FSA has operated a rather straightforward, but nonetheless powerful system of classification. Firms are assessed along 2 axes, riskiness and impact. The risk axis, I should emphasize, relates to the risk they pose to the regulators' objectives. In other words, how far do they deal with vulnerable retail customers? How inherently risky are the types of products they are selling? Then there is an impact axis, which roughly relates to size and significance. It is not straightforwardly a measure of size, since there are some relatively small institutions which play a particularly significant role in the financial system as a whole.

It may be that one could use a taxonomy along those lines to determine which institutions should be subject to enhanced host supervision, even in a regime which endows the consolidated home supervisor with a high degree of authority. Of course the impact measure will be different, country by country, but if the host supervisor could plausibly argue that an institution was of high impact in its jurisdiction, then it could similarly maintain that it needed an enhanced degree of oversight. It would then be possible to agree, between supervisors, on the kinds of information exchange and coordination which were appropriate in those circumstances.

The advantage of such an approach is that I think it is within the gift of current regulatory authorities to deliver. It does not require changed legislation, or the creation of new authorities. What it requires is enhanced practical cooperation across borders, respecting the different legal frameworks which apply.

It may be possible, to deal with the lender of last resort problem, to include similar understandings between the respective central banks, about who would do what in the event of a crisis. It would seem to me to be logical that an increase in the powers of host supervisors would bring about some increase in their responsibilities also.

I recognize that this approach is not intellectually pure. It leaves many complex theoretical issues unresolved. It certainly does not work in theory, but there is a chance it might work in practice, and having been burdened with the personal responsibility for banking supervision in London for over 8 years, I have a bias in favor of solutions which work in practice but not in theory, rather than the other way round.

Howard Davies is the director of the London School of Economics and former chairman of the UK Financial Services Authority.

Survey of the Current Landscape

European Banking Integration and the Societas Europaea: From Host-Country to Home-Country Control

Jean Dermine*

INSEAD, Fontainebleau

1. Introduction

Following the 1992 Treaty on European Union (EU), legal barriers to an integrated European banking market have been progressively dismantled. As banking integration proceeds, a debate arises on the allocation of banking supervision and deposit insurance to the various countries involved. Should it be the "home country" (that of the parent bank), the "host" country (that of the branch or subsidiary), or a newly created European authority?

This paper is divided into two sections. In Section 2, we observe that cross-border consolidation in Europe has often taken the form of subsidiaries, not branches. Special attention is paid to the case of the Scandinavian bank Nordea, which has announced its plan to adopt the statute of *Societas Europaea*, a single corporate legal entity operating across borders with branches. Careful attention to this case helps to identify the regulatory challenges. In Section 3, we evaluate the current system of home-country supervision and deposit insurance. Conclusions follow.

2. The Choice of Corporate Structure: Branches versus Subsidiaries

The grand vision of the single European market was to push the boundaries of each country in order to create the equivalent of an enlarged EU-wide national market. The intention was to decrease the regulatory costs, to facilitate entry into foreign countries, to increase competition, and to facilitate legal proceedings in the event of a wind-up of an international bank. However, to be allowed to go freely cross-border, a bank would need to operate within one corporate structure and a series of branches. If it were operating with subsidiaries, the European passport would not apply, as subsidiaries are considered as local banks in each country. The corporate structure choice by European banks is discussed first. We then review a very recent development, the adoption of a new corporate statute, the *Societas Europaea*, which facilitates branch banking greatly. The move from subsidiaries to branch banking is fundamental as it shifts deposit insurance and supervision from the host to the home country.

A striking feature of the process of cross-border European banking is that it often took place via subsidiaries, not branches. In 2003, there were, in total, 563 branches and 390 subsidiaries for banks from European Economic Area countries. More significant for the purpose of this study, is the fact that cross-border mergers involving banks of significant size have all resulted in holding company structures with subsidiaries. This is, at first glance, a very surprising outcome of the single banking market, as it would seem that a single corporate bank structure would have reduced the regulatory costs significantly.

This questions the choice of the subsidiary-structure when branch banking is facilitated by European law. Insights are gleaned from the corporate finance literature, the international business literature, and interviews conducted in two international banks (Dermine, 2003).

The corporate finance literature helps to understand the nature of imperfections, which can lead to the creation of subsidiary structures. In a world with no transaction costs, corporate structures would not matter. However, conflicts of interest can arise between several parties: bank shareholders, depositors, deposit insurers, borrowers, and bank managers. This has raised interest in financial contracting. Although very much applied to the debt versus equity financial structure issue, it has also been applied to the choice of corporate structure.

A subsidiary structure for a bank could make sense for three reasons. First, it would reduce the dilution cost of outside finance if the financiers did not have to worry about risk shifting in a far away and "opaque" subsidiary. Kahn and Winton (2004) argue that the problem of risk shifting is particularly acute when two entities have very different degrees of risk. The creation of a corporate subsidiary helps to insulate a business from other sources of risk. Second, a subsidiary structure could help to exploit the put option created by deposit insurance. In a single corporate entity, there would be some form of co-insurance between the results of the national entities such that the probability of default states would be low (with a lower expected payout by the deposit insurer). With separate corporate subsidiaries, the probability of states in which one of the subsidiaries might default would be higher.[1] Of course, one could argue that, in order to protect its reputation, the holding company would not let its subsidiaries default. The argument is certainly a valid one, but one cannot rule out cases in which the cost of bailing out a subsidiary would be greater than the loss of reputation. A third reason for a subsidiary structure is that it allows a separate public listing which can solve asymmetric information problems between uninformed investors, informed investors, and managers of the firm.

The international management literature (for example, Rangan, 2000) gives additional reasons why cross-border mergers of equals can lead to a subsidiary structure, at least in the early years of the joint entity. The first argument is that a subsidiary structure can help to break managerial resistance to a merger. By committing to keeping in place a local structure, the staffs of both entities are reassured. This argument is of a short-term nature and should disappear after a few years. The second argument is that international firms must balance the benefits of economies of scale with proximity. Proximity is facilitated by subsidiaries. As a local corporate firm and as a member of the local bankers' association, a company can influence its environment better. A second benefit of proximity is that clients and suppliers can sue the distressed firm under local laws. So, irrespective of the existence of a single market, the international management literature predicts that international firms will operate with a mix of branches and subsidiaries to optimize the proximity/scale trade off.

The third source of insights was interviews conducted at ING Group and Nordea. Both banks explain that, in principle, a single corporate entity will facilitate the exploitation of economies of scale. The motivation to keep a subsidiary structure for banks is driven by eight arguments. The first four are of a temporary nature, likely to disappear overtime. The others are more permanent.

A first argument in favor of the subsidiary structure at the time of the merger is to keep "business as usual" and not to change the brand. A second argument is one of reassurance of the local management that key-functions will not be transferred. The reassurance of shareholders so as to

---

[1] In the option pricing literature, in which deposit insurance is viewed as a put option (Merton, 1977), a portfolio of put options on a series of assets is worth more that one put on the sum of the assets.

get their approval is the third argument. The fourth argument is that of the need to reassure nations that they will keep their bank. When acquiring the Norwegian Christiania Bank, Nordea stated that it would continue to operate as a legal entity. A fifth, and major, reason concerns corporate tax. A subsidiary structure is often more flexible from an international corporate tax point of view than a branch structure. In other words, in case of future group restructurings, start-up losses are more easily preserved and taxable capital gains are more easily avoided in a subsidiary structure. Moreover, the conversion of a subsidiary into a branch could create a corporate tax liability. A sixth argument, to be developed further below, is deposit insurance. If Nordea, based in Sweden, transformed its Norwegian subsidiary into a branch of its Swedish bank, it would have to contribute extra deposit insurance premia to the home-country Swedish guarantee fund, while losing all contributions made to the Norwegian insurance fund. The seventh argument for a subsidiary structure is ring-fencing (protection form risk-shifting) and the ability to do a separate listing. Finally, the eighth argument put forward in favor of a subsidiary structure is the ease with which a business unit can be sold.

Of the eight arguments advanced to explain the choice of a subsidiary structure, four appear temporary (protection of the original brand, management trust, nationalistic feelings, and shareholder approval), two stem from the incomplete process of European integration (corporate tax and deposit insurance), but the last arguments are permanent features of business (asymmetric information and risk shifting, listing, and flexibility).

To conclude, it appears that the European bank operating abroad, exclusively with branches, is currently a myth. Operating abroad with subsidiaries, banks are subject to host-country supervision. However, the creation of the European company statute, *Societas Europaea,* is likely to increase branch banking very significantly. This brings a fundamental change, as branches will be supervised by the home-country authority.

2.1. *Societas Europaea*

In 2003, Nordea AB announced its plan to move to a single corporate structure with the use a European Company (formally, the Societas Europaea, or SE). Officially coming into effect on 8 October 2004, the SE is a limited liability corporation. Its formation and corporate structure are partly governed by EU Law (Regulation on the Statute of a European Company[2] and the Directive Supplementing the Statute for a European Company with Regard to the Involvement of the Employees[3]), partially by the law of the EU member State in which it is incorporated, and partly by its articles and bylaws (IBFA, 2003; Friedfrank, 2004). The importance of the SE statute, the expected economic benefits, and the remaining obstacles to the transformation into an SE are discussed successively.

Before October 2004, there were legal obstacles to the transformation of subsidiaries into branches. Previously, legal mergers between corporations incorporated in different Member states posed numerous legal and practical issues. Because of the lack of EU legislation that would determine which country's laws prevailed in the event of a cross-border merger, such combinations have been rare and costly (Friedfrank, 2004). For instance, the transfer of rights of clients or bond holders from the subsidiary to a new legal entity presented a complex legal challenge. The SE presents a much simpler vehicle to transform subsidiaries into branches.

The stated economic advantages of a single company structure are stated as follows: corporate efficiency, reduction in operational risk, transparency, reduction of value added tax (VAT), and efficient use of capital. Corporate efficiency allows the firm to run a business line across countries, for instance retail banking or asset management, without a burdensome double-reporting at country and business line level. More technical, but relevant for corporate clients, a single bank deposit account, instead of the need to have one in different countries, eases cash management. Reduction in operating legal risk comes from the fact that one does not need to worry in which country and by which persons a contract has to be approved, as it can be drawn up by the single SE. Transparency is relevant for the rating agencies and counterparties who will evaluate more easily the counterparty risk on a single entity as opposed to a web of subsidiaries. Reduction in VAT is due to the fact that shared-services center can be established in a branch, not anymore in a subsidiary. This means not only the avoidance of VAT, but also the absence of costly tax reporting. Note that, as the SE directive is not dealing with taxation, there is still some uncertainty on the treatment of VAT, which, at the time of writing, was in the process of clarification. Finally, in the context of the Basel II capital regulation which apply the

---

[2]Council regulation 2157/2001.
[3]Council directive 2001/86/EC.

regulatory capital ratio to the group and each subsidiary, a single corporate structure with branches will avoid the problem of costly transfer of capital across subsidiaries.

However, the transformation of a bank *cum* subsidiaries into an SE has come up against several obstacles.[4] Deposit insurance appears to be the most important obstacle on the way. It raises both a financial and a commercial issue.

The current rule is that the deposit insurance system of the home country of incorporation of the SE, Sweden in the case of Nordea, would be in charge of insurance deposits raised across the four Nordic countries. If a host country offers a better coverage, the bank can opt for a *top up*, meaning that a complementary deposit insurance coverage is offered by the host country against payment of an additional premium. As shown in Table 1, Denmark offers a deposit insurance coverage of Dkr 300,000 (circa €40,000), while Sweden has a coverage of SEK 250,000 (circa €27,000). If Nordea adopts the SE structure, it implies that the host insurer in charge of subsidiaries would be replaced by a common insurer, that is, that of the Swedish deposit insurer system. A financial implication is that Nordea would lose the money it has already contributed to the Norwegian and Finish insurance funds. The reason is as follows. Deposit insurance premia are collected in the four Scandinavian countries until the guarantee fund reaches a certain percentage of insured deposits, for instance 2 percent of insured deposits in Finland. When this amount is reached, the annual deposit premium is either reduced or returned. As the 1994 Deposit Guarantee directive did not provide for exit rule, Nordea would not be able to claim back the money invested in the Norwegian or Finish guarantee funds.

A second issue is fair competition in the deposit market. Since the funding of deposit insurance was not covered by the 1994 EU directive, the insurance premium charged on foreign branches of banks licensed in different countries, but operating in the same host country, can differ. Moreover, the deposit insurance coverage of foreign branches could exceed that offered to local banks. As an example, the coverage of branches of Danish banks operating in Sweden exceeds that of Swedish banks. The third issue is that depositors in one country might be doubtful about the coverage and the speed of payments by the deposit insurer of an other country. To resolve this issue, Mr. Schütze, member of Nordea Group executive Management, announced in June 2004: "Nordea will apply to Internal Market Commissioner Frits

---

[4]A complete discussion is available in Dermine (2005).

Table 1. Bank size

Country	Bank	Equity/ (book value) (€bn, 2004)	Equity GDP (2004)	Equity/GDP (2000)	Equity/GDP (1997)
UK	HSBC	75.6	4.8%	2.26%	2.00%
UK	RBS	52.3	3.3%	2.43%	0.51%
Spain	SCH	41	5.5%	4.3%	1.75%
F	BNP-Paribas	35	2.2	1.69%	0.8%
NL	ING Groep	30	6.5%	6.65%	5.94%
F	Crédit Agricole	29	1.86%	1.86%	1.55%
CH	Crédit Suisse	27	13.1%	10.55%	5.63%
DE	Deutsche Bank	26	1.2%	1.34%	0.9%
CH	UBS	25.8	12.5%	12.37%	8.65%
UK	Barclays	24	1.5	1.52%	1.28%
NL	Rabobank	22	4.8	3.73%	2.84%
F	SocGen	22	1.4	1.16%	0.89%
NL	ABN AMRO	19	4.1	4.09%	3.88%
B	Fortis[a]	14	1.9	2.27%	1.33%
S	Nordea	12.4	4.5%	na	na
B	KBC	12	4.48	2.85%	1.28%
U.S.	Bank of America	88.5	0.91%	0.59%	0.24%
U.S.	Citigroup	97.3	1%	0.75%	0.5%

[a]In the case of the Belgian-Dutch Fortis, the ratio is equity to the sum of GDPs from Belgium and the Netherlands.
Source: Thomson Analytics, author's calculations.

Bolkenstein for a 'grandfather clause' for the 1994 Directive to exempt SE formed by the merger of existing banks in different countries from the home-country requirement for deposit guarantees and thereby simply continue in local schemes" (Nordea, 2004). A response by the European Commission is expected, and it is not clear what it will be, but a grandfathering rules would take us back to the situation before the 1994 Deposit Guarantee Directive, time when all deposits were insured at the host-country domestic level. Its home-country format was adopted to ensure a matching of responsibility and accountability between deposit insurance and bank supervision (Baltensperger and Dermine, 1987). If the Swedish supervisors have the home-country control task of supervising the whole Scandinavian group Nordea, they should be in charge of providing the deposit insurance scheme. Two different logics are at stake. A business logic that favors a single corporate entity to minimize the regulatory/supervisory costs and risks, as well as proximity to the clients with deposit insurance provided by the local host country, and an accountability logic that recommends allocating supervisory power to the deposit insurer.

Although the commercial logic is understandable, we favor the accountability logic. As the quality of banking supervision is fundamental to the stability of banking systems, the country in charge of supervision should bear the cost (deposit insurance or bailing-out) resulting from poor supervision. In reverse, as in the case of the insurance industry, any insurer would want to control the risk being taken. These arguments lead to accountability and the matching of supervision and deposit insurance. Supervision and deposit insurance could take place at the home-country level (the current system under the 1994 directive), at the host-country level, or at the European Union level. This core policy issue raised by cross-border European banking is discussed next.

3. European Banking Integration, Home vs. Host Supervision

Market failures (Diamond and Dybvig, 1983) explain the introduction of banking regulations and the creation of safety nets to guarantee the stability of banking markets. These have taken the form of deposit insurance, lender-of-last-resort interventions, and public (Treasury-led) bailouts. Deposit insurance funds are unlikely to contribute much to reducing systemic risk because they cover small deposits only. Runs are likely to be initiated by large firms or financial institutions. Therefore, lender-of-last-resort interventions by central banks or public bail out remain the most likely tools in order to avoid bank runs and systemic crises. European banking history shows that public bail out is most often the case, given the need to call on tax-payers to finance credit losses (Goodhart, and Schoenmaker, 1993; Goodhart, 2003a,b).

In the context of cross-border European banking, three specific issues are identified These issues concern, successively, (1) the presence of cross-border spillover effects; (2) the financial ability of some countries to deal with bailout costs and large and complex financial institutions; and (3) the ability to reimburse depositors rapidly in case of bank closure. A discussion of the adequacy of current EU institutional structure follows.

3.1. *Cross-border spillovers*

The first and main issue concern cross-border spillovers and the fear that the provision of financial stability (a public good) by national authorities might not be optimal. Four types of potential cross-border spillovers can be identified: (1) cross-border cost of closure; (2) cross-border effects of shocks to banks' equity; (3) cross-border transfer of assets; and (4) cross-border effects on the value of the deposit insurance liability.

Cross-border cost of closure. Imagine that a foreign bank buys a Dutch bank, and convert it into a branch. According to EU rule on home-country control, the Dutch branch would be supervised by the authority of the foreign parent. However, Dutch authorities remain in charge of financial stability in the Netherlands. The Dutch treasury could be forced to bail it out for reasons of internal stability, but would not have the right to supervise the branch of a foreign bank because of home-country control. Since the lender-of-last-resort and the treasury will be concerned primarily with their domestic markets and banks operating domestically, and since they will bear the costs of a bailout, it is legitimate for the insurers to keep some supervisory power on all institutions (branches and subsidiaries) operating domestically. In other words, home-country control has to be complemented by some form of host control as long as the cost of bailing out remains domestic. This positions appears to have been partly recognized by the European Commission which states that "in emergency situations the host-country supervisor may — subject to ex-post Commission control — take any precautionary measures" (Walkner and Raes, 2005, p. 37).

Cross-border effects of shocks to banks' equity. Peek and Rosengren (2000) demonstrated the impact on the real U.S. economy of a drop in the equity of Japanese banks, resulting from the Japanese stock market collapse in the 1990s. The transmission channel runs through a reduction in the supply of bank credit. Since in a branch-multinational bank, the home country will control solvency (through policy on loan-loss provisioning and validation of probability of default in the Basel II framework), it could have an impact on the real economy of the foreign country.[5]

---

[5]The Basel Committee on Banking Supervision (2003) discusses the respective role of host and home country in validation of probability of default (PDs). It calls for adequate cooperation between host and home authorities, and a lead role for the home-country authority. In the case of Nordea, the Swedish supervisory authority will have the final control of PDs across the group.

Cross-border effects of transfer of assets. In a subsidiary-type multinational, in which the host country retains supervision of the subsidiary, there could be a risk that the home country colludes with the parent bank to transfer assets to the parent bank This risk has been discussed in the countries of Central and Eastern Europe (Goldberg *et al.*, 2004).

Cross-border effects on deposit insurance. The general argument is related to diversification of risks in a branch-based multinational, which, because of co-insurance, reduces the value of the put option granted by deposit insurance (Repullo 2001; Dermine, 2003). There is an additional dynamic consideration to take into account. A multinational bank could be pleased with its overall degree of diversification, while each subsidiary could become very specialized in local credit risk. This implies that banks in a given country could find themselves increasingly vulnerable to idiosyncratic shock. One could argue that, for reasons of reputation, the parent company will systematically bailout the subsidiaries as if they were branches. This could be true in many cases, but there will be cases where the balance of financial costs versus reputation costs may not be so favorable.

Cross-border spillovers raise the question of whether coordination of national intervention will be optimal (Freixas, 2003). This will be discussed in our assessment of the European institutional framework.

3.2. *Bailing out costs: Too big? Too complex?*

A second issue is that the bailout of a large bank could create a very large burden for the Treasury or deposit insurance system of a single country. To assess the potential cost of a bail out, we report in Table 1 the level of equity (book value) of seventeen European banks as a percentage of the gross domestic product (GDP) of the home country. Not surprisingly, the highest figures are found mostly in small countries, Belgium, the Netherlands, Sweden, and Switzerland. The 2004 equity-to-GDP ratio is 12.5 percent for the United Bank of Switzerland and 4.5 percent for Nordea, as compared to 1.2 percent for Deutsche Bank. For the sake of comparison, the equity of Bank of America and Citigroup represents, respectively, 0.91 percent and 1 percent of U.S. GDP. Over the years 1997 to 2004, one observes a marked increase in that ratio, highlighting the impact of consolidation. If one takes as a reference point the fact that the bail out of Crédit Lyonnais has cost the French taxpayers twice the book value of its 1991 equity (admittedly, an arbitrary case), the cost of bailing out the largest Swiss bank could amount to 24 percent of Swiss GDP, as compared to 2.7 percent of German GDP in the case of a Deutsche Bank scenario.

3.3. *Freeze of deposits*

A third issue relates to the real costs incurred through bank failures. As the financial distress cases of the major Swedish banks showed in the early 1990s, it appears very difficult to put a large bank into liquidation. The issue is not so much the fear of a domino effect, whereby the failure of a large bank would create the failure of many smaller ones — strict analysis of counterparty exposures has reduced substantially the risk of a domino effect. The fear is, rather, that the need to close a bank for several months to value its illiquid assets would freeze a large part of its deposits and savings, causing a significant negative effect on national consumption. Kaufmann and Seelig (2002) and Demirgüç-Kunt *et al.* (2005) document the timing of the availability of deposits in the case of a winding up. This is reported in Table 2. In most European countries, insured deposits could be frozen for up to three months. The need to scrutinize more carefully the bankruptcy process for large financial institutions appears timely as a major restructuring trend has reduced the number of banks in a number of European countries to a very few large ones.

Three cross-border banking issues related to financial stability have been analyzed: cross-border spillover effects, size and complexity of bail out, and freeze of deposits. Let us now review the adequacy of the current EU institutional structure.

3.4. *Adequacy of EU institutions*

Accepting the accountability principle, according to which banking supervision, deposit insurance, and bailing-out should be allocated to the same country, it appears that, in European banking, there are three ways to allocate banking supervision: to the host state, to the home country, or to a European entity. The pros and cons or the three approaches are reviewed.

In the host-state approach, multinational banks operate with a subsidiary structure. The national central bank retain control on banking supervision,

Table 2. Deposit insurance systems in EU, 2005

Country	Coverage (euro, 2005)	Funds Availability (average time)
Austria	20	3 Mo
Belgium	20	12 Mo
Denmark	Dkr 300,000 (ca 40,000)	3 Mo
Finland	25	
France	70	na
Germany	Official: 90% of deposits up to maximum euro 20,000) Private: 30% of bank's equity	
Greece	20	3 Mo
Ireland	(20,000 ; 90%)	
Italy	103	
Luxembourg	20	3 Mo
Netherlands	20	3 Mo
Norway	NOK 2,000,000 (ca euro 238,000)	1 Mo
Portugal	25	
Spain	20	3 Mo
Sweden	SEK 250,000 (ca euro 27,000)	
United Kingdom	100% of £ 2000 33,000 +90% of next £	6 Mo
Cyprus	€20,000	na
Czech Rep	€25,000 ; 90%)	3 Mo
Estonia	€12,782 (2007: €20,000)	9 Mo
Hungary	€24,300 ; 90%	3 Mo
Latvia	€9,000 (2008: 20,000)	na
Lithuania	€14,481 (2008: 20,000)	3 Mo
Malta	€20,000 (90%)	na
Poland	€22,500	4 Mo
Slovakia	€20,000 (90%)	3 Mo
Slovenia	€21,267	na

Source: Kaufman and Seelig (2002), Demirgüç-Kunt *et al.* (2005).

deposit insurance, and bailout.[6] As discussed above in the European banking context, this system suffers from four drawbacks. First, it does not allow

[6]It must be observed that the host-country approach is often applied in Europe when many banks operate abroad with subsidiaries.

banks to realize fully the operating benefits expected from branch banking. These benefits were defined in the case of Nordea. Second, a subsidiary structure contributes to the creation of large and complex financial institution (LCFI). Subject to different bankruptcy proceedings, the closure of a large international bank would become very complex. In a branch structure, the European directive on winding up would be applicable, subjecting the bankruptcy proceedings of one country. Third, the resolution of a crisis could be hampered, as discussed above, by problems linked to transfer of assets from subsidiaries to the parent, or to problem of sharing of information. It appears that a host-country-based system would not allow banks to realize fully the expected benefits of European integration.

The second system, the home-country approach, currently applicable to cross-border branches in the European Union, suffers from two drawbacks. The first is that small European countries, such as Sweden, Belgium, Switzerland, or the Netherlands, may find it difficult to bear the cost of the bailout of a large international bank. European funding might be needed. The second is related to the cross-border spillover effects. The decision to close a bank could affect other countries. In principle, cooperation among countries could take place in such a situation, but one can easily imagine that conflicts of interest between countries on the decision to close a bank will arise, and that the sharing of the bailing out costs among countries will not be simple (Schoenmaker and Oosterloo, 2004). These conflicts of interest could, at times, even limit the cross-border exchange of information among regulators. In May 2005, it was announced that an emergency plan for dealing with a financial crisis had been agreed by the European Union finance ministers, central bankers and financial regulators. A Memorandum of Understanding among the 25 EU members, which should facilitate the exchange of information, will be tested next year with a full scale simulation of a financial crisis (FT, 16 May 2005).

4. Conclusion

The recent acceleration of European banking integration and the move to branch-banking questions the adequacy of the home-country approach in the future. Goodhart (2003b) argued that a European supervisory agency cannot exist as long as the cost of the bailing-out is borne by domestic authorities, with reference to a British saying "He who pays the piper calls the tune." There is no disagreement with this accountability principle, but the recommendation to move banking supervision, deposit insurance, and bailing-out to the EU is motivated first by the fact that, de facto, the bailout of large banks from small countries will be borne by European taxpayers, and, second, that spillover effects demand a coordinated resolution. A discussion of cross-border bailout will turn rapidly into an issue of taxpayers' money and into a constitutional debate. A discussion on the preference of citizens to define the border of the nation at the country or European level cannot and should not be avoided. It will guide the choice among host country or EU-wide control of international banks.

References

Baltensperger, E. and J. Dermine, 1987, "Banking Deregulation in Europe," *Economic Policy*, 4, pp. 63–109.

Basel Committee on Banking Supervision, 2003, "High-Level Principles for the Cross-border Implementation of the New Accord," August, Basel, pp. 1–7.

Brealey, R.A. and M. Habib, 1996, "Using Project Finance to Fund Infrastructure Investments," *Journal of Applied Corporate Finance*, 9(3), pp. 25–38.

Demirgüç-Kunt, A., B. Karacaovali, and L. Laeven, 2005, "Deposit Insurance around the World: A Comprehensive Database," WPS 3628, World Bank, pp. 1–59.

Dermine, J., 2003, "European Banking, Past, Present, and Future," in *The Transformation of the European Financial System* (Second ECB Central Banking Conference), V. Gaspar, P. Hartmann, and O. Sleijpen (eds.), Frankfurt: ECB.

Dermine, J., 2005, "European Banking Integration, Don't Put the Cart before the Horse," mimeo, INSEAD, pp. 1–58.

Diamond, D. and P. Dybvig, 1983, "Bank Runs, Deposit Insurance, and Liquidity," *Journal of Political Economy*, 91, pp. 401–419.

Esty, B., 1999, "Petrozuata: A Case Study of the Effective Use of Project Finance," *Journal of Applied Corporate Finance*, 12(3), pp. 26–42.

Freixas, X., 2003, "Crisis Management in Europe," in *Financial Supervision in Europe*, J. Kremers, D. Schoenmaker, and P. Wierts (eds.), Cheltenham: Edward Elgar, pp. 102–119.

Friedfrank, 2004, "The Societas Europaea, Thirty Years Later," pp. 1–15.

Goldberg, L., R. Sweeney, and C. Wihlborg, 2005, "From Subsidiary to Branch Organization of International Banks: New Challenges and Opportunities for Regulators", mimeo, pp. 1–24.

Goodhart, C. and D. Schoenmaker, 1993, "Institutional Separation Between Supervisory and Monetary Agencies," LSE Financial Markets Group, No. 52, pp. 1–30.

Goodhart, C., 2003a, "Panel Discussion," in *Second ECB Banking Conference The Transformation of the European Financial System*, V. Gaspar, P. Hartmann, and O. Sleipen (eds.), ECB.

Goodhart, C., 2003b, "The Political Economy of Financial Harmonization in Europe," in *Financial Supervision in Europe*, J. Kremers, D. Schoenmaker, and P. Wierts (eds.), Cheltenham: Edward Elgar, pp. 129–138.

International Bureau of Fiscal Documentation, 2003, "Survey on the Societas Europaea," pp. 1–78.

Kahn, C. and A. Winton, 2004, "Moral Hazard and Optimal Subsidiary Structure for Financial Institutions," *Journal of Finance*, 59(6), pp. 2531–2576.

Kaufman, G.G. and S.A. Seelig, 2002, "Post-Resolution Treatment of Depositors at Failed Banks: Implications for the Severity of Banking Crises, Systemic Risk, and Too-Big-To-Fail," *Economic Perspective, Federal Reserve Bank of Chicago* (formerly WP 2000-16), pp. 27–41.

Kremers, J., D. Schoenmaker, and P. Wierts, 2003, *Financial Supervision in Europe*, Edward Elgar, Cheltenham: United Kingdom.

Nordea, 2004, "Pioneering the Move Towards a European Company," press release, 23 June (www.nordea.com).

Peek, J. and E. Rosengren, 2000, "Collateral Damage: Effects of the Japanese Banking Crisis on Real Activity in the United States," *American Economic Review*, 90(1), pp. 30–45.

Rangan, S., 2000, "Seven Myths to Ponder Before Going Global," in *Mastering Strategy*, London, Pearson Education, pp. 119–124.

Repullo, R., 2001, "A Model of Takeovers of Foreign Banks," *Spanish Economic Review*, 3, pp. 1–21.

Schoenmaker, D. and S. Oosterloo, 2004, "Cross-border Issues in European Financial Supervision," in *The Structure of Financial Regulation*, D. Mayes and G. Wood (eds.), London: Routledge.

Walkner, C. and J.P. Raes, 2005, "Integration and Consolidation in EU Banking, an Unfinished Business," *European Economy*, 226, April, pp. 1–48.

Jean Dermine is a professor of banking and finance at the Institut Européen d'Adminstration de Affaires (INSEAD) in Fontainebleau, France. The author is most grateful for insightful discussions with L.-O. Andreasson, P. Schütze and K. Suominen of Nordea, M. Massa (INSEAD), D. Schoenmaker (Dutch Ministry of Finance) and to P. Hartmann (ECB) for earlier discussions on related issues.

Risks in U.S. Bank International Exposures

Nicola Cetorelli*
Federal Reserve Bank of New York

Linda S. Goldberg
Federal Reserve Bank of New York and National Bureau of Economic Research

1. Introduction

U.S. banks carry substantial exposures to foreign markets, occurring through cross-border activities, through the local activities of their subsidiaries or branches, and through positions they take in derivatives markets. The amounts and forms of these exposures have evolved dramatically over time, as have the associated risks. In this paper, we focus on this evolution and, of particular interest, on the differences in exposures across types of banks, specifically very large banks versus smaller ones. We contrast the risks in these exposures across respective types of U.S. banks and show how these risks and their capitalization have changed over time. Such differences are the result of the diverse strategies pursued (or perhaps simply attainable) by large and small banks in expanding their exposure in countries characterized by varying risk profiles.

The paper looks at this set of risk issues, taking the perspective of the home country banks. Many studies on other home country and host country themes are explored elsewhere (Bank for International Settlements, 2004; Hawkins and Mihaliek, 2001; Goldberg, 2005; and Litan *et al.*, 2001). Riskiness of positions and associated bank capital reserves, the focus of our paper, has been established as centrally important for financial system stability in Basel II.

Our analysis begins with detailed data contained in quarterly reports filed by U.S. banks or bank holding companies as part of the bank supervisory process. Each reporting bank provides a country-by-country delineation of its foreign claims[1] and of the form of these claims, i.e. whether they are cross-border, extended by their local affiliates, or valuations of derivative positions held. The report also contains some information on maturity composition and broad categories of recipients of U.S. claims by destination market, distinguishing borrowers among foreign banks, public entities or private sector ones.

Houpt (1999) and Palmer (2000) initially used these data to examine trends over the 1980 and early to mid-1990s. Houpt provided an especially clear comparison of different concepts of risk embedded in U.S. bank foreign exposures. Goldberg (2002, 2005) provided a perspective on key trends in this data and the underlying reporting banks. U.S. banks engaged in international lending have become more diverse since the 1980s, with fewer banks overall, and the remaining banks increasingly polarized in terms of size and portfolio allocations. Starting from highs of 185 reporting banks in the mid-1980s, the number of U.S. banks with foreign exposures declined to 140 by the mid-1990s and further declined to 71 banks in 2004. In the 1980s banks were broadly distributed across small, medium, and large asset ranges. By 2004 the distribution was more bimodal.

A few very large banks increasingly dominate overall external claims of U.S. banks. By the late 1990s, many of the other U.S. banks reporting foreign exposures were smaller banks with a strong focus on European and Latin American markets. Lending by the smaller banks, especially with respect to Latin American and Asian markets, was more volatile than the lending by larger banks, a pattern we also observe with the additional years of data reported in the present paper.[2]

In this paper, we extend this analysis, and highlight a number of important risk-related features of U.S. bank foreign exposures. First, despite consolidation in the number of reporting banks, overall exposure has continued to grow. The trend is driven by the growth in foreign exposures of a small number of money center banks (MCBs).

The country composition of total foreign exposure has been fluctuating over time. Especially for MCBs, there has been a shift in recent years away from Asia and the Middle East and towards positions in the "safest" countries — where degrees of safety or riskiness of countries are proxied by

---

[1]This process also informs the Federal Deposit Insurance Corporation and state banking regulators. The use of the term "U.S. banks" in this paper generally includes U.S. owned banks and U.S. subsidiaries of foreign banks.

[2]For details from the host-country perspective, see Crystal, Dages, and Goldberg (2001).

Fitch ratings — or towards less risky forms of exposure. Honing in on the geographical composition of exposure, we highlight the increasing importance of industrialized Europe for the average MCB and the changing role of Latin America, after significant withdrawals in the previous decade. Interestingly, the recent run up in Latin American exposure for the average MCB was achieved mainly as a result of a significant increase in local claims.

We present analysis of the distribution of transfer risk across investment grade and speculative grade countries over time, and differences across MCBs and non-MCBs. Exposure to the riskiest countries has been trending down for MCBs. This trend is not observable for the average non-MCB, which has a much larger relative transfer risk exposure in speculative grade countries than the average MCB.

When paired with an analysis of these positions relative to bank-specific assets and capital, we show that while levels of foreign exposure are increasing, exposure as a share of total bank assets has been declining recently for MCBs and, to a lesser extent, non-MCBs. With capital to asset ratios rising for average banks, the result is that foreign exposure as a fraction of banks' equity capital is less than 200 percent for non-MCBs, versus over 500 percent for MCBs. On average, only MCBs have increased their foreign exposure's weight on banks' equity capital in recent years. Simultaneously, these banks have reduced the incidence of transfer risk and raised the share of investment grade countries in their international exposures.

The body of this paper is divided into three sections. Section 2 discusses the broad patterns in U.S. bank foreign exposure data, and shows the composition of these exposures by type, meaning cross-border or locally generated, and geography. Section 3 explores the risk features of these exposures, showing implied transfer risk and combining the exposures with measures of country risk. Section 4 offers concluding remarks.

2. Broad Patterns in U.S. Bank Foreign Exposures

A Federal Financial Institutions Examinations Council (FFIEC) report 009 must be filed by every U.S. chartered insured commercial bank in the 50 States of the United States, the District of Columbia, Puerto Rico, and U.S. territories and possessions, provided that the bank has, on a fully consolidated bank basis, total outstanding claims on residents of foreign countries exceeding \$30 million in aggregate. In these reports, bank claims are itemized by country, and separately encompass credit extended to foreign country banks, public entities, and other recipients including individuals and businesses. In addition to direct international flows, bank claims also include revaluation gains on interest rate, foreign exchange, equity, commodity and other off-balance sheet contracts. Banks provide some details on time remaining to maturity (one year and under, 1 to 5 years, and over five years). Other quarterly reports filed by banks contain information on bank total assets located in the United States and abroad. There have been changes over time in reporting conventions, but much of this data is consistently available by bank, starting with reports from 1986 and continuing to the present time (2005). Aggregate data are published in the *Country Exposure Lending Survey* (E.16) statistical release (http://www.federalreserve.gov/releases/) and are made available to staff at the BIS for their statistical publications on the overall indebtedness of various countries throughout the world. Microdata, which are what we use in this paper, are confidential.

As shown in Table 1, the total foreign exposure of U.S. banks has grown from $355 billion in 1990 to $1.25 trillion in 2005. Fifty percent or more of this exposure is through cross-border claims. Currently the share to non-bank, non-public sector borrowers is 43 percent. MCBs represent 80 percent of the total exposure and nearly 90 percent of the holdings of foreign derivatives.

We report statistics and trends for money center banks (MCBs) and for all other banks. Each *Country Exposure Lending Survey* lists banks classified as MCBs. As of the third quarter of 2005, four organizations comprised the group of money center banks: Bank of America Corp., Taunus Corp., JPMorgan Chase & Co., and Citigroup.[3] Although MCBs are not necessarily the largest U.S. banks by asset size, they do represent the majority of total foreign exposure of all U.S. banks. As indicated in Table 1, there were 9 banks classified as MCBs in 1990 controlling a total market share

---

[3]Another category, called Other Large Banks, includes data from: Bank of New York Co., Wachovia Corp., HSBC Holdings PLC, and State Street Corp. As of June 30, 2005 the capital and assets in these categories are reported, http://www.ffiec.gov/PDF/E16/E16_200506.pdf, as follows.

Banking Organization Category	Tier 1 Capital	Total Assets
All Reporting Banks	$417.5 billion**	$7,110.0 billion
Money Center Banks	$208.3 billion*	$4,138.2 billion
Other Large Banks	$61.2 billion	$1,062.4 billion
All Other Banks	$148.0 billion	$1,909.4 billion

Table 1. Summary statistics on total U.S. bank foreign exposures

All Banks	1990:Q4	1995:Q4	2000:Q4	2005:Q3
Number of reporting banks	163	137	99	68
		millions of U.S. dollars*		
Total exposure	354,532	440,334	827,553	1,247,655
Cross-border	214,268	255,683	409,733	632,874
exposure	140,264	184,651	329,977	515,311
Local exposure				
Derivative exposure	—	—	87,843	99,470
Composition of total exposure		percent		
Cross-border claims	60.4	58.1	49.5	50.7
Local claims	39.6	41.9	39.9	41.3
Derivatives	—	—	10.6	8.0
Composition of cross-border claims		percent		
To public borrowers	24.0	23.1	28.5	28.7
To banks	50.8	38.4	33.1	28.6
To other private borrowers	25.2	38.6	38.4	42.8
Money Center Banks	**1990:Q4**	**1995:Q4**	**2000:Q4**	**2005:Q3**
Number of MCBs	9	7	6	4
		Percent of U.S. Total accounted for by MCBs		
Total exposure	70.1	78.9	79.8	80.9
Cross-border	58.2	70.1	75.3	80.1
exposure	88.3	91.1	81.7	80.5
Local exposure				
Derivative exposure	—	—	93.8	87.5
Composition of total exposure		percent		
Cross-border claims	50.2	51.6	46.7	50.2
Local claims	49.8	48.4	40.8	41.1
Derivatives	—	—	12.5	8.6
Composition of cross-border claims		percent		
To public borrowers	34.4	29.1	34.4	32.4
To banks	34.4	28.1	25.6	21.6
To other private borrowers	34.4	29.1	34.4	32.4

of about 70 percent. As a result of mergers, that number declined to 4, and their market share increased to 80 percent. Table 1 provides these data, and a range of summary statistics for U.S bank foreign exposures at four different dates, starting in 1990 and extending to the third quarter of 2005, the latest observation available.

There are different ways of presenting and analyzing data of foreign exposure of banks. Publicly available sources add up exposures across all banks and then report the total amounts of U.S. bank exposures in each country or in each type of claim. Such figures correspond to what we call "totals" across the exposures of all U.S. banks. Alternatively, we can discuss the data in a way that reflects the average portfolio of a bank in each category, MCB or non-MCB, without regard for the actual size of the bank. We present this type of analysis as "unweighted" averages across banks.

We report cross-border exposure adjusted on an ultimate risk basis and use this figure in calculating total exposure and transfer risk. Reporting on an ultimate risk basis means that loan made to a borrower in one country but guaranteed by an entity in another country is considered a loan to the guarantor's country, not the borrower's country.

Despite consolidation in the number of banks reporting foreign exposures, the overall foreign exposures of U.S. banks have continued to grow. Figures 1 through 3 show, in billions of 2000 $U.S., the evolution of foreign exposure of U.S. banks, focusing on the totals (Figure 1), and then cross-border (Figure 2) and local claims (Figure 3). After declining over the late 1980s and into the early 1990s, the foreign exposures of U.S. banks have been growing strongly. The charts differentiate between the aggregate over all banks, the amount accounted for by MCBs, and the amount from all other U.S. banks reporting foreign exposures. The amount of total exposure from all other banks has only recently recovered, in real terms, to levels last seen in the mid-1980s. In Figure 2, all of the growth in cross-border lending has been concentrated in money center banks, with flat (in real terms) cross-border claims from all other banks with foreign exposures. Figure 3 shows that MCBs dominate totals in local claims,[4] although other banks as a group have a low but increasing focus on this form of exposure. This dominance is also shown in the second panel of Table 1, which show that while the MCB dominance of local claims is less than what it was in the 1990s (around 90 percent), it still exceeds 80 percent of the total.

---

[4]Local claims are loans issued, in any currency, by a foreign branch of a U.S. bank to borrowers in the country where the branch is located.

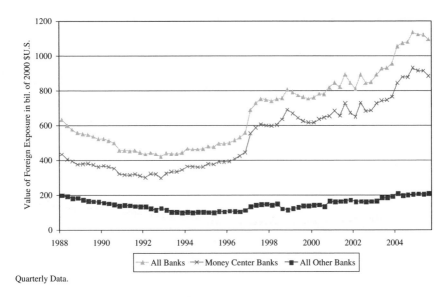

Quarterly Data.

Figure 1. Total foreign exposure of U.S. banks

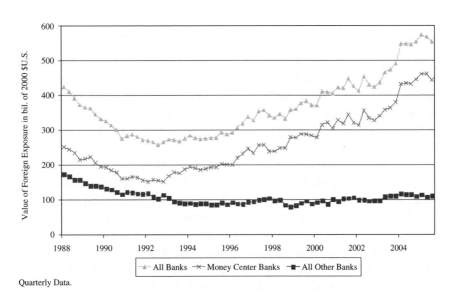

Quarterly Data.

Figure 2. Total cross-border exposure of U.S. banks

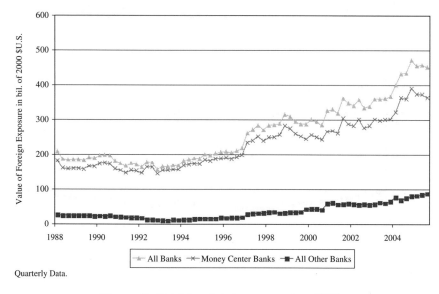

Quarterly Data.

Figure 3. Total local claims exposure of U.S.

2.1. *Geographic distribution on U.S. bank foreign exposures*

The geographical distribution of foreign exposures of U.S. banks has evolved over time. Tables 2 and 3 show this distribution, reporting totals across categories of banks and then for the average MCB or non-MCB. Each table presents details at five-year intervals since 1990, with distinctions made between money center banks and all other banks. Looking first at the total averages in Table 2, foreign exposures are dominated by other industrialized countries, which make up 65 percent of MCB foreign exposure and 86 percent of non-MCB foreign exposure. Particularly for MCBs, exposures to industrialized countries are increasingly concentrated in Europe. The increasing importance of Europe has been driven by cross-border exposures, at the cost of cross-border exposure to Latin America and Asia. In local claims, Europe's share has declined for MCBs as these banks have expanded their local operations in Latin America. Non-MCBs developed substantial Latin American and Asian local claims in the mid-1990s, but have recently returned their focus to Europe and Canada.

A different pattern emerges when we show the geographical breakdown of the average MCB and the average non-MCB. In this (unweighted) approach, the relative importance of industrialized countries for MCBs and

Table 2. Geographical breakdown of total exposures across banks, allocated on an ultimate risk basis

Breakdown of Total Exposure (in percent)	MCBs Only				non-MCBs			
	1990q4	1995q4	2000q4	2005q3	1990q4	1995q4	2000q4	2005q3
Industrialized Countries*	65.9	59.7	68.7	64.9	77.6	60.4	69.6	85.7
Emerging Markets*	34.1	40.3	31.3	35.1	22.4	39.6	30.4	14.3
Europe	47.5	42.6	53.8	55.6	39.5	37.2	47.4	59.2
Latin America	16.7	15.5	12.4	14.0	9.1	25.0	21.9	6.3
Asia and the Middle East	23.7	32.1	24.5	22.2	40.2	26.3	10.7	7.2
Other Regions	12.0	9.8	9.3	8.2	11.1	11.5	20.1	27.4
Breakdown of Cross Border Exposure								
Europe	38.3	42.7	67.9	71.6	39.0	39.0	56.1	70.5
Latin America	27.0	20.9	12.6	10.0	9.1	22.0	18.7	10.7
Asia and the Middle East	25.6	29.7	13.2	12.2	41.1	29.2	14.6	10.3
Other Regions	9.2	6.7	6.3	6.1	10.8	9.7	10.6	8.5
Breakdown of Local Claims Exposure								
Europe	56.8	42.6	34.4	31.2	42.5	28.9	30.7	43.1
Latin America	6.5	9.8	13.7	20.9	9.1	39.0	28.9	0.8
Asia and the Middle East	21.8	34.6	40.1	37.5	35.4	12.5	3.9	3.5
Other Regions	14.9	13.1	11.8	10.4	12.9	19.7	36.5	52.6

*Industrialized/emerging classification from IMF.

Table 3. Geographical breakdown of exposures, unweighted averages across banks in each category

Breakdown of Adjusted Total Exposure (in percent)	MCBs Only				non-MCBs			
	1990q4	1995q4	2000q4	2005q3	1990q4	1995q4	2000q4	2005q3
Industrialized Countries*	65.9	62.9	76.7	71.1	73.2	52.8	51.5	54.6
Emerging Markets*	34.1	37.1	23.3	28.9	26.8	47.2	48.5	45.4
Europe	44.5	42.9	62.1	60.5	31.8	33.5	34.8	41.5
Latin America	18.8	14.4	9.6	13.6	14.6	31.9	32.7	28.1
Asia and the Middle East	26.7	34.0	18.7	17.5	40.7	23.7	19.0	17.2
Other Regions	10.1	8.8	9.6	8.5	12.9	10.9	13.5	13.1
Breakdown of Cross Border Exposure								
Europe	35.3	41.6	70.9	69.3	31.5	33.4	34.3	43.5
Latin America	27.4	19.5	10.4	10.0	14.7	32.1	33.1	27.7
Asia and the Middle East	28.5	32.6	11.8	12.9	40.8	24.3	20.2	18.3
Other Regions	8.8	6.3	6.9	7.7	13.0	10.3	12.3	10.5
Breakdown of Local Claims Exposure								
Europe	62.4	49.9	40.2	42.9	55.0	40.9	47.6	32.3
Latin America	5.8	8.4	12.9	29.6	7.4	25.6	15.0	20.5
Asia and the Middle East	20.3	30.1	32.6	20.5	29.5	17.3	11.0	12.2
Other Regions	11.5	11.6	14.2	7.0	8.2	16.2	26.3	34.9

*Industrialized/emerging classification from IMF.

non-MCBs are reversed, with industrialized countries making up 71 percent of the average MCB's foreign exposure but only 55 percent for the average other bank. The difference thus underscores a distribution of non-MCBs characterized by the presence of a few banks of large size with significant exposures in industrialized countries and many, smaller size banks with a larger presence in non-industrialized countries. In particular, the average non-MCB has maintained a Latin American share in total exposure of around 30 percent since the mid-90s. For MCBs, the unweighted approach reveals a significant dip in total Latin American exposures in 2000, followed by a recent recovery to mid-90s levels. This recovery has been driven entirely by local claims, with cross-border claims to Latin America remaining at 2000 levels for MCBs. The average MCB and the average non-MCB have both shown decreasing exposure to Asia and the Middle East.

3. Risks in U.S. Bank Foreign Exposures

This section explores the risks in U.S. bank foreign exposures, beginning with the concept of transfer risk and then introducing country risk considerations. While aggregate and publicly available reports provide numbers on total transfer risk and breakdowns across countries, we specifically use information on individual bank data to evaluate such risks for the average bank in each category. Through our bank-specific analysis we are able to relate these risks to other bank-specific information, like bank assets and bank capital, thus providing a clearer view of the risks in such U.S. bank foreign exposures, and the extent to which these risks appear to be well capitalized.

Transfer Risk is defined as the portion of a bank's foreign exposure that is vulnerable to default because a country is unable to provide local borrowers with sufficient access to foreign currencies to meet their foreign obligations denominated in a currency other than the local currency of the borrower. Houpt (1999) states that "the supervisory measure of transfer risk has become the sum of cross-border claims, net local country claims, and claims resulting from revaluation gains [that is., derivative claims]" (p. 9).[5]

---

[5]In our analysis, provided below, we calculate a bank's transfer risk to a specific country as follows, following Houpt's definition. We sum cross border and derivative claims, then add in net local claims (local claims — local liabilities) only if this net balance is positive.

Table 4. Capital ratios of exposed banks (unweighted averages across banks)

Mean	MCBs only				non-MCBs			
	1990:Q4	1995:Q4	2000:Q4	2005:Q3	1990:Q4	1995:Q4	2000:Q4	2005:Q3
total exposure/total equity capital	7.72	5.95	4.66	5.17	1.97	1.70	2.05	1.55
standard deviation	*3.47*	*1.99*	*3.43*	*4.37*	*2.59*	*2.69*	*3.82*	*2.80*
transfer risk/total equity capital	5.70	4.43	3.58	4.27	1.90	1.66	1.98	1.44
standard deviation	*2.33*	*1.38*	*2.87*	*4.63*	*2.53*	*2.67*	*3.81*	*2.78*
total exposure as a share of total assets	0.36	0.37	0.28	0.23	0.13	0.14	0.16	0.14
standard deviation	*0.14*	*0.11*	*0.21*	*0.14*	*0.17*	*0.19*	*0.21*	*0.20*
transfer risk as a share of total assets	0.27	0.28	0.21	0.16	0.13	0.14	0.15	0.13
standard deviation	*0.09*	*0.06*	*0.17*	*0.08*	*0.17*	*0.19*	*0.21*	*0.20*
total equity capital/total assets	0.05	0.06	0.06	0.06	0.07	0.09	0.10	0.10
standard deviation	*0.01*	*0.01*	*0.01*	*0.03*	*0.03*	*0.05*	*0.07*	*0.05*

Total Equity Capital = Common Equity + Preferred Equity + Retained Earnings + Treasury Stocks.
Total Assets = Cash + Securities + Federal Funds Sold + Loans + Trading Assets + Fixed Assets & Real Estate + Intangibles.
Data are from quarterly Call Reports (banks) and Y-9C filings (bank holding companies).
Definitions of equity and assets are identical for banks and bank holding companies.

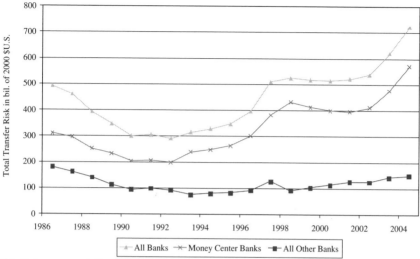

Note: Each year represented by q4 data.

Figure 4. Total transfer risk of U.S. banks

As shown in Figure 4, transfer risk displays an increasing trend, follow-ing the pattern we observed in Figure 1 on total foreign exposure of U.S. banks. Over the past five years, total exposure has grown by about 40 per-cent, in real terms, while transfer risk has grown by just over 30 percent. This slower growth in transfer risk has been a persistent trend. Figure 5 shows the ratio of transfer risk to total exposure for all banks, money center banks, and all other banks. As unweighted averages across individual banks in each category, these figures capture the average increase in importance of local branches and subsidiaries of within types of U.S. banks and the increased importance of netting out with local liabilities the total volume of their local country claims. This pattern is especially relevant for MCBs, which have been able to reduce total exposure by 23 percent to 30 percent in recent years (making the ratio of transfer risk to total exposure between 77 percent and 70 percent). The chart indicates a much smaller reduction for all other banks.

The money center banks' ability to reduce transfer risk while increasing total exposure is also apparent in Table 4, which shows the capital ratios of the average MCB and non-MCB. For MCBs, the ratios of total exposure and transfer risk to total capital declined during the 1990s, but have reverted to their mid-90s level in more recent years. The ratio of exposure or transfer

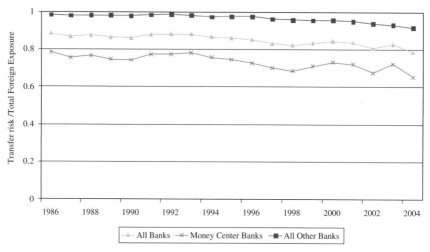

Note: Unweighted average across banks in each category.

Figure 5. Ratio of transfer risk to total exposure for U.S.

risk to equity capital is far higher for MCBs than for non-MCBs, typically up to four times as high for exposure and at least three times as high for transfer risk. Part of this discrepancy across types of banks is explained by foreign exposure playing a larger role in bank assets among MCBs as compared with non-MCBs. As the third row of the table demonstrates, on average MCBs are more internationally active as measured by the share of total exposure in total assets. The fifth row of the table show that overall capital-to-asset ratios are more similar for MCB and non-MCB, though the average non-MCB is increasingly somewhat better capitalized. The fourth row of the table shows that the gap between bank types in transfer risk relative to assets has become far less pronounced than the gap in total exposure relative to assets. MCBs have more exposure, relative to their assets, but the risks associated with every dollar of exposure are lower.

Within this table we also provide standard deviations in each row at each date. The standard deviations are used to illustrate the extent to which bank specific information tends to differ from the mean data that we just discussed. There has been a dramatic rise in the differences across MCBs in their exposure and transfer risks relative to equity capital. The differences in exposure capitalization ratios are mainly driven by differences across banks in equity capital relative to overall assets.

Further insights into the composition and degree of risk involved in foreign exposures are gained when we add into our analysis country risk considerations. *Country Risk* ratings are intended to reflect each country's ability to pay back its international debt. Country risk includes assessments of liquidity constraints, sovereign default, political instability, the possibility that the government will confiscate foreign property or refuse to enforce foreign claims on local lenders, and other relevant concerns.[6] Since country risk covers a variety of features of a country it is generally reported as an index or letter grade. Most published classifications measure sovereign country risk, which is used as a proxy for overall country risk. Moody's, Standard and Poor's, Fitch, and the Organization for Economic Cooperation and Development all publish well-regarded sovereign country risk ratings. In our analysis below we use the Fitch data, which has been published since 1994. Fitch's country coverage has expanded since 1994 and now covers about 90 countries. The Fitch ratings are reported as A through D letter grades, with multiple letters denoting lower risk, so AAA is the best possible credit rating. Fitch groups its country rankings into investment grade, at BBB-rated and above, and speculative grade, at BB and below.[7]

Figures 6 through 8 use the information on the exposures of each bank to specific countries, and present constructed distributions of the risk in portfolios for different types of banks over three dates, 1995:Q4, 2000:Q4, and 2005:Q3. The risks for the average MCB are tracked in Figure 6, for the average non-MCB in Figure 7, and a comparison of relative risks of portfolios in 2005 for both types of banks in Figure 8. A distribution that is skewed more to the right means that a portfolio contains a higher share of exposures in safer countries.

As mentioned in introduction, U.S. banks have produced significant changes in the portfolio composition of total foreign exposure over time, both through changing the form of exposure — via cross-border versus via local claims — and through a change in the proportion of "safer" or "riskier" countries. As shown in Figure 6, MCBs had similar distributions of country risk for 1995, 2000, and 2005. By contrast, Figure 7 shows that the average non-MCB had higher-risk countries in its portfolio in 2000 than in 1995,

---

[6]Houpt (1999) defines country risk as "all risks from economic, social, legal, and political conditions in a foreign country that may affect the status of loans to parties in that country" (p. 8).
[7]Further details on Fitch classification details can be found at http://www.fitchratings. com/corporate/fitchResources.cfm?detail=1&rd_file=ltr.

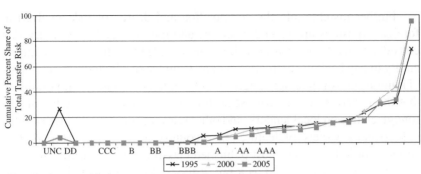

Note: Shares are unweighted averages across all banks in each category.

Figure 6. Detailed distribution of country risk for MCBs over time

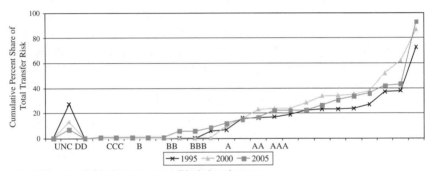

Note: Shares are unweighted averages across all banks in each category.

Figure 7. Detailed distribution of country risk for non-MCBs over time

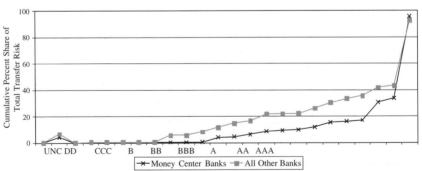

Note: Shares are unweighted averages across all banks in each category.

Figure 8. Detailed distribution of country risk classification, 2005q3

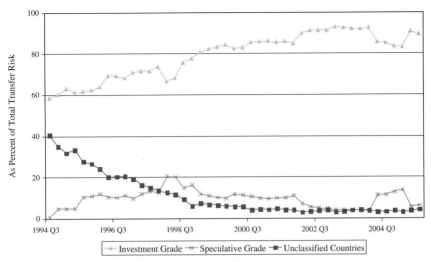

Note: Shares are unweighted averages across all money center banks.

Figure 9. Country risk within transfer risk for money center banks

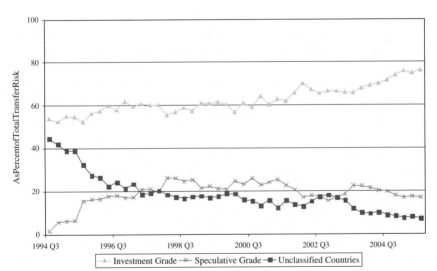

Note: Shares are unweighted averages across all non-money center banks.

Figure 10. Country risk within transfer risk for non-MCB

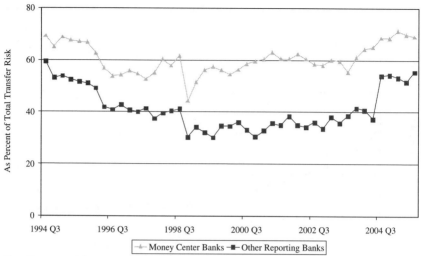

Note: Shares are weighted averages across all banks

Figure 11. AAA grade exposure within investment grade

with this riskier portfolio largely maintained in 2005. Figure 8 shows that in 2005, the non-MCBs had substantially more country risk in their transfer risk than non-MCBs.

Another way of describing the riskiness of bank portfolios is by considering the shares within transfer risk of investment grade versus speculative grade countries. The shares over time for the average MCB banks and for the average non-MCB banks are presented in Figures 9 and 10. Over the past decade the investment-grade held share of transfer risk has risen for most banks, from 58 percent to 89 percent for the average MCB and from 54 percent to 76 percent for the average non-MCB. The increase in the speculative-grade share over the second half of the 1990s is due to absorption into this category of previously "unclassified" countries. By 2005, most of the remaining unclassified foreign exposure is to offshore banking centers, mainly the Cayman Islands, or to regional organizations. Non-MCBs, on average, maintain a much higher share of transfer risk in riskier countries, as compared with the average MCB. As shown in Figure 11, the share of AAA-grade countries in the investment grade part of bank foreign exposures has risen across the average MCB and non-MCB since the late 1990s. Particularly for MCBs, the overall portfolio of foreign exposure has tilted heavily toward investment grade, and toward the safer countries within investment grade.

4. Concluding Remarks

The total foreign exposures of U.S. banks, especially MCBs, have continued to grow over time. On average across MCBs, exposure relative to equity capital has begun to rise toward levels last seen in the mid-1990s. At the same time, the incidence of foreign exposure on banks total asset portfolio has diminished. Non-MCBs reporting foreign exposure have generally improved their overall capitalization, and as a result, on average, foreign exposure has reduced its weight on the average non-MCB's equity capital.

Both MCBs and non-MCBs have increased their share of foreign exposure towards safer countries. Some of the exposure of MCBs to riskier countries — especially Latin American countries — is now achieved mainly through the activities of local branches and subsidiaries that take on liabilities as well as assets. Hence, MCBs have maintained their exposure to riskier countries while reducing its relative impact on transfer risk. MCBs have now nearly 90 percent of their transfer risk in investment grade countries, with the investment grade share increasingly dominated by the safest countries in this category. While the move toward a safer portfolio also characterizes the average non-MCB, the tendency is less dramatic and there is more variation across these smaller banks.

References

Bank for International Settlements, Committee on Global Financial Stability, 2004, "Foreign Direct Investment in the Financial Sector of Emerging Market Economies," working group report #22 March 2004, ISBN 92-9197-666-0.

Bomfin, Antulio and William Nelson, 1999, "Profits and Balance Sheet Developments at U.S. Commercial Banks in 1998," *Federal Reserve Bulletin*, 85, pp. 369–395.

Crystal, Jennifer, B. Gerard Dages, and Linda Goldberg, 2001, "Does Foreign Ownership Contribute to Sounder Banks in Emerging Markets? The Latin American Experience," in *Open Doors: Foreign Participation in Financial Systems in Developing Countries*, R. Litan, P. Masson, and M. Pomerleano (eds.), Brookings Press.

Dages, B. Gerard, Daniel Kinney, and Linda Goldberg, 2000, "Foreign and Domestic Bank Participation in Emerging Markets: Lessons from Mexico and Argentina" *Federal Reserve Bank of New York Economic Policy Review*, 6(3), pp. 17–36.

Goldberg, Linda, 2002, "When Is Foreign Bank Lending to Emerging Markets Volatile?" in *Preventing Currency Crises in Emerging Markets*, Sebastian Edwards and Jeffrey Frankel (eds.), NBER and University of Chicago Press.

Goldberg, Linda, 2004, "Financial Sector Foreign Direct Investment: New and Old Lessons," NBER working paper, #10441, April.

Hawkins, John and Dubravko Mihaljek, 2001, "The Banking Industry in the Emerging Market Economies: Competition, Consolidation and Systemic Stability: An Overview," in *The Banking Industry in the Emerging Market Economies: Competition, Consolidation and Systemic Stability*, Bank for International Settlements Papers, no. 4, August.

Houpt, J. V., 1999, "International Activities of U.S. Banks and in U.S. Banking Markets," *Federal Reserve Bulletin*, September, pp. 599–615.

Litan, R., 2001, *Open Doors: Foreign Participation in Financial Systems in Developing Countries*, Brookings Press.

Palmer, David, 2000, "U.S. Bank Exposure to Emerging-Market Countries during Recent Financial Crises," *Federal Reserve Bulletin*, February, pp. 81–96.

Santor, Eric, 2004, "Contagion and the Composition of Canadian Banks' Foreign Asset Portfolios: Do Crises Matter?," Manuscript, Bank of Canada.

Data Appendix

Banking exposure data

U.S. FFIEC 009 and 009a reports are filed quarterly by all U.S. banks with significant exposures.

Background: The report was initiated in 1977 as the FR 2036 report and was used to collect data on the distribution, by country, of claims on foreigners held by U.S. banks and bank holding companies. The FDIC and OCC collected similar information from institutions under their supervision. In March 1984, the FR 2036 became a Federal Financial Institutions Examination Council (FFIEC) report and was renumbered FFIEC 009. It was revised in March 1986 to provide more detail on guaranteed claims. In 1995 (1997), the report was revised to add an item for revaluation gains on off-balance-sheet items and an item for securities held in trading accounts,

Appendix Table: Country Risk Classifications in 2004q4

Countries Classified as AAA-rated	Countries Classified as other A-rated	Countries Classified as B-rated or Below
Austria	Australia	Argentina
Denmark	Bahrain	Azerbaijan
Finland	Belgium	Bolivia
France	Bermuda	Brazil
Germany	Canada	Bulgaria
Ireland	Chile	Cameroon
Luxembourg	China	Colombia
Netherlands	Cyprus	Costa Rica
Norway	Czech Republic	Croatia
Singapore	Estonia	Dominican Republic
Spain	Greece	Ecuador
Sweden	Hong Kong	Egypt
Switzerland	Hungary	El Salvador
U.K.	Iceland	India
	Israel	Indonesia
	Italy	Iran
	Japan	Kazakhstan
	Korea	Lebanon
	Kuwait	Malawi
	Latvia	Mali
	Lithuania	Mexico
	Malaysia	Mozambique
	Malta	Panama
	New Zealand	Papua New Guinea
	Portugal	Peru
	Saudi Arabia	Philippines
	Slovakia	Poland
	Slovenia	Romania
	Taiwan	Russia
		Serbia
		South Africa
		Thailand
		Tunisia
		Turkey
		Uganda
		Ukraine
		Uruguay
		Venezuela
		Vietnam

Share of 2004q4 Countries that were similarly classified in 2000q4

71.4	72.4	94.9

Share of 2004q4 Countries that were similarly classified in 1994q4

50	58.6	89.7

Source data: Fitch.

and several items were combined. Another revision which will, among other changes, make the FFIEC report more directly comparable to the BIS foreign exposure reports will be implemented starting with the 2006q1 report.

Respondent Panel: The panel consists of U.S. commercial banks and bank holding companies holding $30 million or more in claims on residents of foreign countries. Respondents file the FFIEC 009a if exposures to a country exceed 1 percent of total assets or 20 percent of capital of the reporting institution. FFIEC 009a respondents also furnish a list of countries in which exposures were between 3/4 of 1 percent and 1 percent of total assets or between 15 and 20 percent of capital. Participation is required.

Nicola Cetorelli is a senior economist in the banking studies function and Linda S. Goldberg is a vice president of international research, both at the Federal Reserve Bank of New York. They thank Philipp Hartmann, Ken Lamar, Leon Taub, and the participants to the 2005 World Bank — Chicago Fed Conference on Cross-Border Banking: Regulatory Challenges for useful comments. The views expressed in this paper are those of the individual authors and do not necessarily reflect the position of the Federal Reserve Bank of New York or the Federal Reserve System. Anthony Cho and Eleanor Dillon provided research support. Address correspondences to Linda S. Goldberg, Federal Reserve Bank of NY, Research Department, 33 Liberty St, New York, N.Y. 10045. email: Linda.Goldberg@ny.frb.org or Nicola.Cetorelli@ny.frb.org.

Cross-Border Banking in Asia: Basel II and Other Prudential Issues

Stefan Hohl*, Patrick McGuire and Eli Remolona
Bank for International Settlements

1. Introduction

The 1997 crisis led to a sharp decline in cross-border banking activity in East Asia. In recent years, however, foreign bank activity has started to recover but it has done so in ways that differ from the previous activity. Much of foreign bank lending in Asia is now in the form of local currency loans. Moreover, instead of extending commercial loans, these banks now tend to either hold government securities or lend to households in the form of consumer loans or mortgages. While such foreign bank activity remains limited, it is helping to transform the way domestic banks do business and is fostering a general trend towards consumer and mortgage lending.

In the meantime, bank supervisory agencies in the region have welcomed the new framework of Basel II as a way to avoid the vulnerabilities that led to the Asian crisis. In doing so, the authorities have been trying to avoid the possibility of domestic banks' relying on the standardized approach while foreign banks take advantage of the advanced approaches. Even with a still limited foreign bank presence, the authorities are finding themselves confronted with challenging home-host issues and with the need to give their domestic banks more time to collect the data needed to implement the more advanced approaches, especially for mortgages and consumer loans.

Another important cross-border issue for banking systems in East Asia has been the question of how to deal with the systemic risk of contagion. These are risks that are difficult to capture with just the tools of pillar 1. The Basel II framework does provide pillar 2 as a way to deal with such risks. Banks in the region, however, may have little incentive to assess this risk on their own. Supervisors will have to insist that the banks do so and set aside the appropriate amount of capital. The relatively large judgmental element of pillar 2, however, requires a degree of supervisory assertiveness that may be difficult to find in some countries in Asia.

In what follows, we first characterize the nature of cross-border and foreign bank activity in East Asia. In the following two sections, we then describe the implementation of Basel II in the region and explain why pillar 2 is so important in dealing with cross-border systemic risk, and why this pillar is nonetheless difficult to apply in the region.

2. Cross-border Banking in East Asia

The financial crisis which erupted in 1997 changed the landscape of international banking in Asia. While some countries remained insulated from the crisis, others experienced large cutbacks in domestic and foreign bank credit. This section builds on previous surveys[1] of the crisis, and provides a broad overview of recent developments in foreign banks' activities in Asia. We first survey the size Asia's debt markets, and then propose simple indicators which capture the degree of foreign bank participation in individual countries. These indicators imply that, overall, foreign bank participation remains low in many Asian countries relative to other regions, although there is considerable heterogeneity across countries. Despite this, in several countries, the presence of foreign banks appears to have stimulated growth in certain market segments, particularly consumer finance.

Banking markets differ considerably across countries in Asia. Indeed, "Asia" can be defined broadly, for example by using a strict geographic definition, or more narrowly by grouping countries with similar levels of economic development. The analysis in this section is based on one such classification, motivated by broad similarities across countries and data availability. At one end of the spectrum are Asia's *advanced economies*, typified by Australia, Japan, and New Zealand. At the other are Asia's emerging economies, or *emerging Asia*, which includes China, India, Indonesia, Korea, Malaysia, the Philippines, Thailand, and Taiwan (China).[2] The

---

[1] See for example Bustelo (1998), Coppel and Davies (2003), and Lubin (2002).
[2] Hereinafter, Taiwan.

regions' *financial centers*, Singapore and Hong Kong, play an important role in the distribution of credit throughout emerging Asia by hosting the regional operations of many foreign banks. While the primary focus of this section is to assess cross-border banking in emerging Asia, it does highlight along the way the special role of these financial centers.

For many emerging markets, *loan financing* has become relatively less important than *bond financing* over the last decade. However, banks remain the key source of *debt* financing for nonbanks through their extension of loans and holding of securities. This is especially true in emerging Asia, where debt markets are considerably larger than those in Latin America or emerging Europe. Total credit provided by banks (both domestic and foreign) to nonbank borrowers in emerging Asia has risen as a share of aggregate gross domestic product (GDP) since at least 1995, and now stands at close to 120 percent.[3] This is in contrast to the relatively flat ratios of 40 percent to 50 percent in Latin America and emerging Europe over this same period.[4]

The 1997 crisis is a useful point of departure in analyzing banking flows in emerging Asia. After the Thai baht collapsed in July 1997, credit to nonbank borrowers in emerging Asia contracted significantly during the rest of the year. By the end of 1997, the stock of outstanding corporate and government bonds had fallen by 20 percent, largely reflecting the depreciation of local currencies relative to the U.S. dollar. Total credit provided by banks fell by 10 percent over this same period, reflecting both local currency depreciation and the unwinding of short-term positions. Debt markets in China, Taiwan, and India remained relatively insulated from the crises, as did those in the region's more advanced economies. In contrast, many of the other emerging economies, in particular Indonesia, Korea, and Thailand, have only recently shown signs of credit growth.

The crisis affected both domestic and foreign headquartered banks. Short-term claims, primarily cross-border loans to corporates and banks

---

[3]Total bank financing to nonbank borrowers (government, corporate, and household) in a particular country is the sum of domestic credit (DC), which includes claims (loan and debt security claims) of resident banks, and Bank for International Settlements (BIS) reporting banks' cross-border claims on nonbanks (XB).

[4]Bond markets in emerging Asian countries are also large in absolute terms, with total outstanding bonds (both international and domestic issues) for India, China, and Korea ranking with Mexico and Brazil amongst the top five for emerging economies. However, emerging Asia's bond market in aggregate is similar to that in other emerging market regions when measured as a share of GDP (at roughly 35 percent).

In billions of US dollars

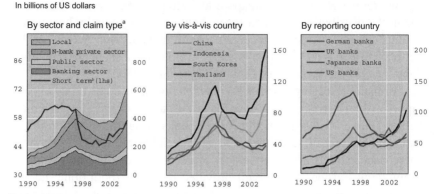

^aForeign claims is composed of *international* claims (cross border claims and local claims in foreign currency) and claims in local currency booked by reporting banks' local affiliates. A sectoral breakdown is available only for international claims. ^bAs a share of total international claims; in per cent.

Source: BIS.

Figure 1.   Foreign claims on Asia-Pacific

in the region, had been on the rise since the mid-1980s (Figure 1).[5] This was particularly evident in Korea, Thailand, and Indonesia, which saw a large run up in credit from Japanese, U.S. and European banks prior to the crisis. After substantial unwinding in the wake of the crisis, U.S., UK, and German banks' lending to the region started to grow within three years, while the lengthy retrenchment by Japanese banks has only recently bottomed out.

The crisis led to significant changes in how credit is channeled in emerging Asia, including the *direction* of net flows vis-à-vis these borrowers. These changes are particularly evident in the regional operations of banks operating in Hong Kong and Singapore. Foreign banks dominate cross-border lending from these centers, accounting for over 80 percent of their

[5]In the BIS consolidated statistics, claims comprise financial assets such as loans, debt securities, and equities, including equity participations in subsidiaries. Claims refer to on-balance-sheet financial assets, and exclude derivatives and other off-balance-sheet transactions. Financial assets of branches and subsidiaries in which the parent bank has a controlling interest (typically 50 percent or more of the outstanding shares) are consolidated with the assets of the parent bank. Intragroup positions, such as loans from the head office to a foreign office, are mostly netted out. In principle, all claims are valued at market prices, but in practice many instruments are valued at either face or cost price.

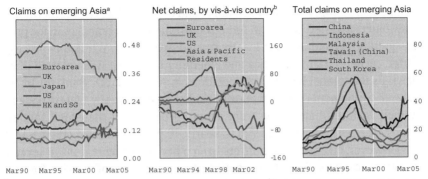

^aAs a share of total BIS reporting countries' cross-border claims on emerging Asia. ^bTotal claims minus total liabilities of all banks in Hong Kong and Singapore, by vis-à-vis country.

Source: BIS.

Figure 2. Cross-border claims of banks in Hong Kong and Singapore

total cross-border claims.[6] In the three years prior to the crisis, roughly half the total worldwide cross-border credit to borrowers in emerging Asia was provided by banks located in these financial centers (Figure 2, left-hand panel). This share has since fallen to roughly 35 percent. Banks in these financial centers are now a hub through which capital is exported from the emerging Asian countries. Total net claims of banks located in Hong Kong and Singapore vis-à-vis residents in emerging Asia hit a high of $101 billion in the second quarter of 1997. Net claims have subsequently turned negative, reflecting the recycling of emerging Asia's current account surpluses through greater deposits placed in banks in these financial centers (Figure 2, middle panel).

With the change in the role of the region's offshore financial centers after the crisis, foreign banks' region-wide operations evolved. Most noticeable is the expansion of foreign banks' local positions. During the 1990s, traditional cross-border lending gave way to other types of business, as global banks

---

[6]Note that these figures include cross-border credit to all borrowers worldwide (as opposed to borrowers in only emerging Asia), as the BIS data does allow for a vis-à-vis country breakdown by parent bank for individual reporting countries. In Hong Kong, Japanese banks had the largest cross-border positions in 1997, but have since fallen behind UK and U.S. headquartered banks.

became increasingly active in derivative and capital markets.[7] Furthermore, many banks invested heavily in foreign subsidiaries and branches in the process greatly expanding their locally funded operations. While this process started earlier in Latin America and emerging Europe, it was not until after the crisis that global banks' local positions in Asia took off. Bank for International Settlements (BIS) reporting banks' local currency claims booked by their local affiliates grew from about 15 percent of their total foreign claims on emerging Asia in 1996 to nearly 40 percent in 2004 (Figure 1).

However, emerging Asia differs from other emerging regions in several important respects. With the exception of a few pockets of activity, foreign bank activity has remained relatively low in emerging Asia. This is evident in two simple measures designed to capture the degree to which foreign banks have made inroads into domestic banking markets.[8] The first measure captures the importance of direct cross-border, or "offshore," banking for a national lending market, financing which is typically missed by domestic banking statistics. The measure is calculated as the ratio of cross-border (XB) to total bank credit to nonbanks, or $XB/(XB + DC)$. The denominator of this ratio is the sum of cross-border (XB) and domestic bank credit (DC) to nonbanks, and includes both loan and security claims. The second measure captures foreign bank participation more fully by incorporating foreign banks' local lending in local currency. It is calculated as the ratio of BIS reporting banks' cross-border *and* locally extended claims to total bank credit to nonbanks, or $(INT + LL)/(XB + DC)$. In the numerator, international claims (INT) include cross-border and local claims in foreign currencies on nonbanks. Local claims in local currencies, LL, are not broken down by sector, and thus also include lending to other banks. Hence, the measure is presented as a range — with LL included and excluded from the numerator — in the graphs below. A best-guess point estimate within this range is calculated by applying to LL the sectoral breakdown available for international claims (INT).

These measures suggests that foreign banks supply a smaller share of bank credit in emerging Asia than in Latin America and emerging Europe (Figure 3). Cross-border or "offshore" banking, captured by the first measure, has remained mostly flat in all three regions, at near 20 percent of

---

[7] See McGuire and Wooldridge (2005), McCauley *et al.* (2002) and Domanski *et al.* (2003).
[8] These measures, discussed in detail in the June and September 2005 *BIS Quarterly Reviews*, capture the positions of BIS reporting banks only. This can lead to an underestimation of foreign banks' participation in a particular country if banks located in non-reporting countries have a significant presence.

Asia-Pacific[b]   Emerging Europe[f]   Latin America[g]

[legend] Foreign bank range[c] — Estimated share[d] — Cross-border share[e]

[a]Data up to the fourth quarter of 2004. [b]China, India, Indonesia, Korea, Malaysia, the Philippines, Thailand and Taiwan (China). [c]The lower bound is the ratio of international claims on non-banks (which include local claims in foreign currency) to total credit to non-banks (domestic credit plus cross-border claims). The inclusion of local claims in local currency (on all sectors) in the numerator yields the upper bound. [d]Implied foreign bank share from applying the sectoral breakdown available for international claims to local currency claims. [e]Ratio of BIS reporting banks' cross-border claims on non-banks to total credit to non-banks. [f]The Czech Republic, Hungary, Poland, Russia and Turkey. [g]Brazil, Chile, Mexico and Venezuela.

Sources: IMF; BIS calculations.

Figure 3. Foreign bank participation in emerging markets, by region[a]

total bank credit in Latin America and emerging Europe, but below 10 percent in emerging Asia. With the growth in local claims in local currencies, the estimated *total* participation of foreign banks is higher in each region, but still relatively low in emerging Asia. Even though foreign banks' exposure to emerging Asia is comparatively large in absolute terms,[9] these banks account for only 7 percent of total bank credit in the region, in contrast to an estimated 40 percent to 45 percent in emerging Europe and Latin America.

Nonetheless there is considerable heterogeneity in the degree of foreign bank participation across countries in emerging Asia. This partially reflects differences (across countries) in the capital controls and restrictions on foreign lending, although the relationship is murky. For example, capital controls and regulations in China have effectively shut out foreign banks, while foreign bank participation in India has just become more difficult.[10] In

[9]BIS reporting banks' foreign claims (ultimate risk basis) on all sectors in Asia-Pacific stood at $600 billion in the first quarter of 2005, compared with $495 billion vis-à-vis emerging Europe and $515 billion vis-à-vis Latin America.

[10]Bank lending accounted for 98.8 percent of all business financing in China in the first quarter of 2005, compared to 93.8 percent in the same period last year and a low of 75.9 percent for the whole of 2001 (*Financial Times*, May 28, 2005). The Reserve Bank of India announced in February 2005 that foreign banks cannot acquire Indian banks, and that their Indian subsidiaries will not be able to open branches freely. These restrictions will remain until 2009 ("Welcome, yet unwelcome," *The Economist*, March 10, 2005).

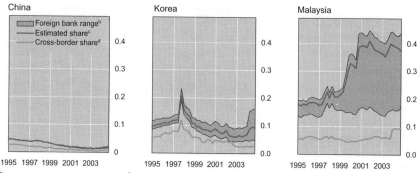

^aData up to the fourth quarter of 2004. ^bThe lower bound is the ratio of international claims on non-banks (which include local claims in foreign currency) to total credit to non-banks (domestic credit plus cross-border claims). The inclusion of local claims in local currency (on all sectors) in the numerator yields the upper bound. ^cImplied foreign bank share from applying the sectoral breakdown available for international claims to local currency claims. ^dRatio of BIS reporting banks' cross-border claims on non-banks to total credit to non-banks.

Sources: IMF; BIS calculations.

Figure 4. Foreign bank participation in China, Korea and Malaysia^a

contrast, regulation on foreign banks' operations in Thailand, Malaysia, the Philippines, and Korea are relatively less binding. The measures discussed above are broadly consistent with this. China stands out with exceptionally low foreign bank penetration, at less than 2 percent of the total credit to nonbanks in the country (Figure 4).[11] Foreign bank participation is relatively low in other emerging Asian countries as well, at an estimated 10 percent in Korea, India, and Taiwan. In contrast, Malaysia (at 36 percent) and the Philippines (at 26 percent) are on par with emerging markets in other regions.

The lifting of restrictions on foreign direct investment (FDI) in some countries contributed to the rise in foreign banks' activities.[12] Prior to the Asian crisis, many emerging Asian economies encouraged FDI in manufacturing, which helped to fuel export led growth, but restricted FDI in the service sector. As these restrictions were loosened, foreign banks moved

---

[11] In absolute terms, BIS reporting banks' exposure to China is large. Foreign claims (ultimate risk basis) stood at $80 billion in the fourth quarter of 2004, fourth behind Mexico, Brazil, and Poland. Just over 10 percent of these claims are accounted for by local claims in local currency. Moving forward, foreign bank participation in China should expand as (1) the Pacific Basin Research Center develops a uniform set of rules governing domestic and foreign banks, and (2) the privatization of major Chinese banks moves forward, possibly putting substantial equity interests in the hands of foreigners.

[12] See Domanski (2005) for a detailed discussion of financial sector FDI in emerging markets.

into sectors that were previously off limits, and started to compete directly with domestic banks (Coppel and Davies, 2003).With the retrenchment of Japanese banks over the 1990s, U.S. and European headquartered banks have emerged as the dominant foreign banks in the region (Figure 1, right-hand panel). In particular, Citibank is the largest foreign bank in many emerging Asian countries, while HSBC, Standard Chartered, Deutsche Bank, and ABN Amro also have a significant presence in the region.[13]

The widening "bands" of the foreign bank participation measures in Figures 3 and 4 highlight the growth in BIS reporting banks' local positions. Although the BIS data do not permit a finer analysis of these local currency claims, data from the CEIC Data Company's Asia database can shed light on the nature of these operations in individual countries. Consistent with the measures presented above, foreign banks account for a relatively small, but in some countries increasing, share of total *domestic* banking assets (Figure 5). In particular, foreign banks control roughly 9 percent of total domestic banking assets in Korea, up from 6 percent three years ago. Similarly, foreign banks account for roughly 10 percent of domestic bank assets in Taiwan and Indonesia, from 5 percent and 8 percent, respectively, in 2000.[14]

The importance of *intra-regional* credit within emerging Asia is more difficult to assess. Very few emerging economies report international banking statistics to the BIS. Banks located in those emerging Asian countries that do report data — India and Taiwan — have relatively small cross-border positions. For example, banks resident in Taiwan account for a mere $6 billion out of the $442 billion in total cross-border claims on emerging Asia in the BIS data. Similarly, the cross-border claims of banks in India vis-à-vis emerging Asia are less than $1 billion.[15] Data on syndicated loan structures suggests that cross-border lending by banks headquartered in the region

---

[13]The CEIC database indicates that Citibank accounts for an estimated 1–2 percent of total bank assets in Indonesia, India and Thailand, and as much as 8 percent in the Philippines. HSBC has a similar presence in Indonesia and India, but has a much smaller presence in the Philippines.

[14]These measures depend critically on the threshold used in determining foreign ownership of domestic banks. For example, Lim (2004) points out that in the case of Korea, foreign banks' share of domestic banking assets jumps considerably when a 40 percent rather than 50 percent threshold is applied.

[15]Taiwanese banks' consolidated foreign claims have trended upwards since mid-2002. This is primarily the result of greater credit to the United States and euro area, while total credit to borrowers in emerging Asia has remained roughly flat at $8 billion.

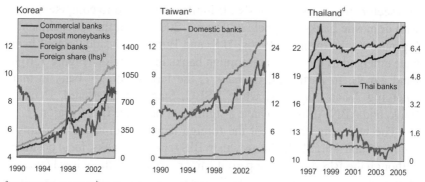

[a]In trillion of Korean won. [b]For Korea as a share of total assets of deposit money banks, for Taiwan as a share of total banking assets and for Thailand as a share of commercial banks' total assets; in per cent. [c]In billions of New Taiwan dollars. [d]In trillions of Thai baht.

Source: CEIC Asia Database.

Figure 5. Bank assets in Korea, Taiwan and Thailand

is a small share of the total. In contrast to Latin America and emerging Europe, where U.S. and European headquartered banks have provided the bulk of syndicated credit, regional banks have been the largest providers in emerging Asia. However, most of this syndicated credit has been essentially domestic lending, for example Thai banks participating in syndicates for borrowers in Thailand.[16] Most of this business has taken place in China, Korea and Taiwan, with the banks (and borrowers) of other Asian countries participating significantly less in syndicated loans.

The growth in foreign banks' local currency operations in many countries has gone hand-in-hand with changes in the asset composition of their balance sheets. For example, since the Asian crisis, foreign banks operating in Korea, Taiwan, and Thailand have channeled funds into securities and other assets (Figure 6), leading to a fall in the share of loans in their total (host-country) assets.

Loans themselves have shifted away from the traditional customer base, that is, manufacturers, and towards consumer and mortgage lending in many countries (Figure 7). In Thailand for example, despite a recent pickup, lending for construction, manufacturing, and commerce trended downward

---

[16]Banks headquartered in emerging Asia have provided over 50 percent of the total syndicated loans to nonbanks in the region over the 1999–2005 period. This share has risen since the Asian crisis, primarily reflecting the retrenchment of Japanese banks. See the box by Blaise Gadanecz in the September 2005 BIS Quarterly Review for discussion.

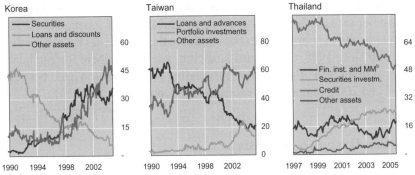

^aAs a share of foreign banks' total domestic assets; in per cent. ^bFinancial institutions and money market.

Source: CEIC Asia Database.

Figure 6. Foreign banks' assets in Korea, Taiwan and Thailand^a

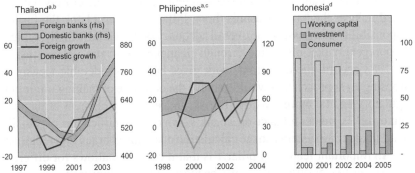

^aGrowth rates in per cent. ^bStocks in billions of Thai baht. ^cStocks in billions of Philippine peso. ^dAs a share of foreign banks' total locally extended loans to borrowers in Indonesia; in per cent.

Sources: CEIC Asia Database.

Figure 7. Consumer lending in Thailand, Philippines and Indonesia

between 1997 and 2004. In contrast, consumer lending in Thailand grew by roughly 30 percent over this same time period. While foreign banks in Thailand have small positions (relative to domestic banks) in the mortgage market, they have been much more active in other areas of consumer finance, for example in credit card loans where they accounted for 35 percent of the total in 2004 (down from 41 percent in 1999). As in Thailand, consumer lending in Indonesia and the Philippines has also picked up since 2000. Foreign banks' consumer loans have grown to 24 percent of their total credit to borrowers in Indonesia in 2005, from roughly 6 percent in 2000. Overall, consumer loans in Indonesia grew at an annual rate of 9 percent in 2004. Similarly, outstanding loans to households in the Philippines have more than doubled since 1998. Credit card financing, a segment where foreign banks control more than 70 percent of outstanding loans, almost tripled between 1998 and 2004, to reach 37 percent of total consumer loans.

3. Basel II Issues in East Asia

Most Asian supervisory authorities have embraced the Basel II framework as something that will bolster reforms after the Asian crisis. The framework is seen as a way to encourage banks to move from collateral-based lending to "risk management".

The Basel II framework consists of three mutually reinforcing "pillars". Pillar 1 aligns a bank's minimum capital requirements more closely with its actual risks as the bank measures them. Pillar 2 assigns a bank the further responsibility of assessing the overall adequacy of its capital. Finally, pillar 3 encourages market discipline through financial disclosure. In contrast to the 1988 accord, the new framework gives banks considerable leeway in choosing an approach that would achieve the objective of making minimum regulatory capital more sensitive to risk. Indeed, a key element of the new framework is greater reliance on a bank's own risk quantification, especially on internal rating systems, in the calculation of capital charges for credit risk.

An important feature of pillar 1 is that it explicitly allows for different approaches to measuring risk, with the more advanced approaches designed to lead to somewhat smaller capital charges for the same exposure. The least sophisticated approach to measuring credit risk is the standardized approach (SA), which simply modifies the approach of the 1988 accord. The advanced approaches are the internal ratings based approach (IRBA)[17] for credit risk and the advanced measurement approach (AMA) for operational risk. Both methods allow banks to use their own estimates for calculating minimum regulatory capital.

---

[17]The risk parameters of the IRBA are the probability of default (PD), loss given default (LGD), the exposure at default (EAD), and maturity (M). The Foundation IRB approach (FIRBA) requires banks to only estimate PDs for their internal rating grades, while the Basel Committee provides supervisory estimates for all other risk parameters.

Pillar 2 requires supervisors to evaluate a bank's own risk assessment. This review encompasses a bank's internal capital allocation practices and any risks not covered under pillar 1. It is supposed to cover, for example, interest rate risk in the banking book. Hence, pillar 2 makes greater demands on supervisory discretion and judgment and thus places greater importance on the supervisor's technical expertise and experience.

Most bank regulators in East Asia have expressed an intention to implement Basel II in the near future. As shown in Table 1, Australia, Hong Kong, New Zealand, and Singapore are the quickest, with plans to implement the advanced approaches in the framework in 2007–08 along with most of the Group of 10 (G-10) countries that decided on the framework. Malaysia, the Philippines, and Thailand plan to implement in 2009. China plans to implement "Basel 1 $1/2$" — that is, Basel 1 plus some elements of Basel II — by 2007.

The schedules depend largely on the amount of time the authorities think their banks will need to gather the data required by the advanced approaches. Nonetheless, these plans have tended to be quite ambitious. This may be in part because of a perceived urgency to enhance risk management by their banks. It may also be because of a desire to keep to a minimum the periods in which home and host supervisors apply different approaches. Finally, it may be because of the peer pressure the different supervisors in the region exert on one another.[18] The advanced approaches are perceived to be especially advantageous in mortgage and consumer loans. Hence, foreign and domestic banks are not only trying to shift their portfolios towards such loans but also racing to build the data bases that will allow them to apply the advanced approaches as soon as their supervisors allow them.

An important cross-border banking issue in Asia, as it is elsewhere, is the cooperation and division of labor between home and host supervisors. As pointed out by Bollard (2004), two supervisors may have different mandates, one to protect depositors, the other to maintain the soundness and efficiency of the financial system. This is an especially difficult issue when a supervisor is dealing with a foreign branch or subsidiary that is systemically important in the host country but not in the home country. In times of stress, the differences are likely to be most pronounced: two supervisors may have different views on whether the problems of a distressed branch or

---

[18]All EMEAP member countries (except New Zealand) and India participated in the third quantitative impact study (QIS 3) carried out by the BCBS.

Table 1. Implementation of the new framework (NF) — Expected approaches in selected Asian economies[a]

NF		Credit Risk — SA	Credit Risk — FIRB	Credit Risk — AIRB	Op Risk — BIA	Op Risk — SA	Op Risk — AMA	Specifics
AU	All banks, 2007	2007	2007	2007 Combined with AMA, IMA (MR)	2007	2007	2007	All approaches at the same time
CN	Basel 1.5	2007, 1988 Accord	No	No	No	No	No	Basel 1 plus Pillar 2 and 3
HK	All banks, 2006	2006	2006	2007	2006	2006	No	Basic approach, more flexibility for FIRB banks
ID	All banks, 2008	2008	2010	2010	2008	2008	Not specified yet	Market risk in parallel with CR (SA) 2008
IN	All banks, 2007	Mar 2007	Not specified yet	Not specified yet	Mar 2	Not specified	Not specified yet	Two phases, 2007 and later
JP	All banks, Mar 2007	Mar 2007	Mar 2007	Mar 2008	Mar 2007	Mar 2007	Mar 2008	4% ratio for domestic banks
KR	All banks, 2007	2007	2007	2007	2007	2007	2007	Some specifics not yet clear

(Continued)

Table 1. (*Continued*)

NF	Credit Risk—SA	Credit Risk—FIRB	Credit Risk—AIRB	Op Risk—BIA	Op Risk—SA	Op Risk—AMA	Specifics
MY All banks, 2007	2007	2009	Not specified yet	2007	2007	Not specified yet	Two phases, 2007 and 2009
NZ All banks, 2007	2007	2007	2007 Combined with AMA, IMA (MR)	2007	2007	2007	All approaches at the same time
PH All banks, 2006	2006	2009	2009	2006	2006	2009	Some risk weights earlier adopted; Basel 1 type approach
SG All banks, 2006	2006	2006	2007	2006	2006	2007	Flexibility in use test possible
TH All banks, 2008	2008	2008	2009	2008	2008	2009	Encouraging improving risk management
TW All banks, 2006	2006	2006	2007	2006	2006	2007	Encouraging on IRBA

Note: AUS = Australia; CN = China; HK = Hong Kong; ID = Indonesia; IN = India; JP = Japan; KR = Korea; MY = Malaysia; NZ = New Zealand; PH = Philippines; SG = Singapore; TH = Thailand; TW = Taiwan.
[a]Dates indicate either year end or month end.
Sources: National authorities and authors' own estimates.

subsidiary of a foreign bank are systemic, and if support is required, who provides it.

Implementing Basel II heightens the need for cross-border cooperation. In 1992, the "Basel Concordat" recommended that the home supervisor be responsible for a banking group as a whole and the host supervisor for the legal entities within its jurisdiction. This does not solve all problems. In Asia, the host supervisors implementing the advanced approaches later than are the home supervisors will have to deal with the fact that they will in effect often be requiring foreign banks to calculate capital twice, once under the standardized approach and again under the advanced approaches. In the case of the Philippines, for example, large foreign banks are expected to adopt the standardized approach even while they consolidate their risks at the global level using more advanced approaches. When home and host supervisors are both implementing the advanced approaches, avoiding double calculations of capital will require the two supervisors to somehow agree on how to validate the specific models used by a bank.

Cooperation among supervisors is paramount in Hong Kong, where the Hong Kong Monetary Authority (HKMA) is both an important host and an important home supervisor. The required information flows between all the foreign home and host countries can be quite demanding. The HKMA plans to implement all approaches of the new framework within the agreed timetable, with the exception of the provision of the AMA for operational risk. In some instances, the entry criteria for the IRB approach being adopted by the HKMA may differ from those adopted by the relevant home supervisor. The HKMA has engaged in discussions with the home supervisors of the major foreign banks to harmonize requirements and build in flexibility so that these banks can adhere to their home supervisory requirements in most circumstances.

Internationally active banks with significant subsidiaries in Hong Kong which will most likely be applying the AMA for operational risk on a group-wide basis but be required to use a simpler approach for the Hong Kong bank. On the face of it, this will place a regulatory burden on the bank involved, requiring a double calculation of regulatory capital. However, the HKMA is understood to be planning to take make adjustments under pillar 2 for the fact that a bank is operating on AMA. When moving to the advanced approaches, the HKMA also requires 75 percent coverage of credit-risk weighted assets, and this may override less stringent requirements on two sides — the banks' home and host supervisors.

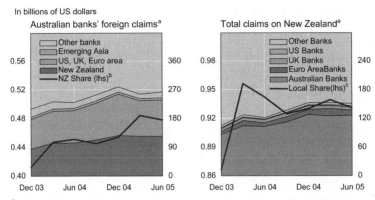

bForeign claims on residents of New Zealand as a share of Australian banks' total foreign claims. cLocal currency claims extended by offices of foreign banks in New Zealand as a share of their total foreign claims (immediate borrower basis) on New Zealand.

Source: BIS.

Figure 8. The Australia-New Zealand link

Like the HKMA, the regulatory authorities in Australia and New Zealand face an unusual set of home-host regulatory issues. Both economies are highly bank dependent. However, this reliance is more pronounced in New Zealand, with banks holding roughly three quarters of financial system assets as opposed to roughly half in Australia. At present, Australian headquartered banks own roughly 85 percent of New Zealand's banking assets, despite the fact that Australia does not have large, systemically important foreign banks. As shown in Figure 8, exposure to borrowers in New Zealand constitutes more 50 percent of their total foreign exposure on an ultimate risk basis, primarily through their local positions in local currency. From New Zealand's perspective, Australian banks account for over 90 percent of total foreign claims on the country.

Bilateral discussions over the past two years have focused on closer integration in trans-Tasman banking regulation and supervision. Among the issues to be resolved are depositor preference, crisis resolution and capital allocation. Discussions have focused on whether systemically important banks in New Zealand should be required to be locally incorporated, and whether they must be able to function on a stand-alone basis in a banking crisis. One question is whether the local board in New Zealand can be made to act in the interest of the New Zealand entity. The Reserve Bank of New

Zealand (RBNZ) now harmonizes its approach with that of the Australian Prudential Regulation Authority (APRA), which insisted at an early stage that their four major banks use the advanced approaches. Banks operating in New Zealand, when meeting certain criteria, will now have the option to use the advanced approaches for credit and operational risk.[19] The "Terms of Engagement" between APRA and RBNZ contains each supervisor's right to set its own minimum levels of capital while trying to minimize the cost for implementation. It goes even further by requiring both institutions to conduct joint supervisory reviews in both jurisdictions and to share necessary information.

4. Pillar 2 and the Risk of Another Asian Crisis

Pillar 2 serves as an overarching supervisory escape clause. In principle, pillar 1 focuses only on credit, market and operational risks faced by an individual bank as a consequence of *the individual items in its own asset portfolio*. To the extent that these risks are not satisfactorily addressed by pillar 1, banks and supervisors are supposed to turn to pillar 2. For example, if the portfolio lacks diversification — that is, has "concentration risk" — this would be an issue for pillar 2.

Systemic risk is also supposed to be addressed by pillar 2. De Bandt and Hartmann (1999) point out that "at the heart of systemic risk are contagion effects" and the concept "includes financial instabilities in response to aggregate shocks." Procyclicality in financial systems can lead to biases in the measurement of risk. Borio, Furfine, and Lowe (2001) argue that risks to the financial system tend to build up during economic booms, and these risks may be underestimated by pillar 1. Recessions may lead to bad loans and an increase in measured risk even when there really is no such increase in risk. If properly applied, pillar 2 should allow banks and supervisors to recognize the build up of risk during booms and to ignore what may seem to be a rise in risk during busts.

Moreover, systemic risk may not be entirely exogenous. Archarya and Yorulmazer (2002) show that banks have an incentive to herd — that is, to

---

[19]See Bollard, A., Governor, Reserve Bank of New Zealand, "Address to the Australasian Institute of Banking and Finance", Sydney, 23 March 2005.

hold "correlated portfolios" — because if there is a problem, the government is more likely to bail them out if the problem is systemic. In other words, a bank is more likely to take excessive risk if other banks are taking the same kinds of risk. If something goes wrong, the bank is likely to fail with other banks and the government is more likely to step in with a rescue package. This is a moral hazard that can only be addressed under pillar 2.

In Asia, these systemic risks seem to apply in spades. Moreover, banks in the region face an important cross-border dimension to these risks. The "contagion effects" to which De Bandt and Hartmann refer are often regional in nature. The region is vulnerable to contagion because of capital flows, which tend to be highly correlated and procyclical. Alba *et al.* (1998) suggest that the buildup of risk leading up to the 1997 Asian crisis was partly a result of "pro-cyclical macroeconomic policy responses to large capital flows". Kaminsky *et al.* (2004) have documented such pro-cyclicality for emerging markets in general: "periods of capital inflows are associated with expansionary macroeconomic policies and periods of capital outflows with contractionary macroeconomic policies". In an earlier paper, Kaminsky *et al.* (2003) have also pointed out that contagion tends to arise when a surge in capital flows is followed by a shock.

Can pillar 2 deal with contagion risk? Compared to pillar 1, pillar 2 relies to a high degree on judgment and supervisory discretion. To assess cross-border systemic risks, banks in the region would need to undertake stress tests for various scenarios of crisis and contagion. For the same reasons that banks would herd in the Archarya-Yorulmazer world, there is little incentive for banks to assess such systemic risks on their own. Supervisors would have to make them do so. In Asia, this would require a high degree of assertiveness on the part of supervisors, which may be lacking for historical reasons. For some countries in Asia, it is hard to imagine a bank examiner telling the bank's risk officer to account properly for a qualitative, judgmental type of risk. When it is the bank examiner's view against that of the bank's risk officer, it is not clear that the examiner's view will prevail.

In a regional crisis involving foreign banks, cooperation will be important not only between host supervisors in the region and home supervisors outside the region but also between just the host supervisors within the region. It will be important that the various Asian supervisors be prepared for such an eventuality.

5. Conclusion

While the presence of foreign banks in Asia remains limited, these banks are making their presence felt in some of the fast-growing market segments. These segments include those where the advanced approaches under Basel II are most advantageous. The supervisory authorities are finding themselves having to cope with home-host issues and with the perceived need to give their domestic banks time to collect the data needed to implement the more advanced approaches and thus be able to compete with foreign banks. Another important cross-border issue for banking systems in East Asia has been the question of how to deal with the systemic risk of contagion. While the Basel II framework would point to pillar 2 as a way to deal with such risks, banks in the region have little incentive to assess this risk on their own. Supervisors will have to insist that the banks do so. The large judgmental component of pillar 2, however, may call for a degree of supervisory assertiveness that may still be lacking in some countries in Asia.

References

Alba, P., A. Bhattacharya, S. Claessens, S. Ghosh and L. Hernandez, 1998, "Volatility and Contagion in a Financially Integrated World: Lessons from East Asia's Recent Experience," World Bank Policy Research Working Paper No 2008, December.

Acharya, V. V. and T. Yorulmazer, 2002, "Information Contagion and Inter-Bank Correlation in a Theory of Systematic Risk," London Business School Working Paper, December.

Bollard, A., 2004, "Being a Responsible Host: Supervising Foreign Banks," address to the Federal Reserve Bank of Chicago Conference: Systemic Financial Crises — Resolving Large Bank Insolvencies, Chicago, 2 October.

Borio, C., C. Furfine and P. Lowe, 2001, "Procyclicality of the Financial System and Financial Stability: Issues and Policy Options," in *Marrying the Macro- and Microprudential Dimensions of Financial Stability*, BIS Papers No 1, March.

Bustelo, P., 1998, "The East Asian Financial Crises: An Analytical Survey," ICEI Working paper no 10.

Coppel, J. and M. Davies, 2003, "Foreign Participation in East Asia's Banking Sector," contribution to the CGFS working group on FDI in the financial sector of emerging market economies, http://www.bis.org/publ/cgfs22cbpapers.htm

De Bandt, O. and P. Hartmann, 1999, "What is Systemic Risk Today?" in *Risk Measurement and Systemic Risk: Proceedings of the Second Joint Central Bank Research Conference*, November 1998, Bank of Japan, Tokyo.

Domanski, D., 2005, "Foreign Banks in Emerging Market Economies: Changing Players, Changing Issues," *BIS Quarterly Review*, forthcoming.

Domanski, D., P. D. Wooldridge and A. Cobau, 2003, "Changing Links Between Mature and Emerging Financial Markets," *BIS Quarterly Review*, September, pp. 45–54.

Moreno, R., G. Pasadilla and E. Remolona, 1998, "Asia's Financial Crisis: Lessons and Policy Responses", in *Asia: Responding to Crisis*, ADB Institute.

Kaminsky, G., C. M. Reinhart and C. A. Vegh, 2003, "The Unholy Trinity of Financial Contagion," NBER Working Paper No. W10061, November.

Kaminsky, G., C. M. Reinhart and C. A. Vegh, 2004, "When It Rains, It Pours: Procyclical Capital Flows in Macroeconomic Policies," NBER Working Paper No. W10780.

Lim, S., 2004, "Foreign Capital Entry in the Domestic Banking Market in Korea: Bitter Medicine or Poison".

Lubin, D., 2002, "Bank Lending to Emerging Markets," discussion paper no. 2002/61, World Institute for Development Economics Research, United Nations University, June.

McCauley, R. N., J. Ruu and P. D. Wooldridge, 2002, "Globalizing International Banking," *BIS Quarterly Review*, March, pp. 41–51.

McGuire, P. and P. Wooldridge, 2005, "The BIS Consolidated Banking Statistics: Structure, Uses and Recent Enhancements," *BIS Quarterly Review*, September.

Schmukler, S. L. and M. Kawai, 2001, "Crisis and contagion in East Asia: Nine Lessons," World Bank Policy Research Working Paper No. 2610, June.

Schnabel, I. and H. S. Shin, 2004, "Liquidity and Contagion: The Crisis of 1763," May. http://ssrn.com/abstract=600746.

Stefan Hohl is a Senior Financial Sector Specialist in the Financial Stability Institute of the Bank for International Settlements (BIS). Patrick McGuire is an economist at the BIS. Eli Remolona is the Head of Economics for Asia and the Pacific and the Deputy Chief Representative of the BIS Office for Asia and the Pacific in Hong Kong. The views expressed are those of the authors and do not necessarily reflect those of the BIS or the Basel Committee of Banking Supervision.

Discussion of the Session
"Survey of the Current Landscape"

Philipp Hartmann*

European Central Bank

The Federal Reserve Bank of Chicago has again proven its ability to ask the right questions at the right time. The present conference on cross-border banking touches on major policy issues, not only on the continent where I am based but also in most other parts of the world. In Europe, for example, the September 2004 informal EcoFin meeting in Scheveningen, Netherlands, discussed why cross-border consolidation was so low and asked the European Commission to study the obstacles leading to this situation. In April 2005, the Commission launched an online survey to collect evidence. The conclusions drawn from this survey were issued almost contemporaneously with the present conference (European Commission, 2005a). It is a pleasure and an honor for me to have the opportunity to discuss the papers presented by three outstanding experts in this area in the opening session of this conference.

Given the quite extensive material provided by the three papers, I decided to be relatively systematic in this discussion. First, I should like to summarize the papers, delimitating them from each other in their main perspectives and messages. Second, I should like to add a brief discussion on the determinants of cross-border banking. Next, I turn to the economic implications of cross-border banking, focusing on two specific issues (the relationship between financial integration and financial stability and the risk implications of foreign exposures). In the following two parts, I shall comment on some issues raised in the papers and provide my own perspective on them. This concerns the degree of integration achieved in European banking and the debate on branch-based versus subsidiary-based cross-border banking activities.

1. Summary and Comparison of the Papers

All the three papers (Dermine, Cetorelli and Goldberg, and Hohl, McGuire, and Remolona) survey the cross-border banking landscape from different angles. They have in common that they all provide evidence on cross-border activities by banks and discuss related policy issues. The angles substantially differ, however, at least in two respects, the geographical scope of the evidence presented and the type of policy issues put at the center of the discussion.

Regarding geographical scope, Jean Dermine looks at European banks in Europe. Stefan Hohl, Patrick McGuire and Eli Remolona cover Asian-Pacific banks, but also a few global banks operating in the Asian-Pacific region. Nicola Cetorelli and Linda Goldberg study U.S. banks' activities abroad but not those of foreign institutions in the U.S. So, the first two papers are relatively symmetric, whereas the last is highly asymmetric. In any case, the session covers a large share of the globe with this evidence, even if not fully complete.

Regarding policy issues, Dermine addresses corporate structures, safety nets, and supervisory structures. Cetorelli and Goldberg, in contrast, concentrate just on the risk-taking of U.S. banks. Finally, the paper by the group from the Bank for International Settlements (BIS) analyzes the implementation of Basel II in Asia. So, with few exceptions the policy issues addressed are really quite different. While the choice of policy questions reflects very likely the "hot issues" in the respective regions, one should not be misled to think that the policy issues addressed in one of the papers is not relevant for the regions covered by the other papers.

Let me now briefly summarize my understanding of the main messages of each paper. Jean Dermine reminds us of the objectives and implications of the Single European Market. Building on his smashing 2003 piece on "European banking: Past, present and future," he notes that if the single market for financial services was working perfectly, then one would expect banks to organize their foreign operations with branches, which do not require a separate banking license or heavier supervisory burdens abroad. This is, however, not really what happens, as a larger part of cross-border operations of European banks are undertaken through subsidiaries.

What has changed since 2003? Since October 2004, firms can adopt a European Company structure, the new Societas Europea. Moreover, a major European bank, Nordea AB, announced to adopt this structure to better pursue its cross-border activities.[1] In principle, this should simplify significantly the operation with branches across European Union (EU) countries. And, indeed, some increases in cross-border activities can be observed. Nevertheless, Dermine identifies at least one major obstacle to European banks reaping the benefits of the Societas Europea, namely current deposit insurance arrangements. The main argument seems to be that a company like Nordea, which has paid in the deposit insurance schemes of several countries would not be able to recover the money after turning into a branch structure. It would only benefit from the funds paid into its home-country scheme.

Broadening the perspective to supervision and bank safety nets more generally, Dermine points out that recent advances in European banking integration argue more and more against the existing home country approach. Whether the next regime should be a more centralized European solution or a host country approach needs to be decided on the basis of a constitutional debate and, ultimately, the preferences of the European citizens.

Nicola Cetorelli and Linda Goldberg track U.S. banks' foreign exposures to a large number of industrial, emerging, and developing countries over the last two decades. These exposures include both cross-border claims and local claims by U.S. banks operating in those countries. They are dominated by a small number of large "money center banks" and by activities in EU countries. Whereas overall absolute foreign exposures decline in the second half of the 1980s and increase since the early 1990s, foreign exposures relative to total assets show the opposite, rather "hump-shaped" evolution. This suggests (plausibly) that in a domestic upturn U.S. banks tend to be less interested in foreign activities. Local claims are predominantly to Europe, whereas cross-border claims are more to Latin America. Over time, however, Latin America gains and Europe loses.

An important variable in the authors' study is what they denote as "transfer risk". This risk is measured *vis-à-vis* a specific country by the sum of a bank's cross-border claims, derivative claims as well as net local claims (if the latter is positive). The intention is to capture the risk that agents in a given country are unable to serve a foreign currency liability for lack of foreign exchange. This risk seems to follow the cycle of total exposure,

---

[1]Nordea is a bank with a balance sheet of 320 billion euros and about 29,000 employees, which operates in 20 countries, in particular in the Nordic and Baltic regions of Europe.

although it somewhat declines as a share of it. Moreover, within the transfer risk, credit ratings of countries have improved since the late 1990s. Both observations lead to the conclusion that the expanding activities of U.S. banks abroad may be less of a concern for their stability.

The data presented by Stefan Hohl, Patrick McGuire and Eli Remolona suggest relatively limited cross-border banking in the Asia-Pacific region, in particular when compared to Latin America or to Central and Eastern Europe. There are, however, some specific exceptions, such as Australia and New Zealand, where the former country basically possesses all the remaining banks in the latter. The cross-border lending that does take place originates increasingly from U.S. and European banks, which expand *inter alia* in fast-growing market segments for which the advanced approaches under the Basel II Capital Accord are most advantageous. These banks give also a special role to Hong Kong and Singapore, which serve as "hubs" for their regional activities.

Asian and Pacific rim countries have greeted the adoption of Basel II with astonishing enthusiasm, announcing often to adopt the new framework relatively early. An implication of this enthusiasm is, however, that local banks — condemned to start with the standardized approach under pillar 1 — may face competitive disadvantages to major foreign banks operating under potentially more capital friendly advanced approaches. So, early adoption of Basel II in the Asia-Pacific region together with local authorities' concerns to preserve a domestic banking industry, may interfere with the implicit objective of the new Accord to allow banks to operate under the same approach worldwide on a consolidated basis. A further challenge for local supervisors is to make sure that under the new regime another systemic crisis like the 1997 one is less likely. Capitalization to shelter banks from systemic risk could in principle be achieved under pillar 2. Hohl, McGuire, and Remolona point out, however, that the pre-condition of sufficient supervisory power to enforce such inherently more judgmental risks cannot be taken for granted for many of the authorities in this region.

2. The Determinants of Cross-Border Banking

All three papers make an excellent contribution to reviewing the evidence on cross-border banking for the specific regions they are interested in or in raising important policy issues. Except perhaps for Jean Dermine's, the papers are, however, relatively silent about economic explanations for the patterns observed. For example, why is cross-border banking activity more limited in the Asia-Pacific region? Or why is U.S. foreign exposure increasing in absolute terms and why more in Latin America than in Europe? I should like to use this section to at least list some of the general driving forces for, and obstacles to, cross-border banking.

Classic explanations for cross-border banking include the profit motive (some countries offer higher profit margins), risk management advantages (improved diversification through investment in countries that have different economic shocks than the home country) or, perhaps less flattering, regulatory and tax arbitrage (including risk shifting in response to potentially lighter supervisory regimes or more generous safety nets in some countries). More recent explanations for enhanced cross-border activities include advances in communication technology (such as internet banking), financial development and innovation (making financial services more tradable, for example, securitization), deregulation, and financial liberalization (see, e.g., Berger and DeYoung, 2006, and Degryse and Ongena, 2004). Also, financial consolidation in smaller countries may reach levels at which competition authorities become more resistant to further banking mergers and institutions have to go abroad to pursue further growth strategies.

What are the obstacles to cross-border banking that prevent it to become very widespread? In particular, in retail banking distance is still associated with asymmetric information. Next, there are language and cultural barriers, which may also be related to preferences for different products and product characteristics. The need for different product specifications may lead for example, to difficulties in consolidating back-office functions that might be important for realizing economies of scale. And the greater uncertainty about the prospects of loans to foreign projects may offset the benefits from diversification. There is indeed some research that suggests that cross-border activities tend to be less efficient or profitable than domestic banking activities, at least among industrial countries. For example, DeYoung and Nolle (1996) or Berger *et al.* (2000) present efficiency studies suggesting this. Amihud *et al.* (2002) find negative abnormal returns for acquiring banks when they announce to take over a foreign bank. Berger *et al.* (2000), however, detect that U.S. banks are different from their foreign counterparts in that they operate also relatively efficiently abroad. Consistently with this, Berger *et al.* (2004) find that the U.S. has comparative advantages in both exporting and importing bank management via mergers and acquisitions (M&As).

In addition, to these "natural" obstacles, there are also the ones implied by public intervention. First, differences in banking regulations and supervisory practices can be powerful deterrents to the crossing of national borders. They may prevent the realization of scale economies and increase the costs of supervision for financial institutions. Jean Dermine's papers illustrate this in a telling way. Finally, the obstacle that made the headlines of the financial press in Europe over the last months, but which is in no way limited to Europe, is the attitude of national authorities *vis-à-vis* foreign entrants to their domestic banking sectors.

3. The Economic Implications of Cross-Border Banking

In this section I should like to turn from the determinants of cross-border banking to its implications. I shall first look at the implications for financial integration and financial stability and in particular at the relationship between the two. Second, I want to add a few observations from the point of view of risk management. The first discussion focuses on the macro-prudential implications, whereas the second is micro-prudential in nature.

Let us start by looking at the economic benefits of cross-border banking. First, it fosters financial integration. The associated improvements in risk sharing should help the household and corporate sectors in terms of consumption and investment. Cross-border banking should also contribute to larger and more liquid financial markets, with better execution and lower transaction costs. Last, increased cross-border banking usually leads to more competition and, in the case of emerging or developing countries, to the export of financial know how.

What are the risks associated with cross-border banking? A major concern for domestic authorities is the risk that foreign banks might transmit financial instability from abroad to their countries. One should not forget, however, that apart from enhanced cross-border contagion risk, there are also stabilizing effects of cross-border bank activities. For example, better risk sharing should help to stabilize the household and corporate sectors in the long run and more liquid financial markets should be more resilient to shocks. A second, and broader, national concern may be the loss of national policy autonomy, for example, related to widespread foreign ownership of banks. In particular, in extreme situations, such as a war, a country may be more constrained with respect to some financing possibilities. Finally, the concept of "essential service" may argue against foreign ownership. In some

rural areas for example, bank branches might be rather rare. Foreign institutions may be less sensitive to continue operating in such areas if they are
less profitable than other activities. This may enhance the risk that a country experiences the emergence of regions where citizens find it difficult to
gain convenient access to basic financial services, such as current accounts.
Several of these aspects illustrate how cross-border banking brings to the
fore the typical tension between the mobility of economic activity and the
immobility of political borders.

A particularly important issue for policy — addressed in various ways in
the three papers — are the stability implications of cross-border banking and
related greater banking integration. The discussion above suggests that —
in theory — the integration-stability relationship has an ambiguous sign. It
is probably fair to say that the literature provides only very limited evidence
helping to determine this sign. In the light of this shortage of knowledge,
I should like to display in what follows some new research trying to shed
some light on the integration-stability relationship.

Hartmann, Straetmans, and de Vries (2005) use very extreme co-
movements between individual banks' stock returns as a measure of banking
system risk. Figure 1, for example, displays the evolution of a recursively
estimated tail dependence parameter η that measures the dependence in
extreme crash situations for an arbitrary large number of institutions con-
stituting a banking system. The case displayed in the figure concerns the
25 systemically most important (and publicly listed) euro area banks for
the period 1992 to 2004. The case of independence (low systemic risk) is
described by a parameter value of $\eta = 1/N = 0.04$ and the case of complete
dependence (high systemic risk) by the value $\eta = 1$.

The figure suggests that the system risk of the major euro area banks is
relatively low and increasing very gradually. The low level in this figure is
mainly related to the still relatively limited linkages between euro are banks
across borders, which contrasts with more substantial domestic linkages. It
is worth noting that the first third of the sample period is characterized by a
number of major policy initiatives fostering financial integration, including
for example, the full liberalization of capital flows and the Second Banking Directive. In fact, a formal test of the stability of η over time finds
a structural break around the year 1997, even though the change is not
very large. Overall the picture is suggestive of a slowly advancing banking
integration process in Europe that has been accompanied by a very gradual increase in cross-border banking risks. This would lend some support

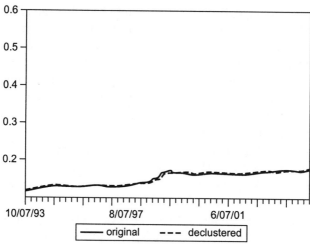

Note: The figure shows recursive estimates of the evolution of extreme negative tail dependence in the stock market excess returns of the 25 systemically most important euro area banks between April 1992 and February 2004. Points on the lines in the figure describe the degree to which extreme crashes of the stock market values for these banks occur together or separately. A value of 0.04 would mean that such crashes are independent and a value of 1 that they are fully dependent. The solid line is for plain excess returns and the dashed line for excess returns cleaned of GARCH effects. They are almost identical.

Source: Hartmann, Stractmans and de Vries (2005), Figure 1.

Figure 1. Evolution of banking system risk in the euro area

to the view that expanding cross-border banking should be accompanied by appropriate surveillance and supervisory policies that help to deal with banking problems that spill over political borders. While this particular evidence looks somewhat muted compared to the one referred to in Jean Dermine's paper, one should not forget that η here considers the full 25-dimensional systemic risk.

Next, I should like to address how to analyze the more micro-prudential risk implications of cross-border bank activities from the point of view of the home supervisor. Cetorelli and Goldberg look at country exposures and the credit ratings of countries. I should like to argue that this relatively focused perspective deserves to be extended by some standard approaches in finance. First, portfolio effects should ideally be taken into account. For example, some excellent work conducted at the Federal Reserve Bank of New York strongly underlines the value of country diversification in credit risk management (see Pesaran, Schuerman, and Treutler, 2005). Considering portfolio effects would further strengthen the relatively benign interpretation of U.S. banks' foreign exposures by the authors. Second, as pointed out above, information problems are likely to be a major source of risk in cross-border banking. Amihud *et al.* (2002) for example, suggest that they may fully offset any diversification benefits, as acquiring banks in cross-border mergers neither show increasing nor decreasing risks. Hence, considering information problems could qualify the main conclusions by Cetorelli and Goldberg.

4. Integration of European Retail Banking

One of the basic assumptions in Jean Dermine's paper is that banking integration has advanced lately in the European Union. This is undoubtedly the case when looking, for example, at banks' interbank and wholesale activities (see, for example, Hartmann *et al.*, 2004, and ECB, 2005). Now even a few larger cross-border mergers, such as the purchase of Crédit Commercial de France by HSBC in 2000 or of HypoVereinsbank by UniCredito in 2005, have occurred. I also agree with Dermine and his sources that these developments are basically significant enough to now think about more far-reaching European solutions with regard to supervision and safety nets, however difficult they may sound.

All this should, however, not blur the view on the fact that European banking integration still has to go a long way to reach a satisfactory level. The devil, here, is in the details of the retail markets. Figure 2 shows the evolution of cross-border loans by banks to nonbanks as a share of total loans in the euro area between 1997 and 2005. It is very clear that cross-border lending is extremely low. In the first half of the sample it increased from about 2.2 percent to about 3.5 percent and then remained at that level.

This observation goes hand in hand with persistent differences in retail lending rates across countries (ECB, 2005). So, it does not come as a surprise that the European Commission's (2005b) "Green paper on financial services policies (2005–10)" singles out retail financial services as one of the areas in which more progress is needed after the Financial Services Action Plan of 1999–2004.

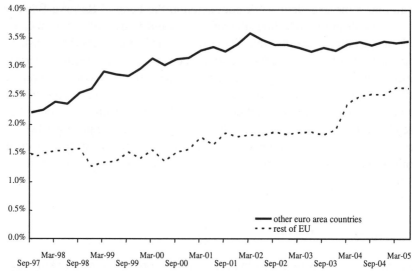

Note: The figure shows the evolution of cross-border loans by Monetary and Financial Institutions (MFIs) to non-MFIs between September 1997 and June 2005. The solid line refers to cross-border corporate loans from euro area countries to other euro area countries and the dashed line from euro area countries to non-euro area EU countries. The composition of the country groups change when countries join either the euro area or the EU. Greece is included in the euro area aggregate as of January 2001, the ten new EU member states are included in the EU aggregate as of May 2004. The values indicated on the vertical axis represent percentages of the outstanding amounts of cross-border loans as a share of total outstanding MFI loans (excluding the Eurosystem).
Source: ECB (2005), Figure 11.

Figure 2.   Evolution of cross-border corporate lending in the euro area

5. The Debate on Branches versus Subsidiaries

Let me close my discussion with a few observations on an issue which seems to be very much at the core of policy debates on cross-border banking, the choice between branches and subsidiaries in establishing a presence in foreign markets. Dermine puts it very much at the center of his paper and the BIS paper addresses it in the context of Trans-Tasman regulation and supervision.

There are two strands of thinking in the policy debate on the form of foreign bank presence. One looks at it from the perspective of financial integration, the other from the perspective of financial stability. As Dermine puts it, branch structures are better for financial integration and therefore more compatible with the idea of a Single Market for financial services. This concern seems to dominate now in EU policy circles, but not really in national policy makers' thinking. National authorities, in particular supervisors, tend often to stress more the benefits of subsidiary structures for domestic financial stability. For example, New Zealand wants the small number of Australian banks that now constitutes its entire banking system to operate as subsidiaries. The idea seems to be that the host country can then still "ring-fence" its financial sector, consumers and firms from stability problems that originate from abroad. An assumption is of course that one cannot fully trust a foreign safety net.

Who is right? And, is there a panacea? I would argue that the right answer on branch versus subsidiary structures depends on the specific situation of a country or region. If a region has already reached a high degree of financial integration, such as it seems to be the case between Australia and New Zealand, then the establishment of subsidiary structures may be less of a concern. In contrast, when a region is more fragmented and wants to integrate financial services better, then the existence of subsidiary structures could constitute a strong obstacle to further progress in financial integration. Hence, the dominant subsidiary structures in the EU may be more worrying then the efforts of New Zealand authorities to also turn the last remaining Australian branch into a subsidiary.

The specific regulatory environment is also relevant. In particular, one formal reason for the attitude of New Zealand authorities in Trans-Tasman regulation and supervision is that the Australian safety net clearly refers only to its own citizens. For example, in case of an Australian banking crisis the home authorities would have no legal basis for caring about New Zealand depositors in the foreign branches. By turning Australian branches into subsidiaries, New Zealand can use its own safety net to protect the citizens using these banks. Moreover, it is interesting to observe that the notion of "essential service" already referred to above seems to play a role in the Trans-Tasman approach, as New Zealand authorities pointed out that the domestic banks must continue operating in a crisis.

The question of branches versus subsidiaries for foreign bank operations has also become important in Central and Eastern Europe and the new EU member states. Many of these countries after privatization and liberalization of their financial sectors experienced a very high share of foreign ownership (often as high as 60 percent or even 80 percent of total assets). It will be interesting to see whether the European financial integration perspective or the domestic supervisory perspective is going to prevail in this region.

References

Amihud, Y., G. DeLong, and A. Saunders, 2002, "The Effects of Cross-Border Bank Mergers on Bank Risk and Value," *Journal of International Money and Finance*, 21, pp. 857–877.

Berger, A., R. DeYoung, H. Genay, and G. Udell, 2000, "Globalization of Financial Institutions: Evidence from Cross-Border Banking Performance," *Brookings-Wharton Papers on Financial Services*, 2000, pp. 23–120.

Berger, A., C. Buch, G. DeLong, and R. DeYoung, 2004, "The Comparative Advantage of Nations at Exporting Financial Institutions Management via M&As," *Journal of International Money and Finance*, 23(3), pp. 333–366.

Berger, A. and R. DeYoung, 2006, "Technological Progress and the Geographic Expansion of the Banking Industry," *Journal of Money, Credit, and Banking*, forthcoming.

Degryse, H. and S. Ongena, 2004, "The Impact of Technology and Regulation on the Geographical Scope of Banking," in X. Freixas, P. Hartmann and C. Mayer (eds.), *European Financial Integration*, Special Issue of the *Oxford Review of Economic Policy*, 20(4), pp. 571–590.

Dermine, J., 2003, "European Banking: Past, Present and Future," in V. Gaspar, P. Hartmann, and O. Sleijpen (eds.), *The Transformation of the European Financial System*, Frankfurt: European Central Bank, pp. 31–95.

DeYoung, R. and D. Nolle, 1996, "Foreign-Owned Banks in the U.S.: Earning Market Share or Buying It?," *Journal of Money, Credit, and Banking*, 28(4), pp. 622–636.

European Central Bank, 2005, "Indicators of Financial Integration in the Euro Area," Frankfurt, September.

European Commission, 2005a, "Cross-Border Consolidation in the EU Financial Sector," Commission Staff Working Document, SEC(2005)1398, 26.10.2005, Brussels.

European Commission, 2005b, "Green Paper on Financial Services Policies (2005–2010)," COM(2005)177, 3.5.2005, Brussels.

Hartmann, P., A. Maddaloni, and S. Manganelli, 2004, "The Euro Area Financial System: Structure, Integration and Policy Initiatives," *Oxford Review of Economic Policy*, 19(1), pp. 180–213.

Hartmann, P., S. Straetmans, and C. de Vries, 2005, "Banking System Stability: A Cross-Atlantic Perspective," NBER Working Paper, No. 11698, October.

Pesaran, H., T. Schuerman, and J. Treutler, 2005, "Global Business Cycles and Credit Risk," NBER Working Paper, No. 11493, July.

Philipp Hartmann is the head of the Financial Research Division in the Directorate General Research of the European Central Bank.

Competitive Implications

Why is Foreign Bank Penetration So Low in Developed Nations?

Allen N. Berger*

*Board of Governors of the Federal Reserve System and
Wharton Financial Institutions Center*

1. Introduction

Foreign banks control only about 10 percent of banking assets in most developed nations. While there are some exceptions, foreign bank penetration is generally quite low in developed nations, particularly when compared to most developing nations. The average foreign share is over 40 percent in both Latin America and the transition nations of Eastern Europe. In some developing nations, foreign banks have virtually taken over the banking markets.

The relatively low foreign penetration in developed nations may be surprising. Most of the developed nations have removed explicit governmental regulatory barriers to foreign bank entry. In addition, improvements in information processing, telecommunications, and financial technologies have facilitated greater reach across borders by allowing banks to manage information flows from more locations, and to evaluate and manage risks at lower cost without geographic proximity. Globalization of trade and enlarged cross-border activities of nonfinancial companies have also increased demand for banks that can provide services across many borders.

The low foreign shares in developed nations relative to developing nations may also be surprising since developing nations more often have high explicit barriers to foreign entry. Developing nations often present particular difficulties as well in processing "soft" information about local conditions and for dealing with cultural and market differences for banks headquartered in developed nations. In many cases, developing nations also have significant market shares for state-owned banks that may "crowd out" foreign competition with subsidized services and lax enforcement of loan repayments.

The European Union (EU) helps illustrate the surprisingly low foreign bank penetration despite intentions and expectations to the contrary. Over the last several decades, the EU has been implementing the Single Market Program (SMP) designed to make the EU as close as possible to a single banking market. The SMP has dramatically reduced explicit government barriers to cross-border competition among member nations, including a single banking license that is valid throughout the EU. As well, many of the regulations have been harmonized and most of the countries now share a single currency — both changes which would also be expected to result in increased cross-border consolidation by reducing the costs of operating in multiple EU nations. Most of the EU nations are also geographically contiguous and have relatively short distances among them, allowing for cross-border banking opportunities without substantial distance-related diseconomies.

Table 1 shows data from 2004 on cross-border banking in the EU taken from the EU Banking Structures October 2005 report supplied by the European Central Bank (ECB). I give the proportions of assets in credit institutions (CIs) in each nation in foreign-owned branches and subsidiaries. I separate the host nations into the 15 members before 2004 that were part of the SMP and other reforms for many years (EU15), and the 10 nations that joined in 2004 (ASCENDING 10), which cannot be considered to have been substantially affected yet by the reforms and differ from the EU15 in many other ways. I also compile statistics for the EU15 without the United Kingdom (E15\UK). This is because the UK is arguably an exceptional case with strong foreign presence primarily due to the status of London as an international banking and financial center.

Using the ECB's organization of the data, the foreign penetration for each nation is tabulated separately for banking organizations from home countries in the European Economic Area (EEA) — the EU15 plus Norway, Iceland, and Liechtenstein — and for non-EEA home countries. The foreign penetration of the EU15\UK by banks from EEA home countries is fairly close to the ideal experiment for illustrating the effects — or lack of effects — of the removal of explicit government barriers, harmonized regulations, common currency, and geographic proximity.

The total share of foreign banks from EEA home countries in the EU15\UK is just 13.34 percent of bank assets despite government

Table 1. Proportions of assets in European Union (EU) Credit Institutions (CIs) in branches and subsidiaries from Foreign European Economic Area (EEA) countries (EU15 plus Norway, Iceland, and Liechtenstein) and non-EEA countries, 2004

	Total Assets of CIs (€ mill)	Proportion Assets in branches from foreign EEA countries	Proportion Assets in subsidiaries from foreign EEA countries	Proportion Assets in branches or subsidiaries from foreign EEA countries	Proportion Assets in branches from foreign non-EEA countries	Proportion Assets in subsidiaries foreign non-EEA countries	Proportion Assets in branches or subsidiaries from foreign non-EEA countries	Proportion Assets in branches or subsidiaries from all foreign countries
Austria	635,347	0.0068	0.1833	0.1901	0.0000	0.0041	0.0041	0.1942
Belgium	914,391	0.0320	0.1827	0.2146	0.0130	0.0042	0.0172	0.2319
Denmark	607,107	0.0437	0.1031	0.1468	0.0000	0.0147	0.0147	0.1615
Finland	212,427	0.0676	0.5270	0.5946	0.0000	0.0000	0.0000	0.5946
France	4,415,475	0.0250	0.0688	0.0939	0.0029	0.0169	0.0197	0.1136
Germany	6,584,388	0.0107	0.0385	0.0491	0.0034	0.0103	0.0137	0.0628
Greece	230,454	0.0982	0.1481	0.2463	0.0017	0.0000	0.0017	0.2480
Ireland	722,544	0.1118	0.2524	0.3643	0.0000	0.0902	0.0902	0.4544
Italy	2,275,652	0.0475	0.0245	0.0721	0.0031	0.0019	0.0049	0.0770
Luxembourg	695,103	0.1573	0.7377	0.8950	0.0077	0.0381	0.0459	0.9409
Netherlands	1,677,583	0.0181	0.0902	0.1082	0.0007	0.0118	0.0125	0.1207
Portugal	345,378	0.0589	0.1950	0.2539	0.0000	0.0074	0.0074	0.2613
Spain	1,717,364	0.0711	0.0392	0.1103	0.0017	0.0030	0.0048	0.1151
Sweden	582,918	0.0744	0.0077	0.0821	0.0000	0.0045	0.0045	0.0866

Table 1. (*Continued*)

	Total Assets of CIs (€mill)	Proportion Assets in branches from foreign EEA countries	Proportion Assets in subsidiaries from foreign EEA countries	Proportion Assets in branches or subsidiaries from foreign EEA countries	Proportion Assets in branches from foreign non-EEA countries	Proportion Assets in subsidiaries foreign non-EEA countries	Proportion Assets in branches or subsidiaries from foreign non-EEA countries	Proportion Assets in branches or subsidiaries from all foreign countries
United Kingdom	6,970,009	0.2216	0.0423	0.2639	0.1659	0.0828	0.2487	0.5126
EU15	28,586,140	0.0817	0.0835	0.1652	0.0427	0.0301	0.0728	0.2380
EU15_UK	21,616,131	0.0366	0.0967	0.1334	0.0030	0.0131	0.0161	0.1494
Cyprus	38,336	0.0124	0.2151	0.2275	0.0728	0.0000	0.0728	0.3002
Czech Republic	86,525	0.0956	0.7730	0.8686	0.0000	0.0496	0.0496	0.9182
Estonia	8,537	0.0944	0.8852	0.9796	0.0000	0.0000	0.0000	0.9796
Hungary	64,970	0.0000	0.5586	0.5586	0.0000	0.0312	0.0312	0.5898
Latvia	11,167	0.0000	0.3940	0.3940	0.0000	0.0407	0.0407	0.4348
Lithuania	8,509	0.0000	0.7415	0.7415	0.0000	0.0000	0.0000	0.7415
Malta	20,391	0.0000	0.3909	0.3909	0.0000	0.0000	0.0000	0.3909
Poland	131,904	0.0063	0.5816	0.5879	0.0000	0.0866	0.0866	0.6745
Slovakia	29,041	0.1032	0.7723	0.8755	0.0000	0.0000	0.0000	0.8755
Slovenia	24,462	0.0000	0.1879	0.1879	0.0000	0.0000	0.0000	0.1879
ASCENDING 10	423,842	0.0315	0.5695	0.6011	0.0066	0.0429	0.0495	0.6506

Separate statistics also shown for EU15 (members before 2004), EU15 without United Kingdom (EU15\UK), and ASCENDING 10 (joined in 2004).
Note: In cases of 1 or 2 branches or subsidiaries, underlying data are not disclosed due to confidentiality reasons. We report these as zero.
Source: EU Banking Structures October 2005, European Central Bank, Tables 2, 11, and 13.

encouragement to become a single banking market. In addition, the total foreign share of non-EEA foreign nations is 1.61 percent, for a total average foreign penetration of only 14.94 percent. These figures are quite small compared to the 60.11 percent EEA penetration and 65.06 percent total foreign penetration in the ASCENDING 10, a mix of developing nations, mostly transition nations of Eastern Europe. Most of the EEA foreign share in the EU15\UK, 9.67 percentage points, is in subsidiaries of foreign banking organizations, rather than in branches, which have 3.66 percentage points. Thus, in most cases, the multinational banking organizations do use the single license privilege.[1] The three largest host nations in the EU15\UK in terms of banking assets — Germany, France, and Italy — all have less than 10 percent presence of EEA-based foreign banks despite the SMP, their similar levels of development, their common currency, and their common borders with one another.[2] These data suggest the presence of strong impediments to cross-border banking at work other than explicit government barriers, differences in regulation, differences in currency, and diseconomies associated with distance.

The focus of this paper is help determine why foreign banks have often been so unsuccessful in penetrating banking markets in developed nations, and generally been much more successful in entering and expanding in

[1]There are a number of reasons why these organizations may prefer the subsidiary structure to the branch structure, including (1) the ability to insulate the main banking organization from country risk, or "ring fencing" (Kahn and Winton, 2004); (2) exploitation of deposit insurance/government safety net in the foreign nation; (3) monitoring and discipline of foreign operations when there are significant managerial agency problems; and (4) time to "digest" or integrate operations after international mergers and acquisitions (M&As) before removing the subsidiary's structure. Consistent with this last motive, many of the banking M&As in the 1980s and 1990s in the U.S. originally kept the acquired institutions as separate holding company subsidiaries — even where branching networks were legally allowed — then later merged the subsidiaries into larger branching networks. The branching form of cross-border banking may also become more prevalent in the EU with the creation of the Societas Europaea or single corporate structure in October 2004 that may reduce the legal costs and problems of multinational branching operations (Dermine, 2005).

[2]A few of the developed small nations in the EU15\UK, such as Luxembourg, have very high foreign penetration by EEA-based banking organizations. These may be related to a phenomenon also noted regarding the New Zealand banking market. New Zealand is dominated by foreign banks from Australia, a much larger developed nation that is geographically proximate (Hohl, McGuire, and Remolona, 2005). It may be easier to have foreign domination in these circumstances than to develop a "national champion" to compete with banks from the much larger nearby developed nations.

many of the developing nations. I use a simple analytical framework to address this question. Under this framework, the primary determinants of the intensity of cross-border competition and foreign bank market shares are (1) the economic comparative advantages and disadvantages of foreign banks; and (2) the explicit and implicit government barriers to foreign bank competition. To the extent that the economic advantages of foreign ownership outweigh the disadvantages, foreign banks should be more efficient relative to domestic institutions, giving stronger incentives for cross-border expansion to exploit these net advantages. To the extent that disadvantages dominate in more cases, the associated inefficiencies should discourage foreign penetration. However, even if foreign banks are relatively efficient, their market shares may be relatively small if explicit or implicit government barriers are relatively high and thwart the economic rationale for cross-border banking. To illustrate, this framework suggests that the relatively low cross-border penetration within the EU15\UK may be primarily the result of either dominating economic disadvantages of foreign bank ownership in these developed nations, relatively high implicit government barriers, or both, given that the explicit government barriers are much lower than elsewhere in the world.

In the remainder of the paper, I review the findings of the research literature and take a brief look at data on variation in cross-border banking around to world to (1) identify the important economic advantages and disadvantages of foreign banks; (2) identify the important explicit and implicit government barriers; and (3) examine whether the findings are roughly consistent with the framework. The next section discusses the economic comparative advantages and disadvantages of foreign banks, some of which differ for developed and developed nations. The third section reviews the empirical research on the relative efficiency of foreign and domestic banks in both categories of nations. A finding that foreign banks are relatively efficient may suggest that the economic advantages of foreign ownership tend to outweigh the disadvantages and vice versa if the foreign banks are found to be relatively inefficient. The fourth section highlights some of the major explicit and implicit government barriers to foreign bank competition in developed and developing nations. The fifth section displays data on cross-border banking around the world to illustrate the net effects of the economic comparative advantages and disadvantages and the explicit and implicit government barriers. The final section draws conclusions regarding the likely reasons why foreign bank penetration is so low in developed nations relative to developing nations based on the analytical framework, arguments, research, and data presented.

2. Economic Comparative Advantages and Disadvantages of Foreign Banks

One potential comparative advantage for foreign banks is that their organizations may be able to diversify and absorb risks across nations and regions of the world. This may raise profits and/or lower costs by providing superior financial stability for which customers may be willing to pay, reducing other costs of risk management, lowering the organization's cost of capital (that is, allowing the organization to operate with a lower equity/asset ratio and/or with lower interest rates on debt), or allowing the institution to invest in some higher risk–higher expected return investments. Research on the correlations of bank earnings across nations suggest strong possibilities for risk diversification through international expansion, including some negative correlations even among EU nations (for example, Berger, DeYoung, Genay, and Udell, 2000, Table 1). Also consistent with research on cross-border risk diversification potential in the EU, a recent study based on the tails of the distributions finds that cross-country spillover of extremely high bank risk in the 12 euro-area nations is low relative to the spillover within individual nations, and this has remained so even after the introduction of the common currency (Hartmann, Straetmans, and de Vries, 2005).[3]

In terms of abilities to serve specific types of customers, the multinational presence of foreign banks may help these institutions serve multinational corporations by providing services in multiple nations. Many studies give evidence that some banking organizations engage in the "follow-your-customer" strategy of setting up offices in nations in which

---

[3]Recent research also suggests that U.S. banking organizations have been able to increase their cross-border exposures without significantly increasing their risks by shifting to safer foreign nations and other changes (Cetorelli and Goldberg, 2005). While there is relatively little research on the diversification benefits to multinational banking organizations, international diversification has been found to improve the risk-expected return tradeoff and profit efficiency in the reinsurance industry (Cummins and Weiss, 2000). Research on domestic banks also shows substantial improvements in performance from geographical diversification within the U.S. (for example, Hughes, Lang, Mester, and Moon, 1996, Akhavein, Berger, and Humphrey, 1997; Demsetz and Strahan, 1997).

their home-nation corporate customers have foreign affiliates (for example, Goldberg and Saunders, 1981).

Foreign banks headquartered in developed nations may have additional advantages over domestic institutions in developing nations. These may include managerial expertise and experience, access to capital, ability to make larger loans, a seasoned labor force, market power over suppliers, and so forth. These institutions also likely have advantages in the use of lending technologies based on "hard" information that is quantitative and verifiable — such as credit scoring or lending based on financial statements or easily valued fixed assets pledged as collateral — given their experience and economies of scale in processing such information (for example, Berger and Udell, 2006).

Another possible advantage of these foreign institutions in developing nations is their stability. This stability may be particularly important in developing nations that are subject to high probabilities of financial crises. For example, some research finds that foreign banks in Argentina and Mexico may provide credit smoothing and financial stability during financial crises (Dages, Goldberg, and Kinney, 2000).[4]

Turning to potential comparative disadvantages for foreign banks, these institutions are sometimes located at significant distances from their organization headquarters, which may be associated with organizational diseconomies to operating or monitoring from a distance, although some evidence suggests that this disadvantage may be falling over time with technological progress.[5] Other disadvantages for foreign banks may be differences in the economic environment in the nation of operations from those in their home country. Differences in language, culture, economic development, and so forth may increase the costs of management, impede the flow of information, or reduce efficiency in other ways. Some empirical research suggests that longer distances, language and cultural differences, and dissimilar levels of economic development all tend to deter cross-border mergers and acquisitions and lending, but these differences are often difficult to distinguish from differences in legal systems and regulation, which fall under my heading of implicit government barriers below (for example, Buch, 2003; Berger,

---

[4] It is alternatively possible that the foreign institutions may be perceived as likely to leave during a financial crisis, which may put them at a disadvantage.

[5] Research on banking within the U.S. suggest that distance-related efficiency problems are declining over time (Berger and DeYoung, 2006) and that banks are increasing the distances at which they make small business loans over time (for example, Petersen and Rajan, 2002; Hannan, 2003).

Buch, DeLong, and DeYoung, 2004; Buch and DeLong, 2004). Note that the diseconomies based on differences between home and host nation may be more severe for foreign institutions from developed nations operating in developing nations.

Foreign banks may also be at comparative disadvantages in technologies based on "soft" information about local conditions. This type of information is difficult to process and communicate for large organizations with layers of management, and these problems may be exacerbated by long distances and differences in culture and development (for example, Berger and Udell, 2002; Stein, 2002; Berger, Miller, Petersen, Rajan, and Stein, 2005). This makes it difficult to serve informationally opaque small- and medium-sized enterprises (SMEs) that rely on relationship lending because they do not have quality hard information on which to base credit decisions. In some cases, even multinational corporations may prefer domestic banks for some services, presumably due to the "concierge" benefits of soft information about local economic conditions, suppliers, and customers.[6]

3. Empirical Evidence on the Relative Efficiency of Foreign Banks

A number of recent papers have compared the average efficiency of foreign and domestic banks, which may suggest whether the economic comparative advantages or disadvantages dominate. Efficiency measures differ from profitability and other financial ratios mainly in that they remove from measured bank performance some of the factors over which management likely has little control (at least in the short run) using statistical or linear programming methods. For example, profit and cost efficiency estimates are often derived from the residuals of profit and cost equations that specify market input prices, output quantities, and local market business conditions. Thus, bank efficiency is based on expected profits or costs for producing the same outputs under the same market conditions.[7]

---

[6]Consistent with this "concierge" effect, one study finds that foreign affiliates of multinational corporations operating in Europe usually chose domestic banks for cash management services, including short-term credit (Berger, Dai, Ongena, and Smith, 2003).

[7]The efficiency comparisons discussed here are based on research studies that compare operations within a single nation, in effect, comparing foreign and domestic institutions against the best-practice frontier for banks operating in the same host nation. Although some studies compare the efficiencies of bank operations across different nations, such results are unreliable in my view because the economic environments in which the banks in different nations compete are simply too different. See Berger (2006) for more discussion.

The research design and findings often differ for developed and developing nations. The research in developed nations generally suggests that foreign institutions are less efficient on average than domestic banks, but there are exceptions, particularly when the home nation of the banking organizations is the U.S. A number of studies compare the efficiency of foreign and domestic banks in the U.S., but do not identify the home nation of the foreign banks. These studies generally find that foreign banks in the U.S. are relatively inefficient (for example, DeYoung and Nolle, 1996; Hasan and Hunter, 1996; Mahajan, Rangan, and Zardkoohi, 1996; Chang, Hasan, and Hunter, 1998). However, similar research using data on banks in other developed nations finds that foreign banks are approximately equally efficient (for example, Vander Vennet, 1996; Hasan and Lozano-Vivas, 1998) or more efficient than domestically banks (for example, Sturm and Williams, 2004).

Studies of banks in developed nations that take account of the home-nation identity of the foreign banks often find that those headquartered in the U.S. are more efficient than domestic institutions (for example, Berger, DeYoung, Genay, and Udell, 2000; Miller and Parkhe, 2002). In one study using Australian data, U.K.-owned institutions are also found to be particularly efficient (Sturm and Williams, 2005). Thus, in terms of overall measured efficiency in developed nations, the data suggest that the disadvantages of foreign banks often dominate the advantages, with some possible exceptions that depend on home-nation identity.

The research in developing nations differs in that there is often a three-way comparison among foreign, state-owned, and private, domestic banks, given the significant presence of state ownership in many of these nations. Another key dimension in developing nations is that a relatively high proportion of the foreign banks are headquartered in more developed nations than the host nation because multinational banking organizations are frequently headquartered in developed nations. Thus, any advantages or disadvantages to having a home-nation identity in a developed nation may generally apply to the foreign banks.

The most common findings for developing nations are that on average, foreign banks are more efficient than or approximately equally efficient to private, domestic banks. Both of these groups are typically found to be significantly more efficient on average than state-owned banks, but there are variations on all of these findings. For example, some research using data from the transition nations of Eastern Europe finds foreign banks to be the most efficient on average, followed by private, domestic banks, and then state-owned banks (Bonin, Hasan, and Wachtel, 2005a,b). However, another study of transition nations finds the mixed result that foreign banks are more cost efficient, but less profit efficient than both private domestic banks and state-owned banks (Yildirim and Philippatos, 2003). A study using 28 developing nations from various regions finds foreign banks to have the highest profit efficiency, followed by private, domestic banks, and then state-owned banks (Berger, Hasan, and Klapper, 2004). For cost efficiency, the private domestic banks rank higher than the foreign banks, but both are still much more efficient than state-owned banks. Two studies using Argentine data (prior to the crisis in 2002) find roughly equal efficiency for foreign and private domestic banks, and that both are more efficient on average than state-owned banks (Delfino, 2003; Berger, Clarke, Cull, Klapper, and Udell, 2005). A study employing Pakistani information finds foreign banks are more profit efficient than private domestic banks and state-owned banks, but all of these groups have similar average cost efficiency (Bonaccorsi di Patti and Hardy, 2005). Finally, a study of banks in India finds that foreign banks are more efficient on average than private domestic banks (Bhattacharya, Lovell, and Sahay, 1997). This study also finds the unusual result that state-owned banks are relatively efficient, which may be partially or wholly due to accounting practices, cross-subsidies from other government agencies, or relatively low-cost accounts by other government-owned firms, but this is not known.

Thus, the efficiency findings using data from developing nations suggest that the advantages of foreign ownership more often dominate the disadvantages than in developed nations. This is also consistent with results from the studies on profitability and performance in developing nations using conventional measures (for example, Claessens, Demirgüç-Kunt, and Huizinga, 2001; Martinez-Peria and Mody, 2004). The difference may be due in part to some of the advantages for foreign banks with home-nation identities in more developed nations.

4. Explicit and Implicit Government Barriers to Foreign Bank Competition

Explicit government barriers to foreign competition include rules and regulations that explicit limit the entry and behavior of foreign banks or treat these institutions in a differently in a formal way from domestic banks.

Historically, explicit restrictions on foreign entry were quite common, but many of these barriers have been lowered over time, including the single banking license in the EU discussed earlier. Empirical research on entry barriers found that these restrictions were more important than the actual penetration of foreign banks to the exercise of market power (for example, Levine, 2003).

Some nations also have explicit rules that limit the behavior and expansion of foreign banks after entry, although again, many nations have reduced these explicit barriers. A current effective example is in India, where foreign banks that purchase shares of local Indian banks are restricted to a ceiling of 10 percent of voting rights and also face explicit additional capital requirements and permissions for branch expansions (Berger, Klapper, Martinez-Peria, and Zaidi, 2005). Similarly, foreign banks face branching and activities restrictions in China, as well as limits on financial ratios and minority foreign ownership, although many of these barriers are being reduced over time as part of their World Trade Organization (WTO) agreement in December 2001 (Berger, Hasan, and Zhou, 2005).

There are at least three types of implicit government barriers to foreign competition. The first are rules and regulations that govern banks and their market environment that do not explicitly target foreign banks. These include having a distinct bank regulatory system/supervisory environment, currency, legal/judicial system, accounting/information system, payment/settlement system, tax code, and so forth. Simply having differences across nations in these conditions may reduce the efficiency of banking organizations that operate across borders in similar ways to differences in economic environments discussed above. Although the EU harmonized many regulations and most now have a common currency, significant differences remain in some of the other dimensions of the banking environment that may hinder cross-border consolidation (for example, Giddy, Saunders, and Walter, 1996; Lannoo and Gros, 1998).

Some rules and regulations may create disproportionate difficulties for foreign banks as well. For example, weak legal/judicial systems and poor accounting and information systems may create more problems for the use of hard-information lending technologies than for soft-information technologies that depend on relationships and local reputations. As examples, financial statement lending depends on auditing standards, credit scoring depends on credit bureaus that share credible information, and fixed-asset lending depends on creditor rights and their enforcement to protect collateral liens (for example, Berger and Udell, 2006). As discussed, foreign banks tend to have advantages in using hard information and disadvantages in processing soft information.

To some extent, this first set of implicit barriers has fallen. The EU has harmonized many regulations and most of its nations adopted the euro as a common currency. The Basel I and II capital accords also make some of the regulation of internationally active banking organizations more similar. However, the extent to which poor legal/judicial and accounting/information systems have progressed remains unclear.

The second type of implicit barrier is actions of government officials, that may or may not become public knowledge, to try to prevent foreign entry and expansion in favor of domestically based institutions. These include delaying/denying foreign merger/acquisitions, encouraging domestic institutions to merge with each other to become larger and more difficult to acquire, and perhaps to conduct their own foreign acquisitions, that is, creating "national champions" or "international champions." It has long been argued that these tactics have been effective in suppressing cross-border competition in Europe (for example, Boot, 1999).

One example of this type of behavior recently became public knowledge. Italian prosecutors allegedly have wiretap evidence implicating the Italian central bank governor, Antonio Fazio, in aiding Banca Popolare Italiana in the attempted takeover of another Italian bank, Banca Antonveneta, rather than by acquirers based elsewhere within the EU, including Dutch ABN Amro (Kahn and Cohen, 2005). After this was made public, however, ABN Amro was able to complete the transaction and buy a 39.4 percent stake in Antonveneta. Assuming that ABN Amro acquirers a majority share in 2006 as planned, it will be the first foreign bank to gain majority control over a large Italian lender, more than a decade since the EU introduced the single banking license (Taylor and Kahn, 2005). While it is difficult to generalize from one example, this episode is consistent with the hypothesis that actions to create "champions" may be more effective if the actions remain secret.

The third type of implicit barrier is direct ownership and subsidy of banks by the government. As discussed, state-owned banks are usually found to be relatively inefficient. However, unlike the case of private-sector agents, this inefficiency does not necessarily imply that they are not strong competitors that are able to "crowd out" other competitors. These institutions are often subsidized and have mandates to make loans at below-market rates to targeted customers, such as specific industries, sectors, or regions, new entrepreneurs, and so forth. Another consequence of the subsidy is that the state-owned institutions do not necessarily require repayment of credit to stay in business, and so they may offer the attraction to some borrowers of less monitoring and enforcement of repayment. Consistent with this, some empirical evidence suggests that state-owned banks often have very high nonperforming loan ratios (for example, Hanson, 2004; Berger, Clarke, Cull, Klapper, and Udell, 2005). Thus, the subsidized rates and lax repayment standards of state-owned banks may provide significantly more competition for the targeted customers, but these institutions may provide less competition for other customers. Presumably, in most cases, it is more likely that private, domestic banks are "crowded out" than foreign banks, given that foreign banks are more likely to compete for large customers than for the targeted customers. However, in cases in which the state-owned banks have very large market shares, virtually all competitors are "crowded out" to some degree.

While state-owned bank presence is generally more of an issue in developing nations, it also affects some important developed nations. The second and third largest economies in the world both have significant state-owned bank presence. In Japan, the $3 trillion postal system is, by some measures, the world's largest "bank," although it does not fit the definition of a commercial bank that takes deposits and makes commercial loans. Japan Post manages about one-quarter of Japan's household financial assets, and invests them primarily in government bonds, which are spent on public projects, such as roads and bridges that may directed by political interests. Prime Minister Koizumi recently called and won an election in which privatization of Japan Post was a key issue (Moffett, 2005). Germany also has a nationwide system of state-owned Landesbanken that compete with private commercial banks for deposit and loans.

5. Brief Look at Worldwide Data on Cross-Border Banking

I next examine data on the extent of cross-border banking around the world to show the net effects of the economic comparative advantages/disadvantages and explicit/implicit government barriers. Figure 1 and Table 2 illustrate some of the variation in foreign bank market shares across regions and within regions. To be comprehensive, I use the most recently available data from the World Bank that covers most of the nations of the

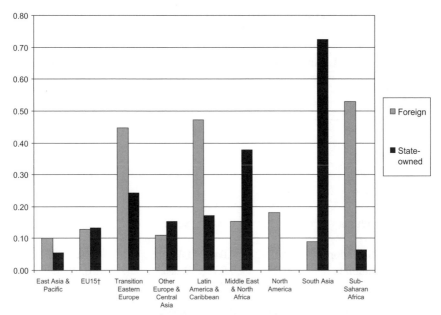

Source: World Bank data base described in Barth, Caprio, and Levine (2001).
Notes: Correlation between proportion foreign-owned and proportion state-owned shares = –0.38***. (*** indicates statistical significance at the 1% level.)
†EU15 includes the 15 member nations of the European Union as of 2001.

Figure 1. Foreign-owned and state-owned market shares for selected regions as of year end 2001

world. The data are as of year end 2001 are drawn from the World Bank data base described in Barth, Caprio, and Levine (2001) and were graciously provided by Sole Martinez-Peria. I include the state-owned market shares as well as the foreign shares to illustrate the relationship between the presence of the two bank ownership types. The data set includes information on shares for 130 nations for the foreign banks and 135 nations for state-owned banks. In all cases, a bank is considered to be foreign or state-owned based on majority ownership.

Figure 1 aggregates the data for the individual countries into 9 regions, and shows the weighted averages of foreign and state-owned bank market shares for each region. The data in Figure 1 suggest that in most of the regions dominated by developed nations — North America, the EU15, and East Asia, both foreign and state banking shares are low relative to most of the developing regions. The foreign bank proportions are generally higher in

Table 2. Foreign and state-owned market shares for selected nations with very high and low shares

	Latin America			Transition Eastern Europe		
	Country	Foreign	State-Owned	Country	Foreign	State-Owned
Foreign						
High	Belize	0.95	0.00	Estonia	0.99	0.00
	Mexico	0.83	0.00	Czech Republic	0.90	0.04
	Ecuador	0.70	0.14	Croatia	0.89	0.05
Low	Honduras	0.19	0.00	Serbia/ Montenegro	0.13	0.04
	El Salvador	0.12	0.04	Ukraine	0.11	0.12
	Guatemala	0.09	0.03	Russia	0.09	0.36
State-Owned						
High	Costa Rica	0.23	0.62	Belarus	0.26	0.74
	Uruguay	0.43	0.43	Albania	0.46	0.54
	Brazil	0.30	0.32	Romania	0.47	0.42
Low	Puerto Rico	0.30	0.01	Estonia	0.99	0.00
	Peru	0.42	0.00	Latvia	0.65	0.03
	Honduras	0.19	0.00	Hungary	0.89	0.09

	Africa			Asia		
	Country	Foreign	State-Owned	Country	Foreign	State-Owned
Foreign						
High	Guinea Bissau	1.00	0.00	Macau	0.88	0.01
	Lesotho	1.00	0.00	Jordan	0.64	0.00
	Tonga	1.00	0.00	Armenia	0.59	0.00
Low	South Africa	0.08	N/A	Tajikistan	0.01	0.05
	Sudan	0.04	0.12	Turkmenistan	0.00	0.96
	Egypt	0.13	0.65	Kuwait	0.00	0.00

Table 2. (*Continued*)

	Africa			Asia		
	Country	Foreign	State-Owned	Country	Foreign	State-Owned
State-Owned						
High	Algeria	0.04	0.96	Turkmenistan	0.00	0.96
	Egypt	0.13	0.65	China[†]	0.02	0.73
	Togo	0.18	0.51	India	0.07	0.75
Low	Benin	0.91	0.00	Japan	0.07	0.00
	Botswana	1.00	0.00	Jordan	0.64	0.00
	Kenya	0.39	0.01	Armenia	0.59	0.00

Notes: The state-owned figure may be understated because it includes only the "Big Four" wholly state-owned banks — other banks are also partially or fully owned by the state or by state-owned enterprises (SOEs).
Source: Data for China are for 2003 from Berger, Hasan, and Zhou (2005).

most of the regions dominated by developing nations. For instance, Figure 1 suggests that the foreign share is quite high in many nations in Latin America, the transition nations of Eastern Europe, and Sub-Saharan Africa. In most of the developing regions, the state-owned share is also relatively high, exceeding 20 percent in Eastern Europe, the Middle East/North Africa, and South Asia.

Figure 1 also shows some significant heterogeneity among the developing regions. In some cases — such as in many of the nations of South Asia — the foreign share is quite small — below that of the developed nations. The data in Figure 1 suggest that this may be due to the large presence of state-owned banks in many of these nations — the third implicit barrier to foreign competition according to my analytical framework. These institutions may offer subsidized credit with lax repayment standards, which may "crowd out" private banks that need to recover costs and earn returns on their loans. As discussed above, state-owned banks generally provide more competition for private, domestic banks than foreign banks, but virtually all domestic and foreign competitors may be "crowded out" when the state-owned share is very large, such may be the case in some nations in South Asia in Figure 1. As shown at the bottom of Figure 1, there is a strong negative, statistically significant correlation of –0.38 between foreign and state market shares across all 130 nations with data available on both types of shares. This suggests that government operation of commercial banks often provides a significant implicit barrier to foreign bank entry and expansion.

To investigate the heterogeneity among the developing regions further, Table 2 shows the shares for individual nations in four regions of interest that are primarily composed of developing nations, Latin America, the transition nations of Eastern Europe, Africa, and Asia. For each region, I select the 3 banks with the highest and lowest foreign shares and those with the highest and lowest state-owned shares. The data show some interesting similarities and differences across regions as well as remarkable variation within regions.

All four regions have several nations with majority foreign ownership and a number of other nations with majority state ownership. However, an important difference across regions is that almost all Latin American and Eastern European countries have significant foreign bank presence. In contrast, Africa and Asia both have a number of countries with little or no foreign bank penetration.

The reasons for the widespread significant foreign presence in Latin America and Eastern Europe differ somewhat. In Latin America, much of the foreign bank ownership stems from financial market liberalizations and financial crises. The Mexican banking crisis in 1994–95 (the Tequila crisis) had substantial contagion effects throughout much of the Latin American region, resulting in failures, consolidation, and flight to quality that attracted foreign entrants. Over 1996–1998 alone, foreign direct investment in Latin America's banking sector has been estimated at over $10 billion, particularly in Argentina, Chile, Brazil, and Mexico (Raffin, 1999). Another contributing factor is the relatively small role for state-owned banks. As shown in Table 2, many of the nations have little or no state bank ownership due to either privatization or traditions of private-sector banking.

In the transition nations of Eastern Europe, in contrast, the driving forces behind the high foreign ownership are the combination of the privatization of state-owned institutions and the dearth of private, domestic banks with expertise to take over these institutions. In most cases, these countries were traditionally dominated by state-owned institutions, so no large private, domestically-banks existed. In a number of these nations, the state-owned institutions went through some evolution in early 1990s, and then massive privatizations in the late 1990s in which foreign banks took ·

over most of the banking assets (for example, Bonin, Hasan, and Wachtel, 2005a,b). As shown in Table 2, in many of these nations, the sum of foreign and state-owned bank shares is at or near 100 percent, as the private, domestic banks typically have little or no presence. Thus, even in the Eastern European nations that maintained relatively high state-owned market shares like Belarus, Albania, and Romania, the foreign shares are still quite large relative to those in developed nations.

Finally, I draw attention to a few significant present and future economic powerhouses in Asia that do not appear to have very dynamic banking industries, at least as far as foreign bank penetration is concerned. China and India, the two most populous nations, are both rapidly growing due to globalization of trade, and yet both have yet to "globalize" their banking sectors. Chinese banking is dominated by four very large state-owned banks (the "Big Four") with 72.62 percent of total assets as of 2003, and many of the remainder are partially or fully owned by the state or by state-owned enterprises (SOEs), in some cases with minority foreign ownership. Banks with majority foreign ownership hold only 1.57 percent of assets, and some of them may not compete effectively because they do not have permission to take deposits/make loans in the local currency (yuan). The very large market share for the state-owned banks is likely a significant barrier to foreign entry, and the explicit restrictions on foreign banks are also important. However, there are plans to partially privatize three of the Big Four banks and take on minority foreign ownership of these institutions by large U.S., European, and Asian financial organizations. One of the Big Four, China Construction Bank, has already begun its partial privatization. Evidence on the relatively low efficiency of the Big Four and favorable efficiency effects of minority foreign ownership of other state-owned and private, domestic banks in China suggests that this reform may boost performance significantly (Berger, Hasan, and Zhou, 2005).

India similarly has a very large state ownership of its banking sector, which may help explain why its foreign share is only 7 percent. As noted, foreign banks in India also face explicit barriers to expansion.

Finally, Japan has had a banking crisis for more than a decade, which has affected their economic growth, but their foreign share remains only 7 percent. This country has no state ownership of commercial banks, but as noted, the state-owned Japan Post is larger than any of the commercial banks and controls a large share of household deposits. The extent to which this implicit government barrier versus other government barriers and economic disadvantages for foreign banks explain the relatively low foreign share is not known.

6. Conclusions

I analyze the important research and policy issue of why foreign bank competition as measured by market share has been surprisingly weak in developed nations and much stronger in many of the developing nations. Under my analytical framework, the main determinants of foreign bank penetration are the economic comparative advantages and disadvantages of foreign banks and the explicit and implicit government barriers to foreign bank competition. I analyze the available research literature to date using this framework and illustrate some of the points using data on foreign bank competition around the world.

To highlight some of the key elements of the framework, some of the important economic comparative advantages of foreign banks are their generally superior managerial expertise/experience, access to capital, use of hard-information technologies, and ability to diversify risk in most developing host nations where the private, domestic institutions have not acquired comparable skills. Some of the important economic disadvantages of foreign banks include distance-related diseconomies, language and cultural differences, dissimilar levels of development, and use of soft-information technologies — disadvantages that are likely more severe in developing host nations.

The empirical bank efficiency research suggests that the comparative disadvantages of foreign banks dominate in developed nations and the comparative advantages dominate in developing nations. Studies usually find that foreign banks are inefficient relative to domestic banks in developed nations, and are equally or more efficient than domestic banks in developing nations. The net economic disadvantage in developed nations may occur because foreign banks have to compete on a more equal footing with domestic banks that have comparable management, capital, ability to use hard information, and diversification, in contrast to the relatively weak competition in these dimensions from domestic institutions in most developing nations. This disadvantage of having to compete "in the lions' den" against comparably-skilled domestic competitors in host developed nations may dominate the other economic differences between developed and developing host nations, even though most of the other comparative disadvantages of foreign banks related to distance, language/culture, dissimilar development, and soft information are likely more severe in developing nations. In developing nations, the superiority of the foreign banks over domestic banks in management, capital, hard information, and diversification appear to dominate all the other economic disadvantages.

The major explicit government barriers to foreign bank competition are rules/regulations that explicitly limit foreign entry and/or restrict foreign banks that have entered. I also distinguish three types of implicit government barriers: (1) differences and weaknesses in regulations, legal/judicial/information systems, and so forth; (2) actions of government officials to delay/deny foreign entry and encourage private, domestic institutions to combine into "national" or "international champions;" and (3) subsidized state bank ownership that "crowds out" private competition.

In terms of differences between developed and developing nations, all of the government barriers except the second implicit barrier are generally more restrictive in developing nations. The second implicit barrier — actions to delay/deny foreign entry in favor of domestic "champions" may be more likely in developed nations because of the greater abilities of private, domestic institutions in these nations to reach "championship" scale. Most developed nations have relatively low explicit government barriers to foreign competition (particularly within the EU). The first implicit government barrier — rules and regulations that do not explicitly target foreign banks, but create more difficulties for them than for domestic banks — is generally lower in developed host nations. The regulatory environments, legal/judicial systems, information systems, and so forth are also more similar in developed nations (particularly within the EU), which should create fewer difficulties for potential entrants from developed home nations. As well, the more developed legal/judicial and information infrastructures in developed nations should pose fewer problems for the use of hard-information technologies by foreign banks than the weaker structures in developing nations. The third implicit barrier — state ownership and subsidy of banks — is also clearly more of a problem in developing nations than in developed nations. However, state ownership may not significantly impede foreign competition unless the state-owned share is relatively high.

To the extent my framework captures the primary determinants of foreign bank market shares, the relatively low foreign penetration in developed nations reflects greater net economic disadvantages of foreign bank ownership than in developed nations, higher explicit and/or implicit government barriers, or some combination of these factors.

Based on my analytical framework and the arguments, research, and data presented here, I can now suggest the likely reasons why foreign bank penetration is so low in developed nations relative to developing nations. A key reason appears to the net economic advantage of foreign banks in developed host nations and net economic advantage of these institutions in developing host nations. The empirical research suggests further that these incentives are present in both developed and developing nations, not just on a relative basis between them. That is, the finding that foreign banks are generally inefficient relative to domestic banks in developed nations suggests a net dominance of economic disadvantages in these nations (not just relative to developing nations), reducing incentives to cross-border banking. The findings for developed host nations conversely increase incentives to expand into these nations.

The arguments are also reasonably clear for the effects of government barriers to foreign competition, but there is relatively little evidence on their effects. The only barrier identified here that could help explain the relatively low foreign penetration in developed nations is the second implicit barrier or actions that favor of domestic "champions" over foreign banks. However, there is little objective evidence of these actions, perhaps because their effectiveness may depend on their secrecy. The other government barriers are generally higher in developed nations, but in most cases it is difficult to assess the strength of their effects. One important exception may be the "crowding out" of foreign competition when state-owned banks have commanding market shares. The raw data on market shares by foreign and state-owned banks suggests that this may have occurred and kept foreign bank presence low is some regions and some individual nations, possibly including China and India.

References

Akhavein, J.D., A.N. Berger, D.B. Humphrey, 1997, "The Effects of Bank Megamergers on Efficiency and Prices: Evidence from the Profit Function," *Review of Industrial Organization*, 12, pp. 95–139.

Barth, J.R., G. Caprio, Jr., R. Levine, 2001, "The Regulation and Supervision of Banks Around the World: A New Database," in *Brooking-Wharton Papers on*

Financial Services, Litan, R.E. and Richard Herring (eds.), Washington, DC: Brookings Institution, pp. 183–250.

Berger, A.N., 2006, "International Comparisons of Banking Efficiency," in Raj Aggarwal, ed., *A Companion to International Business Finance*, forthcoming.

Berger, A.N., C.M. Buch, G. DeLong, R. DeYoung, 2004, "Exporting Financial Institutions Management via Foreign Direct Investment Mergers and Acquisitions," *Journal of International Money and Finance*, 23, pp. 333–366.

Berger, A.N., G.R.G. Clarke, R. Cull, L. Klapper, G.F. Udell, 2005, "Corporate Governance and Bank Performance: A Joint Analysis of the Static, Selection, and Dynamic Effects of Domestic, Foreign, and State Ownership," *Journal of Banking and Finance*, 29, pp. 2179–2221.

Berger, A.N., Q. Dai, S. Ongena, D.C. Smith, 2003, "To What Extent will the Banking Industry be Globalized? A Study of Bank Nationality and Reach in 20 European Nations," *Journal of Banking and Finance*, 27, pp. 383–415.

Berger, A.N., R. DeYoung, 2006, "Technological Progress and the Geographic Expansion of the Banking Industry," *Journal of Money, Credit, and Banking*, forthcoming.

Berger, A.N., R. DeYoung, H. Genay, G.F. Udell, 2000, "The Globalization of Financial Institutions: Evidence from Cross-Border Banking Performance," *Brookings-Wharton Papers on Financial Services*, 3, pp. 23–158.

Berger, A.N., I. Hasan, L.F. Klapper, 2004, "Further Evidence on the Link between Finance and Growth: An International Analysis of Community Banking and Economic Performance," *Journal of Financial Services Research*, 25, pp. 169–202.

Berger, A.N., I. Hasan, M. Zhou, 2005, "Bank Ownership and Efficiency in China: What Will Happen in the World's Largest Nation?" Board of Governors of the Federal Reserve System working paper.

Berger, A.N., L.F. Klapper, M.S. Martinez-Peria, R. Zaidi, 2005, "The Effects of Bank Ownership Type on Banking Relationships and Multiple Banking in Developing Economies: Detailed Evidence from India," Board of Governors of the Federal Reserve System working paper.

Berger, A.N., N.H. Miller, M.A. Petersen, R.G. Rajan, J.C. Stein, 2005, "Does Function Follow Organizational Form? Evidence from the Lending Practices of Large and Small Banks," *Journal of Financial Economics*, 76, pp. 237–269.

Berger, A.N., D.C. Smith, 2003, "Global Integration in the Banking Industry," *Federal Reserve Bulletin*, November, pp. 451–463.

Berger, A.N., G.F. Udell, 2006, "A More Complete Conceptual Framework for SME Finance," *Journal of Banking and Finance*, 30.

Berger, A.N., G.F. Udell, 2002, "Small Business Credit Availability and Relationship Lending: The Importance of Bank Organizational Structure," *Economic Journal*, 112, pp. F32–F53.

Bhattacharya, A., C.A.K. Lovell, P. Sahay, 1997, "The Impact of Liberalization on the Productive Efficiency of Indian Commercial Banks," *European Journal of Operational Research*, 98, pp. 332–345.

Bonaccorsi di Patti, E., D. Hardy, 2005, "Bank Reform and Bank Efficiency in Pakistan," *Journal of Banking and Finance*, 29, pp. 2381–2406.

Bonin, J.P., I. Hasan, P. Wachtel, 2005a, "Bank Performance, Efficiency and Ownership in Transition Countries," *Journal of Banking and Finance*, 29, pp. 31–53.

Bonin, J.P., I. Hasan, P. Wachtel, 2005b, "Privatization Matters: Bank Efficiency in Transition Countries," *Journal of Banking and Finance*, 29, pp. 2155–2178.

Boot, A.W.A., 1999, "European Lessons on Consolidation in Banking," *Journal of Banking and Finance*, 23, pp. 609–613.

Buch, C.M., 2003, "Information versus Regulation: What Drives the International Activities of Commercial Banks?" *Journal of Money Credit and Banking*, 35, pp. 851–869.

Buch, C.M., G.L. DeLong, 2004, "Cross-Border Bank Mergers: What Lures the Rare Animal?" *Journal of Banking and Finance*, 28, pp. 2077–2102.

Cetorelli, N., L.S. Goldberg, 2005, "Risks in U.S. Bank International Exposures," New York Federal Reserve Bank working paper.

Chang, C.E., I. Hasan, W.C. Hunter, 1998, "Efficiency of Multinational Banks: An Empirical Investigation," *Applied Financial Economics*, 8(6), pp. 1–8.

Claessens, S., A. Demirgüç-Kunt, H. Huizinga, 2001, "How Does Foreign Entry Affect the Domestic Banking Market?" *Journal of Banking and Finance*, 25, pp. 891–911.

Cummins, J.D., M.A. Weiss, 2000, "The Global Market for Reinsurance: Consolidation, Capacity, and Efficiency," *Brookings-Wharton Papers on Financial Services*, 3, pp. 159–209.

Dages, B.G., L. Goldberg, D. Kinney, 2000, "Foreign and Domestic Bank Participation in Emerging Markets: Lessons from Mexico and Argentina," *Federal Reserve Bank of New York Economic Policy Review*, 6(3), pp. 17–36.

Delfino, M.E., 2003, "Bank Ownership, Privatisation and Efficiency. Empirical Evidence from Argentina," Working paper, University of Warwick.

Demsetz, R.S., P.E. Strahan, 1997, "Diversification, Size, and Risk at Bank Holding Companies," *Journal of Money, Credit, and Banking*, 29, pp. 300–313.

Dermine, J., 2005, "European Banking Integration: Don't Put the Cart before the Horse," INSEAD University working paper.

DeYoung, R., D.E. Nolle, 1996, "Foreign-Owned Banks in the U.S.: Earning Market Share or Buying It?" *Journal of Money, Credit, and Banking*, 28, pp. 622–636.

Djankov, S., R. La Porta, F. Lopez-de-Silanes, A. Shleifer, 2003, "Courts," *Quarterly Journal of Economics*, 118, pp. 453–516.

EU Banking Structures October 2005, European Central Bank, Frankfurt, Germany.

Giddy, I.H., A. Saunders, I. Walter, 1996, "European Financial Market Integration: Clearance and Settlement Issues," *Journal of Money, Credit and Banking*, 28, pp. 986–1000.

Goldberg, L.G., A. Saunders, 1981, "The Determinants of Foreign Banking Activity in the United States," *Journal of Banking and Finance*, 5, pp. 17–32.

Hannan, T.H., 2003, "Changes in Non-Local Lending to Small Business," *Journal of Financial Services Research*, 24, pp. 31–46.

Hanson, J.A., 2004, "Indian Banking: Market Liberalization and the Pressures for Market Framework Reform," in A.O. Krueger and S.Z. Chinoy, eds.: *Reforming India's External, Financial, and Fiscal Policies*, New Delhi: Oxford University Press.

Hartmann, P., S. Straetmans, C. de Vries, 2005, "Banking System Stability: A Cross-Atlantic Perspective," European Central Bank Working paper series No. 527 (September), European Central Bank, Frankfurt, Germany.

Hasan, I., W.C. Hunter, 1996, "Efficiency of Japanese Multinational Banks in the United States," *Research in Finance*, 14, pp. 157–173.

Hasan, I., A. Lozano-Vivas, 1998, "Foreign Banks, Production Technology, and Efficiency: Spanish Experience," Working Paper presented at the Georgia Productivity Workshop III, Athens, Georgia.

Hohl, S., P. McGuire, E. Remolona, 2005, "Cross-Border Banking in Asia: Basel 2 and other Prudential Issues," Bank for International Settlements working paper.

Hughes, J.P., W. Lang, L.J. Mester, C.-G. Moon, 1996, "Efficient Banking Under Interstate Branching," *Journal of Money, Credit, and Banking*, 28, pp. 1043–1071.

Kahn, C.M., A. Winton, 2004, "Moral Hazard and Optimal Subsidiary Structure for Financial Institutions," *Journal of Finance*, 59, pp. 395–422.

Kahn, G., S. Cohen, 2005, "Wiretaps of an Executive in Italy Put Central Banker in Hot Seat," *Wall Street Journal* (September 13, vol. 246, no. 51), A1, A14.

Lannoo, K., D. Gros, 1998, "Capital Markets and EMU: Report of a CEPS Working Party," Centre for European Policy Studies.

Levine, R., 2003, "Denying Foreign Bank Entry: Implications for Bank Interest Margins," University of Minnesota mimeo.

Mahajan, A., N. Rangan, A. Zardkoohi, 1996, "Cost Structures in Multinational and Domestic Banking," *Journal of Banking and Finance*, 20, pp. 238–306.

Martinez-Peria, M.S., A. Mody, 2004, "How Foreign Participation and Market Concentration Impact Bank Spreads: Evidence From Latin America," *Journal of Money, Credit, and Banking*, 36, pp. 511–537.

Miller, S.R., A. Parkhe, 2002, "Is There a Liability of Foreignness in Global Banking? An Empirical Test of U.S. Banks' X-Efficiency," *Strategic Management Journal*, 23, pp. 55–75.

Moffett, S., 2005, "Japan's Leader Suffers Defeat in Privatization Push," *Wall Street Journal* (August 9, vol. 246, no. 27), A1, A6.

Petersen, M.A., R.G. Rajan, 2002, "The Information Revolution and Small Business Lending: Does Distance Still Matter?" *Journal of Finance*, 57, pp. 2533–2570.

Raffin, M., 1999, "A Note on the Profitability of the Foreign-Owned Banks in Argentina," Banco Central de la Republica Argentina, Technical Note Number 6.

Stein, J.C., 2002, "Information Production and Capital Allocation: Decentralized vs. Hierarchical Firms," *Journal of Finance*, 57, pp. 1891–1921.

Sturm, J.E., B. Williams, 2005, "What Determines Differences in Foreign Bank Efficiency? Australian Experience," Bond University working paper.

Sturm, J.E., B. Williams, 2004, "Foreign Bank Entry, Deregulation and Bank Efficiency: Lessons from the Australian Experience," *Journal of Banking and Finance*, 28, pp. 1775–1799.

Taylor, E., G. Kahn, 2005, "ABN Amro Wins Fight for Antonveneta Stake," *Wall Street Journal* (September 27, vol. 246, no. 63), C4.

Vander Vennet, R., 1996, "The Effect of Mergers and Acquisitions on the Efficiency and Profitability of EC Credit Institutions," *Journal of Banking and Finance*, 20(9), pp. 1531–1558.

Yildirim, H.S., G.C. Philippatos, 2003, "Efficiency of Banks: Recent Evidence from the Transition Economies of Europe 1993–2000," EFMA 2004 Basel Meetings Paper.

Allen Berger is a senior economist at the Board of Governors of the Federal Reserve System and a senior fellow at the Wharton Financial Institutions Center. The opinions expressed do not necessarily reflect those of the Federal Reserve Board or its staff. The author thanks the Lamont Black, John Boyd, Phillip Hartmann, Iftekhar Hasan, Mingming Zhou, and other participants at the Federal Reserve Bank of Chicago/World Bank Conference on Cross-Border Banking: Regulatory Challenges conference for helpful suggestions, Sole Martinez-Peria for providing data, and Phil Ostromogolsky for outstanding research assistance.

Competitive Implications of Cross-Border Banking

Stijn Claessens*
World Bank

1. Introduction

Cross-border banking has long been an important part of the trend towards increased globalization and financial integration. In terms of this paper, cross-border banking refers to both cross-border capital flows as well cross-border entry in banking. Cross-border capital flows have been for long important drivers of financial integration. Particularly in the form of cross-border entry, cross-border banking has increased sharply in the last decade and has affected countries' financial systems in many ways and dimensions. Research has long studied the determinants and implications of cross-border capital flows and has started to analyze the determinants and cost and benefits of the recent wave of foreign entry in banking systems. In particular, a growing number of papers, using cross-country, individual and country bank evidence, have investigated the effects of foreign banks entry on local banking systems. The purpose of this paper is to review this literature, taking a broad view of cross-border banking as well as of its competitiveness implications, but focusing on the policy implications of the findings. In reviewing the literature, I focus on a number of aspects.

First, are the determinants of cross-border banking. These determinants are important to identify as they point towards the countries and circumstances under which one can expect cross-border banking to occur — or the degree to which it might occur and affect the local financial systems. Many of the determinants of cross-border banking identified in the literature are as expected — countries' creditworthiness, quality of institutional environment and growth opportunities. Furthermore, there appears to be a regional or proximity bias, including clustering, in cross-border flows and banking. I highlight that these factors often correlate with the strength of the local financial system. In other words, good financial systems are more likely to also have more cross-border banking. As such, one can expect the determinants of cross-border banking to complicate the analysis of any competitiveness implications. In other words, it will be hard to separate any "implications" of cross-border banking on the local banking system, including its competitiveness, from the determinants of the strength of the local system.

Second, I review the costs and benefits associated with cross-border banking. In terms of impact, one can distinguish effects on the development and efficiency of the local financial system, on the access to financial services by firms and households, and on the stability of the local financial system and the overall economy. A growing number of papers have studied the effects of cross-border banking on efficiency and development, access to financial services and stability. I report that these studies find largely beneficial effects, although there are some questions regarding the impact on relationship type lending based on softer information, particularly in low-income countries, and on financial stability.

Third, I draw some lessons from the (more recently studied) integration in international capital markets. Here, the effects of integration and competition have been observed in several dimensions: micro-financial, for example, lower cost of capital, higher rates of return on investment, more access to financing; institutional, for example, better quality of local rules and enforcement thereof; and overall market development, for example, beneficial as well as adverse effects on liquidity and prospects for a sustainable local market. The lessons from capital markets' financial integration and competition are relevant for cross-border banking not only as banking and capital markets are converging in many respects, but also as developments in capital markets tend to proceed faster than in banking. The capital markets' experiences suggest some specific lessons for cross-border banking: competitiveness' impacts extend beyond purely financial dimensions; there can be important impacts on overall market development; and there may be path dependency.

Fourth, I review more generally the fast changing global landscape of financial services provision. As financial systems, globally and nationally, absorb new technologies and distribution channels, see barriers among products and between markets being rapidly reduced, and as consolidation in many markets progresses, much is happening to the nature of the competition in financial services industries. I argue that these trends heighten the need to redefine competition policy broader than it has been done to date, including revisiting the special nature of banks. For all markets, I argue that there is a need to go beyond purely institutional approaches to competition policy — focusing on the contestability of entry and exit of players in a market — and beyond functional approaches — focusing on the level playing field in a market for a particular financial service. Rather, the need is to assure that the institutional environment for financial services provision is pro-competitive, implying (relatively) open access to all networks used, including payments, information and key distribution systems.

Fifth, I discuss the special circumstances of developing countries. Financial services industries in developing countries are undergoing changes similar to rest of the world. While institutional weaknesses in many developing countries are severe, they often represent deeper causes related to political economy factors related to the power of incumbents and associated with of a large public sector role. I argue that developing countries may benefit more than developed countries do from committing to a pro-competitive framework since credibility is more at a premium, and competition policy authorities are often weaker and have greater difficulty in implementing effective competition policy and resolving conflicts with prudential authorities.

Finally, I conclude with lessons for competition policy as they relate to financial services in general and to the role played by the World Trade Organization (WTO) and regional free-trade types of arrangements. I argue that a horizontal approach negotiating to financial services is preferable. Under a horizontal approach, no single segment is negotiated separately but rather all services (and goods) are considered jointly. I highlight that this also means the prudential carve-out for financial services may need to be revised in scope and applicability. I also suggest that it will be useful to complement the forthcoming round of market access commitments in General Agreement on Trade in Services (GATS) with a set of pro-competitive principles of sound regulation. For developing countries the WTO/GATS can help in committing to pro-competition, especially as it relate to the institutional and functional approaches.

The structure of paper itself is as follows. I first define the forms of cross-border banking that I want to analyze: capital flows and entry by foreign banks. I also review what has been found to drive banking system integration, as (lack of) integration determines the scope for competitive implications. I next review how to define and measure the competitive effects of cross-border banking, focusing on several dimensions: efficiency, access, and stability. And I review studies on these aspects conducted so far. As an inter-mezzo, I review whether there are lessons from the recent global financial integration in capital markets for the (potential) competitiveness effects of cross-border banking. I then analyze the implications of broader trends in national and international financial markets, and particular what the changing competitive landscape implies for competition policy in some important dimensions. I discuss the special circumstances of developing countries and the role of the WTO/GATS next. Finally, I end with some areas of unknowns where further research can be useful.

2. Forms of Cross-Border Banking, Determinants and Scope of Consequences

Forms of cross-border banking. Under the GATS framework, there are four forms of cross-border use or provision of (financial) services (Key, 2004). The first mode is cross-border supply, that is, the traditional trade in good and services, which in the context of finance means capital flows. The second mode is consumption abroad, for example, obtaining some financial services while traveling. The third mode is by commercial presence, that is, the production of a good or service within the country, which means the foreign establishment in a host market. The fourth mode is delivery by the presence of persons in host country, for example, solicitation of insurance products by agents traveling to the country. I focus on the first and third forms, that is, the consumption or delivery of financial services produced by a financial institution located abroad or produced domestically by a foreign-owned financial institution. In financial services, these two forms are the most important forms of trade in financial services.

It is important to note that there are important interfaces between capital account liberalization and financial services liberalization, and thus between the two modes (Dobson and Jacquet, 1998). Obviously, some aspects of domestic financial services provision by foreign banks (mode 3) will be impeded if there is little capital account freedom. Vice-versa, the degree of capital account liberalization and ability to deliver financial services through capital flows will affect the incentives to establish local operations. Another aspect is the relationship between financial services liberalization and domestic (de-)regulation. The degree of domestic reform will affect the incentives of financial services providers' ability to produce and market financial services. This interface more generally relates to the issue of the determinants of cross-border banking. The degree and motivation of cross-border banking are important to acknowledge as they determine the scope for competitiveness effects. It is not just that without cross-border capital flows or entry, there will be no impact, but more generally the determinants condition the potential impact.

Determinants of cross-border banking. The literature has found capital flows and entry to be functions of the quality of countries' institutions, economic and financial openness, political stability and growth opportunities (see Eichengreen, 2000, for a review of capital flow determinants and Clarke *et al.*, 2003 for a review of foreign bank entry). Financial centers seem to play a special role as they experience more entry relative to these factors (Buch, 2003; Buch and DeLong, 2004; see also Focaselli and Pozzolo, 2003). The literature has found capital flows to be motivated by perverse factors, for example, moral hazard in the form of a safety net provided by the government (Dooley, 2000). For entry, besides these, more general factors, a residual role has been found for indirect barriers, such as limits on mergers and acquisitions (Berger, Buch, DeLong and DeYoung, 2004). Anecdotal evidence and industry studies (Financial Leaders Group, 1997) show that these barriers can sometimes be quite subtle and raised by incumbents, as when access to the payments system is limited to incumbents through specific pricing or other policies (as has been argued in South Africa) or when there are limits on payments of interest on demand accounts (as was the case in France). The general point is that the determinants condition the possible effects of cross-border banking. Put differently, the competitiveness effects may be limited in those countries most in need of increased competition, for economic or political reasons, as cross-border banking is limited for exactly these countries (see further Berger in this volume).

Banking integration. While we would like to know the degree of effective financial integration as an input into any competitiveness study, in practice the degree of integration is hard to measure, even for developed countries where data are better than for many developing countries. When measured, it is typically done imperfectly using prices (for example, interest rates) and quantities (for example, actual capital flows or entry). Among developed countries that otherwise face limited barriers and otherwise well functioning institutions, such the EU, integration has been found to be high in wholesale banking and certain areas of corporate finance, modest in relationship, and low in retail banking (Center for Economic Policy Research, 2005). For example, Dermine (in this volume) shows that in terms of quantities, cross-border banking penetration in the EU has been the least in retail banking. In terms of prices, differences in spreads have been found to be the lowest in corporate banking and the highest in retail markets (European Central Bank, 2005; see also Baele *et al.*, 2004). For the most part, integration has thus been the highest where theory predicts, even when some barriers to integration remain. The competitiveness effects have been correspondingly, at least at face value, that is, less in naturally more "segmented" markets, such as retail and relationship lending. Note that one needs to add "at face value" since theory suggests — and empirics show it is difficult to determine the competitiveness of some financial markets.

Consistent with their weaker economic fundamentals and institutions, the degree of banking integration for developing countries is more limited. The competitive impact of capital flows is often (further) limited to a subset of borrowers — highly rated corporations, financial institutions, possibly connected to government or political powers — and a subset of depositors and lenders (for example, capital flight) as typically only those have international access (Claessens and Perotti, 2005). For banking entry in developing countries, though, competitive effects possibly cover a much wider spectrum of borrowers, lenders and others, as entry can be large (50% or more of market share is not uncommon in emerging markets; see Hohl and Remolona in this volume and Levy-Yeyati and Micco, 2003). At the same time, the economic environments in developing countries are not always stable and financial and corporate sector reform processes are often underway or incomplete. This means the entry impact effects can be harder to discern from other factors, for example, are the changes due to increases in competition, changes in governance, regulatory and supervisory improvements, or other reforms?

Possible competitive effects. What types of effects can one distinguish? I consider three dimensions: development and efficiency, access, and stability. Under the first, development and efficiency, I consider questions like: is the system more developed, for example, is it larger, does it provide better quality financial products/services; is it more efficient, that is, exhibit a lower cost of financial intermediation, is it less profitable; and is it closer to some competitive benchmark? Under access, I consider whether access to financing, particularly by smaller firms and poorer individuals, but also in general for households, large firms and other agents is improved, in terms of volume and costs. And in terms of stability, I consider whether the banking system has less instability, fewer financial crises and is generally more robust and its financial integrity higher. I look at all these dimensions as they can be important relationships among them, making analyzing any individually not complete.

2.1. *Theory*

It is useful to consider what to expect given theory on some of these dimensions. First, the general competition and contestability theory suggests that the market structure and the actual degree of entry or exit are not the most important factors in determining competition. The degree of contestability, rather than actual entry, matters for competitiveness (Baumol, Panzar, and Willig, 1982). Furthermore, competition can be expected to affect several dimensions: not only efficiency and costs, but also the incentives of institutions and markets to innovate. Financial sector specific theory on competition effects adds to this some additional considerations (see Claessens and Laeven, 2005 for a review). It has been found that the structure of systems can matter, but in many ways, including the ownership of the entrants and incumbents, the size and the degree of financial conglomeration (that is, the mixture of banking and other forms of financial services, such as insurance and investment banking). It has also analyzed how access depends on the franchise value of financial institutions and how the general degree of competition can negatively or positively affect access. With too much competition, for example, banks may be less inclined to invest in relationship lending (Rajan, 1992). Because of hold-up problems, however, too little competition may tie borrowers too much to an individual institution, making the borrower less willing to enter a relationship (Petersen and Rajan, 1995 and Boot and Thakor, 2000).

The quality of information interacts with the size and structure of the banking system. There is evidence, for example, for the U.S. that consolidation has led to a greater distance and thereby to less lending to more opaque small and medium enterprises (SMEs) (Berger, Miller, Petersen, Rajan and Stein, 2005; see also Carow, Kane and Marayaman, 2004; Karceski, Ongena and Smith, 2005; Sapienza, 2002; Degryse, and Masschelein and Mitchell, 2005). The fact that too much competition can undermine stability and lead to financial crises has been often argued (Allen and Gale, 2004 review), although difficult to document systematically (see Beck, Dermirguc-Kunt and Levine, 2002). These complex relationships and tradeoffs among competition, financial system performance, access to financing, stability, and finally growth already make it clear that it is not sufficient to analyze a narrow concept of competitiveness alone.

The theory on the effects of competition in financial services has shown some further complications. Some have highlighted that competition is partly endogenous as financial institutions invest in technology and relationships (for example, Hauswald and Marguez, 2004). This in turns means there are often ambiguous effects of technological innovations, access to information, and the dynamic pattern of entry and exit on competition, access, stability and efficiency (for example, Dell'Ariccia and Marquez, 2004, Hauswald and Marquez, 2003 and Marquez, 2002). The effects are further complicated by the fact that network effects exist in many supply, demand or distribution aspects. As for other network industries, this is making competition more complex (Claessens, Dobos, Klingebiel and Laeven, 2003). Importantly, financial services industries are continuously changing — due to removal of barriers, globalization, increased role of non-bank financial institutions, technological progress and increased importance of networks, which is affecting the degree and type of competition, something I will analyze further below in Section 3.

2.2. Empirics

Although theory alone is giving mixed insights into the effects of cross-border banking on competition, the empirical findings are fairly clear. In terms of development and efficiency, competition through cross-border capital flows has led to lower cost of capital for borrowers, higher rates of return for lenders, that is, lower margins and lower costs of financial intermediation (Agénor, 2001; Bekaert and Harvey, 2003), spurring growth (Bekaert, Harvery and Lundblad, 2005). Interestingly, there is some evidence that foreign banks' international activities are not necessarily more profitable. (DeYoung and Nolle, 1996 and Chang, Hasan and Hunter, 1998), involving possibly some cross-subsidies (as has been noted for Japanese banks; see Hasan and Hunter, 1996 and Peek, Rosengren and Kasirye, 1999) or evidence that diversification benefits of international activities make lower profitability still attractive (Berger, DeYoung, Genay and Udell, 2000). The effects of cross-border capital flows on access are found to be positive as well, although as noted increased access has largely been for selected groups of borrowers. Finally, the effects on stability of international capital flows have generally been found to be favorable — as international financial integration allows for greater international specialization and diversification (for example, Obstfeld, 1998). Of course, international capital flows can add to financial risks, among others, through contagion (Dornbusch, Park and Claessens, 2000 and Claessens and Forbes, 2001).

The entry of foreign banks has generally had favorable effects on the development and efficiency of domestic, host banking systems (Micco, Panizza and Yanez, 2004; Mian, 2003). These generally positive results have occurred through various channels. Lower costs of financial intermediation (measured in the forms of margins, spreads, overheads) and lower profitability have generally been documented (see Claessens, Demirgüç-Kunt, and Huizinga, 2001 and follow-up studies, for example, Berger, Clarke, Cull, Klapper, and Udell, 2005). Also, researchers have found some evidence of a better quality of financial intermediation, for example, as one observes less loan-loss provisioning with more foreign entry beneficial (Martinez-Peria and Mody, 2004). The qualitative aspects have by nature been harder to document, but have possibly been most important. These include the emergence of new, more diverse products, the greater use of technologies, and the spillovers of know-how (for example, as people learn new skills in foreign banks and migrate over time to the local banks). An additional channel has been pressures of foreign banks to improve regulation and supervision, increase transparency, etc., and more generally be a catalyst for reform (see further Levine, 1996 and Dobson, 2005, for reviews).

The effects of the entry of foreign banks on development and efficiency appear to depend, though, on some conditions. The general development and any remaining barriers can hinder the effectiveness of foreign banks (Garcia-Herrero and Martinez-Peria, 2005; Demirgüç-Kunt, Laeven and Levine, 2004). Also, the relative size of foreign banks' entry seems to matter. With more limited entry (as a share of the total host banking system), fewer spillovers seem to arise, suggesting some threshold effect (Claessens and Lee, 2003). In terms of individual foreign bank characteristics, it seems that larger banks are associated with greater effects on access for SMEs, perhaps as they are more committed to the market, while smaller banks are more niche players (Clarke *et al.*, 2005). The health of both the home banks as well as the local host bank matters, with the healthier banks showing better credit growth (Dages Goldberg and Kinney, 2000; see also Haber and Musacchio, 2005 and de Haas and van Lelyveld, 2005).

It should be noted that these effects of the entry of foreign banks are not necessarily competitiveness effects since the studies reviewed so far are not tests of formal competition models. Fully specified empirical competitiveness studies are scarce, with mostly single country studies, but only a few cross-country studies (Berger, 2006). To the extent available, however, cross-country evidence using formal empirical contestability tests suggests that foreign bank ownership is the most consistent factor associated with improved competitiveness of local banking systems (Claessens and Laeven, 2004). Next in importance are less severe entry and activity restrictions on banks. This same study suggests that there is little evidence that the structure of banking system matters in terms of competitiveness. Bank concentration and competitiveness are actually sometimes positively correlated, that is, more concentrated banking systems exhibit more competitive behavior and the number of banks is never positively, and sometimes even negatively related to measures of competitiveness, that is, more banks make for less competition. This confirms the importance of contestable system rather than a certain structure.

The effects on access by foreign banks can be separated in terms of access to foreign capital and access to domestic financing. Access to international financing is surely enhanced for some borrowers and lenders. Indeed, evidence suggests that both in normal times, but especially during time of crises, borrowers have enhanced access to finance with more foreign banks present (Goldberg, 2002). In terms of access to domestic capital, maybe in part since this is being more recently studied, the findings are not as clear. Generally, though, it has been found that access is enhanced by direct provision by foreign banks and indirectly by putting pressure on local banks (for example, more competition and stability driving local banks to provide more access). It has been found, for example, that firms report financing obstacles to be lower with more foreign banks, that even SMEs benefit and no evidence has been found that these SMEs are harmed by the presence of foreign banks (Clarke *et al.*, 2001 see also Beck, Demirgüç-Kunt and Maksimovic, 2004). There is some evidence to the contrary though. Detragiache, Gupta and Tressel (2005) for example, find that foreign banks presence in low-income countries leads to a reduction in credit and higher operating costs.

Foreign banks seem to lead to more entrepreneurial activity, although the effects are lesser for smaller firms. Interesting, more "connected" firms, that is, those having access based on non-economic factors, seem to suffer in access from foreign banks, which would be a positive effect (Giannetti and Ongena, 2005). Two aspects are not yet well known: whether the effects come about in a mostly direct or indirect way; and whether entry is less beneficial in softer-information lending as foreign banks may rely more on hard information to do their lending (see Berger, Klapper and Udell, 2001 for some evidence). These aspects are still to be investigated further.

Finally, the effects of entry of foreign banks on stability are generally found to be positive. There appears to be less risks of financial crises, and banks, foreign as well as domestic, display higher provisioning, less non-performing loans, suggesting better quality lending (Demirgüç-Kunt, Min and Levine, 1998 and Barth, Caprio and Levine, 2001). There is also evidence of less pro-cyclical lending behavior of the local operations of foreign banks relative to the cross-border operations of foreign banks (Goldberg, 2005) and lower sensitivity to the risk of financial contagion (Goldberg, 2002). There are, however, some possible negative effects. These include negative effects on franchise value, although often hard to determine given recent entry in many markets (Boyd, DeNicolo, and Smith, 2006). There can also be the risk of undiversified home countries (Buch, Carstensen and Schertler, 2005), which have to be weighted against the risk of an undiversified banking system without entry. Then there is the risk of new technologies and new financial instruments being introduced pre-maturely. Again, these risks may arise in principle, but are hard to quantify. Finally, there is the risk of easier capital flows, possibly capital flight, as a consequence of banks that have greater access to international financial markets. And there are the risks to the home countries (Cetorelli and Golberg in this volume).

Much of these empirical findings on cross-border banking have to be qualified by the fact that, even without formal barriers, financial integration remains imperfect. One observes that even in fully integrated markets, such as the U.S. or increasingly so the EU, that there still is a familiarity bias in capital flows and entry decisions, for example, more investment and entry closer to home. This means that the competitiveness effects can remain limited to some markets, regions or market segments (Mian, 2006). Of course, any further removal of barriers may still facilitate entry. While evidence of immersion effects of foreign banks entry in the presence of distortions is limited, many observers (for example, Center for Economic Policy Research, 2005) and market participants have argued that achieving the full gains from entry requires more (minimal) harmonization of regulations, legal and other institutional infrastructure.

Furthermore, it is important to consider the interactions between capital account liberalization, financial services liberalization and domestic deregulation. Generally, liberalizing along all three dimensions, is considered mutually reinforcing. There are, however, issues of consistency and coherence between the three forms of liberalization to consider. Financial services liberalization can require some degree of capital account liberalization as foreign banks need access to international financial markets to operate effectively. Domestic deregulation and capital account liberalization can both involve the removal of lending restrictions, which needs to be done in a consistent fashion across the two forms. Inconsistencies, for example, when firms are allowed to access certain forms of international capital freely, while still being restricted in their borrowing domestically, can lead to the buildup of external vulnerabilities.

Cross-border banking through capital flows and through entry can be alternative to reach a market (Buch and Lippner, 2004) and tradeoffs can arise. Using data from Italian, Spanish and U.S. banks, Garcia-Herrero and Martinez-Peria (2005) found that foreign banks open branches in countries with better profit opportunities and greater "banking freedom," that is, countries that do not impose restrictions on bank activities, controls on foreign currency lending or high taxes on banking. In smaller, less secure developing markets, though, banks rely more on cross border lending. There is also some evidence that stock markets liberalization before financial services liberalization increases the benefits of foreign banks, but that capital account liberalization first reduces the benefits (Bayrakta and Yang, 2004 see also Claessens and Glaessner, 1999).

Lessons from capital markets. A short intermezzo useful here concerns the lessons from capital markets' integration for cross-border banking. Capital markets, both equity and bond markets, have for long time experienced much cross-border financial flows and in the recent decades have also seen more services being consumed cross-border (for example, in the form of the listing and trading of securities at international exchanges). And there has been some foreign entry in capital markets in the last few years. Capital markets integration is not the main topic here, but still can provide some useful lessons for three reasons. One, for a number of reasons, including easier adoption of technology, capital markets are evolving faster than banking markets are. As such, one may learn from capital markets for changes coming to banking markets. Second, and more debatable, capital markets are less subject today to natural and policy barriers than banking markets are. The traded nature of assets and the lesser importance of soft information, for example, make cross-border trading in securities easier than in banking products. Financial integration in capital markets is then often also deeper than in cross-border banking. And third, there has been some convergence of banking to capital markets in terms of products and approaches, as, for example, in the form of credit derivatives.

While there are many similarities between capital markets and cross-border banking, there are some important differences. Not only are barriers (institutional and technological) less in capital markets than in banking, integration appears to a lesser degree than for banking markets a function of the quality of institutional environment. One has, for example, seen near complete price integration in the capital markets of some more developed emerging markets, while cross-border banking flows still remain limited for the same countries. There are also more distinct scale effects in capital markets, more so than in banking, with small scale hindering the development of the local markets and encouraging internationalization of financial services (Claessens, Klingebiel and Schmukler, 2005). Most importantly, the implications of financial integration in capital markets are experienced not only in supply and demand dimensions but also in institutional aspects. In international capital markets, as for cross-border banking, suppliers and demanders benefit from a lower cost of capital, lower trading costs, more liquidity, higher returns, greater quantity of external financing, etc. In equity markets, however, there is also evidence that the institutional environment is affected as a consequence of competition. Generally, the local institutional environment improves, that is, when faced with competition, countries engage in a race to the top more likely than to the bottom (Coffee, 1999). In terms of impact on overall market development and prospects, however, it appears that local liquidity declines, not just for stocks listed and traded abroad, but also for the local-only stocks (Levine and Schmukler, 2003). Competition can thus have some negative effects on the overall development of local capital markets.

The lessons from capital markets for cross-border banking would be that competition effects can be broad. Competition can affect efficiency and access, but also the evolution of rules and institutions. Furthermore, competition can even affect the presence of markets. Since scale effects appear important in capital markets, small local markets may be at risk from competition, including through negatively affecting the scope for the development of local services supporting capital markets (for example, accounting and investment banking services). As such there can also be path dependency, for example, the development of local markets prior to introducing competition might provide greater scope for ending up with functioning local markets. Arguments for infant industries are very tricky, though, given political economy factors, and as such may not provide the desired results.

3. Changing Competitive Landscape

So far, I have analyzed the forces that drive cross-border banking and the impact cross-border banking can have on domestic banking markets. While I have highlighted that many of the impacts of cross-border banking are similar to those usually subscribed to increased competition, there are some important differences, particularly in turns of access, stability and market development. This analysis was, however, largely still within the paradigm of the typical goods markets and a relatively stable global financial system. But competition in the financial sector can be very different from that in other goods or services markets. Furthermore, financial services industries are in flux and the nature of competition is changing as a consequence. This has implications not only for the nature of competition, but also for competition policy. In this section, I will analyze the basic difficulties with applying competition policy in finance as well as the forces for change in financial services industries today, ending up with some suggestions on how competition policy might need to be adapted.

Competition in finance. Competition policy in financial services provision is complex (see Vives, 2001, for a review). The presence of large sunk costs and high fixed costs in the production of financial services mean significant first mover and scale advantages, possibly leading to natural monopoly and market power. Large switching costs mean that customers do not easily change financial services providers and make the adoption of new technologies exhibit critical mass properties. Financial services provision also involves the use of a great number of networks, such as payments, distribution and information systems. This means barriers to entry can arise due to a lack of access to essential services. More general, network externalities can complicate the application of competition policy. Finally, the "special nature" of financial sector, with its emphasis on financial stability has always meant that competition policy was considered more complicated. "Free entry", for example, even when subject to fitness test, has generally been considered to pose risks to financial stability as it would undermine franchise value. While arguably these arguments are less relevant today — as many financial services can be provided by non-bank financial institutions and the role of banks as liquidity providers is less crucial today — it still affects the application of competition policy in finance in practice.

In addition to these complications, recent trends have made competition, and competition policy, more complex (see Claessens, Dobos, Klingebiel, and Laeven, 2003, for a review). For one, market and product definitions have become (more) difficult. It is trite, but nevertheless very important from a competition policy point of view to state that financial markets today are global in nature, making any application of competition policy to national markets of lesser value than two decades ago. Second, markets are rapidly consolidating around the world (Berger, Demsetz, and Strahan, 1999).

In addition, the definition of a specific financial service and its market has become more complicated, affecting competition policy. Today, for example, there are little differences between the market for pension and that for assets management services. And with many nonfinancial institutions providing (near) banking and other financial services, the boundary between non-bank financial institutions and banks has become blurred. More generally, the production of financial services has changed in many ways, with large investments in information technology and brand name necessary to operate effectively and to gain scale. There are also some forces towards vertical integration in some aspects, especially in capital markets (for example, integration of trading systems with clearing and settlement), while other forces push towards more separation (for example, clarity in functions) or horizontal consolidation (for example, economies of scale). In addition, there are increasing links between banking and commerce (for example, between banking and telecommunications).

Revisit competition policy. These changes point to a need to revisit competition policy in the financial sector. I suggest that the "new" competition policy combines three approaches: an *institutional* approach, to assure contestable markets by entry/exit of institutions, domestic and cross-border; a *functional* approach, to assure contestable markets by leveling the playing field across similar financial products (in all dimensions); and a *production* approach, to assure efficiently provided and equally accessible and affordable network services (information, distribution, settlement, clearing, payment, etc.) and to take into account any network externalities. Combined, these approaches can make competition policy resemble that in other network industries, for example, telecoms. So far, however, only the institutional and somewhat the functional approaches have been used.

I will next expand on these three approaches (see further Claessens, 2003 for more detail).

3.1. *Institutional approach*

The institutional approach to competition means that the entry and exit regime for different type of financial institutions should be pro-competitive, or at least as contestable as possible after considering issues arising from financial stability. As in other sectors, applying the institutional approach in the financial sector involves, among others, a review of entry and exit barriers for a market at a regional, country, or, global level; a review of actual entry and exit decisions, mergers and acquisitions of financial institutions; and investigations of market power and dominance of institutions. As noted above, this approach is generally accepted, but is nevertheless not always used, especially not at the global level.

3.2. *Functional approach*

The functional approach uses the same concept of contestable markets, except it applies it to a specific service, rather than to a set of financial institutions. The functional approach implies a need to level the playing field for each financial service and between similar types of financial services across all types of providers. It means a proper entry and exit regime for each financial service and avoiding differences in the regulatory treatment of similar types of financial services. Few countries have adopted this approach. And even when tried in earnest, the principle of a level-playing field across functions is difficult to put in practice. One reason is that the substitutability between specific financial services can be high in most dimensions, but involve subtle differences in some dimensions, such as credit risks or access to the safety net. Whether remaining differences are distortionary will often be very difficult to establish. Furthermore, historical differences can be difficult to correct as many other aspects come into play.[1]

---

[1]Even when attempts have been made to level the playing field for financial service providers and across financial services, regulatory and other differences may continue to create barriers to full competition. Standards may conflict, for example, such as the need to require capital for local branches of foreign banks, but not for branches of domestic banks. Information requirements may differ by product, for example, although otherwise similar, securities markets products may require more information disclosure than pension products. Differences in the tax treatment between pension and other forms of savings can be large, although they are in many ways equivalent financial instruments.

Even when distortions in treatment across products have been minimized, however, it will be difficult to assess whether markets for specific financial products are fully competitive or contestable. One reason is that financial institutions typically bundle financial services together and/or cross-subsidize services. This can be because financial institutions derive their comparative advantage from the bundle of services they provide, rather than from any specific individual service. But, it may also be because regulatory or other advantages (for example, access to a distribution network) allow the financial institution to provide the bundle of services in a way more advantageous than a single service provider can. Open entry in one market segment may as a consequence not guarantee a competitive market for each specific product. Or it can be that predatory cross-subsidization in the presence of natural entry barriers gives existing institutions an unfair advantage, allowing them to build up a market share. More generally, given the network properties analyzed, it is difficult to ascertain that there are no anti-competitive barriers remaining. It is therefore necessary to go beyond the institutional and functional approaches with a more production-based approach to competition policy.

3.3. *Production approach*

The production approach would mean that the various inputs, including network services, required for the production and distribution of financial services need to be available to all interested in using them, be fairly and uniformly priced and efficiently provided. For no part of a specific financial service production and distribution chain, should there be any undue barriers or unfair pricing. For most inputs (labor, services, etc.), this in turn simply requires competitive supply markets. Since the production and distribution of financial services rely much on common infrastructure with network properties, however, this approach requires more. Specifically, it requires an "efficient" market infrastructure, which itself is not an easily defined concept, in part as many elements of financial infrastructure have been subject to changes recently.

The market infrastructure for financial services involves many parts, such as trading systems, payment and clearing systems, ATM systems, and information systems. Differences are many, but competition issues can arise from differences in access, ownership — public versus private ownership — and forms of control, oversight, and corporate governance. The commonly shared infrastructure of a payments system, for example, can be run by a central bank, by banks themselves, or by a third party. Choices further vary between for-profit and not-for-profit organizations, and related, mutual and demutualized structures. Stock exchanges, for example, can be organized as mutual, not-for-profit organizations or as for-profit corporations. The various oversight structures — self-regulatory, government or purely private arrangements — can vary, by explicit design or historical consequences.

Each of these differences can give rise to its own set of competition policy issues. Private ownership of the market infrastructure may lead to direct forms of rent-seeking by the owners. Self-regulation of a market may lead to rules that favor insiders. Competition is, however, only one of the dimensions according to which one can evaluate the various arrangements for the provision of market infrastructure services and the recent changes. Dimensions such as the efficiency of providing relevant (supportive) services, risk management, integrity, incentives to innovate and upgrade, are often equally or more relevant. The general assessment is that the trend toward demutualization and privatization of stock markets, for example, has led to efficiency gains in the delivery of these services, without necessarily compromising (and often even enhancing) the objectives of proper risk management, integrity, and stability. But whether the recent changes are also always pro-competitive is not clear, at least not as of yet, as little time has passed and research been very limited. Similar lack of clarity exists with respect to competition implications of the new alternative trading systems for stocks and other financial assets. More generally, the type of competition policies applicable to the market structure supporting forms of financial services is not yet clear.

4. The Special Issues of Developing Countries

In many ways, financial services industries in all countries have been subject to similar trends. Despite differences among countries — including factors such as the state of the financial system, readiness of the telecommunications infrastructure and the quality of the regulatory framework — there is much commonality and convergence in the way financial services industries are being reshaped. In securities markets, global trading is becoming the norm. Increased connectivity has accelerated the migration of securities trading and capital raising from emerging markets to a few global financial centers. In banking, consolidation is proceeding in many markets and integrated financial service provision has become the norm around the world.

Despite similarities in the evolution of financial services industries around the world, there remain large differences among countries in terms of overall development, the stages of their financial sector development, and the quality of their institutional frameworks. This raises the question whether there is a need to approach the issues of cross-border banking and competition policy differently by level of development.

For a variety of reasons, countries are at different level of development of their regulatory and supervisory capacity, quality of legal and judicial systems, and other institutional dimensions. Reaping the full gains of cross-border banking can require a certain minimum level of financial sector regulation and supervision. Many of developing countries' deficiencies are being identified in the assessment of compliance with international standards. Deficiencies in each of these areas are expected to be addressed over time in the follow-up and through general pressures associated with this process (such as through disclosure of deficiencies and pressures from peers and investors).

These reforms will take time. Furthermore, one has to acknowledge that there will often be deeper reasons why failures in regulation and supervision do not allow developing countries to reap the full benefits of their liberalization efforts. In particular, the failure of countries to take appropriate regulatory actions when liberalizing often relates to political economy reasons, involving often moral hazard and (too) extensive forms of deposit insurance. To change this will require achieving greater political openness itself a gradual process in many cases (Barth, Caprio and Levine, 2005). Nevertheless, one should consider how reforms in cross-border banking could help overcome some of these political economy constraints. Entry by foreign financial institutions will often bring with it not only foreign expertise, but can also reduce political pressures on the supervisory system. Similarly, broadening the scope of institutions able to provide financial services can reduce the political influence of incumbent banks.

Beyond the need for a consistent approach in the three forms of liberalization and the need to deal with political economy factors, arguably there are no fixed preconditions to allow effective internationalization of financial services. Countries with weak and strong regulation and supervision can both do well under large foreign entry; in the first case, foreign entry brings with it improved regulation and supervision, enhancing the quality of the overall domestic sector; in the second case, strong domestic regulation and supervision assure that entry does not lead to any concerns.

It may be that the intermediate cases of moderately developed frameworks present the most risks as foreign financial institutions compete away franchise value of incumbents, thus creating incentives for imprudent behavior, and as domestic and foreign investors misjudge the stability of the system and the robustness of the regulatory response. In such cases, good closure rules for weak financial institutions and quantitative restrictions on financial exposures may be the most appropriate response while liberalizing.

Country conditions surely have relevance, however, for the way in which competition policy, including the disciplines associated with GATS/WTO, is conducted. In spite of reforms, many developing countries' financial sectors are still characterized by a lack of "effective" competition. They may have a quite concentrated market structure, extensive links between financial institutions and corporations, and a high ultimate ownership concentration of the financial sector. While in principle many developing countries are open today, entry by foreign financial institutions may be limited to some niche areas, in part because of country risk perceptions. Important, incumbent financial institutions may have a lock on networks essential for financial services provision. Existing incumbents may block new initiatives via a variety of means. The net results will be less pressure to reduce costs, to improve the quality of financial services and to move down the credit scale into lower-income retail and small-enterprise lending.

While again it is difficult to generalize on how competition policy ought to be differentiated by level of development, it is likely more important for developing countries to include competition issues when designing reforms including changes to the payments system, credit information arrangements, and telecom regulatory and legal frameworks. Specifically, one needs to be careful in the design of networks, whether they involve financial service specific systems only or are telecom related as these can become important barriers to entry, including for foreign banks. In the area of retail payments, for example, the use of a third party provider (not a consortium of banks) for the provision of different forms of retail payment services could be more appropriate from a competition point of view when the market structure is very concentrated.

An effective competition commission is critical, but that will require adequate support, jurisdiction and backing vis-à-vis other supervisory agencies. In case of many developing countries, the overall capacity and independence of competition authorities is limited and proper enforcement tools are mission. Often, political support will be lacking and conflicts may exist between the competition policy agency and the agency that deals with prudential regulation. Also, a case for more restrictions on cross-holdings can be made, particularly in smaller developing countries. Limits on groups and banking-commerce may be necessary to assure effective competition.

5. The Role of GATS and WTO

The GATS can be an important force for a more pro-competition policy in financial services. The past financial services negotiations, however, have been arduous and extended (Sorsa, 1997). Final success has arguably been relatively limited as many countries have commitments that are much less binding than their existing practices. In others words, most countries have not used the process to bind themselves to an (accelerated) process of liberalization. In part, this outcome has arisen because the approach to date for financial services has been sector-specific and largely outside the normal GATS-negotiations (Kono *et al.*, 1997 and Key, 2004).

Going forward, similar to other goods and services, a horizontal approach is preferable for financial services given the increased inputs from other sectors in the production and distribution of financial services, including those from networks industries such as telecommunications. Liberalizing financial services industries alone may not lead to the full possible gains if other sectors do not liberalize equally. A horizontal approach is also more feasible today as financial services have become less special and the horizontal approach is thus less likely to lead to conflicts with prudential concerns. A key argument for a horizontal approach, however, is that political economy factors, that are so prevalent in financial services, have dominated the negotiation outcome. When there was no ability to tradeoff interests with those in other sectors, the political powers led to a limited liberalization. As financial services are increasingly being recognized as essential inputs in overall economic production, the support from other sectors for efficient financial services provision, and consequently for liberalization, has increased, making a horizontal approach more attractive.

Applying the horizontal approach to financial services liberalization may require a revisiting of the prudential carve-out of GATS (Sauve, 2002). The carve-out has already been used as an argument to keep financial services out of the Uruguay Round negotiations. There are some issues as to the interpretation of the scope of the carve-out. Under some interpretations, the carve-out cannot be used to evade other GATS commitments and needs to be aimed primarily at prudential regulation. Even with this strict interpretation, however, the issue remains what constitutes justifiable prudential regulation. On one hand, a more standard view on prudential regulation has developed through, among others, the promulgation of international banking and other standards, thus reducing the likelihood of differences in frameworks leading to non-trade barriers. At the same time, there may be a need to rethink prudential regulation given changes in the financial services industries globally. As noted, in many countries regulation has stifled competition and countries political economy may mean that more rules will encourage this behavior. The current emphasis on global standards, as part of the new international financial architecture, implies that there are legitimate concerns that the approach will overshoot in concerns for safety, soundness and stability at the expense of concerns over free trade in financial services.

The potential anti-competitive way in which the prudential carve-out can be applied does not imply that it needs to be removed fully. For one, it is likely to be used sparingly. Countries realize the reputation costs of invoking the carve-out and applying prudential regulation in an anti-competitive way. Particularly in the context of developing countries, investors will look for signs of credibility and invoking the carve-out will provide the opposite signal, especially when in a financial crisis. It is also unclear what type of regulations can reduce risks of financial contagion and volatility, arguably the more likely causes of crises going forward. Useful regulations will include some prudential banking systems regulations (for example, requiring certain loan-loss provisioning), but they could also be more macro-economic in nature (for example, limiting exposures to certain sectors), or aimed specifically at some balance-of-payments objectives (for example, restrictions or taxes imposed on short-term capital flows). Whether these fall (or ought to fall) under the prudential carve-out is unclear. Nevertheless, there might be circumstances when a form of carve-out will be useful, although it can be more circumscribed than currently formulated.

In addition to assessing the scope of the prudential carve-out under GATS, it will be useful to complement the forthcoming round of market access commitments in GATS with a set of pro-competitive principles of sound regulation. Proposals in this respect have been made by many in the financial services industry. They center around commitments on improved transparency and regulatory reform, including transparent domestic rules and administrative procedures. This emphasis on increased transparency would be consistent with the general need highlighted in this paper that trade liberalization needs to be complemented with a more active competition policy.

6. Areas Lesser Known

Rather than present conclusions, I like to raise some areas that are less well-known. A number of these will be taken up in the other parts of the volume. I am raising them here as they can also have competitive impact. One is what to do to further foreign bank entry. If, as evidence suggests, entry by foreign banks can be useful, are there specific measures countries can put in place to attract foreign banks? Since there is also some evidence that the size of banks and the nature of the home country affect the behavior of entrants, it can be suggested that policy makers try to affect the size and home country of foreign banks entering. Furthermore, since lending can been hindered by the more formal approaches used by foreign banks, and distance more generally creates obstacles, it is tempting to suggest using a different regulatory approach to foreign banks' international operations. This, of course, is quite difficult and can create uneven approaches. This seems to deserve some further research. Also, can the right type of banks — size, host, diversified — specifically be attracted at all? And if so, are such, possible preferential treatments consistent with the WTO-principles? In terms of the overall sequence of reforms — capital account liberalization, financial services liberalization, domestic deregulation — there are questions on sequence to be followed that maximizes the impact of foreign banks. I am skeptical research caused much light on this in general, but nevertheless one can try to review some case studies as to their experiences with sequencing.

A broader question is what to do in small economies. Clearly, there are many scale issues to consider here beyond cross-border banking and foreign banks entry specifically. It raises the "economies of scale" of an own currency, regulation and supervision, etc. But one can try to address whether there are more special approaches, or sequences to be followed. There are experiences of countries like the Baltics that adopted at the same time currency boards, had large cross-border banking and harmonized rules as they got ready to enter the EU. Perhaps these and other small economies experiences are relevant to review. Furthermore, regional solutions and some of the arrangements in the Africa currency unions on common institutional infrastructures (stock exchanges and regulation and supervision) may be relevant to review. Also, might there be ways to open up particular aspects of financial services provision chain that are more suited to small economies? For example, in the area of banking, could gross value payments system be outsourced to foreign markets, while retail payments system are developed domestically? Again, these are issues that could have implications for competition.

The minimal requirements on rules and the necessary degree of harmonization of rules and practices are typically considered regulation and supervision issues. Yet, there is a competitiveness angle to them as well. Apart from the need to assure contestability, there could also be an argument to adapt rules given the special focus of foreign banks. If indeed foreign banks focus more on hard-information, foreign banks may be more conservative in their local lending behavior in developing countries, thus potentially making less of a contribution. This behavior can be part of their general practices (see de Haas and Naaborg, 2005) — and should thus not be discouraged (Stein, 2002), but could in part also because they apply their de-facto more strict home standards (whether Basel II, AML, etc.) to their local lending operations. To the extent this more formal approach creates too great a distance from the borrower, and undermines productive lending, should the rules consequently be adopted? Put differently, there may be some specific regulatory responses that increase the competitive impact of entry of foreign banks. For example, whether subsidiaries or branches are allowed for foreign banks can perhaps consider the development and competitiveness impact.[2] More generally, is there an argument to avoid over-regulation of foreign banks, operations and if so what regulatory elements specifically can be adjusted?

Finally, what does the "new" view of competition policy mean for the tools for identifying and addressing competition issues? Clearly, the tools typically used to date are quite limited (Herfindahl/or concentration indexes) and need to be enhanced. Yet, the analytical tools developed for measuring competition in financial services industries are hard to apply empirically. What to use in practice? Related, what is the specific role of WTO/GATS and regional free-trade agreements (FTA) in this process? How can GATS/FTAs help with entry by fostering deeper reforms? There clearly is a commitment

[2]Cerutti, Dell'Ariccia, and Soledad Martinez-Peria (2005) study the differences between motives of foreign banks to go abroad as subsidiaries or branches. See also Gkoutzinis (2005).

role of GATS/FTAs in domestic competition, but how to implement is not as clear. At the same time, how can one avoid the equivalent of trade diversion in any FTAs, given the strong home bias that already exists in financial services provision (for example, regional financial institutions may dominate cross-border banking but this may reduce the diversification and other benefits)?

References

Agénor, Pierre-Richard, 2001, "Benefits and Costs of International Financial Integration: Theory and Facts," Policy and Research Working Paper No. 2699, The World Bank.

Allen, Franklin and Douglas Gale, 2004, "Competition and Financial Stability," *Journal of Money, Credit and Banking*, 36(3), pp. 453–480.

Baele, Lieven, Ferrando, Annalisa, Hoerdahl, Peter, Krylova, Elizaveta and Monnet, Cyril, 2004, "Measuring Financial Integration in the Euro Area. European Central Bank," (Frankfurt, Germany) Occasional Paper No. 14, May.

Barth, James, Gerard Caprio and Ross Levine, 2001, "Banking Systems Around the Globe: Do Regulation and Ownership Affect Performance and Stability?" in Frederick Mishkin (Ed). *Financial Supervision and Regulation*: What Works and What Doesn't? NBER, Cambridge, MA.

Barth, James, Gerard Caprio and Ross Levine, 2005, *Rethinking Bank Supervision and Regulation: Until Angels Govern*. Cambridge, UK: Cambridge University Press.

Baumol, William J., John C. Panzar, and Robert D. Willig, 1982, *Contestable Markets and the Theory of Industry Structure*, San Diego, CA: Harcourt Brace Jovanovich.

Bayraktar, Nihal and Yan Wang, 2004, "Foreign Bank Entry, Performance of Domestic Banks and Sequence of Financial Liberalization," Policy Research Working Paper No. 3416, World Bank.

Beck, Thorsten, Asli Demirgüç-Kunt and Ross Levine, 2002, "Bank Concentration and Crises," Mimeo, World Bank and University of Minnesota.

Beck, Thorsten, Asli Demirgüç-Kunt and Vojislav Maksimovic, 2004, "Bank Competition, Financing Constraints and Access to Credit," *Journal of Money Credit and Banking*.

Bekaert, G., and C. R. Harvey, 2003, "Emerging Markets Finance," *Journal of Empirical Finance*, 10(1–2), pp. 3–56.

Bekaert, Geert, Campbell Harvey, and Christian Lundblad, 2005, "Does Financial Liberalization Spur Growth," *Journal of Financial Economics*, 77, pp. 3–56.

Berger, A. N., 2006, "International Comparisons of Banking Efficiency," in Raj Aggarwal, ed., *A Companion to International Business Finance*, forthcoming.

Berger, A. N., Buch, C. M., DeLong, G., DeYoung, R., 2004, "Exporting Financial Institutions Management via Foreign Direct Investment Mergers and Acquisitions," *Journal of International Money and Finance*, 23, pp. 333–366.

Berger, Allen N., George R. G. Clarke, Robert Cull, Leora Klapper and Gregory F. Udell, 2005, "Corporate Governance, and Bank Performance: A Joint Analysis of the Static, Selection and Dynamic Effects of Domestic, Foreign and State Ownership," Policy Research Working Paper No. 3632, World Bank.

Berger, Allen N., Rebecca S. Demsetz, and Philip E. Strahan, 1999, "The Consolidation of the Financial Services Industry: Causes, Consequences, and Implications for the Future," *Journal of Banking and Finance*, 23(February), pp. 135–194.

Berger, A. N., DeYoung, R., Genay, H., Udell, G. F., 2000, "The Globalization of Finanical Institutions: Evidence from Cross-Border Banking Performance," *Brookings-Wharton Papers on Financial Services*, 3, pp. 23–158.

Berger, Allen N, Leora F. Klapper, and Gregory F. Udell, 2001, "The Ability of Banks to Lend to Informationally Opaque Small Businesses," *Journal of Banking and Finance*, 25.

Berger, Allen N., Nathan H. Miller, Mitchell A. Petersen, Raghuram Rajan, and Jeremy Stein, 2005, "Does Function Follow Organizational Form? Evidence from the Lending Practices of Large and Small Banks," *Journal of Financial Economics*, 76, pp. 237–269.

Boot, Arnoud, and Anjan V. Thakor, 2000, "Can Relationship Banking Survive Competition?" *Journal of Finance*, 55(2), pp. 679–713.

Boyd, John, Gianni DeNicolo, and Smith, 2006, Banking Crises and Competition, *Journal of Money, Credit and Banking*, forthcoming.

Buch, C. M., 2003, "Information versus Regulation: What Drives the International Activities of Commercial Banks?" *Journal of Money, Credit and Banking*, 35, pp. 851–869.

Buch, C. M. and G. L. DeLong, 2004, "Cross-Border Bank Mergers: What Lures the Rare Animal?" *Journal of Banking and Finance*, 28, pp. 2077–2102.

Buch, C. M., Carstensen, K., Schertler A, 2005, "Macroeconomic Shocks and Foreign Bank Assets," Kiel Working Paper No. 1254, Kiel Institute for World Economics, July.

Buch, C. M., and A. Lipponer, "FDI versus Cross-Border Financial Services: The Globalisation of German banks," Discussion Paper Series 1: Studies of the Economic Research Centre, No.05/2004, Deutsche Bundesbank.

Carow, K. A., Edward Kane, and R. Narayanan, 2004, "How Have Borrowers Fared in Banking Mega-Mergers?" Unpublished manuscript, Boston College.

Cetorelli, Nicola and Linda S. Goldberg, 2006, "Risks in U.S. Bank International Exposures," in this volume, forthcoming.

Center for Economic Policy Research (CEPR), "Integration of European Banking: The Way Forward," *Monitoring European Deregulation*, 3, London, UK.

Cerutti, Eugenio, Giovanni Dell'Ariccia, and Maria Soledad Martinez-Peria, 2005, "How Banks Go Abroad: Branches or Subsidiaries?" Unpublished manuscript, IMF and World Bank.

Chang, C. Edward, Iftekhar Hasan, William C. Hunter, 1998, "Efficiency of multinational banks: an empirical investigation," *Applied Financial Economics*, 8(6).

Claessens, Stijn, 2003, "Regulatory Reform and Trade Liberalization in Financial Services," in Aaditya Mattoo and Pierre Sauvé (Eds.), *Domestic Regulation and Service Trade Liberalization*, World Bank, Oxford University Press, Washington, D.C., pp. 129–146.

Claessens, Stijn, Asli Demirgüç-Kunt, and Harry Huizinga, 2001, "How Does Foreign Entry Affect the Domestic Banking Market?" *Journal of Banking and Finance*, 25(5), pp. 891–911.

Claessens, Stijn, Gergely Dobos, Daniela Klingebiel, and Luc Laeven, 2003, "The Growing Importance of Networks in Finance and Its Effects on Competition," in Anna Nagurney (Ed.), *Innovations in Financial and Economic Networks*, Edward Elgar Publishers, Northampton, MA, U.S., pp. 110–135.

Claessens, Stijn, and Kristin Forbes, Eds, 2001, *International Financial Contagion*, Boston: Kluwer Academic Press.

Claessens, Stijn, and Thomas Glaessner, 1999, "Internationalization of Financial Services in Asia," in James A. Hanson and Sanjay Kathuria (Eds.), *India A Financial Sector for the Twenty-first Century*, Oxford University Press, pp. 369–433.

Claessens, Stijn, Daniela Klingebiel and Sergio Schmukler, 2005, "Stock Market Development and Internationalization: Do Economic Fundamentals Spur Both Similarly?" *Journal of Empirical Finance*, forthcoming.

Claessens, Stijn and Luc Laeven, 2004, "What Drives Banking Competition? Some International Evidence," *Journal of Money Credit and Banking*, 36(3), pp. 563–583.

Claessens, Stijn and Luc Laeven, 2005, "Financial Dependence, Banking Sector Competition, and Economic Growth," *Journal of the European Economic Association*, 3(1), pp. 179–201.

Claessens, Stijn and Jong-Kun Lee, 2003, "Foreign Banks in Low-Income Countries: Recent Developments and Impacts," in *Globalization and National Financial Systems*, James Hanson, Patrick Honohan and Giovanni Majnoni (Eds.), World Bank, Washington, D.C., pp. 109–141.

Claessens, Stijn and Enrico Perotti, 2005, "The Links between Finance and Inequality: Channels and Evidence," Background paper for the 2005 *World Development Report*, World Bank.

Clarke, George R. G., Robert Cull, and Maria Soledad Martinez-Peria, 2001, "Does Foreign Bank Penetration Reduce Access to Credit in Developing Countries? Evidence from Asking Borrowers," Mimeo, Washington: The World Bank.

Clarke, George, Cull, Robert, Maria Soledad Martinez-Peria, and Susana M. Sánchez, 2003, "Foreign Bank Entry: Experience, Implications for Developing Countries, and Agenda for Further Research," *World Bank Research Observer*, 18(1), pp. 25–40.

Clarke, George, Robert Cull, Maria Soledad Martinez-Peria and Susana M. Sánchez, 2005, "Bank Lending to Small Businesses in Latin America: Does Bank Origin Matter?" *Journal of Money, Credit, and Banking*, 37(1), pp. 83–118.

Coffee, John, 1999, "The Future as History: The Prospects for Global Convergence in Corporate Governance and its Implications," *Northwestern Law Review*, 93, pp. 641–708.

Dages, G. B., L. Goldberg and D. Kinney, 2000, "Foreign and Domestic Bank Participation in Emerging Markets: Lessons from Mexico and Argentina," *Economic Policy Review*, 6(3), pp. 17–36.

Degryse, Hans, Nancy Masschelein, and Janet Mitchell, 2005, "SMEs and Bank Lending Relationships: The Impact of Mergers," CEPR Working Paper No. 5061.

Dell'Ariccia, Giovanni, and Robert Marquez, 2004, "Information and Bank Credit Allocation," *Journal of Financial Economics*, 71, pp. 185–214.

Demirgüç-Kunt, Asli, Luc Laeven, and Ross Levine, 2004, "Regulations, Market Structure, Institutions, and the Cost of Financial Intermediation," *Journal of Money, Credit, and Banking*, 36(3), pp. 593–622.

Demirgüç-Kunt, Asli, H. Min, and Ross Levine, 1998, "Opening to Foreign Banks: Issues of Stability, Efficiency, and Growth," in *Proceedings of the Bank of Korea Conference on The Implications of Globalization of World Financial Markets*, December 1998.

Detragiache, Enrica, Poonam Gupta, and Thierry Tressel, 2005, "Foreign Banks in Poor Countries: Theory and Evidence," Working paper, IMF.

De Young, Robert and Daniel E. Nolle, 1996, "Foreign-Owned Banks in the U.S.: Buying Market Share or Earning It?" *Journal of Money, Credit, and Banking*, 28, pp. 622–636.

Dobson, Wendy, 2005, "Background paper — Trade in Financial Services," Mimeo, World Bank, Trade Division.

Dobson, Wendy, and Pierre Jacquet, 1998, *Financial Services Liberalization in the WTO*, Washington, D.C.: Institute for International Economics.

Dooley, Michael P., 2000, "A Model of Crises in Emerging Markets," *Economic Journal*, 10, pp. 256–272.

Dornbusch, Rudiger, Yung Chul Park, and Stijn Claessens, 2000, "Contagion: Understanding How It Spreads," *World Bank Research Observer*, 15(2), pp. 177–197.

European Central Bank, 2005, "Indicators of Financial Integration in the Euro Area," September.

Eichengreen, Barry, 2003, *Capital Flows and Crises*, MA: MIT Press.

Financial Leaders Group, 1997, *Barriers to Trade in Financial Services: Case Studies*, London: Barclays.

Focarelli, Dario, and Alberto Pozzolo, 2003, "Where Do Banks Expand Abroad? An Empirical Investigation," Mimeo, Bank of Italy.

Garcia-Merro, Alicia and Maria Soledad García Herrero and Martínez Pería, 2005, "The Mix of International Banks' Foreign Claims: Determinants and Implications," Mimeo, World Bank.

Gelos, Gaston, and Jorge Roldós, 2004, "Consolidation and Market Structure in Emerging Market Banking Systems," *Emerging Markets Review*, 5, pp. 39–59.

Giannetti, Mariassunta and Steven Ongena, 2005, "Financial Integration and Entrepreneurial Activity: Evidence from Foreign Bank Entry in Emerging Markets," CEPR working paper 5151.

Gkoutzinis, Apostolos, "How Far is Basel from Geneva? International Regulatory Convergence and the Elimination of Barriers to International Financial Integration," University of London, at http://ssrn.com/abstract=699781.

Goldberg, Linda S., 2002, "When Is Foreign Bank Lending to Emerging Markets Volatile?" in *Preventing Currency Crises in Emerging Markets*, edited by Sebastian Edwards and Jeffrey Frankel, NBER and University of Chicago Press.

Goldberg, Linda S., 2005, "The International Exposure of U.S. Banks," NBER Working Paper 11365, Boston, MA.

de Haas, Ralph and Iman van Lelyveld, 2005, "Foreign Banks and Credit Stability in Central and Eastern Europe, A Panel Data Analysis," *Journal of Banking and Finance*, August.

de Haas and Naaborg, 2005, "Internal Capital Markets in Multinational Banks: Implications for European Transition Countries," mimeo, De Nederlandsche Bank, Amsterdam.

Haber, Stephen, and Aldo Musacchio, 2005, "Foreign Banks and the Mexican Economy, 1997–2004," unpublished, Stanford University.

Hasan, Iftekhar and Hunter W. C., 1996, "Efficiency of Japanese Mutinational Banks in the United States," *Research in Finance*, 14, pp. 157–173.

Hauswald, Robert and Robert Marquez, 2003, "Information Technology and Financial Services Competition," *The Review of Financial Studies*, 16(3), pp. 921–948.

Karceski, Jason, Steven Ongena, and David C. Smith, 2005, "The Impact of Bank Consolidation on Commercial Borrower Welfare," *Journal of Finance*, 60, pp. 2043–2082.

Key, Sydney, 2004, *The Doha Round and Financial Services Negotiations*, Washington, DC: American Enterprise Institute.

Kono, Masamichi, Patrick Low, Mukela Luanaga, Aaditya Mattoo, Maika Oshidawa and Ludger Schuknecht, 1997, *Opening Markets in Financial Services and the Role of the GATS*, Geneva: World Trade Organization.

Levine, Ross, 1996, "Foreign Banks, Financial Development, and Economic Growth," In *International Financial Markets*, ed. by Claude Barfield, Washington: American Enterprise Institute Press.

Levine, Ross and Sergio Schmukler, 2003, "Migration, Spillovers, and Trade Diversion: The Impact of Internationalization on Domestic Stock Market Liquidity," NBER Working Paper No. 9614.

Levy-Yeyati, Eduardo, and Alejandro Micco, 2003, "Concentration and Foreign Penetration in Latin American Banking Sectors: Impact on Competition and Risk," Research Department Working Paper No. 499, Inter-American Development Bank.

Marquez, Robert, 2002, "Competition, Adverse Selection, and Information Dispersion in the Banking Industry," *Review of Financial Studies*, 15(3), pp. 901–926.

Martinez-Peria, Maria Soledad and Ashoka Mody, 2004, "How Foreign Participation and Market Concentration Impact Bank Spreads: Evidence from Latin America," *Journal of Money, Credit, and Banking*, 36, pp. 511–537.

Mian, Atif, 2003, "Foreign, Private Domestic, and Government Banks: New Evidence from Emerging Markets," Unpublished manuscript, University of Chicago.

Mian, Atif, 2006, "Distance Constraints: The Limits of Foreign Lending in Poor Economies," *Journal of Finance*, forthcoming.

Micco, Alejandro, Ugo Panizza, and Mónica Yañez, 2004, "Bank Ownership and Performance: Are Public Banks Different?" Unpublished, Inter-American Development Bank.

Obstfeld, Maurice, 1998, "The Global Capital Market: Benefactor or Menace?" *Journal of Economic Perspectives*, 12(4), pp. 9–30.

Peek, Joe, Eric Rosengren and Faith Kasirye, 1999, "The Poor Performance of Foreign Bank Subsidiaries: Were the Problems Acquired or Created?" *Journal of Banking and Finance*, 23(2/4), pp. 579-604.

Petersen, Mitchell A., and Raghuram Rajan, 1995, "The Effect of Credit Market Competition on Lending Relationships," *Quarterly Journal of Economics*, 110, pp. 407–443.

Rajan, Raghuram, 1992, "Insiders and Outsiders: The Choice between Informed and Arm's-Length Debt," *Journal of Finance*, 47(4), pp. 1367–1400.

Sapienza, Paola, 2002, "The Effects of Banking Mergers on Loan Contracts," *Journal of Finance*, 57, pp. 1891–1921.

Sauve, Pierre, 2002, "Completing the GATS framework: Safeguards, Subsidies and Government Procurement," In Hoekman, Bernard, Aaditya Mattoo and Philip English, (eds.), *Development, Trade and the WTO: A Handbook*, Washington, DC: World Bank.

Sorsa, P, 1997, "The GATS Agreement on Financial Services: A Modest Start to Multilateral Liberalization," IMF Working Paper WP/97/55. Washington, DC: IMF.

Stein, Jeremy, 2002, "Information Production and Capital Allocation: Decentralized Versus Hierarchical Firms," *Journal of Finance*, 57, pp. 1891–1921.

Vives, Xavier, 2001, "Competition in the Changing World of Banking," *Oxford Review of Economic Policy*, 17, pp. 535–545.

Stijn Claessens is a senior adviser in the financial sector vice presidency of the World Bank. The author would like to thank John Boyd and conference participants for comments. The opinions expressed do not necessarily represent those of the World Bank. Contact: Stijn Claessens, Senior Adviser, Operations and Policy Department, Financial Sector Vice-Presidency, The World Bank, 1818 H Street, N.W., Washington, D.C. 20433, phone 1- 202-473-3484, secretary 1- 202-473-3722, fax 1-202-522-2031, Email sclaessens@worldbank.org.

Bank Concentration and Credit Volatility

Alejandro Micco*
Central Bank of Chile

Ugo Panizza
Inter-American Development Bank

1. Introduction

This paper studies the relationship between bank concentration and credit volatility. This topic is closely linked to cross-border banking activity because there is a widespread concern that the globalization of the banking industry may, by increasing concentration, reduce bank competition, efficiency, and access to credit.

This paper is related to the literature on the relationship between bank concentration and interest margins (see Berger and Hannan, 1998; Corvoiser and Gropp, 2001; and Demirguç-Kunt *et al.*, 2003, among others), the relationship between bank concentration and growth (Cetorelli and Gambera, 2002), and the relationship between bank concentration and financial fragility (see Allen and Gale, 2004, for a theoretical analysis and Beck *et al.*, 2004, for an empirical analysis). However, we focus on an additional possible effect of bank concentration and test whether bank concentration is correlated with the way in which external shocks affect domestic credit. This is important because it is well known that external factors are important determinants of economic activity (this is especially the case in developing countries, see Calvo *et al.*, 1993) and that there is a causal relationship going from credit availability to gross domestic product (GDP) growth. Hence, any mechanism that would amplify, through credit availability, the effect of an external shock would also play a role in amplifying the high degree of macroeconomic volatility that characterizes the majority of developing countries (Inter-American Development Bank, 1995).

There are several channels through which concentration may affect how bank credit reacts to external shocks and, interestingly, some of these channels predict opposite effects. On the one hand, there are at least three reasons why higher concentration may play a role in smoothing external shocks. First of all, a higher degree of concentration could be associated with larger and more diversified banks. This higher degree of diversification would allow banks to take more risk and, hence, continue lending during recessions. One caveat with this view is that it is not clear that concentration is associated with more diversification (Boyd and Runkle, 1993). Second, if a higher level of concentration is associated with higher profitability, banks with some monopoly power could be able to build a buffer that would allow them to take more risk (Boot and Greenbaum, 1993) and to reduce margins during economic downturns, especially if increasing lending during bad times allows them to extract more rents during periods of economic expansion (for a similar logic, see Petersen and Rajan, 1995). Finally, banks with a lager market share could internalize the positive counter-cyclical effects of expanding credit during recessions or have incentives to reduce financial contagion (for a discussion on the latter point see Allen and Gale, 2004).

On the other hand, it is possible that bank concentration may lead to higher intermediation margins which, in turn, could increase macroeconomic instability. Smith (1998) studies this channel by building a general equilibrium model in which banks with market power can increase efficiency by improving the asset transformation mechanism but where market powers is also associated with higher cost of funds for all classes of borrowers, independently from their level of collateral. By calibrating his model, Smith (1998) shows that there is a wide range of parameters that yield the conclusion that a less competitive banking system is associated with lower economic activity and higher macroeconomic volatility.

Finally, while Boyd and de Nicolò (2005) find that bank concentration increases fragility, Allen and Gale (2004) and Boyd *et al.* (2003) find that there is no clear theoretical relationship between bank concentration and financial stability. In particular, Boyd *et al.* (2003) build a general equilibrium model in which the relationship between the degree of bank competition and the probability of a banking crisis depends on the level of inflation. According to their model, monopolistic banking systems tend to be more crisis prone (with respect to a competitive banking system) in low inflation environments but this result reverses when inflation is above a certain threshold. Beck *et al.* (2004) empirically test the relationship between concentration and financial fragility and find that concentration is associated with a lower probability of observing a systemic banking crisis.

It is important to note that several of the theoretical models discussed above assume a one to one relationship between concentration and bank competition. Although this interpretation is consistent with the traditional "structure conduct performance" approach in which the causality goes from market structure to market performance (see Molyneux *et al.*, 1994, for a survey applied to the banking system), recent advances in industrial organization made it clear that this direction of causality is not warranted and that it is perfectly possible for performance to affect market structure. Claessens and Laeven (2003) recognize this possibility and test whether there is a causal effect from concentration to (lower) competition and find no evidence for such a causal effect. In fact, the theory of contestable markets (Baumol *et al.*, 1982) suggests that a high level of concentration is not inconsistent with the presence of a competitive market. According to this view, some banks may have large market shares simply because they are more efficient than their competitors (Berger, 1995), and a situation where more efficient banks have a larger market share is clearly a desirable outcome and not one that reduces social welfare.

As theory cannot help us in identifying a clear direction in the relationship between bank concentration and macroeconomic volatility, in this paper we will take an agnostic stand and use an empirical approach to evaluate whether such a relationship exists and in which direction the relationship goes. Our main finding is that in countries with higher bank concentration domestic credit reacts less to external shocks, suggesting that bank concentration is associated with lower credit volatility. In our empirical analysis we also make an effort to separate the effect of concentration from that of competition (as proxied by entry barriers) and find some evidence indicating that it is concentration and not lack of competition that reduces volatility. In fact, our results provide some evidence (albeit not very robust) suggesting that entry barriers increase credit sensitivity to external shocks.

2. Data

Throughout the paper, we will study how concentration affects credit by focusing on real credit growth (CRGR). We measure real credit growth using data from the International Financial Statistics' (2003) entry for "Credit to the Private Sector (lines 22d.f plus 22zw for Europe) deflated by the CPI (line 64). Focusing on the 1990–2002 period, we were able to identify 54 countries with data on credit growth for the whole period (13 observations per country) and other 39 countries with at least 9 years of data, yielding a total of 93 countries and 1,162 observations. In order to avoid possible problems due to extreme values, we then dropped the country-years in the top and bottom 2 percent of the distribution of our credit growth variable and obtained our final sample consisting of 1,116 observations.

The second key variable in the empirical analysis is our measure of real external shocks (*SHOCK*). The real external shock is defined as the weighted average of GDP growth in country i's export partners. Formally, we define the external shock as follows:

$$SHOCK_{i,t} = \frac{EXP_i}{GDP_i} \sum_j \phi_{ij,t-1} GDPGR_{j,t},$$

where $GDPGR_{j,t}$ measures real GDP growth in country j in period t, $\phi_{ij,t}$ is the fraction of export from country i going to country j, and EXP_i/GDP_i measures country i average exports expressed as a share of GDP. An advantage of our SHOCK measure is that it is highly correlated with GDP and credit growth (if we regress GDP growth over our SHOCK variable and control for country and year fixed effects, we find a coefficient of 1.5 and a t-statistics of 7.5) but it is exogenous with respect to these variables.

Our third key variable is bank concentration (*C3L*). Our main source of data is the Bankscope (BSC) database that includes information on bank balance sheets in 179 countries. In building an index of bank concentration, we faced three types of choices. The first had to do with the type of index to be used. The second had to do with the variable that should be used to measure concentration (assets or loans). The third had to do with the time dimension (purely cross-sectional or panel). With respect to the first choice, we decided to measure concentration using the C3 index (share of the three largest banks over total banking system). This choice was driven by the fact that C3 is the simplest measure of concentration and tends to work better in small countries with few banks. With respect to the second choice, we decided to compute concentration by using loans rather than assets (so, C3 is defined as share of loans of the three largest banks over total loans). We chose loans instead of assets because loans are closer to the concept of sales. It is worth nothing, however, that the two indexes of concentration yield identical results. With respect to the third choice, we followed

Beck *et al.* (2004) and, rather than computing indexes of concentration year by year, we computed average concentration for the 1995–2002 period. One possible problem with this strategy is that our sample starts in 1990 and, as concentration is measured after some of the events we consider, this may lead to reverse causality. We think that this is not a very important problem because our estimation strategy focuses on the interaction between concentration and external shocks and it is hard to think that credit growth could have a large effect on this interaction. In their study of the relationship between bank concentration and fragility, Beck *et al.* (2004) investigate the possibility of reverse causality going from fragility to concentration and find no evidence in support to this hypothesis.

Our fourth key variable is financial development (*FINDEV*). We measure financial development by averaging the ratio between domestic credit and GDP (all data are from the World Development Indicators). In our sample, financial development averages 55 percent and ranges from 3.5 percent (Sudan) to 195 percent (Japan).

3. Empirical Analysis

In this section, we run a set of fixed effects regressions aimed at estimating how concentration affects the relationship between external shocks and credit growth. Our basic specification takes the following form:

$$CRGR_{i,t} = \alpha_i + \tau_t + SHOCK_{i,t}(\beta + \gamma * C3L_i + \delta * FINDEV_i) + \lambda CR_{i,t-1} + u_{i,t},$$

where α_i is a country fixed effect and τ_i is a time fixed effect. The variable β is a coefficient that captures how credit growth reacts to external shocks. The variable γ is our parameter of interest and it measures how bank concentration mitigates (if the coefficient is negative) or amplify (if the coefficient is positive) the impact of external shocks on credit growth. The variable δ measures how the size of the financial system affects the impact of external shocks on credit growth. We expect δ to be negative because countries with a larger financial system should be able to cope with external shocks better than countries with small financial systems. Finally, we control for mean reversion by including the lagged log value of real credit.

Table 1 reports our basic results. Column 1 shows that, as expected, real credit growth is positively and significantly correlated with the external

Table 1. Concentration and real credit growth

	(1)	(2)	(3)	(4)	(5)
Log real credit t-1	−0.117	−0.199	−0.132	−0.021	−0.118
	(0.013)***	(0.006)***	(0.016)***	(0.017)	(0.013)***
Shock	16.551	15.184	16.712	16.254	13.301
	(3.739)***	(1.733)***	(4.867)***	(4.765)***	(4.364)***
Shock*C3-Loan	−13.713	−12.840	−14.451	−8.970	−12.121
	(4.674)***	(2.403)***	(6.264)**	(4.292)**	(4.768)**
Shock*FINDEV	−4.612	−5.367	−4.651	−7.629	
	(1.663)***	(0.668)***	(1.955)**	(3.919)*	
Shock*Pub.Own.					10.499
					(6.351)*
Shock*For.Own.					−0.535
					(3.243)
Observations	1116	1002	830	286	1116
R-squared	0.2688		0.2671	0.4717	0.2709
Test OIR		0.152			
Test AR 1		0.0005			
Test AR 2		0.470			
Period	1990s	1990s	1990s	1990s	1990s
Sample	All	All	Developing	Industrial	All
Estimation Method	OLS FE	GMM AB	OLS FE	OLS FE	OLS FE

Robust Standard errors in parentheses; *significant at 10%; **significant at 5%; ***significant at 1%.
OIR: Sargan test of overidentification restrictions.

shock and that the data exhibit mean reversion ($\lambda = -0.12$). We also find that the coefficient of the interaction between the external shock and financial development is negative and statistically significant, indicating that in countries with larger financial systems, credit growth tends to be less responsive to external shocks.

What is more interesting for our purposes is the negative, large, and statistically significant coefficient of the interaction between the external shock and bank concentration. This coefficient suggests that countries with more concentrated banking systems tend to respond less to external shocks with respect to countries with less concentrated banking systems. This finding seems to support the theoretical models that associate higher concentration with higher financial stability and is in line with the empirical findings of Beck *et al.* (2004) who suggest that the frequency of banking crisis tends to be negatively correlated with bank concentration. The coefficient also suggests that the impact of concentration is quantitatively important. Take for instance a country with an average level of financial development (0.54) and the lowest level of concentration (0.20). In this case, a one standard deviation change in the external shock (0.01) would affect credit growth by approximately one standard deviation (0.11). If we consider, instead, a country with the same level of financial development but the highest level of bank concentration (0.96), we find that a one standard deviation change in the external shock (0.01) has a minuscule effect (0.009, corresponding to less than one tenth of one standard deviation) on credit growth. If we repeat the same exercise but consider a change in the level of bank concentration from the 25th to the 75th percentile of the cross-country distribution, we find that a higher level of concentration reduces the effect of an external shock on credit growth by approximately 50 percent (from 8 percent to 4.6 percent).

One possible problem with the estimation of column 1 is that we used ordinary least squares (OLS) to estimate a fixed effect model that includes a lagged dependent variable. To address this issue in column 2, we re-estimate the baseline model using the generalized method of moments (GMM) estimator proposed by Arellano and Bond (1991). We find that the model performs well in terms of the various specification tests (OIR test and AR2 test) and that our results are basically unchanged.

In columns 3 and 4 we split the sample between industrial and developing countries. We find that the results are qualitatively similar to those of column 1, but we also find that the mitigating effect of concentration is much stronger in developing countries. The difference in coefficients, however, is not statistically significant. In order to compare column 1 of Table 1 with columns 3 and 4, we simulated the effect of a one standard deviation change in the external shock for the two groups of countries (industrial and developing) and for the whole sample under different levels of bank concentration. In performing the simulation, we used group-specific average values of financial development and measured the impact of the shock as share of the group-specific standard deviation in credit growth. Our main finding is that, when we adjust for the fact that in industrial countries credit is less volatile than in developing countries, the impact of bank concentration in developing countries is similar to the impact of bank concentration in industrial countries.

In column 5 we check whether controlling for bank ownership affects our results. This important because Levy Yeyati *et al.* (2003) argue that state owned banks may have the explicit objective of stabilizing credit (in Micco and Panizza, 2004, we provide some evidence in this direction). If this were the case and if there were a correlation between state ownership of banks and bank concentration, then our results could just proxy for the effect of ownership. Foreign ownership may also be important. In particular, Caballero (2002) argues that foreign owned bank may have played a destabilizing role during the negative shock that affected Chile in 1998 and Galindo *et al.* (2004) discuss that, depending on the type of shock, foreign owned banks may either stabilize or destabilize credit. When we augment our baseline regression with the interaction between the external shock and the share of total loans that are issued by state owned banks and the interaction between the external shock and the share of total loans that are issued by foreign owned banks we find that the ownership variables do not affect our basic result.

Column 5 shows that the coefficient on foreign participation is negative although not statistically significant. Galindo *et al.* (2004) suggest that this should be the expected sign if foreign banks have an advantage at canalizing foreign liquidity and our shock variable is a better proxy of domestic liquidity than of domestic investment opportunities. The coefficient on public ownership is positive and marginally significant (at the 10 percent confidence level) suggesting that the presence of state owned banks is correlated with higher credit volatility. This result seems at odds with our previous study (Micco and Panizza, 2004) where we showed that individual public banks tend to be less procyclical than their private counterparts. These contrasting results have to do with the fact that the exercise of this paper focuses on cross-country variation in public ownership and the exercise in Micco and Panizza (2004) focuses on bank-level data. Taken together these results suggest that countries with more public banks are more sensitive to external shocks (perhaps because public participation is associated with country characteristics that may increase aggregate credit volatility for example, lack of sound institutions) but individual public banks react less to external shocks than their private counterpart within each country.

4. Robustness Analysis

One possible problem with the specifications of Table 1 is that financial development is likely be endogenous with respect to credit volatility (countries with a more volatile credit market tend to develop a smaller financial sector). To address this issue, we substitute *FINDEV* with a dummy variable that takes value one for countries that have a common law legal system and zero otherwise (common law is clearly exogenous and strongly correlated with financial development La Porta *et al.*, 1998). We find that substituting financial development does not affect our basic results.[1] We also investigate whether using asset concentration makes a difference. We find that when we repeat our baseline regression but replace loan concentration with asset concentration we find that the results are unchanged.

To test whether our result is purely due to banking crises or whether concentration also affects credit volatility in normal times, we augment our baseline specifications with a dummy that takes value one during banking crises (we use data from Caprio and Klingebiel, 2003) and with the interaction between this dummy and our measure of bank concentration. We find two noteworthy results. As expected, the crisis dummy is negative and statistically significant; indicating that credit growth tends to be low during episodes of systemic banking crises. However, we also find that the interaction between the crisis dummy and bank concentration is positive and statistically significant, indicating that credit contractions due to banking crises tend to be smaller in countries with more concentrated banking systems. The effect is economically important. The point estimates indicate that a one standard deviation increase in bank concentration would reduce

---

[1] In order to save space, we do not report the results of our robustness analysis. All the results are available upon request.

the negative impact of a banking crisis by approximately 25 percent. This is another indication that bank concentration stabilizes credit. Furthermore, we still find that the interaction between the external shock and bank concentration is negative, large, and significant.

5. Can We Say Anything about the Channels?

After having shown that there is a robust negative correlation between concentration and sensitivity to external shocks, we now explore some of the possible channels discussed in the introduction. In particular, we check whether this relationship is due to the fact that higher concentration is due to the presence of larger (and possibly more diversified) banks or whether this relationship is due to regulations that restrict the competitiveness of the banking system and generate monopoly rents.

To test the first hypothesis, we augment our baseline specification with the interaction between the external shock and a variable measuring absolute bank size (*SIZE* is defined as the time-invariant average of the log of the sum of loans issued by the 3 largest banks). If the relationship between concentration and credit volatility were due to the fact that more concentrated banking system tend to have larger (and possibly more diversified) banks, we should find that *SHOCK*SIZE* has a negative coefficient and that controlling for this interaction reduces the explanatory power of *SHOCK*C3*. Columns 1 and 2 of Table 2 show that *SHOCK*SIZE* has the expected negative coefficient but that the coefficient is not statistically significant. Moreover, the regression results show that controlling for *SHOCK*SIZE* has no effect on the coefficient of *SHOCK*C3*. This seems to indicate that the smoothing effect of concentration is not due to bank size. This result is consistent with the previous finding that large banks do not seem to be more diversified than smaller banks (Boyd and Runkle, 1993).[2]

The last four columns of Table 2 look at the effect of regulations that restrict competition. Again, if the effect of concentration on credit growth were to go through lower competition, we should expect that controlling for these factors should reduce the coefficients and the explanatory power of *SHOCK*C3*. We start by augmenting our baseline specification with the

---

[2]In principle, economies of scale do not affect our *Shock*C3* coefficient unless these are increasing or decreasing. Increasing (decreasing) economies of scale would induce a positive (negative) coefficient.

Table 2. Real credit growth and regulation

	(1)	(2)	(3)	(4)	(5)	(6)
Log real cr. t-1	-0.118	-0.117	-0.135	-0.133	-0.147	-0.147
	(0.013)***	(0.013)***	(0.016)***	(0.016)***	(0.016)***	(0.016)***
Shock	20.993	21.532	14.605	15.015	12.087	8.312
	(6.062)***	(5.601)***	(4.394)***	(4.202)***	(5.610)**	(4.922)*
Shock*C3-Loan	-14.236	-13.477	-17.504	-16.901	-12.153	-11.282
	(4.708)***	(4.743)***	(5.559)***	(5.527)***	(4.445)***	(4.440)**
Shock*FINDEV	-2.655		-0.438		-3.608	
	(2.681)		(2.709)		(1.942)*	
Shock*SIZE	-0.596	-0.774				
	(0.641)	(0.448)*				
Shock*CL		-2.564		-4.518		-1.978
		(1.660)		(2.194)**		(1.513)
Shock*DENY			5.922	9.349		
			(3.588)*	(3.912)**		
Shock*REST					0.613	1.219
					(1.660)	(1.602)
Observations	1116	1116	712	712	873	873
R-squared	0.2695	0.2705	0.3229	0.3274	0.2937	0.2921
Period	1990–2003					
Sample	All Countries					

Robust Standard errors in parentheses; *significant at 10%; **significant at 5%; ***significant at 1%.

interaction between the external shock and a variable that measures barrier to entry in the banking system. In particular, we use a variable assembled by Barth *et al.* (2001) that measures the number of denied entry application as a share of total entry application received from both foreign and domestic institutions (*DENY*). While this variable is far from being problem-free and its use greatly reduces the size of our sample, it can give us some idea on the mechanism that drives the relationship between concentration and credit growth.[3] If entry restrictions have a positive impact on profit without greatly reducing efficiency, we should find a negative coefficient for the *SHOCK*DENY* interaction and also find that controlling for this variable reduces the explanatory power of *SHOCK*C3*. If, instead, entry restrictions only increase the inefficiency of the banking system, we should find that *SHOCK*DENY* increases credit volatility and that including this variable in the regression does not affect the coefficient and explanatory power of *SHOCK*C3*. Column 3 of Table 2 shows that this is the case. In particular, we find that the coefficient of *SHOCK*DENY* is positive (although not statistically significant) and that the coefficient of *SHOCK*C3* remains negative and highly significant. Column 4 shows that using Common Law instead of financial development does not affect the results described above.

As a last experiment, we use Barth *et al.*'s (1999) index of regulatory restrictions on bank activity (*REST*). The effects of these restrictions are ambiguous. On the one hand, they could make banks safer and (by restricting competition) more profitable and hence more able to perform countercyclical lending. On the other hand, they could limit diversification, reduce efficiency and explicitly limit lending activity (through margin requirements) during recessions. Column 5 shows that *SHOCK*REST* has a positive (although not statistically significant) coefficient and that including this variable in the regression does not affect our basic results. Again, the results are unchanged if we substitute *FINDEV* with Common Law (column 6).

---

[3]There are two types of problems with this variable. The first one has to do with the fact that the variable is only available for the late 1990s. Barth *et al.* (2005) show that this is not a very serious problem because banking regulations tend to be stable over time. The second, and more serious problem, has to do with the fact that a low number of denied application may not signal free entry but could signal that nobody bothers to apply because but it could signal that nobody bothers to apply because the probability of approval is extremely low.

6. Conclusions

Economic theory yields ambiguous predictions on the relationship between bank concentration and credit volatility. In this paper, we analyze the empirical relationship between bank concentration and credit volatility using an unbalanced panel of 93 countries during the period 1990–2002. To identify this relationship, we study credit reaction to external shocks in countries with different level of loan concentration. We find that there is a strong and negative relationship between loans concentration and credit sensitivity to external shocks and that this result is robust to different samples (industrial and developing countries), measures of concentration, econometric techniques, and that it is not driven by crisis episodes. We also find that the result does not vanish when we control for financial development, bank ownership, bank size and lack of competition (measured by entry barriers).

It is worth noting that although our paper is purely positive, we did implicitly assign a normative connotation to our findings and assumed that the shadow value of an extra dollar of lending is higher during recessions than during economic expansions and, hence, credit stabilization (or countercyclical lending) is socially optimal. This equivalent to believing that over-lending during periods of economic expansion plants the seeds for the successive crisis and that, during crises, there are valuable projects that are not executed or abandoned for lack of financing. Alternatively, one may believe that technology plays a key role in determining the business cycle and, as a consequence, investment projects will have low returns during economic crises and high returns during economic expansion. In this set-up, procyclical lending would be socially optimal and our finding that bank concentration reduces procyclicality should be seen as evidence in favor of policies aimed at reducing bank concentration.

References

Arellano, Manuel and Stephen Bond, 1991, "Some Tests of Specification for Panel Data," *Review of Economic Studies*, 58, pp. 277–297.

Allen, Franklin and Douglas Gale, 2004, "Competition and Financial Stability," *Journal of Money, Credit, and Banking*, 36, pp. 453–480.

Baumol, William, John Panzar, and Robert Willig, 1982, *Contestable Markets and the Theory of Industry Structure*, New York: Harcourt Brace Jovanovich.

Barth, James, Gerard Caprio Jr., and Ross Levine, 2001, "The Regulation and Supervision of Banks Around the World: A New Database," Mimeo, The World Bank.

Beck, Thorsten, Asli Demirgüç-Kunt, and Ross Levine, 2004, "Bank Concentration and Crises," NBER Working Paper no. 9921, National Bureau of Economic Research, Cambridge, MA.

Berger, Allen and Timothy Hannan, 1998, "The Efficiency Cost of Market Power in the Banking Industry: A Test of the "Quiet Life" and Related Hypotheses," *The Review of Economics and Statistics*, 80, pp. 454–465.

Boyd, John and Gianni de Nicolò, 2005, "Bank Risk Taking and Competition Revisited," *Journal of Finance*, 60.

Boyd, John, Gianni de Nicolò, and Bruce Smith, 2003, "Crisis in Competitive versus Monopolistic Banking Systems," IMF Working Papers 03/188, International Monetary Fund.

Boyd, John and David Runkle, 1993, "Size and Performance of Banking Firms: Testing the Predictions of Theory," *Journal of Monetary Economics*, 31, pp. 47–67.

Caballero, Ricardo, 2002, "Coping with Chile's External Vulnerability: A Financial Problem," Unpublished, Department of Economics, Massachusetts Institute of Technology, Cambridge, MA.

Calvo, Guillermo, Leonardo Leiderman, and Carmen Reinhart, 1993, "Capital Inflows and Real Exchange Rate Appreciation in Latin America: The Role of External Factors," *IMF Staff Papers*.

Caprio, Gerard and Daniela Klingebiel, 2003, "Episodes of Systemic and Borderline Financial Crises," World Bank, Mimeo.

Cetorelli, Nicola and Michele Gambera, 2001, "Banking Market Structure, Financial Dependence, and Growth: International Evidence from Industry Data," *Journal of Finance*, 56, pp. 617–648.

Claessens, Stijn and Luc Laeven, 2003, "What Drives Bank Competition? Some International Evidence," Working Paper no. 3113, World Bank, Washington, D.C.

Corvoisier, Sandrine and Reint Gropp, 2002, "Bank Concentration and Retail Interest Rates," *Journal of Banking and Finance*, 26, pp. 2155–2189.

Galindo, Arturo, Alejandro Micco, and Andrew Powell, 2004, "Loyal Lending or Fickle Financing: Foreign Banks in Latin America," Business School Working Papers 08/2004, Universidad Torcuato Di Tella.

Inter-American Development Bank, 1995, *Overcoming Volatility*, Baltimore: The Johns Hopkins University Press.

Inter-American Development Bank, 2004, *Unlocking Credit*, Baltimore: The Johns Hopkins University Press.

Levy Yeyati, Eduardo, Alejandro Micco, and Ugo Panizza, 2003, "The Role of State-Owned Bank," mimeo, IDB.

Micco, Alejandro and Ugo Panizza, 2004, "Bank Ownership and Lending Behaviour," mimeo, IDB.

Molyneux, Phil, D. M. Lloyd-Williams, and John Thornton, 1994, "Competitive Conditions in European Banking," *Journal of Banking and Finance*, 18, pp. 445–459.

Petersen, Mitchell and Raghuram Rajan, 1995, "The Effect of Credit Market Competition on Lending Relationships," *Quarterly Journal of Economics*, 110, pp. 407–443.

Smith, Todd, 1998, "Banking Competition and Macroeconomic Performance," *Journal of Money, Credit and Banking*, 30, pp. 793–815.

Alejandro Micco is a senior economist in the financial policy division of the Central Bank of Chile (amicco@bcentral.cl) and Ugo Panizza is on staff in the Research Department of the Inter-American Development Bank (ugop@iadb.org). The opinions expressed in this paper do not necessarily reflect those of the Central Bank of Chile or the Inter-American Development Bank. The authors would like to thank John Boyd and conference participants for useful comments and suggestions and Dany Jaimovich for excellent research assistance and for useful comments and suggestions. The usual caveats apply.

Cross-Border Banking — Regulatory Challenges: Comments

John H. Boyd*

University of Minnesota

1. Introduction

This session deals with recent trends and developments in international banking competition, and in particular the challenges these developments pose for banking regulatory authorities. Three papers were included and will be reviewed. The first, by Allen Berger, investigates the market share of foreign banks and shows that on average it is much higher in developing than in developed nations. The second study, by Stijn Claessens, presents a review of the recent literature on international bank competition and makes a number of policy recommendations. The third study, by Alejandro Micco and Ugo Panizza, empirically investigates the relationship between competition in banking and a measure of credit market stability.

Before turning to the individual studies, I will attempt to set the stage and put the large related literature in some perspective. It is well documented that cross-border banking competition has increased enormously over the last decade or so, and that almost all parts of the world have participated in this development (de Nicolò, Bartholomew, Zaman and Zephirin, 2004). More and more banks are crossing national borders and invading one another's turf. For purposes of this session, the important questions are, "What are the causes of this trend, and what are the primary economic consequences?"

Many of the reasons for the explosion of cross-border banking are well known from existing literature and further documented in our three studies. First, banks often follow their customers as the latter locate operations abroad. This is not a new trend, but it continues to be important simply because bank relationships with their customers are important. Second, international operations provide banks with opportunities for geographic and product-line diversification. Such diversification benefits are documented in Claessens (2005) and Berger (2005). Third, banks from the developed economies have invested huge sums in sophisticated information, risk management, and payments technologies. In many instances these technologies are superior to those available to generally smaller banks in developing nations.[1] This may provide a competitive advantage to new entrants with sophisticated banking technologies. Fourth, in some instances banking crises have created "financial vacuums" in which domestic banking systems are largely destroyed. When permitted, banks from foreign countries may enter and fill the void. A good example would be what happened in Mexico after the "Tequila Crisis;" essentially, the total domination of Mexican banking by banks from abroad.

It as almost universally believed (at least, among free-market economists) that foreign entry in banking is, on average, pro-competitive. Further, it is widely held that such competition generally results in better service levels, higher deposit rates and lower loan rates, *ceteris paribus*. Moreover, such improvements in financial efficiency are believed to contribute to long-run real growth and economic welfare in developing nations (King and Levine, 1993). Finally, foreign entry may result in improvements in the domestic banking technology and lead to the introduction of new products and services.

When it comes to the effect of foreign bank entry on the stability of the banking industry, however, there is much less consensus in the literature. Indeed, there is little consensus on the more fundamental question: "Is competition in banking good for the stability of the industry?" As will be discussed below, this is an important policy issue in light of the large number of banking crises in many nations over the last several decades.

I next turn to discussion of the three studies. I must be candid that there are many interesting and useful parts of these studies that, because of page constraints, I do not cover. Probably the most egregiously overlooked is the Claessens (2005) study which contains a long and interesting discussion of policy reforms in the context of General Agreement on Trade in Services (GATS) and the World Trade Organization (WTO). I apologize for not covering this material but it simply doesn't fit and (anyway) I am hardly an expert on the topic. In what follows I will concentrate on two main

---

[1]"Superior" in some but not all respects. I will return to this issue later.

issues. The first is the determinants of foreign bank entry, and why entry seems to have been so much more prevalent in the developing as opposed to developed world. The second is the relationship between foreign bank entry, competition, and the stability of the banking industry.

2. Why Is Foreign Banking Entry So Low (High) in Developed (Developing) Nations?

In recent years there has been an enormous surge in cross-border banking in most parts of the world. However, this development has not occurred equally across developed and developing countries. As Berger (2005) puts it, "Foreign banks control only about 10 percent of banking assets in most developed nations. … (However), the average foreign share is over 40 percent in both Latin America and the transition nations of Eastern Europe. … In some developing nations, foreign banks have virtually taken over the banking markets," (p. 1, parentheses added). Among developed markets, the EU is an interesting case in point because the banking authorities there have gone to great strides in recent years to open banking markets and encourage competition. Even so, Berger reports that the total foreign share of bank assets in the EU15/UK is currently only about 15 percent.[2]"

To explain these stylized facts, Berger employs a simple but useful two-part analytical framework. The determinants of foreign entry can be partitioned into: (1) the economic comparative advantages/disadvantages of foreign banks; and (2) Government barriers to foreign bank entry. In turn, government barriers to entry can be sub-partitioned into explicit and implicit barriers. I will not go into detail here on all the potential economic advantages and disadvantages of foreign banks, since this has been done more than adequately in Berger (2005) and Claessens (2005). However, one stylized fact seems to hold as a general rule, and by itself goes a long way toward explaining the facts. Many of the large international banks headquartered in the developed world have relatively efficient intermediation technologies that are (in many, but not all) respects superior to those of developing nations' banks. The obvious implication is that these banks can frequently enter the developing world and compete very effectively, *if they are allowed to do so.* However, such technological differences are generally not so significant when a large bank from one developed nation seeks to

---

[2]EU15 refers to the 15 nations that were EU members prior to 2004.

enter some other developed banking market. In essence, these large international banking organizations all employ relatively similar intermediation technologies. Moreover, I would argue, the differences between their technologies have been declining over time.[3]

There is a darker side to this generally rosy picture of large banks entering the developing world and bringing better intermediation technologies to capture market share. Berger (2005) and Claessens (2005) note that foreign banks are usually at a *relative disadvantage* when it comes to making loans based on "soft" information, to opaque borrowers, and to small and/or newer firms. Both make this point, but neither elaborates on the following fact. These are precisely the kinds of loans that are the most frequently needed for development; and, further, the poorer the host nation the greater the prevalence of such opaque loans. Indeed, there is ample evidence that even within developed economies large international banks are not particularly adept at this kind of lending. (Berger, 2005, and citations therein).

Besides the relative economic advantages/disadvantages of banks, a key determinant of foreign bank entry is government policy in the form of barriers to entry. Berger (2005) makes an interesting case that in recent years what has matter most in Europe has been *informal barriers*. He reviews the high-profile case of Banca Antonveneta, in which there was alleged wiretap evidence implicating an Italian central banker in aiding a takeover by another Italian bank. Because of the leak and storm of publicity that followed, ABN Amro, a Dutch bank, was able to acquire a 39 percent stake in Banca Antonveneta and hopes to acquire full control in 2006. In Berger's verbal presentation he noted that, in all likelihood, what was exceptional about this incident was that the parties happened to get caught. I agree with his assessment and further note that such implicit barriers may not require any government intervention at all. A recent article in *Porsche Panorama* (a magazine targeted at Porsche enthusiasts, not the financial community) discussed Porsche's recent acquisition of a 20 percent stake in badly troubled Volkswagen. Dr. Wiedeking of Porsche described this move as "aiming to insure a 'German solution' to the long-term future of both companies." (Porsche Panorama, 2005, p. 72). Similarly, the Banca Antonveneta incident could have been described as a (failed) "Italian solution" to the future of two Italian banks.

---

[3]On the convergence of large bank technologies see Group of Ten (2001).

Claessens (2005) mentions an interesting and important determinant of foreign bank entry that comes from a very different perspective than that of Berger (2005). As Claessens puts it, "Many of the determinants of cross-border banking identified in the literature are as expected — countries' creditworthiness, quality of institutional environment and growth opportunities. I highlight that these factors often correlate with the strength of the local financial system. In other words, good financial systems have more cross-border banking." (p. 2). This statement is undoubtedly correct and it underscores a vexing question in empirical analyses of cross-border banking and its effects. *What is the direction of causality?* As discussed earlier, there is ample evidence that foreign banking entry is associated with more competition, more efficient intermediation and a host of other *desiderata*. However, it could be the case that foreign banks are entering *because* of these features of the local market but are *not causing them*. Unfortunately, identifying causal relationships (which frequently are bi-directional) remains one of the most vexing tasks in empirical research in financial economics. My personal bottom line is that some of the alleged benefits of cross-border banking should be taken with a grain of salt, until the causality issue has been more carefully addressed.

One should be a bit careful in reading the Berger (2005) study. It strictly investigates market shares, not financial flows or stocks. This has the effect, of course, of heavily weighting foreign banks in developing nations since the denominator is relatively small. Put another way, if one looks at total bank assets, or loans, the picture is completely different and foreign bank activities in developed nations dwarf those in developing nations. This is an obvious point, but the reader can easily overlook it in reviewing the Berger study. For the interested reader, I recommend also looking at De Nicolò, Bartholomew, Zaman and Zephirin (2004), which uses somewhat different data and provides good counter-point to Berger (2005).

There is a substantial literature, some of it cited in Berger (2005), suggesting that government-owned banks are relatively inefficient when compared to private banks.[4] Other work suggests that, government ownership of banks substantially reduces the positive effects of the banking sector on economic development (La Porta, Lopez-de-Salinas and Shleifer, 2002). Berger (2005) makes the observation that government banks' relative inefficiency "... does not necessarily imply that they are not strong competitors that are

---

[4]In this context, government ownership may be by national or regional government entities.

able to "crowd out" other competitors. These institutions are often subsidized and have mandates to make loans at below market rates to targeted customers such as specific industries, sectors, or regions, new entrepreneurs, and so forth." (p. 10). Figure 1 in Berger (2005) suggests that a large presence of government banks may act as an implicit barrier to foreign entry. There, the simple correlation between state owned bank market share and foreign bank market share is −0.38, which is statistically significant at the 1 percent confidence level.

Large government banking sectors may be found in developed and developing economies alike. Examples of the former include the gigantic postal savings system in Japan (not exactly a bank, but still a savings-investment intermediary), and the Landesbanken in Germany which are specialized lenders sponsored by municipal governments. Examples of the latter include India, with a large government banking share, and China where four huge government banks hold about 73 percent of banking assets. Recently, there have been incentives in a number of countries to fully or partially privatize their government-owned banks. This was a major political issue in Japan during the 2005 election, and there is an active debate in Germany today on "what to do about the Landesbanken." Given the large and growing weight of evidence on the many problems associated with government-owned banks, this seems a welcome development.

3. Foreign Entry and Banking Stability

Banking stability is a public policy issue of the highest order, as witnessed by the wave of banking crises world-wide over the last several decades. Such banking crises have been not only frequent, but have also been extremely costly in terms of permanently lost real output (Boyd, Kwak, and Smith, 2006). It follows that any significant development in banking including, obviously, cross-border banking, must be evaluated at least partially in terms of its effect on stability. Claessens (2005) considers these issues in some detail and nicely summarizes the existing literature on the topic. Unfortunately, from my perspective the existing literature is inconsistent and does not (yet) leads to any firm conclusions on the bank entry–bank stability nexus. To clarify thoughts, I quote three statements from Claessens (2005) each of which is intended to summarize a set of research findings.

(1) Formal empirical contestability tests suggest that foreign bank ownership is the most consistent factor associated with improved competitiveness of local banking systems. (p. 7).

The statement is hardly controversial and reflects the broad consensus that, on average, foreign bank entry tends to stimulate competition in local banking markets.

(2) The fact that too much competition can undermine stability and lead to financial crises has been often argued. (p. 6).

This statement reflects what has been the consensus view among both scholars and policy-makers for a long time. It has been believed, at least since the Great Depression, that there exists a trade-off between competition and stability in banking. It follows that policy-makers have been willing to forego some of the efficiency gains associated with competition so as to promote stability. Recently, the conventional wisdom has been challenged. In reviewing the empirical literature, Boyd and De Nicolo (2005) conclude that when researchers have investigated the link between competition and stability in banking the findings have been rather mixed. Further, they argue that existing empirical work has depended either on weak measures of competition, weak measures of banking instability, or both.

Even more important are Boyd and de Nicolò's findings in the area of theory. Previous theoretical studies (for example, Allen and Gale, 2000) had found an unambiguous trade-off between competition (as represented by number of competitors in a market) and banks' level of risk exposure in equilibrium. However, Boyd and de Nicolò show that a simple and intuitively appealing modification of standard models totally reverses their predictions. That is, in the Boyd de Nicolò model, as the number of bank competitors increases, equilibrium risk exposure unambiguously decreases. And all that is required to produce this change is to allow (in a very standard way) for the existence of a loan market. In sum, from my perspective Claessens' literature survey represents a view of the world that has recently come under real challenge.

The final summarizing statement by Claessens (2005) is:

(3) "The effects of entry of foreign banks on stability are generally found to be positive. There appears to be less risk of financial crises and banks, foreign as well as domestic, display higher provisioning, less nonperforming loans, suggesting better quality lending. There is also evidence of less procyclical lending behavior … and lower sensitivity to the risk of financial contagion. (p. 8).

At face value, statements 1, 2, and 3 seem *perfectly inconsistent.* If foreign entry stimulates competition, and competition is bad for banking stability, how can it be that "... the effects of entry of foreign banks on stability are generally found to be positive."? I believe that there are two possible explanations for this inconsistency, and that they are not necessarily mutually exclusive. The first possible explanation is that the conventional wisdom is simply wrong and that, *ceteris paribus,* more bank competition leads to a more stable banking industry. Not surprisingly, this is my preferred explanation since it is supported by my on-going research with De Nicolo. Alternatively, it is possible that empirical researchers have badly misinterpreted a causal relationship that runs primarily *from stability* (perhaps due to good institutions?) *to foreign bank entry.* As mentioned earlier, pinning down causality is often a difficult econometric task, and this case is no exception. I believe that sorting out these alternative explanations will require more and better research than we have seen to date.

The study by Alejandro Micco and Ugo Panizza entitled "Bank Concentration and Credit Volatility" is directly related to the issue of competition and banking industry stability. Indeed, it presents empirical evidence seemingly consistent with the "conventional wisdom" that more competition is *ceteris paribus* associated with more instability in banking. This study finds that more concentrated banking makes credit flows less volatile in the sense of responding less to external macroeconomic shocks. It is a careful and generally well-done empirical investigation, but I have some reservations. Note that what the authors are really reporting is that, the less competitive a nation's banking market, the smaller are *quantity adjustments* to an exogenous macroeconomic shock. This is hardly a surprising result theoretically — in fact it is the expected result from standard models of imperfect competition such as the Cournot-Nash. However, standard theory also tells us that smaller equilibrium quantity adjustments are *not necessarily welfare improving* because price (interest rate) adjustments will be larger, *ceteris paribus.* Loan rates are not considered in this study and I believe it would be difficult to do so given the paucity of reliable bank loan rate data in most countries.

I would like to see a number of robustness checks that are not now in the paper and these are briefly discussed below.

(1) To represent banking concentration, this study relies entirely on 3-firm concentration ratios. With the data set the authors already have, they can easily calculate 5-firm concentration ratios and Hirschman-Herfindahl

indices — and they can do so for loans, deposits and total assets. Since none of these measures of competition is necessarily *a priori* preferred, this seems an obvious thing to do.

(2) The dependant variable in their work is aggregate credit flows through the financial sector, but it is *bank behavior* that is being investigated. An obvious robustness check would be to substitute total bank lending for total credit and see if they get similar results.

(3) The "shock" that these authors study is, essentially, a weighted average of GDP growth in a country's trading partners. This is a very special kind of export-demand-related shock and obviously one can think of many other kinds of shocks that affect any economy. The results reported in this paper are therefore very special and an obvious next step is to study the effects of different sorts of exogenous shocks.

(4) One can think of lots of different ways to test the relationship between bank concentration and credit volatility. Their model is highly parametric and concentration is only entered as an interaction variable. Why not run some tests that are less restrictive structure-wise, for example vector auto-regressions?

Overall, I will be much more confident in this paper's findings if they stand up to the robustness checks. But I don't mean to sound too negative. As mentioned earlier, this is good quality research, interesting, and deals with an important but difficult issue.

References

Allen, F. and D. Gale, 2000, *Comparing Financial Systems*, Cambridge, MA: MIT Press.

Boyd, John H. Sungkyu Kwak and Bruce D. Smith, 2006, "The Real Output losses Associated with Modern Banking Crises," *Journal of Money, Credit and Banking,* forthcoming.

de Nicolò, Gianni, Phillip Bartholomew, Jhanara Zaman and Mary Zephirin, 2004, "Bank Consolidation, Internationalization and Conglomeration: Trends and Implications for Financial Risk," *Financial Markets, Institutions & Instruments,* 13(4), pp. 173–217.

Boyd, John H. and Gianni De Nicolò, 2005, "The Theory of Bank Risk Taking and Competition Revisited", *Journal of Finance*, 60(3), June.

Group of Ten, 2001, "Report on Consolidation in the Financial Sector," *Bank for International Settlements,* January.

King and Levine, 1993, "Finance and Growth: Schumpeter Might be Right," *Quarterly Journal of Economics*, CVIII, pp. 717–738.

Porsche Panorama, 2005. November, Springfield, Virginia, USA.

La Porta, Rafael, Florencio Lopez-de-Salinas and Andrei Shleifer, 2002, "Government Ownership of Banks," *Journal of Economic Perspectives*, LVII (1), February.

John Boyd holds the Kappel Chair in Business and Government at the Carlson School of Management at the University of Minnesota.

Prudential Regulation Issues

Home and Host Supervisors' Relations from a Host Supervisor's Perspective

Piotr Bednarski*
National Bank of Poland

Grzegorz Bielicki
National Bank of Poland

1. Introduction

Since the mid-1990s, we have witnessed the growing presence of cross-border banking in Central and Eastern Europe (CEE) and other emerging markets. While cross-border banking has been visible in other major economies for many years, only recently did this trend become more pronounced. The focus of this paper is to present some aspects of home and host supervisors' relations in the context of the increasing presence of foreign systemically important banks in emerging markets. This paper will address many of the resulting challenges, mostly from the host-supervisor perspective.

The CEE countries predominantly act as a host country, where banking sectors are mostly foreign controlled. Over last ten years, Poland and other CEE countries successfully implemented politically difficult, but economically important, privatization programs for almost all major state-owned banks by their sale to foreign investors. This decision was one of the few options available in the 1990s where domestic, private investment capital was scarce and (after 50 years of communism) and necessary banking expertise and resources were insufficient.

Foreign control of local banking sectors resulted in closer interdependence of local, systemically important banks and their foreign parent companies, as well as between home and host supervisors. Emergence of foreign systemically important banks in CEE necessitates oversight, not only of the local bank but also, to some extent, for the safety and soundness of the parent bank. The parent banks may affect the situation of the local bank as well as the stability of the financial system in host country. In consequence, host supervisors started to emphasize the need to realign Basel and Brussels guidance and directives respectively to address growing information needs of host supervisors towards home or consolidating supervisors. In parallel, for last three years to four years, a new concept has been promoted at the international level, especially in Europe and somewhat stimulated by Basel II and lobbying of banks, to give more decision powers to the consolidating supervisor, especially in the approval of models. All this was under the effort of lowering burden for industry through introduction of the "one-stop shopping" concept, effectively limiting the role of host supervisor without limiting the host's responsibilities. There is a clear imbalance in this concept because more power is given to home supervisor but is not paralleled with more responsibility, including bearing all the related costs, such as crisis resolution. This is not to say that we do not recognize a need for closer supervisory cooperation and greater convergence of supervisory practices. All of this, however, needs to be put in a broader context of the existing safety net and legal architecture which would respect the sovereignty of particular countries' jurisdictions and the interests of home and host supervisors as well as financial groups.

2. Background

2.1. *Banking sectors in CEE under foreign control*

A test case for free movement of capital and openness of Polish and other CEE banking sectors to foreign direct investment (FDI) has gone extremely well. In Poland, the government privatized, amid political discussions, almost all major Polish banks resulting in a higher level foreign control. Similar steps were also taken in other countries in the CEE, Mexico, Brazil, New Zealand, and Hong Kong. As a result, foreign banks dominate the banking sector in Poland through their subsidiaries and, to a lesser extent, branches. In the case of major foreign-controlled banks, all are listed on the Warsaw Stock Exchange and have local minority shareholders.[1] Overall,

---

[1]It is worth mentioning that now more capital is available as rapidly expanding local pension funds seek good investment opportunities and listed banks are considered as such.

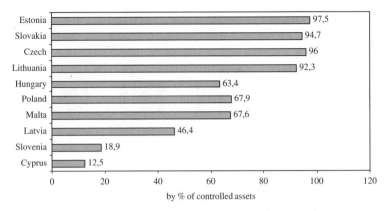

Figure 1. Predominant presence of foreign investors in the banking sector assets in the new member states of the EU
Sources: European Central Bank, at 31.12.03.

they control more than 67 percent of Polish banking assets (Figure 1). In Poland, the Czech Republic, Hungary, and other CEE, almost all systemic banks are foreign controlled.

Furthermore, foreign banks individually hold very substantial market shares in host countries, which are often much higher than the share of the home-country banking sector (Figure 2). In the Group of Ten (G10) countries, it is an almost unknown situation that a single foreign bank controls more than 20 percent of the banking sector, yet this is common in CEE.

Another important feature of CEE banking systems is the asymmetry in the relative size of a subsidiary within its banking group and in the host country. The share of a major foreign subsidiary in a host country like Poland (and other CEE countries) is almost always much bigger than its share within its own banking group, where the foreign subsidiary is almost immaterial from the group perspective. Figure 3 illustrates this disproportion.

This might result in a situation where the parent company is not considered a systemically important bank in the home country, yet the subsidiary or branch is considered systemically important in the host country. The attitudes toward supervision of these entities might be very different from the home-country supervisor's and the host-country supervisor's perspective.

Finally, it should be added that banking sectors of all EU New Member States are relatively small; for example, in comparison to ING Bank, their assets constitute around 63 percent of ING Bank's assets (at 31.12.2004). To illustrate relative small size of CEE banking sectors (assets) it is also worth

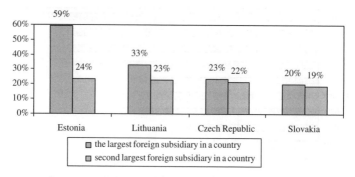

Figure 2. Share of foreign financial groups in the banking sectors in CEE countries via their subsidiaries
Sources: Central banks' reports and banks' financial reports available at their websites, at 31.12.04.

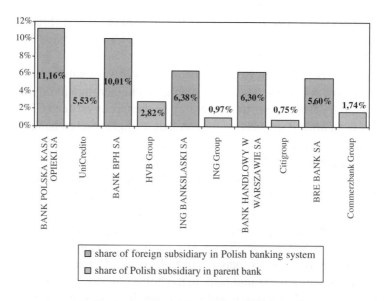

Figure 3. Share of foreign subsidiary in the Polish banking sector as opposed to share in a parent bank
Sources: NBP data and financial reports of the banks available at their websites, at 31.12.04.

Figure 4. Share of Polish banking sector in parent institution assets (in %)
Sources: NBP data and financial reports of the banks available at their websites, at 31.12.04.

comparing them to international banks. Figure 4 illustrates comparison of the size of the Polish banking sector to major foreign banks operating in Poland.

For example, the entire Polish banking sector represents only 49.6 percent of the Unicredito, an Italian parent bank of the second Polish largest bank — Pekao S.A.

2.2. Impact of systemic foreign banks' on the stability of local financial sector

The predominant role of foreign banks in the CEE banking sectors links local financial stability to the standing of foreign parent banks. This is a new and important dimension in terms of prudential supervision and central bank financial stability oversight. There is a dichotomy here: CEE banks being legally separate entities from their parent banks while, at the same time being economically linked to the parent and — indirectly — their home country economies. Furthermore, a spillover of systemic risk across borders has become more likely. A negative event in a parent bank or one of its subsidiaries might result in crystallization of local reputation risk. This in consequence might lead to lower rating by rating agencies (due to lower rating of parent and lower expectation of support by parent), higher cost of funding of local operations, etc. In an extreme case, cascading reputation risk might bring a run on local banks and liquidity problems. This is especially acute when, according to our survey, parent banks neither give a formal guarantee of liquidity assistance nor an offer of responsibility for deposits in times of crisis. That is, why host supervisors now feel a necessity to look not only at the local bank standing, but also at the safety and soundness of the foreign parent bank in designing their supervisory strategies. This is especially the case for local systemically important foreign subsidiaries.

A full picture of the risks posed by a bank in the host country requires the knowledge of the parent bank's global risks, financial situation, products and services, etc. This knowledge is partially included in published information but judgmental information from home supervisor is also crucial. In recent years, there were also cases where the problems of the parent bank, for example, stemming from credit exposures to ailing sectors of home economy, focused the parent bank on home country challenges and contributed to the decision to walk away from foreign subsidiary that needed support.[2] In case of local systemic banks, such move might impact the stability of the financial system in host country and its borrowers in real economy.

Another aspect of the parent bank-foreign subsidiary discussion, which is often overlooked, is the source of funding for local subsidiaries. In many CEE countries, most of the funding comes from local deposits. In Poland, the largest banks, mostly foreign, obtain 60 percent of their funding from local customers. Thus, it is not the shareholder's money that is predominantly at stake but depositors' money and local deposit insurance.

In short, foreign subsidiaries, being of the key importance for CEE and other emerging markets, might be immaterial for home supervisors. Thus, they would receive much less attention from the parent company and home supervisor due to their low impact on group's position. Less attention sometimes translates into less willingness to consider host supervisors information needs. Moreover, such asymmetric relations as between parent bank and its foreign subsidiary or between home and host supervisor might pose a problem in crisis situation. One of the answers to such challenges is supervision based on stand-alone principle, especially in case of systemic foreign banks. According to this principle, the banks should be able to operate independently from parent bank, having adequate core functions, capital, and liquidity to maximize possibility of survival in case of problems in the group. Such approach does not exclude cooperation, exchange of information and cross-border crisis management.

---

[2]See "Rogue trader, rogue bank," *The Economist*, September 12, 2002. See also Goodhart, C. A. E. (2004) with reference to the failure of the healthy subsidiary of BCCI in Hong Kong due to problems of parent bank.

3. The Principles of Foreign Banks' Operations in Host Jurisdiction: A Case for Systemic Banks

3.1. *Systemic foreign subsidiaries should be able to operate on a stand-alone basis*

Interests of foreign parent banks and their local subsidiaries in most cases would be similar. But we cannot exclude situation that they might be divergent and might occur. Customers, shareholders, and authorities of home and host country may have different interests and be subjected to different laws and politics, especially in crisis scenario. The stand-alone principle gives clarity to home-host relations and supports legal certainty in dealing with cross-border banking.

3.2. *Key components of stand-alone basis principle*

Necessary autonomy, respecting interest of legal entity and local stakeholders, and full responsibility of local management. In Poland and other regional countries, foreign subsidiaries are separate legal entities governed by local laws. In the case of European Union countries local laws should be harmonized with EU Directives.

Deposit-taking or credit institutions (in EU terms) are governed by a set of more stringent, specific laws compared to unregulated companies. Such laws and related corporate governance principles provide for an important degree of autonomy of the subsidiary management and keeps local management fully responsible for its actions. Thus, the influence of the parent company is only within the limits of law. The group-wide interest cannot prevail over the interest of the subsidiary; the group must not force any decision unfavorable to the subsidiary or any group of stakeholders, like minority shareholders or creditors. It is in line with Basel Committee and Organization for Economic Cooperation and Development (OECD) principles that recognize the interest of all stakeholders.

In practice, management of all areas should be in the hands of the local management board (not transmitted at the group level) which should not follow any instructions from parent bank that would result in a breach of local laws or discriminate interests of local stakeholders.

Effective local risk management. It is also crucial for effective risk management that responsibilities, necessary expertise, and adequate infrastructure stay at legal entity level. Such a position does not exclude group-wide risk management or strategy. Both can be carefully implemented at local level, following local laws and corporate governance rules.

Local capital and solid earnings. A foreign subsidiary should be well capitalized and manage its risks in prudent manner. However, parent bank financial strength and reputation might have impact on local subsidiary. In addition, parent bank ability to support its operations in host jurisdiction is an important factor. But it cannot be assumed that parent bank would always support its subsidiary. Currently, no foreign parent bank offers its Polish subsidiary an explicit guarantee in case of liquidity or solvency problems in that subsidiary. Such decision is usually a result of cost/benefit analysis where reputation or legal risk of walking away might be judged as lower to rescue package. Basel II, with its advanced methods of calculation of capital charge for credit of operational risks within centrally developed models, puts an extra stress for host supervisors. They need to ensure that any supervisory concession like lower regulatory capital, which is highly probable under the internal ratings based (A-IRB) or advanced measurement (AMA) approaches, is coupled with strong enough local risk management capacity. However, some elements might escape local control.

As global or regional groups tend to run its businesses on consolidated or portfolio basis, their strategic decisions on business in host countries may indirectly impact local ability to generate earning stream (for example, transfer pricing, business directions). What is good for the whole group does not always make good for local operations. Therefore, arm-length's relations between parent and subsidiary, business relations (including intra-group transactions) based on market terms are essential conditions. There is a room for supervisors' insight into the effectiveness and terms of these transactions.

3.3. Justification for stand-alone principle: Broader legal and economic framework

As we demonstrated above, neither the parent bank nor the home country authority offers explicit guarantee for foreign subsidiary liquidity or solvency. On the other hand, host countries are responsible for maintaining local financial stability. Their responsibilities, also financial, go hand in hand with right to regulate and supervise. We would like to concentrate on these responsibilities.

First, deposit guarantee schemes are locally funded and based on local laws. That is why a failure of a foreign bank would result in major costs of local safety including, potentially, fiscal costs.

Second, key stakeholders of major foreign banks in CEE are depositors as these banks are funded predominantly locally (for example, in Poland nearly 60 percent of banks' funding for the nine largest foreign controlled banks comes from local deposits).

Third, the host central bank — as emergency liquidity supplier — is expected to provide liquidity in case of liquidity pressure for Poland-incorporated banks. The parent bank is not legally liable for subsidiary liquidity and deposits, although a moral obligation may be evident. In other words, emergency liquidity supply is not centralized across countries.

Fourth, in case of failure of a foreign systemically important bank, the final costs — if the government decides to intervene — would have to be borne by the host country state budget as fiscal costs to maintain stability of banking system. Neither the Ministries of Finance and budgets nor deposit schemes are governed centrally in EU or other regions to cover costs of crisis.

Fifth, there is no clear evidence how well cross-border bank insolvency framework would operate. But in the view of current share of responsibilities, a crucial role is vested with the national supervisor, deposit insurance, central bank, and government.

3.4. *Challenges to stand-alone principle: Parent bank and subsidiary bank relations*

There are at least 3 major challenges in this area, which we have outlined in detail below.

Corporate organization. A growing tendency, much stimulated by Basel II, towards more closely-held corporate organization of international banks and an existing trend towards matrix management, pose some challenges to the existing legal set up and division of responsibilities. Under the title of either greater efficiencies (cost-cutting) or consolidated (group-wide) management, certain international banks seem to informally reduce the role of foreign subsidiary to a mere branch even if they are separate legal entities. However, it should be noted that such changes might result in the dilution of effective local management ability and morale to do their job properly. They might be also in non-compliance with the local laws and regulations, not to mention corporate governance rules that clearly state the responsibility of local company management.

For example, foreign bank subsidiaries in CEE belong to large international groups, which tend to operate according to business line divisions. The question is whether the double lines of reporting do not weaken the corporate structure of a bank. Ultimately, it is the local management board (not the head of business line abroad), which is fully responsible for the bank's soundness. It is a bank — as legal entity and not business line — which bears all the costs in case of any problem and potential insolvency. Such misalignment of legal and business status might become a real challenge in case of a failure of large international group.

Centralization of functions, intra- and extra-group outsourcing. The tendency to centralize functions on a group level might be a positive trend, assuming certain safeguards are in place. However, transfer of core functions (for example, risk control functions) from subsidiary to parent bank bears new risks. It deepens the misalignment described above. While the parent banks concentrate management tools and processes, legal responsibility stays with local management.

While it is acceptable to outsource some secondary functions, no core functions should be outsourced. The local management needs these functions as tools to fulfil its legal and corporate governance responsibilities. They are critical to ensure that banks are run in safe and sound manner. In addition, outsourcing itself, even to parent bank, bears its own risks.

Risk management is an example of a core function that should not transferred at the group level but stay close to the local markets. Local risk managers should not be reduced to clerical staff sending data to the parent and receiving "black box" outputs, which might be difficult to interpret or of unknown validity. The risk should be managed (in terms of decision-making, control) where it is generated and accounted for, at local level. This does not contradict group-wide management and support from the group for local risk management. However, the parent bank should not — via core functions' centralization — diminish the local ability to manage risk on a stand-alone basis. From host supervisor's perspective, group-wide risk management or audit is quite useful but they cannot eliminate or replace local risk control.

Relations within a group: Intra-group transactions. In the oversight of the stability of a local subsidiary, attention is being directed to the terms and size of intra-group transactions. The question becomes even more important with regard to recent discussions at the Joint Forum and in the EU on the question of liquidity management in the large international groups. The analysis is driven, among other things, by attempt to answer the question of how to allow more flexible migration of liquidity within the group, across entities and across borders, especially in crisis situation when it might be so much needed. This topic raises at least two fundamental questions:

1. How such intra-group loans would be treated under bankruptcy proceedings;
2. What would be the terms of lending to the parent banks or their subsidiaries if they need liquidity. This includes questions on the terms of transfer of eligible collateral from subsidiary to foreign parent company in order to get liquidity from foreign central bank.

In our view, the principle of arm's length lending should be applied in this context which means that the subsidiary should not be expected to lend to parent or other subsidiary bank in the group if this is too risky. Similarly, parent banks do not offer explicit guarantee of liquidity to subsidiary.

4. Current Legal Framework for Cooperation between Home and Host Supervisors

At a global level, the relations of home and host supervisors are governed by the Basel Committee's guidance, bilateral or multilateral Memoranda of Understanding, and tested in practical, daily collaboration. Within European Union, the principles of home and host supervisor relations provisioned for in the Directive 2000/12 relating to the taking up and the pursuit of business of credit institutions (Codified Banking Directive) and Capital Requirements Directive (CRD).

Following the EU Directives, a consolidating supervisor (a home supervisor) shall coordinate the exchange of information as well as the supervisory activities (also in time of crisis) with a view to avoid unnecessary communication and duplication of tasks for both supervisors and supervised institutions. This role has been substantially expanded and enhanced in the CRD.

Host supervisors, who are responsible for safety and soundness of banks within their jurisdiction, have measures in place to ensure that the financial situation of the supervised bank is safe and sound. In contrast, host country supervisors have very limited role of foreign branch monitoring, which is the more explicit responsibility of the parent bank's home supervisor.

Despite the relatively high level of harmonization of banking regulation in the EU, the duties and powers of bank supervisors are basically limited by the boundaries of their state and their respective obligations under national law. Home and host supervisors have their tasks and responsibilities imposed by their own local legislations, and banks operate as separate legal entities subject to their national supervisor, regulator and legislator.

In our opinion, both solo and consolidated supervision are important, as the first complements the latter. There should be no conflict of interest between them. The last ten years shows that cooperation between supervisors improved substantially and closely follows Basel standards. Interestingly enough, Basel Committee standards increasingly recognize the emergence of systemically important foreign subsidiaries and need for more balanced exchange of information between home and host supervisor. On the other hand, the growing complexity of large groups, functionally integrated and linked by intra-group transactions, causes group-wide monitoring to be increasingly important from a financial stability perspective, but at the same time more difficult to perform without adequate information sharing by all authorities involved.

4.1. *Basel II and cross-border cooperation*

Currently, the role of home supervisor is especially important in implementing Basel II by a banking group. All parties, including the industry, recognize that effective implementation of Basel II will require effective cooperation between home and host authorities. However, both the Basel Committee and the EU Commission recognize that Basel II results in no change of legal responsibilities for supervisors.

The home supervisor is responsible for the oversight of the implementation of Basel II on a consolidated basis, especially group-wide models. Host supervisors would deal with the models applicable to local banks, especially those locally developed. However, in the EU context, if the supervisors of a given banking group do not come to an agreement within six months, the final decision belongs to home supervisor. This is one of the major concessions in EU that host supervisors accepted.

Supervisory review process under pillar 2 is another area of interest where home–host cooperation will be quite important. Furthermore, there is a need for on-going assessment if the banking groups are applying the Basel II models properly and that the conditions for "advanced" approaches continue to be met. That is why the respective role of consolidating supervisor and host supervisor and their cooperation should be clearly settled.

As we see one of the major consequences of Basel II decided by G10 countries, which is also reflected in CRD at EU level, is that much more power is being shifted to home supervisors. Directly or indirectly, both Basel and Brussels expanded the role and powers of the home (or "consolidating") supervisor in the case of international banks operating in various host jurisdictions. Moving model validation process, for models also applicable in host jurisdiction, to the group level highlights the more prominent role of the consolidating supervisor. The host supervisor's role in validation process would be in practice narrowed to the assessment of the local calibration of the central model and its local use test, to ensure that it properly reflects the local circumstances and whether the risks are not understated due to being developed at the parent level. However, host supervisors should be given a clear and strong position in deciding about approval of a model applicable in their jurisdiction. The reason is that IRB or AMA models will most probably produce lower capital requirements than standard approach or Basel I approach used currently. The latter will be predominant option for smaller and medium size (local) banks. In such cases, domestic competition might be distorted.

The new role of the consolidating supervisor would facilitate effective supervision of large cross-border groups through more information sharing and coordination. However, doubts remain as to right of the consolidating supervisor to have final decision on the approval of group-wide advanced models, applicable in host country. The home country supervisor will gain powers, but still responsibility in case of any problems would be in the host supervisors' hands.[3]

5. EU Supervisors and Legislators Response to Industry

Financial institutions are keen to see greater cooperation, coordination, and convergence of supervisory practices both in the EU and globally. Some of the largest regional or global banks go even further promoting in the EU

---

[3]In addition, there is a question of access by host supervisor to working documents prepared by home supervisor on models and demonstrating reliable assessment of IRB or AMA models that will be applicable in that country and will result most likely in lower capital.

the idea of lead supervisor — a single point of contact and decision for all supervisory events.

The idea of lead supervisor is quite radical. Even from the European Central Bank (ECB) there are heard voices that "lead supervisor" as proposed by the financial industry would raise substantial doubts, regarding the credibility and effectiveness of the overall framework. First, present arrangements for crisis management, emergency liquidity assistance, insolvency and winding-up procedures, and deposit insurance are all based on the existing, clear allocation of supervisory responsibilities and potential costs. Therefore, introduction of a concept of a lead supervisor while retaining all other components of the supervisory system intact would result in unbalanced transfer of powers to lead supervisors without transfer of legal and financial responsibility. Second, remaining legal differences between Member States could impair the practical functioning of this approach as lead supervisor may not be adequately equipped to perform supervisory duties that extend to another country where the subsidiary is located, because he may lack the necessary legal power, knowledge and tools. Third, it may be difficult to gain sufficient political support for a transfer of supervisory responsibility to the lead supervisor, especially when the question of allocation of potential fiscal costs is unresolved. Fourth, the commitment of the lead supervisor to the host entities may not always be fully clear and certain, especially in those cases where there might be some divergent interests (for example, when a parent bank is not systemically relevant while its subsidiary is a systemically important bank in the host country). Another factor in this debate is what if the lead supervisor is not completely trusted by the other Member States; what if one of the major EU banks suddenly moves its "home country" to the Member Country that offers lowest regulatory or supervisory burden; would all Member States feel as comfortable as with the new home country and lead supervision as they did with its original home country.

Nevertheless, the European legislators accepted some of these ideas. As a result, a softer version of lead supervisor concept for the model validation in Basel II is proposed. According to CRD, the scope of the home or consolidating supervisor's powers would be broadened. Apart from formal reiteration of existing responsibilities of the consolidating supervisor (for example, supervisory overview and assessment of the group), the consolidating supervisor would plan and coordinate supervisory activities; it would coordinate the gathering and dissemination of information about the group, both on on-going basis and in emergency situations. Further, the consolidating supervisor will also be required to alert central banks and finance ministries. The most important change concerns the right to lead the consultation process of the college of supervisory authorities with regard to the validation of group-wide advanced models and to take the final decision if the competent authorities were unable to come to an agreement within six months. In addition, there has been reduction of national options. The EU supervisors have adopted via the Committee of European Bank Supervisors (CEBS) numerous initiatives to address concerns of the industry. These initiatives are directed towards greater harmonization of reporting requirements (COREP and FINREP projects), convergence of supervisory practices (standards), and intensified on-going cooperation.

6. Prospects for Home and Host Supervisors' Cooperation — Concerns and Hopes

6.1. *Dismantling some elements of existing supervisory architecture without addressing international framework for problem bank resolution*

Countries where systemically important banks are controlled by foreign banks might have serious doubts with regard to this new model of sharing powers. The latter changes supervision, which is just one element of the broader framework, without addressing all other elements like safety net and fiscal costs.

This concern is connected with already mentioned imbalances. One of them is that the share of foreign subsidiaries in an emerging economy is always much bigger than the share of the subsidiary in the banking group itself. Many systemically important banks in host countries are almost immaterial from the group and home supervisor perspective. The latter might not pay sufficient attention to immaterial operations in the host country, under a risk-based supervision paradigm.

Second, if we look at other elements like deposit insurance, international schemes for sharing fiscal costs of cross-border banking group failure or supranational liquidity supplier (Emergency Liquidity Assistance), such a coordinated and comprehensive system does not exist at the international level.

Third, there is no legal liability of the parent bank for its subsidiary — neither deposit insurance nor liquidity support. It is just a moral responsibility. This kind of support is not guaranteed and is purely on voluntary basis, motivated mostly by reputation risk. Therefore, the host country's supervisors, central bank, deposit insurance, and government have to deal with a foreign problem subsidiary bank on their own.

Fourth, host supervisor is still responsible under the laws for the supervision of entities (its standing and soundness) where it has authority. Any dispute regarding foreign subsidiaries and their depositors would be handled in a local court.

Fifth, international banks operate in various legal environments governed by different set of laws like bankruptcy law, various legal regulations for supervision. For example, cross-border insolvency of a major EU bank has never been tested and there are uncertainties how it would be handled (Brouwer *et al.*, 2003). Therefore, the more ambiguity and uncertainty regarding powers and responsibilities in relation of parent bank-subsidiary and home-host supervisors, the more legal uncertainty and less chance for smooth resolution in times of crisis if they affect international groups.

It is worth remembering the basic principle: "one who gets more powers and ability to act also takes more responsibility". This responsibility includes also potential costs of dealing with a problem bank. The transfer of powers from host to home authority should result in transfer of risks and costs. The aforementioned proposals say little about sharing responsibility tough they recognize the need for re-arrangement. The home country government may be reluctant to use its own taxpayers' money to bail out a bank/branch, which may be systemically important in a host country only. This problem is especially acute in case of systemic branches that might emerge in EU under new European Company Statute. On the other hand, host country governments may not want to provide budget help to a foreign institution. Besides, banking groups are usually big enough to make it difficult or even impossible for a single government to bear the costs of support. Furthermore, if the costs were to be split between a few governments, a question arises how the support can be shared and organized. There were some theoretical proposals to put ECB in the role of expert arbiter in charge of the appropriate division of burden sharing between relevant national authorities (Goodhart, 2004). We are not sure whether this kind of solution could prove feasible in practice.

6.2. *Future perspective*

Currently, we are facing at least two possibilities in addressing growing cross-border supervision area. The first one is to clearly reiterate that each country is an independent regulator and has right to decide about requirements for foreign subsidiaries (like approval of the models applicable in calculation of capital requirements). This should be however accompanied by strides, in an evolutionary way, at the convergence of practices and growing supervisory cooperation or even building common supervisory culture like regions like EU. In this way, industry concerns would be at least partially addressed making cross-border supervisory process comparable, easier, and cost-sensitive (Basel II could be a pilot test).

The second option is to develop further the idea of lead supervisor, where a host supervisor would be quite limited in its powers and be a sort of secondary supervisor. More radical version is the overhaul of the existing system of supervision towards a sort of pan-European supervisory framework but not covering safety net and other elements. This option lacks balance and completeness.

A more integrated supervisory system cannot be excluded in the future. But only after we address successfully and fairly questions of global budget in case of crisis, global deposit protection, home or global emergency liquidity assistance. Without prior resolution of these problems more centralized supervision is truly a premature concept. Any change in the supervision structure must be gradual, comprehensive, and considered in details.

However, until the solutions are found, the national supervisors should take efforts to converge their practices and cooperate.

In the cooperation of home and host supervisor, host country supervisors' needs, especially in countries dominated by foreign banks, should be understood and recognized. These needs concern, for example, possibility of receiving judgmental information on the risk and financial strength of the overall group. Such expectation follows from the consolidating supervisor being responsible for the supervision of the group safety and soundness. On the other hand, supervisory powers remain in full with the authorities that have licensed individual institutions. Consolidating supervisors will thus have to further rely on their host peers for effective intervention at subsidiary levels.

Undoubtedly, we do face financial market integration globally, and within EU and globally. So far, it has been mostly evidenced in the wholesale banking while retail banking is often locally owned, except for CEE.

This process will probably continue also in old EU Member States and other parts of the world. The proceeding integration of financial markets needs adjustment of the regulatory schemes to those changes and the supervision must follow positive developments in markets; however, it cannot be realized of ambiguous and misaligned supervisory set up internationally. It should not affect negatively the effectiveness of local supervision and local financial stability.

7. Final Remarks

Supervisors face changing banking structures globally and a strong pressure of the financial services industry to centralize the process of supervision, as the current system is perceived as costly and burdensome. However, this pressure should not result in destabilizing banking sectors, the basic principles of effective supervision and principles of corporate governance.

At this stage, a decentralized system is probably preferable to a centralized system of supervision, due to diversity of different markets and banking sectors, and current share of responsibilities. This does not exclude gradual convergence of common practices and greater coordination managed by the consolidating supervisor, and leveraging substantial progress in home and host supervisors' cooperation. Such cooperation should respect interests of home and host supervisors.

The debate about the future architecture of the European financial system and broader home–host relations is not completed yet. The realism, respecting legal and financial responsibilities, and basic principle of alignment of power and responsibilities, should be leading elements of this debate.

References

Brouwer, H., G. Hebbink, S. Wesseling, 2003, "Problems to be Addressed in Resolving European Banking Crises," in: Mayes, D.G., Liuksila, A., *Who Pays for Bank Insolvency*, Basingstoke: Palgrave.

Goodhart, C.A.E., 2004, "Some New Directions for Financial Stability?," Bank for International Settlements, Per Jacobsson Foundation, June.

Piotr Bednarski and Grzegorz Bielicki are deputy director and director, respectively, in the Banking System Off-Site Analysis Division of General Inspectorate of Banking Supervision, the National Bank of Poland. The views presented in this paper are not necessarily those of the National Bank of Poland. The authors acknowledge substantial assistance of Magdalena Szumielewicz of the National Bank of Poland, in preparation of this paper. We appreciate comments received from Bryn Stirewalt of Bearing Point and Linda van Goor of De Nederlandsche Bank and Conference participants.

Basel II Home Host Issues

Patricia Jackson[*]

Ernst & Young LLP

1. Introduction

Home host issues are not new. Indeed much of the early work of the Basel Committee on Banking Supervision was engaged in defining the division of responsibilities among national authorities to ensure that there were no gaps in the supervisory net caused by the foreign operations of banks. The Basel Concordat (BCBS, 1975) established that the home country supervisor of the parent bank was responsible for the prudential regulation of branches of foreign banks but the local or host supervisor was responsible for subsidiaries. In 1992 (BCBS, 1992) this was expanded, requiring home country supervisors to carry out consolidated supervision for the whole banking group. However, the new Basel II framework (BCBS, 2004), establishing a new more risk sensitive approach to setting minimum capital requirements for Group of Ten (G10) banks and beyond, has brought into stark relief the question of how home and host responsibilities will work in the new environment. This paper looks at why Basel II poses fresh challenges, the issues faced by the banks and some possible ways forward.

2. Home–Host Division of Responsibility

The original division of responsibility recognized that subsidiaries are legal entities in the jurisdiction in which they are established and have to meet local banking law and regulatory requirements. This approach was not affected by the 1988 Basel Accord which established an 8 percent minimum risk weighted assets ratio and a simple approach to weighting defined by type of asset. The basic structure of the capital requirements was additive and could be applied to a local subsidiary and to a consolidated entity with little conflict. Although, the focus in supervision started to shift away from primary reliance on capital and towards assessment of the quality of systems and controls, home and host supervisors started to cooperate in terms of exchange of information as well as, in some cases, joint supervisory visits.

3. Basel II

Basel II (under the internal ratings approach) has moved away from defining capital weights by type of asset towards allowing banks to assess the risk on individual assets — banks assess the components of expected loss — probability of default (PD), loss given default (LGD) and exposure at default (EAD). Fixed functions provided by the Committee convert this expected loss figure into a capital requirement to cover approximately a 99.5 percent/99.9 percent loss. With estimates from the banks driving the capital figures, the rating systems used to produce them have to meet supervisory standards and supervisory inspection.

For credit risk, the requirements are still broadly additive because they do not give separate allowance for diversification (diversification of portfolios was assumed in the calibration). Therefore at first sight standalone requirements for subsidiaries should be consistent with requirements applied at the consolidated level as in the case of Basel II.

However, various aspects of Basel II undermine this:

(1) The Operational Risk requirements under the advanced approach do allow for diversification.
(2) The new Accord will not present a single set of requirements — there are a number of areas where options are offered giving scope for national discretion. This in turn creates differences in treatment across supervisors.
(3) Some supervisors are even tailoring the actual requirements further.
(4) Key supervisory judgements are required with regard to the ratings systems used by the banks, while supervisors differ in the judgements they make, and even the implicit standards applied.
(5) There may be differences in the performance of some rating systems at a group wide level and a subsidiary level reflecting data or risk differences.

This creates scope for friction between the home and host regimes applied.

4. Home State is King?

Bank models are increasingly considering risks at a global level and this is reflected in the ratings systems built and data stored. This follows the way many of the portfolios are managed. Exposures may originate in one jurisdiction and be booked in another reflecting tax or other considerations.

At first sight the solution might therefore seem to be that home state supervisors, with their responsibility for consolidated supervision of the group as a whole, should be the ones to agree world-wide rating systems, options used under the Accord and so on.

But this highlights the clash between two different regimes with different philosophies. On the one hand the risk management systems of the banks and on the other the insolvency regime. Banks may perceive themselves as global entities but if they get into difficulty they are not wound up as a single entity — the subsidiaries are liquidated separately. In some jurisdictions such as the U.S. even branches of overseas banks are treated as separate entities.

This issue has been exacerbated by two different developments over the past ten to fifteen years. One is a shift in view away from the assumption that a solvent but weak bank could not afford to let a loss making subsidiary go to save the rest. The second is the development of approaches to managing the insolvency of banks in some jurisdictions, particularly the U.S., which can worsen the position in a subsidiary relative to the rest of the group. The U.S. bridge bank legislation enables the U.S. authorities to pick and choose among the assets in the U.S. to improve the payout for U.S. creditors. This could move a loss to the next big unsecured creditor which could be an overseas subsidiary having passed funds to the parent.

5. Information Sharing

With local supervisors responsible to their domestic legislatures for the safety and soundness of the banking system, responsibility for subsidiaries cannot simply be handed over to home states. A way has to be found of satisfying their interests without generating a large cost burden for the banks.

The causes of the costs could be as follows:

- Systems costs if data has to be stored in different ways for different supervisors — an example would be differences in the definition of default.
- The cost of stand-alone systems built solely to satisfy local regulators — for example, advanced measurement (AMA) for subsidiaries.
- Systems costs caused by different national discretions.
- Management time if many supervisors try to review the same models/ systems.
- Costs of producing differently designed reports for supervisors on Basel II.

The home–host issue was identified at an early stage by the Basel Committee and the Accord Implementation Group (AIG) was established to consider national discretions and different approaches to implementation. Information sharing between home and host supervisors was seen as the best way forward to avoid the need for duplicative effort on model recognition etc. It has, however, proved hard to reach any multi-national agreements regarding implementation.

In the EU, where there is a common legislative framework, more progress has been made. Generic reports to supervisors have been developed to provide an overall framework and reduce systems costs. Also agreement has been reached on a framework for considering models — final lack of agreement would leave the decision with the home state supervisor.

6. The Views of the Banks

A survey carried out by Ernst and Young LLP indicated that the banks and securities firms remain concerned about the home–host issue.

- There seems to be little commonality in approach across jurisdictions — not helped by the substantial scope for national discretion enabling many minor differences.
- Some countries have been bringing in their own unique modifications that could have far reaching systems implications — for example, the U.S. is considering a unilateral modification to the definition of default.

- There are concerns that some smaller jurisdictions may create heavy demands in terms of information because they are unable or unwilling to rely on information provided by home states.
- Perversely the AIG recommendations are making it harder for overseas banks to get clarity from host state supervisors because they are being told that the discussion must be with the home states.
- Generally the regulators do not seem to be working as closely together as necessary. For the U.S. securities firms operating in Europe this is exacerbated by the Securities and Exchange Commission being new to the consolidated supervision required under EU law.

Part of the difficulty undoubtedly stems from systems overload in both the firms and the regulators. For the banks and securities firms the coinciding of Basel II, the Sarbanes–Oxley Act, and International Accounting Standards has created huge pressures in terms of resource and management time. For some large international banks many hundreds of individual systems have to be adapted.

For the regulators, Basel II is a seismic shift in terms of their role in the credit risk area. Bank internal models had been allowed for market risk since 1996 (BCBS, 1996) but this could be dealt with in many supervisory agencies by small and specialist teams.

Basel II is much more fundamental and has required a complete rejigging of the supervisory approach, techniques, skills etc. Many supervisors are still developing their approaches and rules making it very difficult to provide clarity to the banks.

Basel II is a far harder task to implement than the earlier foray into recognizing internal models for the trading book. Many credit portfolios are bedeviled by lack of data and whereas with daily value at risk (VaR) thousands of observations can be accumulated over time, in credit one cycle is one observation. For many models banks only have a few years worth of data — certainly not a whole cycle. This reduces the reliability of statistical tests and increases the emphasis that needs be placed on judgment by both the banks and the supervisors. In essence the final judgment comes down to whether the figures are actually plausible. This creates substantial demands on regulatory skills and resources. It also creates substantial scope for differences in view across regulators.

The inherent cyclicality of some of the credit books, for example, residential mortgages, exacerbates the issue. Even more data and therefore years of operation of the systems will be needed before supervisors and banks can be sure that the judgements made were the right ones. It has also raised the issue of procyclicality of the capital requirements — point in time systems can indicate a need for capital in booms which is a fraction of the requirements needed for a recession. Some supervisors have encouraged banks to move to more through the cycle modeling and others have not — this too has created lack of consistency in treatments.

Another issue that has created supervisory pressure is the approximate nature of the fixed functions used to translate the expected loss — probability of default, loss given default (LGD), exposure at default — into capital needed to cover a 99.5 percent/99.9 percent event. The curves were built assuming zero volatility in LGD (for lack of good data) and therefore a downturn LGD needs to be used by the banks. But this has created demands for guidance from the banks. The curves also assumed fully diversified portfolios and used average G10 data, again requiring supervisory assessment of the plausibility of the outputs for particular portfolios and particular markets.

The fourth Quantitative Impact Study (QIS4) in the U.S. produced results which surprised the supervisors — both with regard to the variability in the capital requirements produced by the banks for identical exposures and the size of the falls in the minimum capital required against the current Accord for many banks. The U.S. has now announced a delay in implementation of Basel II and a longer period of floors — 2008 parallel run, 2009 a 95 percent floor against Basel I, 2010 a floor of 90 percent and 2011 a floor of 85 percent (FDIC, 2005). Europe will be moving ahead more quickly with implementation of some approaches in 2007, and banks are currently preparing the data sets needed. This is turn may create difficult home host issues vis model validation — if the U.S. regulators have not validated the models of U.S. banks operating in overseas markets when other countries implement the IRB.

Some supervisors outside the G10 are moving rapidly to the advanced approaches even where data on loss given default and probability of default in the market is limited, adding to pressures.

Overall Basel II presents a massive learning curve for the banks and supervisors and this is exacerbating the home–host pressures.

7. Solutions Proposed by Banks

The banks are beginning to develop approaches to reduce the home–host inefficiencies. Besides working with the individual supervisors bilaterally to find ways forward they are trying to find structural solutions. One is to apply IRB to the group but standardized in all but the largest overseas operations. This reduces the time needed to deal with competing issues on validation. Likewise some are using the AMA operational risk approach at the group level but standardized at the subsidiary level.

This seems to be a satisfactory way forward for supervisors in many jurisdictions but not all. In some jurisdictions banks are required to calculate standalone IRB models and/or standalone AMA for subsidiaries.

Some higher risk markets may be concerned that the standardized approach may understate the risk on some credit portfolios for their market relative to the IRB, apparently leaving the subsidiary undercapitalized. But this is probably not an argument for standalone AMA because the charges are likely to be lower under this approach than standardized.

Another issue is competition. Where banks have a large subsidiary, supervisors may be reluctant to see it operate under significantly different rules from the domestic banks — this seems to be a core issue in the U.S.

8. Ways Forward

There are several ways forward that could ease the position:

- A freeze in terms of new rules/developments of Basel II until it has been fully embedded in 2010/2011.
- Much greater willingness to rely at a subsidiary level on pillar 2 adjustments to required capital, than changes in pillar 1, to address any perceived capital shortfalls relative to risk.
- Willingness to accept standardized approaches for subsidiaries with suitable pillar II adjustments where needed.
- Reduction in the range of national discretions.
- Complete avoidance of national changes which create substantial systems costs.

The freeze in changes is very important to enable banks and supervisors to catch up with the extent of the existing change. But this alone would not reduce the costs caused by different pillar 1 rules in different countries. One solution would be for host jurisdictions to place greater reliance on pillar 2 for overseas owned subsidiaries, rather than requiring use of any different pillar 1 rules locally, compared with the home state.

It has been suggested that different approaches to pillar 2 by host state regulators could create an unlevel playing field. But so too can the imposition of different rules across jurisdictions generating much higher systems charges for cross border banks. Indeed, given that most large banks carry at a group level substantially more capital than the regulatory minimum, to achieve their desired credit rating, somewhat different pillar 2 charges across host jurisdictions would just affect the allocation of capital within the group rather than the overall amount of capital held. This would be the case unless a jurisdiction started to impose completely disproportionate pillar 2 charges on subsidiaries leading the total capital needed for the group to rise. In contrast, systems differences impose immediate and actual net costs. It might therefore be preferable for host states to avoid changing rules for overseas owned subsidiaries relative to the home state model and, if concerned that this could result in too little capital in their jurisdiction, simply use pillar 2.

One argument against doing this would be that relying on pillar 2 rather than pillar 1 to align capital charges more closely with risk could affect market discipline. This is probably the case at a group level because only the pillar 1 figure is published. The market cannot distinguish between a bank which is holding a substantial buffer above pillar1 because it is well capitalized and one that holds a large buffer because it is high risk and is required to hold more capital by supervisors. It is therefore preferable that the pillar1 charges reflect risk as closely as possible. But it is not clear that market discipline is as important at a subsidiary level and therefore this may be a less significant consideration for those entities.

Relying more on pillar 2 for fine tuning capital charges for foreign owned subsidies would focus the debate with the host supervisors for those firms at the level which is surely most important — how much overall capital should be held in a jurisdiction to back the risks in that jurisdiction. This would give banks more scope to adopt simpler approaches at a subsidiary level and could have a very real effect on the costs of cross-border banking. In the IRB, given the complexity of the systems needed to support it (with as many as 100 characteristics needed for some borrowers in some systems), these costs should not be underestimated.

References

Basel Committee on Banking Supervision, 1975, "Report to the Governors on the Supervision of Banks' Foreign Establishments (original concordat)," Bank of International Settlements.

Basel Committee on Banking Supervision, 1988, "International Convergence of Capital Measurement and Capital Standards," Bank of International Settlements.

Basel Committee on Banking Supervision, 1992, "Minimum Standards for the Supervision of International Active Banking Groups and their Cross Border Establishments," Bank for International Settlements.

Basel Committee on Banking Supervision, 1996, "Amendment to the Capital Accord to incorporate Market Risks," Bank for International Settlements.

Basel Committee on Banking Supervision, 2004, "International Convergence of Capital Measurement and Capital Standards. A Revised Framework," Bank for International Settlements.

Federal Deposit Insurance Corporation, 2005, "Joint Release Banking Agencies Announce Revised Plan for Implementation of Basel II framework" Board of Governors of the federal reserve system, Federal Deposit Insurance Corporation, Office of the Comptroller of the currency, Office of Thrift Supervision.

Patricia Jackson is a partner at Ernst & Young LLP but the opinions expressed in the paper are her own.

Basel II and Home versus Host Regulation

Giovanni Majnoni*
World Bank

Andrew Powell
*Inter American Development Bank and
Universidad Torcuato Di Tella, Buenos Aires*

1. Introduction

The principle that consolidated supervision is a responsibility of the home (or consolidator) supervisor has grown in large part as a practical response to bank failures such as Herstatt (1983) and Bank of Credit and Commerce International (1991) and the idea that the home supervisor will naturally consider the full set of risks of a global institution. Crisis episodes have helped spark intense diplomacy between bank regulators resulting in the 1974 creation of the Basel Committee on Banking Supervision (BCBS), the 1975 Basel Concordat, its 1983 revision, and its subsequent rebirth in 1992 as the Minimum Standards for the Supervision of International Banking Groups. More recently, the trend towards bank globalization is stretching the limits of international bank supervision and Basel II has refocused the attention on cross-border supervision. Curiously, pillar 2 (that specifically considers the role of supervisors) is silent on cross-border issues. More recently the short document on High Level Principals published by the BCBS attempted to restate the role of the lead supervisor.

What led the BCBS's attempt to clarify the role of home and host supervisor in conjunction with Basel II? Why has the proposed division of responsibilities been received with such a mixed set of reactions? This paper will try to answer both questions and address the causes of what Ben Bernanke suggested, "we may delicately call tensions",[1] with a view to

---

[1]Ben Bernanke (2004).

providing suggestions on how to strengthen home-host coordination. Our conclusion is that as banks have gone global, supervision should also be global but that the lead regulator model needs to be reconsidered. Host supervisors will naturally wish to protect local depositors and local deposit insurance funds. At times this will lead to conflicts of interest between home and host regulators. We suggest alternative coordinating mechanisms that would help to reduce conflicts, increase trust, and enhance regulatory efficiency.

The paper is structured as follows. Section 2 motivates what follows by considering recent trends in banks' cross-border claims. Section 3 suggests arguments why home and host supervisory incentives may diverge. Section 4 provides empirical support to the notion that international banks do not provide unlimited guarantees to their foreign subsidiaries.[2] Section 5 suggests that Basel II has provoked new dynamics into home-host supervisory relations. Section 6 makes policy suggestions to facilitate cooperative behavior in a Basel II world. Section 7 concludes.

2. On the Development of Cross-Border Banking

The Bank for International Settlements (BIS) consolidated banking statistics indicate that, as of September 2004, there were US$1.92 trillion dollars of foreign claims from BIS reporting banks to developing countries.[3] This is a significant number, around 26 percent of total domestic credit in the countries concerned but this figure rises to 69 percent for Latin America and 78

---

[2]In this paper, we do not dwell on the differences between subsidiaries and branches. The legal responsibility of international banks for depositors in branches overseas is perhaps most explicit for U.S. banks given mid-1990's legal changes after particular cases. U.S. banks may negate their responsibility for overseas branches in specified situations. More generally there is still little jurisprudence on this issue and perhaps for this reason some host countries take the approach of either not allowing branches or asking them to have capital as if they were subsidiaries. There is also little jurisprudence on the legal responsibility for depositors in overseas subsidiaries, and whether the "veil of ownership" is relevant. See Del Negro and Kay (2002) for a discussion.

[3]Figures as of December 2004. There are an additional US$1.4 trillion of claims on "Offshore Centers" including US$537 billion on the Cayman Isles, US$300 billion on Hong Kong, US$158 billion on Singapore, US$58 billion on Bermuda, and US$37 billion on Panama.

percent for developing Europe.[4] While total foreign claims on developing countries have grown over the last 20 years, reflecting bank *internationaliza- tion*, local claims in local currency have risen even more strongly reflecting the increase in brick and mortar entry into developing countries. This latter trend is normally referred to as bank *globalization*.

Before 1990, local claims in local currency were less than US$50 billion but now stand at a record of almost US$790 billion or 40 percent of total foreign claims (Figure 1).[5] Notwithstanding this remarkable increase, BIS reporting banks' foreign lending (local and cross-border) to emerging countries as a percentage of foreign lending to all countries has decreased over recent years to about 10 per percent. Hence, while foreign banks in developing countries are very important (especially in Latin America and developing Europe), those countries are less important for the large international BIS reporting banks. Moreover, this conclusion is only strengthened if the ratio of cross-border claims on developing countries to international banks' total assets (including domestic assets in home countries) is considered.[6]

3. Home–Host Tensions

To understand what might lead to home-host tensions in banking supervision, consider the case of a global bank with an investment in a local subsidiary in a host country. Initially the balance sheet of the international bank might be decomposed into the capital, assets, and liabilities of the local bank and those of the bank in the rest of the world where for simplicity we assume that there are no loans or liabilities outstanding between the

---

[4]Domestic credit is line 52 from the International Monetary Fund's international financial statistics report and here we use the BIS definition of developing countries and the BIS's regional breakdown for consistency with the BIS foreign claims data. This figure refers to 2004:Q3.

[5]Local claims are those loans extended by subsidiaries and branches in the country concerned but understate bank globalization as local claims in foreign currency are included in international claims in the BIS figures.

[6]U.S. banks' foreign exposure as a percentage of total assets is as low as 1 percent for the 68 BIS reporting banks and 7 percent for 5 money center banks in March 2005. See Federal Financial Institution Examination Council's E.16 Statistical Release (also known as the Country Exposure Lending Survey) at www.ffiec.gov/E16.htm.

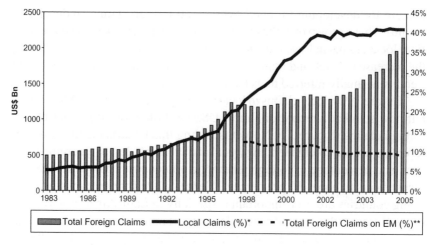

*Local claims as a percentage of total foreign claims on developing economies.**Total foreign claims on emerging economies as a percentage of worldwide foreign claims of BIS reporting banks.

Figure 1. Growth of international, local, and total foreign claims of BIS reporting banks on developing economies

two institutions and hence there are no consolidation issues. The value of the bank at period zero is then simply the same as the bank's capital, the difference between the valuation of assets and liabilities where we use the subscript "*L*" to refer to the capital, loans, and deposits of the local bank and items without subscript refer to the bank in the rest of the world.

$$V^0 = K^0 + K_L^0 = L + L_L - D - D_L. \tag{1}$$

Now suppose that loan recovery rates ($\tilde{a}$ and $\tilde{a}_L$) are uncertain while the interest rate paid on deposits is known (r and r_L). We suppose that this uncertainty is resolved between time period 0 and period 1. Hence the value of the international bank in period 2 is equal to:

$$V^1 = \tilde{a}L + \tilde{a}_L L_L - rD - r_L D_L, \tag{2}$$

which is equal to the new capital of the bank. In other words if loan returns are greater than the amount the bank must pay on its liabilities then those earnings are added to capital and if they are less then the bank's capital is depleted.

In period 1, the international bank may decide whether to maintain a presence in the host country or not. Assume that the bank can only recover the assets if it maintains its presence in the host country but that apart from the return on assets, the bank also values relationships that have been built due to its presence. We will refer to this as F_L for the pure value of the franchise. The bank will then maintain its subsidiary if the perceived return from doing so is greater than the cost of exiting the country, or if:

$$\tilde{a}_L L_L - r_L D_L + F_L > -X, \tag{3}$$

where $X \geq 0$. This indicates that the bank may decide not to exit the country also with negative capital when exit would imply additional losses in terms of reputation costs or legal liabilities.[7] We leave open the possibility that X is a function of the other variables such as D_L. Hence it follows that the bank would decide to exit if:

$$\tilde{a}_L < \frac{r_L D_L - F_L - X}{L_L}. \tag{4}$$

Let us say that the subsidiary is technically insolvent if $\tilde{a}_L L_L - r_L D_L < 0$. There is then a possibility that the international bank would bail out the subsidiary if:

$$\frac{r_L D_L - F_L - X}{L_L} < \tilde{a}_L < \frac{r_L D_L}{L_L}. \tag{5}$$

In general, the bailout would need to ensure that the capital of the subsidiary meets the local capital requirement. However, the implied bailout might threaten the capital position of the overall bank. In other words, the international bank without its problem subsidiary might meet its capital requirement whereas consolidated with the problem subsidiary it would not. In other words, it is possible that:

$$\tilde{a}L - rD \geq K_{REQ1}, \quad \tilde{a}L - rD + \tilde{a}_L L_L - r_L D_L < K_{REQ2}, \tag{6}$$

---

[7]This equation says that the bank will stay if its capital (period 1 value) plus franchise value (right hand side) is greater than any potential liabilities it may face if it leaves (left hand side). The assumption is then that the bank does not have the technology to recover assets, remove capital and then exit. The potential liabilities include reputation effects (although there is little evidence that the reputation of Credit Agricole, Intesa, and Scotia Bank suffered on their exit from Argentina) or legal liabilities from depositors, employees or other creditors.

where K_{REQ1} is the capital requirement without the subsidiary and K_{REQ2} is the capital requirement with the subsidiary.[8] In general any capital injection from the international bank to a subsidiary would weaken the solvency position of the international bank and hence might create tensions between supervisors.

In Figure 2, we present several areas to illustrate these tensions. The lower horizontal line illustrates out-turn asset recovery rates in the host where the international bank would just wish to exit. The upper horizontal line represents the case where the subsidiary is just solvent — although as mentioned this may still require a capital injection to bring the subsidiary to satisfy its local capital requirement. The diagonal lines show regions where the international bank's solvency position is weak such that the bailout of the local subsidiary may threaten the capital requirement (or solvency) of

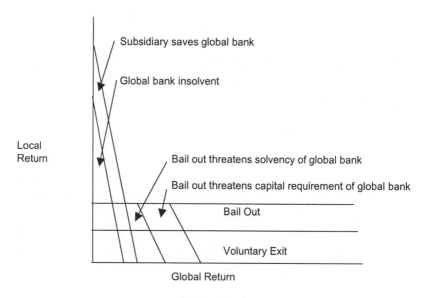

Figure 2. Home–host tensions

---

[8]We have not included the potential liability, X, in this calculation. X itself may be a source of tension. An international bank that decides to exit may argue that a subsidiary is a stand-alone enterprise and there should be no liability beyond the capital invested and the lead regulator may support this position to protect the solvency of the (rest of the) international bank. The host regulator would wish X to be large to prevent exit or protect local depositors if the bank did leave.

the international bank. Finally there is also a logical possibility where the subsidiary might assist and even rescue the global bank but which the local supervisor may resist as this would weaken the local bank. The greater is the economic volatility in the host country then the larger might be the area where the international bank would wish to exit but also possibly the larger the space where the subsidiary is technically insolvent but where the international bank would wish to inject capital.

These examples show that tensions may well arise between local and lead supervisors. While both certainly share priorities; to ensure the bank is efficient, has good management, and especially good risk management, there are clear cases where priorities would differ. Another way to consider these tensions relates to the guarantees that the international bank extends to a local subsidiary. If this guarantee is considered full and transparent, then the international bank would always bail out the subsidiary. However, this may be at the cost of reducing the solvency of the international bank. The higher the economic volatility in the host, the more valuable would be the guarantee to the host country and the more costly to the international bank and the more worrying for the home supervisor. On the other hand, if the guarantee is not full and not transparent, then the solvency of the local subsidiary is surely a valid concern to the local supervisor.

4. Empirical Evidence on the Provision of Cross-Border Guarantees

In this section, we use rating agencies assessments to test empirically whether international banks are perceived to give full guarantees to their local subsidiaries.[9,10] Consider a cross-section regression of the rating of the foreign bank subsidiary against the rating of the parent and the rating of the country in which the subsidiary operates.[11] If the guarantee of the

---

[9]While in the past, rating agencies have restricted international ratings of local companies to below those of the sovereign this is no longer the case for the 3 major agencies: Moody's publish a sovereign ceiling that is not necessarily the same as the rating of the sovereign while Standard and Poors, and Fitch both allow ratings higher than the sovereign. If there is an implicit or explicit sovereign ceiling for banks then the regression is really a truncated.

[10]The regression includes subsidiaries and branches. The data does not allow a test to see if there are differences between the two.

[11]The data for this regression are the ratings of banks in developing countries that are subsidiaries or branches of banks in G10 countries and the rating of their parents.

parent is complete, then one would expect the rating of the parent to be significant and the rating of the country to be insignificant in the regression. If the guarantee were non-existent then the rating of the country in which the subsidiary operates should be significant and that of the parent insignificant.

Subsid $= 7.19 + 0.0449$ Host $+ 0.277$ Parent[12]
(11.14) (2.48) (3.75)

T-statistics are in parentheses.
No. Observations 38, $R^2 = 0.3681$, Adjusted $R^2 = 0.3289$, $F(2, 35) = 10.07$, Prob $> F = 0.0004$

In fact, the regression above shows that both the parent rating and the country rating are significant. The results serve to illustrate that (1) the guarantee is partial; and (2) the environment in which the bank operates affects the risk of the subsidiary or branch. A standard explanation is that it is difficult to imagine a sovereign default without capital controls or other measures that affect the banking sector and hence parental guarantees can only be limited. Still a foreign parent might make good on the outstanding debt of a subsidiary subject to local capital controls.[13,14]

More generally, the decision of how much support to extend might be thought of as a trade-off between the *cost of funding* that the subsidiary might then attract and a *hold-up* problem with respect to the local authorities. If a transparent and full guarantee was extended then the funding costs of the international bank subsidiary should be reduced to that of the parent. However, given such a guarantee, the local authorities might be tempted to take actions that would lower the value of the local bank and increase the probability that the parent would have to make good on that guarantee.

---

[12]Subsid. is the rating of the subsidiary or branch, Host is the rating of the host country and Parent is the rating of the parent bank. While the numerical scale used is the same for both, the average ratings differ so the size of the coefficient may not represent the relative impact of a similar change in the two independent variables.

[13]In the case of Argentina most subsidiaries of foreign banks restructured international bonds although some including HSBC did not and the parent honored the international claims of the local subsidiary. There have also been cases of foreign banks paying local depositors in their home countries; see Del Negro and Kay (2002) for a discussion.

[14]Curiously however rating agencies may dictate that a local bank defaulted on its obligations even if the parent pays in full and this possibility would be reflected in the rating of the subsidiary ex ante. We are thankful for Lorna Martin of Fitch for this observation.

While this might have been thought of as a somewhat academic possibility, this is surely no longer the case after the Argentine crisis.[15]

Considering the arguments in this and the previous section, we then suggest that where economic volatility is low and trust is high guarantees will be close to full and in that case the role of the host supervisor may be delegated more fully to that of the home supervisor. However, where economic volatility is high and trust between the authorities is low then banks are unlikely to give full guarantees and local supervisors will wish to exercise their legal powers to regulate and supervise local banks.

5. On Basel II and Cross-Border Implications

No country is legally obliged to implement Basel II, however more than 100 countries claim to have implemented Basel I and official reports suggest a similar number will implement the new accord.[16,17] Basel II emphasizes that banks, should adopt a consistent approach globally. For large international banks this may imply pressure to implement a consistent internal ratings based (IRB) methodology across all the countries where they operate.[18] While this approach will remove opportunities for regulatory arbitrage within an institution it will come at the cost of potentially higher capital requirements for lending in those countries with lower sovereign ratings. Basel Committee on Banking Supervision (2003) argues that a small- or medium-sized enterprise (SME) with no external rating might attract an internal bank rating 2 or 3 notches below that of the sovereign. This implies that an SME in Brazil, where the sovereign local currency rating is BB

---

[15] In Argentina in early 2002 devaluation and forced and asymmetric pesification lowered bank capital significantly. Through 2002 the central bank implemented an asymmetric assistance policy such that foreign bank subsidiaries and branches were assisted if the parent extended matching funds. Most foreign banks went along with this with Credit Agricole, ScotiaBank, and Intesa being the relatively small exceptions. The government subsequently extended compensation to the banks in the form of government bonds.

[16] See Financial Stability Institute (2004).

[17] See Basel Committee for Banking Supervision (1988) and (2004) for the old and the new Accord. These, together with literally hundreds of comments are available on www.bis.org.

[18] While Basel II includes different approaches, large U.S. banks will have to adopt the Advanced IDB option and the largest European banks are likely to adopt IRB as this will imply a lower capital requirement or due to supervisory pressure.

might be expected to have a rating of B+ or B indicating a default probability of 2.91 percent to 8.31 percent and a capital requirement of 8.3 percent to 13.4 percent.[19] If the same logic is applied to SMEs in Uruguay (local currency rating B), Bolivia (local currency rating B−), and Ecuador (CCC) then the current Basel IRB formula would give capital requirements well in excess of 20 percent.

At the same time, local regulators in emerging economies face tough choices if they wish to implement Basel II. While the standardized approach (SA) may afford little in linking capital to risk, due to a lack of penetration of rating agencies, the IRB approach looks complex and is most likely incorrectly calibrated. In previous work we have therefore suggested an intermediate centralized rating based (CRB) approach.[20] If local authorities adopt SA, international banks that must also use IRB globally will be at a competitive disadvantage in that IRB will yield much higher requirements than SA for the default probabilities found in emerging countries. International banks may then lend more to higher rated local banks and selected corporates and less to SME and retail.[21] If this is the case then bank globalization may revert back to cross-border lending as a local presence may be less of a necessity.

We view this market segmentation as a likely consequence of the proposals as they stand but this does depend on how the cross-border issue is finally resolved. We suggest that there is a choice between rules that focus on consistency within an institution, and hence market segmentation within countries, versus rules that attempt to maintain consistency within a country but that may come at the cost of arbitrage possibilities within institutions. In fact we doubt that these arbitrage possibilities are so great. If say a consistent IRB rule is applied for international banks for sovereign lending and higher rated corporates and local rules are applied for SME and retail, the only potential arbitrage would be for international banks to book SME and retail loans onshore and not offshore, which does not appear a tremendous cause for concern. And these are the requirements where there is most concern regarding market segmentation and a potential negative impact on developing countries' cost of funds.

---

[19]This assumes S&P 12 month default probabilities, sales of 25 million euros and applying the correlation correction for SME's.

[20]See Majnoni and Powell (2005).

[21]The situation may resemble an extreme version of that suggested in Repullo and Suarez (2004) where the more sophisticated foreign IRB banks lend to higher rated clients and the less sophisticated local SA banks lend to SME's and retail clients.

We also noted that the IRB curve is most likely calibrated incorrectly for most developing countries. In particular, we are told that the IRB curve was calculated using Group of Ten (G10) credit portfolios and a value at risk concept with a 99.9 percent tolerance value. Two questions emerge. First, is 99.9 percent the right number, and second, is G10 calibration appropriate for emerging countries? Majnoni and Powell (2005) using corporate loan performance data from public credit registries in Argentina, Brazil, and Mexico find that (1) Basel IRB will result in significantly higher capital requirements than Basel I, *but* that (2) the formula will not yield the 99.9 percent level of protection as advertised. One explanation is that correlations between default risks are typically higher in an emerging economy than in a developed economy. Thus an estimated expected loss in an emerging economy may lead to a higher unexpected loss for a particular tolerance value than that for a G10 nation. For example, Majnoni and Powell (2005) find that in pre crisis Argentina the average default probability for all corporate loans in the public credit registry was 9.6 percent and unexpected losses to be some 21.5 percent whereas the Basel IRB formula yields 17.76 percent.

We therefore suggest the simultaneous adjustment of two parameters of the IRB curve: the correlation (which is too low) and the risk tolerance (which is too high).[22] This modified curve would achieve the double objective of improved calibration for a typical emerging economy and a capital requirement closer to SA. This point is illustrated in Figure 3, where we plot the Basel IRB curve (labeled Tolerance 99.9 percent) and an adjusted curve that roughly fits the experience of pre crisis Argentina with higher assumed covariances. It can be seen that this second curve (labeled 99.9 percent Hi Correlation) suggests that capital requirements to obtain 99.9 percent protection are significantly higher than the original Basel II curve and would yield much higher capital charges than Basel I's 8 percent or Argentina's basic 11.5 percent capital charge at that time, for the average default probability quoted above (9.6 percent). Now suppose that Argentina applied a 97.09 percent standard but with this correlation structure (this is a B+ standard and in line with Argentina's current top bank ratings). This gives the curve labeled 97.09 percent Hi Correlation and is a little flatter than the current Basel IRB curve.[23]

---

[22] In the appendix the technical details of adjusting the statistical tolerance and the covariance assumptions in the Basel IRB curve is discussed.

[23] Basel Committee on Banking Supervision (2003) suggested an adaptation of the tolerance value to match the sovereign credit rating. We find their rule yields capital requirements that would be too low for many national supervisors.

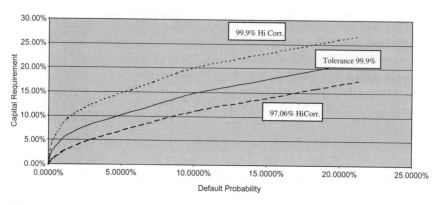

Figure 3. The effect of altering the correlation and statistical tolerance in the IRB curve

6. Suggested Solutions for Selected Cross-Border Supervisory Issues

The decision of a host regulator to cede regulatory and supervisory duties to a lead regulator would be a very significant delegation of responsibilities. Moreover, we have argued above that home and host supervisory incentives may differ and that it is unlikely that international banks will offer transparent and comprehensive guarantees to subsidiaries or even branches. Under such circumstances it appears unlikely that a host country would wish to cede its role as he would wish to adopt rules that (1) ensure adequate protection to local depositors and the deposit insurance agency; and (2) that the local regulator can understand, monitor and enforce. Hence it appears likely that if lead regulators insist on the consistent global implementation of the more advanced approaches, international banks are likely to face multiple regulatory regimes.

At the same time, an objective of Basel II is to use the cross-border supervisory issues as a springboard for supervisory cooperation and where possible for knowledge transfer in order to enhance bank supervision across the globe. Moreover, this is likely to lead to faster regulatory homogeneity and greater trust between home and host regulators. We do not believe that continuing to stress the lead regulator model will achieve these goals. Our first proposal is that *host* supervisors should form a college of supervisors including representatives of supervisors from relevant lead regulators depending on which foreign banks are operating in the country concerned:

Proposal 1: A college of supervisors organized by the host regulator

The college would discuss the appropriate regulatory scheme (Basel I, Basel II SA,[24] CRB, IRB, plus the appropriate choice for credit mitigation techniques, securitization risk, operational risk, related lending, lending to own sovereign, lending in foreign currency and other issues left to national discretion) to be applied in the host country. If an IRB approach is to be used the college would also discuss the appropriate calibration of the IRB curve. In the interests of regulatory efficiency the decisions of the college of supervisors would be adopted by the home regulators for the subsidiaries or branches of foreign banks operating in that jurisdiction.

Cross-border questions are not limited to pillar 1 (Quantitative Capital Requirements) but are also present in pillar 2 (Supervisory Review), and pillar 3 (Market Discipline). Regarding pillar 2, we suggest that there should be explicit measures to enhance cross-border information sharing, cooperation, and technology transfer. Hence we propose joint inspections of foreign subsidiaries and branches:

Proposal 2: Joint inspections

Whenever an on-site inspection is made of an international bank in an emerging country, then the host supervisor should have the option to send its own staff to accompany that inspection. And when the host supervisor inspects the local entity an invitation should be extended to the home supervisor.

For the first time the Accord explicitly asks banks to publish their capital requirements. Under IRB, the contribution of the risk of different portfolios and different risks must be revealed. As written, pillar 3 must be applied at the level of the consolidated entity and at the level of each significant subsidiary. While pillar 3 focuses on transparency, most foreign bank entry into developing countries has been through the purchase of domestic institutions leading to the potential loss of valuable market information. Typically the

---

[24]With regards to the standardized approach (SA), we note that a further topic for the college is that local regulators are likely to wish to employ ratings for domestic corporations according to a local scale while lead regulators may wish to push the use of international ratings.

domestic institution would have been quoted on the local stock market and would have had fixed liabilities outstanding. Foreign purchase in several cases has led to stock market delisting and, depending on the bank and its funding strategy, local debt instruments may also be retired. In effect, market prices of equity and debt are then replaced by non-transparent guarantees. We therefore suggest that an international bank that is important for a country should adopt pillar 3 fully for the local entity whether it is significant to the global institution or not. However, these arguments also suggest that pillar 3 may not go far enough. A foreign bank subsidiary or branch might also be asked to issue local subordinated debt to be held by outside institutional investors. The returns on these debt instruments would then give some market expectation regarding the value of the guarantee from the parent.[25]

Proposal 3: Disclosure requirements

All pillar 3 requirements to reveal capital requirement and its components in terms of the various risks and portfolios should be applied to the local subsidiary or branch at the discretion of the host supervisor. Moreover consideration should be given to the idea of the branch or subsidiary issuing local subordinated debt to make more transparent the market expectation regarding the nature of the parental guarantee.

7. Conclusions

Over the last 30 years, jointly with the extraordinary growth of cross-border banking, the regulatory diplomacy of the BCBS helped to develop a consensus regarding home-host bank supervisory responsibilities across its members. Trends in global banking have made foreign banks very important for developing countries but these economies account for a relatively small

---

[25]We do not comment here on the proposal by Guillermo Ortiz that local subsidiaries of foreign banks should have significant (30 percent) local ownership. We understand that this proposal stems more from concerns regarding corporate governance and the stability of the local economy than a prudential concern *per se* which is the focus of this paper — on these stability issues see Galindo, Micco and Powell (2004).

amount of total cross-border lending and a very low proportion of the total assets of internationally active banks.

We describe above situations where incentives between home and host supervisors may differ and suggest that in general international banks may not wish to extend full and transparent guarantees to their subsidiaries. This result is supported by an empirical analysis and suggests the inherently different nature of supervisory coordination problems among countries where economic volatility is low and the risk of hold up is very small (industrial countries, EU) and countries where those risks are significant. In the first case the provision of (almost) unlimited guarantees may eliminate the need of joint monitoring by home and host supervisors, while in the second case, the ambiguous nature of implicit guarantees strengthens the incentives for host supervisors to resist ceding their responsibilities to home supervisors.

Basel II's multiple regulatory alternatives has brought this discussion to the fore. The consistent application of the IRB approach by large international banks will likely collide with national standards promoted by host supervisors unlikely to cede national responsibilities. The current debate focusing on the lead regulatory model then favors the coexistence of multiple standards with a severe regulatory burden for banks and at the cost of market segmentation between local and international banks; the latter subject also to their lead regulator's requirements.

The recognition of potentially divergent incentives between supervisors is a first step toward the design of effective mechanisms to strengthen regulatory cooperation. We make three specific proposals along these lines. First, we suggest a College of Supervisors coordinated by the *host* supervisor where home supervisors of the relevant foreign institutions active in a country would join efforts with the host supervisor to define a mutually beneficial regulatory approach. The recalibration of the IRB formula to fit local circumstances might be one task for this College depending on local circumstances. Second we propose joint inspections by home and host supervisors for the subsidiaries or branches of foreign banks in host countries to enhance trust and technology transfer and third we propose applying fully pillar 3 and possibly introducing further market discipline measures on those subsidiaries where market data has been lost to assist local depositors to evaluate the strength of the implicit guarantees between the parent and the local bank. We believe that these measures may strengthen supervisory cooperation and trust between international banks and their home and host authorities, facilitating a more extensive and transparent provision of guarantees to local bank depositors and hence reducing the need for a separate home and host supervision.

References

Basel Committee for Banking Supervision, 2004, *The New Basel Capital Accord*, available on www.bis.org.

Basel Committee for Banking Supervision, 2003, *High-level Principles for the Cross-Border Implementation of the New Accord*, available on www.bis.org.

Balzarotti, V., C. Castro, and A. Powell, 2003, "Reforming Capital Requirements in Emerging Countries: Calibrating Basel II using Historical Argentine Credit Bureau Data and CreditRisk+," Universidad Torcuato Di Tella, mimeo.

Bernanke, B., 2004, "Remarks at the International Bankers' Annual Breakfast Dialogue," available on www.federalreserve.gov/boarddocs/speeches/2004/.

Calomiris, C. and A. Powell, 2002, "Can Emerging Economy Bank Regulators Establish Effective Discipline," in F. S. Mishkin (ed.), *Prudential Supervision: Why Is It Important and What Are the Issues*, Chicago: University of Chicago Press and NBER.

Del Negro, M. and S. Kay, 2002, "Global Banks, Local Crises: Bad News from Argentina," *Economic Review, Federal Reserve Bank of Atlanta*, Q3, pp. 89–106.

Financial Stability Institute, 2004, "Implementation of the New Capital Adequacy Framework in Non-Basel Committee Member Countries," FSI Occasional Paper No 4 (July 2004), available on www.bis.org/fsi/fsipapers04.htm.

Galindo, Micco and Powell, 2004, "Loyal Lenders or Fickle Financiers: Foreign Banks in Latin America," Universidad Torcuato Di Tella, Working Paper, 08/2004, available on www.utdt.edu/departamentos/empresarial/cif/pdfs-wp/wpcif-082004.pdf.

Griffith-Jones, S. and S. Spratt, 2003, "CP3 and the Developing World," Submission to the Basel Committee for Banking Supervision, available on www.bis.org.

Jackson, P., 2001, "Bank Capital Standards: the New Basel Accord," Bank of England, *Quarterly Review*, Spring.

Jackson, P. and W. Perraudin, 2000, "Regulatory Implications of Credit Risk Modeling," *Journal of Banking and Finance*, 24, pp. 1–14.

Majnoni, G. and A. Powell, 2005, "Bank Capital and Loan Loss Reserves under Basel II: Implications for Emerging Countries," *Economía*, 5(2) pp. 105–149.

Powell, A., 2002, "A Capital Accord for Emerging Economies?," World Bank Working Paper No. 2808.

Powell, A., 2003, "Basel II and Developing Countries: Sailing Through the Sea of Standards," Policy Research Working Paper Series, World Bank No 3387.

Repullo, R. and J. Suarez, 2003, "Loan Pricing Under Basel Capital Requirements," CEMFI Working Paper No. 0308.

Standard & Poor's, 2002, "Sovereign Rating History Since 1975," available on www.standardandpoors.com.

Standard & Poor's, 2000, "Ratings Performance 2000: Default, Transition, Recovery, and Spreads," available on www.standardandpoors.com.

Giovanni Majnoni is an advisor in the private sector and infrastructure unit of the Latin American and Caribbean Department of the World Bank. Andrew Powell is lead research economist at the Inter American Development Bank and a professor at the Universidad Torcuato Di Tella, Buenos Aires. The findings, interpretations, and conclusions expressed in this paper are entirely those of the authors. They do not necessarily represent the view of the World Bank or of the Inter-American Development Bank, their Executive Directors, or the countries that they represent. The authors wish to thank Jerry Caprio, Mark Carey, Michael Gordy, Patricia Jackson, Lorna Martin, Pascual O'Dougherty, Rafael Repullo, and Eric Rosengren for very useful discussions. They also wish to thank participants in the Federal Reserve Bank of Chicago–World Bank conference on "Cross-Border Banking: Regulatory Challenges" and especially to their discussant, João Santos. Naturally, all mistakes remain their own.

Comments on Jackson, Bielicki and Bednarski, and Majnoni and Powell

João A. C. Santos*

Federal Reserve Bank of New York

These three papers analyze some of the challenges for home and host supervisors of banking organizations that operate in multiple countries. The paper by Patricia Jackson focuses on the challenges that Basel II will bring to the relationship between these supervisors. The paper by Piotr Bielicki and Grzegorz Bednarski, in turn, focuses on the difficulties that host countries' supervisors face when their banks, despite being systemically important in the home country, are controlled by substantially larger foreign banks. Finally, the paper by Giovanni Majnoni and Andrew Powell presents a theoretical model to investigate how banks' incentives can give rise to tensions between home and host supervisors, and an empirical analysis on the guarantees that parent banks extend to their foreign subsidiaries. Below is a brief summary of each of these papers followed by some observations on their main conclusions and policy recommendations.

The paper by Patricia Jackson starts out by noting that the original division of the responsibility to supervise banks that operate in multiple countries recognized that subsidiaries are legal entities in the jurisdiction in which they are established and, therefore, have to meet the local banking law and are subject to supervision by local authorities. The paper goes on to note that while the 1988 Basel Accord did not interfere with this allocation of responsibilities between the home and host bank supervisors, Basel II will likely require a different allocation of responsibilities and additional coordination between supervisors.

Jackson's paper focuses on the challenges that multinational banks which qualify for the advanced approaches to set the capital standards will pose to the current institutional allocation of responsibilities between home and host supervisors. To deal with these challenges, and in particular to determine the level of required capital at the subsidiary level for these banks, Patricia Jackson proposes that supervisors should be more willing to accept banks adopting advanced approaches at the group level and the standardized approach at the subsidiary level in all but the largest foreign subsidiaries. She also advocates the use of pillar 2 to address any potential capital shortfalls at the subsidiary level where needed.

This proposal would greatly facilitate the implementation of Basel II and would lead to important savings for the banks that adopt the new accord. However, it would come at a cost. The additional reliance on pillar 2 would likely reduce the information content of the pillar 1 requirement and would certainly increase the discretion of host regulators with implications for the level playing field. The implementation of this proposal would also require extensive reliance on information sharing agreements between home and host supervisors with their corresponding challenges for supervisors (more on this below).

The paper by Piotr Bielicki and Grzegorz Bednarski also considers the interplay between the home and host supervisors of banks that operate in multiple countries. However, they focus on the difficulties that host supervisors of subsidiaries that are systemically important in their countries (but are small vis-à-vis their parent bank). The authors pay particular attention to the concerns of host supervisors with the spillovers to the subsidiary bank from problems at the parent bank, and the difficulties that host supervisors face to access the information on the parent bank they deem relevant given the importance of the subsidiary bank for the local economy.

The authors consider two alternative arrangements to govern the relationship between the home and host supervisors: centralize the responsibility for supervision of the entire group in the supervisor of the parent bank or institutionalize a system of cooperation between the parent supervisor and the host supervisor of the subsidiary bank. The authors argue that the former arrangement has some important limitations. The supervisor of the parent bank, for example, may not take into account the host country's best interests when evaluating the subsidiary bank, despite its systemic importance for the local economy. The cooperative arrangement has its own problems too, including potential conflicts of interest between the home and host supervisors, and the fact that the host supervisor has limited authority over the parent bank that owns the local subsidiary. Given the difficulties in solving these problems, the authors propose an arrangement in which systemically important subsidiaries of foreign banks operate as a stand alone bank and are supervised by the host supervisor.

The spillovers from the parent bank to its foreign subsidiaries are potentially important. However, more often than not problems originate at foreign subsidiaries rather than the parent bank. Also, once a foreign bank takes control over a local bank, it will be difficult to require the parent bank to let its subsidiary operate as a stand-alone bank without interfering in its management. It may not even be desirable to do so as this will limit the ability of the subsidiary to benefit from the management and other resources of the parent bank. Having said that, this paper highlights one of the challenges that the arrangements built upon the assumption that home and host supervisors will share all information necessary to meet their mandates are likely to face (more on this below).

Finally, the paper by Giovanni Majnoni and Andrew Powell has three parts. The first part presents a theoretical model to investigate how banks' incentives to bail out foreign subsidiaries or even the parent bank can give rise to tensions between home and host supervisors. The second part of the paper attempts to determine the extent of the guarantee that parent banks give their subsidiaries. To this end, the authors investigate the impact of the parent credit rating and the impact of the rating of the country where the subsidiary operates on the rating of the subsidiary. The third part of the paper discusses some implications of Basel II on international banks operating in emerging markets and the corresponding effects on the availability and cost of bank credit in these countries. The authors conclude their paper with a set of proposals to deal with cross border supervisory issues, including the establishment of a college of supervisors organized by the host regulator, and on-site joint inspections (by the host supervisor and the supervisor of the parent bank) of subsidiaries owned by foreign banks.

The authors' attempt to investigate the tensions between the home and host supervisors through a theoretical model is interesting, but their reliance on a reduced form model poses some limitations on their analysis. It would be useful to see, therefore, if their insights continue to hold in a more general setting that models, for example, the objective functions of the home and host supervisors. Similarly, their empirical findings on the guarantee that parent banks grant their subsidiaries should be interpreted with some caution. Their findings are based on credit ratings and a small sample. In addition, the fact that the credit rating of the parent bank helps explain the credit ratings of its subsidiaries does not necessarily imply that the parent bank has committed to extend a guarantee to its subsidiaries. This may also be the result of sample selection. For example, safer banks may be more likely to succeed on their attempts to acquire safer foreign subsidiaries.

Nonetheless, the authors make an important point in their paper, one that is often forgotten in the debate on the design of regulatory and supervisory arrangements for banks operating in multiple countries, namely that the incentives between home and host regulators are not perfectly aligned all of the time and consequently should be taken into account when designing these arrangements.

In sum, a common message of these papers is that differences in the incentives of regulators may lead to conflicts of interest and pose problems for the designers of regulatory arrangements to deal with banks that operate in multiple countries. Despite their importance, these differences have received little attention to date. This is partly because it is often assumed that cooperative agreements and information sharing agreements will make the differences in these incentives innocuous. However, as these papers show, this may not be the case. Also, as Kahn and Santos (2005, 2006) show, some of the very same reasons that lead to conflicts of interest between different regulators of banks also give these regulators incentives not to share information.

References

Kahn, C. M. and J. A. C Santos, 2006, "Who Should Act as Lender of Last Resort? An Incomplete Contracts Model: A comment," Forthcoming in the *Journal of Money Credit and Banking*.

Kahn, C. M. and J. A. C Santos, 2005, "Allocating Bank Regulatory Powers: Lender of Last Resort, Deposit Insurance and Supervision," *European Economic Review*, 49(8), pp. 2107–2136.

João A. C. Santos is a research officer in the Banking Studies Group of the Federal Reserve Bank of New York and can be contact at 33 Liberty Street. New York, NY 10045, 212 720-5583, joao.santos@ny.frb.org. The views expressed here are those of the author and not necessarily those of the Federal Reserve Bank of New York or the Federal Reserve System.

Market Discipline Issues

Confronting Divergent Interests in Cross-Country Regulatory Arrangements

Edward J. Kane*

Boston College

As financial institutions and markets more and more effectively transcend geographic borders, limitations of national systems of regulation become more consequential. Beginning with the five-page Basel Concordat of 1975, banking regulatory agencies in major countries have agreed that multinational banking organizations should be supervised in a cooperative manner by both their "home" and "host" countries. The concordat assigns home-country supervisors responsibility for consolidated oversight of global conglomerate banking organizations, while it leaves host-country regulators responsible both for supervising the local operations of foreign and domestic banks and for sharing relevant information about local operations with home-country regulators. The concordat's conflicting goals were to assure adequate cross-border supervision of multinational banks, while reducing the total regulatory burden generated across the jurisdictions in which the bank might operate and respecting a host country's right to set its own domestic standards for individual-bank safety, system stability, and the accumulation of market power.

Under the aegis of the Basel Committee on Banking Supervision (the Basel Committee), the concordat spurred a search for minimum prudential standards that evolved by 1997 into a 44-page statement of *Core Principles for Effective Banking Supervision*. These fluid principles are gradually congealing into amplifying criteria that teams of outside experts can use to make country-by-country assessments of regulatory effectiveness (Basel Committee, 2001). In turn, these criteria are helping to shape a new and more-complicated system of risk-based capital requirements known as Basel II (Basel Committee, 2003). Basel II focuses the conflict between home and host regulators on how to verify and share information across countries and how to use whatever data they share to allocate a conglomerate institution's capital and diversification benefits between local and home-country exposures to insolvency risk. As in ordinary human affairs, the need to mitigate or overcome bankers' and foreign regulators' incentives to hide embarrassing information is a central feature of conscientious bank supervision.

Although nation-based systems of financial regulation obviously constitute a second-best approach to global welfare maximization, treacherous accountability problems must be acknowledged and resolved before regulatory cooperation can deal fairly and efficiently with cross-border issues. To track and control insolvency risk within and across any set of countries, officials must construct a partnership that allows regulators in every participating country to monitor and to influence counterpart regulators in all partnering nations. Using efforts to partner the Australian and New Zealand regulatory systems as an example, this paper identifies characteristics by which regulatory systems differ and underscores particular features that make harmonization difficult to achieve.

1. Trans-Tasman Regulatory Harmonization as an Illustrative Case

Troubled banks routinely conceal unfavorable information about their performance or condition from outsiders. Bank customers and counterparties acting on their own cannot easily uncover this information. Partly to overcome this coordination problem, government chartering and supervision of banks and payments systems are near-universal phenomena (Aghion *et al.*, 1999). Regulatory activities may be described as efforts by a trusted Third Party that affect the shaping, pricing, and delivery of banking products in one of three ways: by rule making (for example, capital requirements); by monitoring and enforcement; or by detecting and resolving insolvencies (that is, shortages in bank-contributed net worth).

To the extent that the beneficiaries and the regulated are different parties, banking regulation is "other regarding" and "other directing." A principal goal is to protect society from the consequences of excessive risk-taking, capital shortages, and loss concealment at individual banks. To maximize global welfare, contracts under which officials are appointed would have to make them or their agencies explicitly accountable to potential loss-bearers in all partner countries for all costs incurred in preventing, detecting, and resolving bank insolvencies.

The Basel Concordat and its later elaborations call for contact and cooperation between host and parent supervisory authorities. In the absence of harmonizing contact and cooperation, contractual arrangements focus banking regulators in each country on domestic interests. They would be expected to design and operate regulatory enterprises nationalistically, that is, with an eye toward maximizing primarily the welfare of their own citizens.

It is important to recognize that policy coordination cannot eliminate cross-country and within-country incentive conflicts in banking regulation. At best, it may establish a contractable partnership that supplements — without substituting for — policies of sound regulatory discipline in individual countries.

Mishan (1969) emphasizes that economic policy performance should be assessed in two dimensions. Optimal strategies produce outcomes that are simultaneously Pareto-efficient and "distributionally preferred" (that is, they help the representative citizen and avoid anti-egalitarian effects on the distribution of income).[1] The Mishan criterion reminds us that cross-country arrangements to detect, prevent, and resolve bank insolvencies must not result in increased loss exposures that disadvantage the citizens of any partner country.

As stewards of taxpayer resources, the Mishan criterion implies that in each country financial supervisors and regulators owe four duties to the representative citizen:

1. *Vision* (maintaining a capacity to recognize risk-taking and capital shortages in timely fashion);
2. *Prompt corrective action* (being committed to control the value of implicit and explicit government guarantees);
3. *Least-cost resolution* (efficiently curing insolvencies that corrective action fails to avert);
4. *Truth-telling* (keeping voters and taxpayers informed about the true opportunity costs of regulatory strategies).

---

[1] In the words of Andrew Jackson (quoted in Todd, 2002): "In the full enjoyment of ... the fruits of superior industry, economy, and virtue, every man is equally entitled to protection by law; but when the laws undertake to add to these natural and just advantages artificial distinctions to grant titles, gratuities, and exclusive privileges to make the rich richer and the potent more powerful, the humble members of society — the farmers, mechanics, and laborers — who have neither the time nor the means of securing like favors to themselves, have a right to complain of the injustice of government (1832)."

Gaps in vision and reporting obligations engender incentive breakdowns. They reduce society's ability to hold regulators responsible for uncovering the truth about bank losses and acting on it. This weakness in communicating societal disapproval undermines a regulator's incentive to prevent insolvencies and to resolve them efficiently. Being able to hide lapses in performance intensifies incentive conflict. It makes it easier in tough times to pursue short-run political and career rewards that top officials can capture by not closely enforcing economic insolvency.

Sincere efforts to integrate the private banking markets of any two countries — in particular, those of Australia (A) and New Zealand (Z) — must also plan to integrate their private and governmental systems of information disclosure and banking regulation. Regulatory integration is complicated because, even if regulatory strategies and control structures (R_A, R_Z) did not differ greatly between the countries, individual-country regulators are responsible to different sets of taxpayers (T_A, T_Z), and social norms and applicable legislation makes private and governmental regulatory officials accountable to their citizens in disparate contractual ways (C_A, C_Z). To maximize the joint welfare of citizens of both countries, it is not enough to blend the countries' strategies and control structures. To harmonize regulatory incentives, regulatory performance measures and reporting responsibilities must be refocused as well.

A country's regulatory system co-evolves with popular perceptions of what regulatory problems cry out to be solved. When citizens believe their country's incentive-control system is working adequately, it is hard to build a coalition strong enough to win marked changes in regulatory strategies and tactics. This is why substantial regulatory reforms usually occur only in the wake of large-scale crises.

In noncrisis times, lobbying activity can seldom achieve more than a marginal adjustment either in the objectives that officials pursue or in the tradeoffs officials make within the limits of their regulatory culture. How particular policy strategies actually work in practice is co-determined by the *rules* officials adopt and by regulatees' ability to find and exploit circumventive *loopholes* in the enforcement of these rules. One reason that the issue of cross-border regulatory cooperation is on the table around the world is that exploiting loopholes often entails moving activities that one country might tax more heavily or regulate more effectively into the jurisdiction of another.

With large Australian-owned institutions holding over 85 percent of the New Zealand banking market, harmonization is a hot-button issue in both countries. Although the two countries agreed in early 2005 to establish a joint Trans-Tasman Council on Banking Supervision, the initial hopes and fears of officials in A and Z seemed to differ sharply. Australian Treasurer Peter Costello portrayed harmonization as a process of negotiation in which a single system of "seamless" regulation would be the most desirable endpoint, while New Zealand Finance Minister Michael Cullen took care to label a single regulatory system as merely a "possible endpoint" (Joint Press Conference, 2005).

New Zealand citizens could draw little comfort from a follow-up interview that Treasurer Costello offered in the February 19th *Weekend Herald*. He described his vision for the two countries as one in which "goods and services will move as seamlessly across the Tasman in much the same way they now move seamlessly across the Victorian and New South Wales border." To the extent that states' rights in Australia fall short of absolute sovereigty, this vision comes perilously close to expressing an intention to reduce New Zealand financially to Australia's seventh state or third territory.

The overriding task of financial regulation is to resolve diverse incentive conflicts in financial transactions at minimum net cost to society. Treasurer Costello's position assumes that dual supervision generates only "duplication and unnecessary cost." An alternative view is that, especially where bank risk exposures and capital positions are hard to detect and easy to shuffle across jurisdictions, two heads are likely to prove better than one. This view is buttressed by the undeniable value to New Zealand citizens of ensuring that officials in any post-harmonization regulatory enterprise remain *democratically accountable* for identifying and protecting Kiwi (Z) interests and especially for preventing and managing the dangers and costs of future banking crises. It is not for nothing that the New Testament warns of the impossibility of faithfully serving two masters.

Any system of government generates different costs and benefits for differently situated citizens and corporations. It is natural for large Australian banks to ask their government to help them reduce their total taxes and regulatory compliance costs. It is just as natural for New Zealand citizens to worry about how well their interests would be represented in an evolving global banking system if their concerns had to be filtered through the economic interests of Australian banks and the political interests of Australian regulators.

The Trans-Tasman Council's central contracting problem is to recognize and ameliorate conflicts between societal and private interests that exist in Tasman-area markets for banking services. Woolford and Orr (2005, p. 46) define the council's main goal as promoting "maximum coordination, cooperation, and harmoni[z]ation of trans-Tasman bank regulation where sensible." To me, this means integrating one country's regulatory system with that of the other country without eroding the advantages and democratic responsibilities of either. To accomplish this task, conferees must develop transparent measures of bank and regulatory performance and incorporate these measures into a self-enforcing contractual structure that empowers citizens of both countries to hold officials accountable for the tradeoffs they make between joint and national interests (Schüler, 2003).

2. Primacy of Controlling Incentive Conflict

In banking, depositors and other outside stakeholders may be exposed to loss from fraud, leverage, or earnings volatility without being adequately informed or compensated for the risks entailed. To reduce their exposure to these three types of risk shifting, a bank's counterparties deploy three remedies: (1) they require the bank to bond itself in various ways to behave honestly and fairly; (2) they negotiate a deterrent right to punish opportunistic behavior; and (3) they monitor information on the bank's ongoing performance and condition.

Bonding, policing, and monitoring are not costless. The costs vary inversely with the transparency (T) provided by the accounting and disclosure regime under which the bank operates. The more transparent the disclosure regime, the more easily and more accurately outsiders — depositors, investors, and supervisors — can estimate the true value of a bank's assets and liabilities. But policing costs are also a function of outside stakeholders' ability to *appreciate* the implications of the information they receive (that is, their financial expertise) and their ability to *coordinate* deterrent and punitive responses with others (that is, their disciplinary power).

In the absence of credible third-party guarantees, financially sophisticated counterparties act as keynoters whose actions put strong pressure on banks known to be experiencing opportunity-cost losses to adjust their affairs promptly. The market forces that keynoters unleash require troubled banks to do one or all of three things: shrink their footings, raise more capital, or pay higher interest rates on their deposits and other debt.

In monitoring, disciplining, and resolving banks, the incentives of government officials to act promptly differ from the duties and incentives of private creditors in important ways. Because official interventions are unusual and generate a great deal of publicity, officials cannot focus only on the *economic* costs and benefits of the intervention. Given that disadvantaged parties would be all too ready to accuse them of creating or escalating problem situations, regulators must worry about the political and career ramifications of even the most-dutiful interventions. Even small interventions can damage their professional reputations and careers if their policies distress powerful parties.

Although many commonalities of interest exist, governmental systems for setting and enforcing financial rules are infested with incentive conflict. Even within a country, major conflicts exist between and among:

1. Regulators and the firms they regulate;
2. Particular regulators and other societal watchdogs;
3. Regulators and the politicians to whom they must report; and
4. Taxpayers and the politicians and regulatory personnel they put in office.

How a country traditionally approaches and resolves these conflicts is in part hard-wired into its political and institutional structure. To different extents, societies impose bonds of community on individual citizens. Ideally, these bonds restrain corporate and governmental decision making in socially beneficial ways. Communal bonds generate an internally and externally enforced sense of reciprocity that inserts into individual preference functions a concern for one another's welfare that deters at least some forms of opportunistic behavior. To reinforce these implicit controls, a country also works out ways for watchdogs to fill gaps in the bonding, deterrent rights (deterrency), and transparency inherent in its private contracting environment. Over time, efforts to close gaps in private and government contracting generate a country-specific *regulatory culture*.

3. Difficulty of Resolving Divergences in Regulatory Culture

When private corporations merge, the goal of the transaction is to create value by enhancing the capabilities and performance of partner firms. To be successful, managers of the combined enterprise must identify synergies and mitigate conflicts of interest among various stakeholders. Especially in cross-border combinations, empirical evidence indicates that marked differences in either the corporate cultures or strategic orientations of partnering firms reduce the chance that they can be merged successfully (Weston, Siu, and Johnson, 2001, p. 639; Altunbas and Ibáñez, 2004).

This section begins by defining a regulatory analogue to the concept of corporate culture. This concept provides a systematic way to compare and contrast the specific regulatory strategies and tactics employed in Australia and New Zealand. Despite a number of fundamental similarities, important differences in culture can be identified. From an evolutionary perspective, the very persistence of these differences indicates that, within each country, idiosyncratic features manage to resolve incentive conflicts with reasonable efficiency. The Trans-Tasman Council cannot hope to build a system that stitches together in compromise fashion an equal number of pieces from the different regulatory systems without losing the threads of economic logic that underlie them. If these threads are not rewoven carefully enough, the citizens of one or both partner countries will suffer substantial welfare losses.

3.1. The concept of regulatory culture

A culture may be defined as customs, ideas, and attitudes that members of a group share and transmit from generation to generation by systems of subtle and unsubtle rewards and punishments. A regulatory culture is more than a system of rules and enforcement. It incorporates higher-order norms about how officials should comport themselves; these norms limit the ways in which uncooperative or even unscrupulous individual bankers can be monitored and disciplined. It includes a matrix of attitudes and beliefs that define what it means for a regulator to use its investigative and disciplinary authority honorably. These attitudes and beliefs set standards for the fair use of government power. Checks and balances that bound each agency's jurisdiction express a distrust of government power that often traces back to abuses observed in a distant past when the country was occupied, colonized, or run by a one-party government. Underlying every formal regulatory structure is a set of higher-order social norms that penetrate and shape the policymaking process and the political and legal environments within which intersectoral bargaining takes place. These underlying standards, taboos, and traditions are normative in two senses. They simultaneously define what behaviors are "normal" and what behaviors regulators should mimic to avoid criticism or shame.

Prudential regulation imposes on regulators a *duty* to stop excessive risk-taking and to find and resolve hidden individual bank insolvencies in timely fashion. Within any country, the regulatory culture within which this duty is discharged is spanned by six specific components:

- Legal authority and reporting obligations;
- Formulation and promulgation of specific rules;
- Technology of monitoring for violations & compliance;
- Penalties for material violations;
- The regulator's duties of consultation: To guarantee fairness, regulated parties have a right to participation and due process, which imposes substantial burdens of proof on the regulator; and
- Regulatees' rights to judicial review: Intervened parties have an access to appeals procedures that bond the fairness guarantee.

3.2. Similarities in Australian and New Zealand regulatory cultures

In Australia and New Zealand, the last three dimensions of regulatory culture are fundamentally the same. Both countries accept social norms that subject official decisions to intragovernmental checks and balances and require them as well to treat violators as innocent until formally proven guilty and to assure that punishments meted out do not exceed the social importance of the violations at issue. The presumption of innocence protects fraudsters and bumblers from *prompt* regulatory discipline; the other two norms make it impossible to make penalties draconian enough to eliminate risk-shifting incentives completely.

By increasing the difficulty of proving a bank to be insolvent, tests of regulatory authority, fairness, and reasonableness prolong the process of detecting and resolving insolvencies. Even a deeply insolvent institution can delay and ameliorate disciplinary actions in two ways: (1) by delaying the writedown of impaired assets; and (2) by accumulating political clout and using it to generate outside (and not always proper) interference on its behalf.

3.3. Differences in the allocation and implementation of legal authority

Despite sharing almost identical legal norms, the regulatory systems of the two countries differ importantly in each of the first three dimensions. The

Reserve Bank of New Zealand (RBNZ) combines specialized prudential supervision of the NZ banking system with the tasks of conceiving and executing monetary-policy actions. Conduct-of-business regulation and supervision of financial firms in nonbank sectors is conducted by other agencies. In Australia, the relatively new Australian Prudential Regulatory Authority (APRA) follows the British model of leaving monetary policy to the central bank, The Reserve Bank of Australia (RBA), and exercises supervisory authority in an integrated manner over insurance companies, depository institutions, and some types of securities firms.

These different structures of prudential regulation allocate responsibility for preserving financial stability in very different ways. Unlike APRA, the RBNZ at present has no formal responsibilities for supervising nonbank institutions (Mortlock, 2003). Unlike the RBNZ, APRA leaves policy decisions that affect interest-rate and exchange-rate volatility to the RBA, even though monetary-policy decisions can work potentially devastating effects on an individual bank's solvency and risk profile.

Several other ways of allocating legal authority for promoting financial stability are used by other countries. For example, the U.S. central bank combines monetary policy authority with supervisory responsibilities, but competes for and shares supervisory jurisdiction over banks with many other regulators. Several European countries task their central bank with supervising securities firms and banks in tandem.

The great diversity we observe in how supervisory authority is allocated supports this paper's central hypothesis that different ways of dividing supervisory and monetary policy responsibility have particular advantages and disadvantages, with the balance of costs and benefits varying with the character of a country's financial and political contracting environment. Common sense and Samuelson's principle of revealed preference tell us that each country's current structure is better suited to its own particular financial environment than any other country's would be.

3.4. Interaction of differences in monitoring methods, rules, and enforcement

The goal of all systems for supervising banks is the same: to assure a safe and sound financial environment by protecting depositors and the economic health of the nation as a whole from hidden and disruptive bank risk-taking. Ideally, rules and the ways they are enforced are designed to detect losses and imprudent risk exposures and to resolve capital shortages at banks before they can become deep enough to cause widespread disruption.

As explained earlier, authorities' vision is constrained by leeway in accounting standards and by the larger disclosure regime in which their banks operate. The rules and enforcement methods by which authorities pursue financial stability must be tailored to overcome weaknesses not only in their own vision, but also in the vision of partner regulators and in the bonding, deterrency, and transparency present in their private contracting environments.

Disclosure regimes place a web of formal and informal obligations on bank managers, accountants, and directors. These obligations determine what asset and liability items bank accountants must report values for, what changes in value must be reported (either on the balance sheet or in footnotes), and when and how authorities are to be informed about emerging losses.

In all countries, independent external accountants assume a responsibility for reporting accurate information to directors, creditors, stockholders, regulators, and other outsiders, even if the managers that hire them would prefer to cook the books in misleading ways. Similarly, bank directors have a duty to review and test audit reports for accuracy and to assure themselves and regulators that the bank is being managed well.

An effective regulatory partnership must impose sensible and enforceable regulator-to-regulator disclosure obligations all around. When top regulators receive strong evidence that crippling losses may be emerging at an individual bank, duty must also require them to dispatch a team of forensic analysts to measure the extent of these losses. When the special exam is completed, regulators are expected to share the findings with the bank's directors. At this point, directors could request a brief window of time to give them a chance to cure the bank's capital shortages. If sufficient new capital is not subscribed, the bank would be closed, offered to a new owner, or placed in statutory management. The task of statutory managers would be to decide afresh whether and when to liquidate the bank or offer it for sale.

In both Australia and New Zealand, auditors are required to report to the supervisory authority any evidence they uncover of actual or potential insolvency and to alert authorities about possible violations of prudential standards. Accountants must attest that nothing that "has come to their attention" in preparing or reviewing financial statements would cause them to believe that the bank's financial statements and supplementary disclosures do not present a "true and fair view" of the matters to which they relate. Section 96 of the Reserve Bank of New Zealand Act requires auditors to disclose directly to the RBNZ any information that is "likely to assist, or be relevant to the exercise by the bank of its powers under this part of this act" (that is, the RBNZ's supervisory powers). The same section obliges a bank's auditors to alert the RBNZ if they believe the bank is either "insolvent or is likely to become insolvent or is in serious financial difficulties." Section 97 requires auditors to "take reasonable steps to inform the registered bank" of their intention before expressing their concern to the RBNZ, and Section 98 protects auditors that make good-faith disclosures from civil and criminal liability or professional sanctions. The *legal force* of these provisions is to assure that inserting exculpatory clauses into their articles of engagement cannot relieve auditors of legal liability for not reporting evidence of a developing bank insolvency. The *social force* of these provisions comes from an individual's desire to enjoy the esteem of his or her fellow citizens and to avoid disgrace. Experience suggests that most auditors are considerably more concerned about potential lawsuits than their social standing.

The most important difference in the supervisory regimes of Australia and New Zealand is the strength of the obligations that they place on bank directors to uncover and transmit unfavorable information to top regulators (Brash, 1996). In Australia (indeed in most countries other than New Zealand), bank managers, auditors, and directors may (if they are careful about it) use loopholes in accounting rules to delay the transmission of adverse information to regulators. Table 1 lists the alternative ways that news of crippling losses may first come to light. It also lists the ways that managers, directors, and lower-level regulatory staff members may sugarcoat bad news or temporarily blockade the various paths through which bad news can reach top regulators.

For directors of registered banks, New Zealand's disclosure regime imposes self-reporting obligations that all but eliminate impunity for director-supported misrepresentation. All directors must sign *quarterly* statements indicating whether "after due enquiry" they believe: (1) that the General Disclosure statement (Tripe, 2001, describes the content of this document) contains all information required and is neither false nor misleading; (2) that the bank has complied with various regulations (including rules on lending to connected persons); and (3) that the bank has in place and is properly applying systems that adequately monitor and control material risks, a great many of which are named explicitly. Finally, to do business in

Table 1. Paths by which bad news may reach top regulators

Ways in Which Crippling News Surfaces	Initial Source of Corrective Pressure	Ways in Which Bank Management Can Challenge or Stifle Bad News	Ways in Which Regulators Can Lessen the Call to Action Generated by the Bad News
1. Government-Initiated Path	Government examiners discover irregularities in loan underwriting, documentation, or loss reserves during an ordinary bank examination	Exercise rights to appeal examiner writedowns	Higher-ups may modify examiner's "pencil report"
2. Bank-Initiated Path	A conscientious internal whistleblower provides evidence to either: a. the bank's external auditor b. the bank's board of directors c. regulatory staff members	a. Auditors may be persuaded to ignore or marginalize the evidence b. Board members may be persuaded to ignore the evidence c. Managers may succeed in demonizing the whistleblower	a. Not applicable b. Not applicable c. Regulators may treat the whistleblower as a mean-spirited troublemaker
3. Auditor-Initiated Path	Auditor finds irregularities and either quits, is fired, or issues a qualified report	Managers concoct a persuasive cover story for the impasse	Regulators may ignore the audit impasse
4. Creditor-Driven Path	News about auditor issues, leaks, or autonomous rumors undermine depositor confidence or the confidence of suppliers of interbank loans	Managers may collateralize and/or pay very high interest on large deposits or interbank loans	Central bank may replace private funding with discount-window loans

New Zealand, large Australian banks must be locally incorporated. While no explicit residential requirement yet exists, it has been understood that the chief executive should reside in New Zealand so that he or she could be prosecuted for false disclosures without extradition proceedings.

So far, directorial self-reporting has served New Zealand well. The threat of legal and reputational penalties for false attestations have surfaced relevant supervisory issues both as a result of changes occurring at individual banks and as a result of changes made in the wording of RBNZ attestation requirements. Cautious directors of particular banks have on several occasions scheduled meetings with RBNZ senior staff to inform them promptly of concerns that interfere with their signing the required statements. Similarly, when the RBNZ has encountered inconsistencies in attestations and reports, RBNZ staff have initiated the same sort of meetings.

This special channel of verification focuses rule-making on what positions or facts should be disclosed to the RBNZ and how the accuracy of disclosures should be certified. Except for a web of specific restrictions on insurance activities and loans to connected firms and persons, the RBNZ eschews formal limits on the size of particular bank positions. It presumes that directorial disclosure obligations will identify losses and imprudent loss exposures in a more relevant and more timely manner than a rigid program of position caps and periodic inspections for breaches by government examiners could.

In contrast, position caps and confidential government inspections play starring roles in Australia's supervision of banks. Of course, the effectiveness of either regulatory regime is routinely undermined by regulation-induced innovation. Still, government supervisors are never going to know enough about the motives for financial innovation to design ratios that can serve as an effective first line of defense against risk-shifting by troubled banks. The presumption that particular portfolio positions are either prohibitively risky in themselves or signify failure-producing risk-taking ignores both the value that any risky position may have in diversifying other risks and the rich and growing menu of techniques that banks use to hedge or intensify broad categories of risk-taking today. The pace of innovation in techniques of risk-taking and risk management virtually guarantees that with every passing day, balance-sheet ratios that predicted failure in the past become less and less reliable measures of a modern bank's proneness to failure. Both in rule-making and in monitoring, the continuing expansion and growing complication of structured and index derivatives keep government supervisors' risk-assessment capabilities lagging behind those of the banks they regulate. However, impairments to *regulatory vision* and *verification* are less daunting in that many of them can be contracted away.

3.5. *Summary*

In Australia and indeed in most other countries, inspection-based supervision is a game of hide the cheese. The cheese, of course, is adverse information about a bank's true condition or periodic performance. Loopholes in the rules of the game *create incentives* for bank directors to help managers to mislead supervisors and other outsiders. They can do this with impunity as long as the firm makes skillful and legitimate use of an evolving set of professionally certified accounting loopholes. Like night-club illusionists, managers and accountants may even expect ethically challenged directors to admire their proficiency in using smoke and mirrors to make losses and loss exposures invisible to the naked eye.

The distinctive feature of New Zealand's post-1996 regulatory culture is that self-reporting obligations imposed on directors simplify the supervisory burden of uncovering and proving fraud and insolvency. It makes it illegal and disreputable for individual bank directors to assist others in perpetrating an illusion. Directors are required by law to bring to the attention of the supervisor important adverse information they happen to come across. This duty is enforced by substantial criminal and civil penalties and intensified by the reputational harm that timely public exposure of formally illicit behavior inevitably brings.

Even with substantial prior notice, replacing either country's regulatory system by the other would be extremely disruptive for the country whose supervisory traditions would be pushed aside. It seems more sensible to focus on finding ways to network the two systems in a cooperative way and to explore experimentally which particular strategies and tactics can provide enough vision to control economic and financial stress within and across the partner countries.

4. The Role of Regulatory Culture in the Insolvency Detection and Bank Failure Process

Economists define economic net worth (N_E) as the full-information value of a firm's tangible and intangible assets and liabilities. In statistical terms, accounting or book-value net worth (N_{BV}) becomes a poorer and poorer estimator of N_E as the latent variable N_E declines. In troubled times and circumstances, the estimator N_{BV} becomes increasingly more biased and inefficient.

In effect, regulatory vision falters when it is most needed. This makes accounting insolvency a dangerously unreliable threshold for winding up the affairs of a troubled bank. Opportunities to defer the accounting realization of economic losses render accounting net worth a lagging indicator of the extent of a troubled bank's capital shortage. When a financial institution's survival is threatened, adverse information becomes harder and harder to detect in accounting reports. The threshold at which authorities can force stockholders to either recapitalize a troubled bank or surrender their franchise must be set high enough to compensate for this predictable decline in acuity.

Historical experience shows that, with a zero N_{BV} threshold, a financial institutions' ability to conceal risky transactions and impairments in asset values from outside eyes can allow *economic* insolvencies to reach costly depths before authorities can address them (Honohan and Klingebiel, 2003). Weaknesses in loss detection and regulatory intervention rights can spawn a systemic crisis by enabling insolvent institutions to adopt aggressive risk-taking strategies that — by destroying profit margins — spread insolvency to competing institutions.

4.1. Crisis-driven reforms in New Zealand and the United States

According to Honohan and Klingebiel (2003), New Zealand's banking system was in crisis between 1989 and 1992 (see also Ledingham, 1995). Several foreign-owned banks had to be recapitalized by their parents, but a number of financial firms failed, one of which was a major institution: the Development Finance Corporation (DFC, in 1989). Although DFC was not a commercial bank, it was the seventh-largest financial institution in New Zealand. As the first important financial insolvency to occur in many years, the need to resolve its affairs was a systemic event that disrupted credit flows and put the viability of a few other institutions into question. Winding up its affairs took many years and absorbed a great deal of supervisory resources.

According to Brash (2000), the country's largest bank (the Bank of New Zealand) would almost certainly have failed as well if the government (as the majority shareholder at the time) had not been willing on two occasions to provide a "capital injection." The size of the second (1990) injection was disclosed to be NZ$620 million. Honohan and Klingebiel estimate that the total fiscal cost of the crisis was 1.0 percent of GDP. Although this cost is comparatively low, in dollar terms it is substantial. The policy lessons revealed by this turbulent episode prompted authorities to redesign the RBNZ's early warning system to emphasize self-reporting by directors.

Australia experienced a crisis of similar magnitude. Although it also did not offer explicit deposit insurance, its winding-up regime gave depositors preference over other creditors (a feature enacted in 1959). Authorities made minor changes in the substance of its disclosure, intervention, and detection regimes. Without triggering a whistleblowing obligation, directors of a distressed Australian bank can still stand by while managers search out and exploit loopholes that can conceal losses. Governmental intervention rights continue to depend primarily on examiners' ability to uncover and verify hidden problems. However, the Australian Stock Exchange (ASX) imposes disclosure and whistle-blowing obligations on listed banks. These obligations fall on the banking "entity" rather than specific officeholders and shift the burden of further disclosure onto the ASX.[2] This leaves the forensic accounting burden that supervisory officials must meet before they can intervene somewhat higher in Australia than in New Zealand and more subjective than in the U.S.

Although the U.S. operates an insolvency-detection regime similar to Australia's, taxpayer losses in the savings and loan debacle led Congress to beef up and mechanize regulators' intervention and winding-up rights. Along a specified ladder of positive net worth thresholds, U.S. banking law now authorizes an escalating series of interventions and requires regulators to intervene ever more strongly as a bank's accounting net worth declines. The Federal Deposit Insurance Corporation Improvement Act of 1991 instructs bank regulators to demand that banks take particularly strong corrective actions whenever their book-value net worth falls below 4 percent of assets. If these remedies fail to stop the slide in a bank's accounting net worth, regulators must order a stockholder recapitalization. If the recapitalization does not materialize or proves insufficient, authorities must — after due notice — put the bank into a receivership or conservatorship (in most circumstances) once its book-value net worth falls below 2 percent of assets. Putting stockholders on notice lets them avoid closure by injecting new capital or finding a merger partner. They should exercise one of these

---

[2]ASX Listing Rule 3.1 states: "Once an entity is or becomes aware of any information concerning it that any reasonable person would expect to have a material effect on the price or value of an entity's securities, the entity must immediately tell ASX that information."

options if they believe that N_E is still positive. The alternatives that these options offer prevent the 2 percent threshold from being characterized under common law as an "unjust taking" of private assets by the government.

APRA employs triggers for intervention as well. The process is called PAIRS/SOARS. Experts evaluate the financial health of a bank and its systemic significance. This evaluation feeds into a four-way classification scheme for calibrating the need for regulatory attention and discipline: normal; oversight; mandated improvement; and restructuring. Quantitative elements in these assessments influence but do not formally dictate APRA's response.

4.2. *Potential conflict between the Australian and New Zealand strategies for insolvency detection*

The success of any partnership depends on how much the partners disagree and how well they can handle disagreement. Potential conflict between host-country and home-country supervisors intensifies as a bank weakens. Divergences in disclosure and detection regimes allow home and host regulators to compile and react to evidence of bank weakness in different ways.

Mayes (2005) distinguishes four regimes of market and supervisory response to individual-bank accounting reports. In the first regime, market participants and supervisors are satisfied with the bank's condition and performance and impose no penalties. In the second regime, the bank manages to meet all supervisory tests, but market participants begin to impose risk premiums. In the third case, supervisors begin to be concerned and should be acting to strengthen the bank. In the fourth case, the bank is economically insolvent and authorities need to take over the bank and relicense it.

Within Mayes' third regime, home and host supervisors may not be equally concerned. Even when both sets of regulators enjoy the same acuity of vision, nationalistic norms and reputational concern might tempt home-country officials to delay insolvency resolution (Kane, 1989). Home-country delays give managers of a failing institution an opportunity to shift bad assets to the host jurisdiction. When banking problems surface during a top official's watch, his or her reputation is at risk. In some cases, agency leaders may even be grateful that accounting trickery can temporarily hide evidence of weakness from the market. Similarly, in the host country, effective action may also be delayed by the threat of career and reputational penalties that politically important foreign banks may be able to exert on particular ministers both directly and through the press.

As the home-country regulator, it is APRA's job to assess the strength of each cross-country conglomerate institution. Although rumors can speed up the process, Australia maintains a traditional zero-value accounting threshold for failing a bank or banking conglomerate. It is easy to imagine circumstances in which information transmitted by resident directors would lead the RBNZ to recognize the insolvency of an Australian bank's New Zealand subsidiary long before periodic reports and APRA's examination-based verification methods could ascertain whether the economic net worth of the Australian parent was truly strong enough to cover New Zealand losses on a consolidated basis.

These are precisely the circumstances in which preserving RBNZ intervention rights would protect New Zealand taxpayers from potential weaknesses or mistakes in Australian supervision. In cases where the conglomerate organization was in fact weak, home-country managers would not want the RBNZ to force APRA to examine their accounts more closely. Given the RBNZ policy of local incorporation, an Australian parent compliant under the supervisor's measures, but insolvent under economic measures would recognize the value of making sure that, at each quarterly reporting date, it had shuffled enough good assets to its New Zealand subsidiary to keep local accountants and directors from blowing any whistles. Backed by local directors' obligation to inform the RBNZ of any transaction than weakens a New Zealand institution, this incentive protects New Zealand taxpayers from being saddled with losses incurred in Australia. However, this protection would unravel either if Australian banks were allowed to operate in New Zealand through branch offices or if the Australian scheme for insolvency detection were simply to displace the New Zealand one.

5. Summary

Prudential regulation seeks to assure the safety and soundness of the financial sector. As institutions and markets evolve, so must processes for resolving incentive conflicts in financial transactions.

The inherited regulatory cultures of Australia and New Zealand show differences in the structure of legal authority, in their reliance on position limits and other rules, and in the technology used to monitor bank risk-taking and net worth. Lasting differences in regulatory culture evolve experimentally, as tentative solutions to recognized societal problems that prove themselves able to meet the test of time.

The persistence of substantial differences implies that authorities in the two countries have had to respond to fundamental differences in operative political, cultural, and risk-taking environments. Replacing New Zealand's financial regulatory system with that of Australia would simultaneously deny New Zealand citizens the hard-won benefits of this evolutionary process and make it hard for them to hold regulatory officials in Australia accountable politically for costs their policy decisions might impose on the Kiwi economy.

The Mishan welfare criterion tells us that trans-Tasman regulatory arrangements cannot be fairly harmonized unless and until political mechanisms can be established that enable regulators and citizens of both countries to observe and adequately discipline the tradeoffs that responsible officials make between their own and partner-country interests when these interests diverge. Only by crafting the equivalent of a strong and fair prenuptial agreement can efforts to marry the regulation of individual country banking markets be expected to succeed. At a minimum, each prenuptial agreement must impose bilateral obligations to intervene well in advance of book-value insolvency and to disclose emerging concerns to partner regulators promptly. To back up these obligations, the agreement should authorize partner regulators to sue in a neutral court to recover damages from countries whose officials appear to have violated this right.

References

Aghion, Philippe, Patrick Bolton, and Steven Fries, 1999, "Optimal Design of Bank Bailouts: The Case of Transition Economies," *Journal of Institutional and Theoretical Economics*, 55(March), pp. 51–70.

Altunbas, Yener, and David Marqués Ibáñez, 2004, "Mergers and Acquisitions and Performance in Europe: The Role of Strategic Similarities," Frankfurt: European Central Bank, Working Paper No. 398 (October).

Bank for International Settlements, Committee on Banking Regulations and Supervisory Practices, 1975, "Report to the Governors on the Supervision of Banks' Foreign Establishments (the Concordat)," Geneva (September 26).

Basel Committee on Banking Supervision, 1997, *Core Principles for Effective Banking Supervision*, Geneva (September).

———, 2001, *Core Principles: Cross-Sectional Comparison*, Geneva (November).

———, 2003, *High-Level Principles for the Cross-Border Implementation of the New Accord*, Geneva (August).

Brash, Donald T., 1996, "A New Approach to Bank Supervision," Address to the Center for the Study of Financial Innovation, London (June 5).

————, 2000, "Central Banks and Financial System Stability in an Uncertain World," Address to the Belgian Financial Forum (June 6).

Honohan, Patrick, and Daniela Klingebiel, 2003, "The Fiscal Cost Implications of an Accommodating Approach to Banking Crises," *Journal of Banking and Finance*, 27(August), pp. 1539–1560.

Joint Press Conference, 2005, "Transcript of Proceedings Featuring Michael Cullen, New Zealand Finance Minister and Peter Costello, Australian Treasurer," Wellington, NZ (February 17).

Kane, Edward J., 1989, "Changing Incentives Facing Financial-Services Regulators," *Journal of Financial Services Research*, 2(September), pp. 265–274.

Ledingham, Peter, 1995, "The Review of Bank Supervision Arrangements in New Zealand: The Main Elements in the Debate," Reserve Bank of New Zealand: *Bulletin*, 58(September), pp. 163–171.

Mayes, David G., 2005, "Crisis Resolution of Large Banks in Small Countries," Slideshow Prepared for Norges Bank Conference on Banking Crisis Resolution — Theory and Policy (June).

Mishan, E.J., 1969, *Welfare Economics: An Assessment*, Amsterdam and London: North Holland Publishing Company.

Mortlock, Geof, 2003, "New Zealand's Financial Sector Regulation," *Reserve Bank of New Zealand: Bulletin*, 66(December), pp. 5–49.

Schüler, Martin, 2003, "Incentive Problems in Banking Supervision — The European Case," Mannheim, Germany: ZEW Discussion Paper No. 03-62.

Todd, Walker, 2002, "Central Banking in a Democracy: The Problem of the Lender of Last Resort," in P.A. McCoy (ed.), *Financial Modernization after Gramm-Leach-Bliley*, Newark, NJ: Matthew Bender.

Tripe, David, 2001, "Banking Supervision by Disclosure: A Review of the New Zealand Regime," Centre for Banking Studies, Massey University, Palmerston North, NZ (unpublished).

Weston, J. Fred, Juan A. Siu, and Brian A. Johnson, 2001, *Takeovers, Restructuring, and Corporate Governance*, Third Edition. Upper Saddle River, NJ: Prentice-Hall Inc.

Woolford, Ian, and Adrian Orr, 2005, "The Limits to Hospitality," *The Financial Regulator*, 10(June), pp. 41–46.

Edward J. Kane is the James F. Cleary Professor in Finance at Boston College. For helpful comments on earlier drafts, the author wants to thank Richard C. Aspinwall, David Mayes, numerous staff members at the Reserve Bank of New Zealand, and seminar audiences at Victoria University at Wellington.

Market Discipline Issues and Cross-Border Banking: A Nordic Perspective

Thorvald Grung Moe*

Norges Bank

1. Cross-Border Banking Poses New Challenges

Cross-border[1] banking is on the rise. Large, cross-border banks have been established in the Nordic, Baltic, and Benelux countries. Banco Santander's takeover of Abbey National made headline news, and the bid by the Dutch bank ABN Amro for the ninth largest Italian bank Antonveneta was front-page news for months.

As cross-border banks increase in size, it is relevant to ask if stakeholders in these megamergers banks are exposed to the true risks involved, or if they expect the financial safety net to bail them out — should a crisis occur. National authorities could also be exposed in case of a failure in a cross-border bank, but the potential liability facing taxpayers has so far been masked by unclear home–host responsibilities for cross-border banks.

Crisis resolution in a cross-border bank is obviously the responsibility of the bank's owners and management, but previous banking crises have shown that authorities must also have contingency arrangements in place. Cross-border banks pose new challenges for policymakers. Goodhart (2005) has noted that "the interaction of an internationally inter-penetrated banking

---

[1]The term "cross-border banking" will be used here to encompass bank's establishments abroad as either branches or subsidiaries; that is, other representation forms such as direct cross-border lending or lending via a representative office are excluded. Why banks choose to establish overseas offices, or why they choose a specific representation form is not discussed further. See Dermine (2003) for a discussion of these issues.

system with national regulations and burden allocation could well turn out to be a dangerously weak institutional feature."

The policy response has been to seek greater clarity in roles and responsibilities. Supervisory convergence and coordinated liquidity provision are being discussed among supervisors and central banks. Clarke (2005) even asks if an international liquidity concordat for large cross-border banks should be considered. But is this drive for convergence and agreement on intervention principles realistic? And is it desirable? What if greater clarity about roles and responsibilities were to weaken market discipline?

In the following, I review some of the issues involved and discuss their possible impact on market discipline. Most of the home–host discussion has so far been centered on supervisory issues. There has been less attention to the role of central banks, especially in cross-border crisis resolution. I refer to some of the issues that have been discussed among the Nordic central banks. I conclude that international agreements on crisis resolution and burden sharing will be hard to achieve. Private sector solutions should therefore be promoted, while public authorities should take measures that will make their non-intervention policy credible.

2. Market Discipline Requires a Credible No-Bailout Policy

There is broad agreement that market discipline should be enhanced. Market discipline has the potential to reinforce capital regulation and other supervisory efforts to promote safety and soundness in cross-border banks. This has been recognized in the new capital accord, pillar 3. The Basel Committee "believes that market discipline, supported by an appropriate public disclosure regime, can be an effective complement to supervisory efforts to encourage banks to assess risk, maintain capital and develop and maintain sound risk management systems and practices".[2]

Mayes and Llewellyn (2003) argue that market discipline can be a useful complement to prompt corrective action (PCA) by the authorities in handling problem banks. If the conditions are right, market discipline can reinforce the PCA rule, and limit the scope for discretionary intervention. However, as Llewellyn (2005) notes "market discipline is still somewhat of a "black box" and its precise mechanisms are not always clear." Several conditions have to be met for market discipline to work and "central to

---

[2]Basel Committee Consultative Document, January 2001, para. 7.

the effectiveness of market discipline is the requirement that stakeholders should be exposed to losses if a bank fails," that is, there has to be a credible no-bailout policy.

The idea behind market discipline is actually quite simple. By trying to avoid big losses, stakeholders will put pressure on the management of the financial institutions to avoid excessive risk taking. The size of the losses will, however, depend on the authorities' actions in troubled times. The two polar cases are (1) that the authorities will not allow the stakeholders to lose money at all, or (2) that the authorities will allow the bank to fail, leaving the stakeholders to pick up the entire bill. The effect of market discipline will therefore depend on the authorities' resolution strategies, as perceived by the stakeholders.

During the Norwegian banking crisis the equity capital of the affected banks was written down to zero, but uninsured creditors were on the whole not affected (see Moe, Solheim, and Vale, 2004). Uninsured creditors were not affected in the banking crises in Finland or Sweden either, since blanket guarantees were issued. Similar experiences in other countries have led investors to expect public bailouts or excessive forbearance.[3] If bank creditors expect to be bailed out, then the pricing of the securities they hold in banks will not reflect the true risk of default. If these banks expand overseas, investors may continue to expect to be bailed out, even though their risk exposure has increased.

Amihud, de Long, and Saunders (2001) show that this is not necessarily the case. They find that investors expect domestic regulators to assist domestic banks, but not the foreign operations of their own domestic banks or the domestic operations of foreign banks. This is consistent with U.S. regulatory practice. The situation in Europe is slightly different. Table 1 show that some large cross-border banking groups have the same (long-term) rating for home and host banks, while some host banks have lower ratings. Many investors thus expect the parent bank or the authorities to assist the host bank should it get into difficulties. But are these realistic expectations? Could it be that investors are counting on assistance that will not be forthcoming? To answer these questions, it is instructive to review the current status of the home–host discussion.

---

[3]Hanweck *et al.* (2005) shows that strong forbearance expectations could cancel out the disciplining effect of a mandatory subordinated debt rule.

Table 1. Fitch long term ratings

	Home	Host
Nordea (SE)	AA−	
Nordea Norway		AA−
Fortis (BE)	AA−	
Fortis Netherland		AA−
Dexia (BE)	AA+	
Dexia Slovenia		A+
ING (NL)	AAA	
ING Belgium		AA−

3. Who Is "Responsible" for Resolving a Financial Crisis in a Cross-Border Bank?

The responsibility for resolving a financial crisis in a cross-border bank clearly lies with the affected bank.[4] Owners and managers should ensure that the bank does not end up in a critical financial situation and they also have the main responsibility for managing any crises that might arise.[5] However, previous banking crises have shown that authorities must also have contingency arrangements in place.

The division of responsibilities between authorities in different countries for crisis resolution in subsidiary banks and branches of foreign banks has not really been adjusted to accommodate large cross-border banks.[6] Basel 2 has brought more attention to the home–host issue, for example, in the context of validation of internal rating models and operational risk capital. European banking supervisors have also made progress in developing guidelines for home–host cooperation (see Committee on European Banking Supervisors, 2005). However, despite the increased attention, there remain at least three contentious issues:

- Who is responsible for handling a crisis in a subsidiary bank?

[4]For a broader discussion of this issue, see Borchgrevink and Moe (2004).
[5]This principle was adhered to during the Norwegian banking crisis in the early 1990s, when the share capital was written down to zero before the Government committed new funds, Moe (2004).
[6]See for example Lastra (2003) and Herring (2004).

- What is the role for the host state authorities if a systemic branch gets into difficulties?[7]
- Will small states be able to shoulder the resolution burden of a large cross-border bank?

Crisis resolution in a subsidiary. The Basel Committee has addressed the issue of home–host responsibility for subsidiaries in a cross-border banking structure in several reports (1996, 1999, and 2001). The potential tension between home and host regulators arises when cross-border banks transcend national boundaries and operate with global control along global business lines. If the group is allowed to "hollow out" the subsidiary, the host regulator may eventually end up being responsible for only a *de facto* branch.[8] There have been two recent responses to this process. In New Zealand, the central bank has tried to restrict the hollowing out process by requiring foreign banks to appoint local boards and retain core competencies.[9] In Europe, on the other hand, the home ("consolidated") supervisor is supposed to coordinate and sort out any differences with the various host supervisors. The banking industry has advocated a more centralized approach ("lead supervisor"), but the resistance from host supervisors has so far prevailed; see European Financial Services Roundtable (2004). The UK Treasury (2005) noted recently that "… any proposals for significant radical changes to the division of legal responsibilities between home and host supervisory authorities should be approached with great care and are unlikely to be feasible."

In the Nordic countries, the development of the Nordea group has led to similar discussions among the responsible authorities. A central bank working group was established in 2000 to review policies for a liquidity crisis in a large cross-border bank. In 2002, a joint crisis simulation exercise was undertaken together with the Nordic supervisory agencies. The

---

[7]We use the term "host" here to encompass both "branch host" and "subsidiary host". Since a subsidiary is in fact licensed and supervised in the host country, it has previously been common to designate this country as the "home" country for the bank. There has recently been a shift towards the term "subsidiary host", reflecting the de facto shift in responsibilities that has taken place.

[8]See IMF (2004) for an interesting discussion of measures to counter such a development.

[9]The Australian owned subsidiaries are in fact previous branches that were considered to be systemic by the RBNZ, and the new regulation then required them to incorporate in New Zealand.

exercise illustrated that "ring fencing" could easily block a joint crisis solution. A regional memorandum of understanding (MoU) was later signed among the central bank governors. Similar agreements have been signed among the Nordic supervisors. The MoU deals primarily with procedures for information exchange, and clarifies who should take the lead if a large cross-border bank should get into trouble. The MoU does not spell out who would be directly responsible for solving a crisis. The home country central bank, Riksbanken, has so far been reluctant to acknowledge any formal responsibility for liquidity provision in a crisis, as such a statement could create moral hazard problems. In fact, it (Riksbanken, 2003a) even notes that "... it is unlikely that the home country would be willing to bear any costs associated with a rescue. Instead, the host country may be forced to ensure in some way that the foreign group's operations will continue."

Box 1

The Nordea group

Nordea is a Nordic bank with a subsidiary structure founded on the four previously independent Nordic banks Merita Bank, Nordbanken, Unibank and Christiania Bank og Kreditkasse, from Finland, Sweden, Denmark and Norway, respectively. The banking group has market shares of between 15 and 40 percent in the four countries. The bank currently operates as a group of legally independent subsidiaries, but with business segments and risk control managed across the legal structure and across country borders. The HQ of Nordea bank was moved from Finland to Sweden in 2003. Nordea has announced plans to convert the current subsidiary banks into branches and to establish itself as a European company.

Serious liquidity problems in a large cross border bank — like Nordea Norway (described in Box 1) — should in my view primarily be solved by the parent bank and if required be supported by the home country authorities. The fact that the subsidiary is a fully owned entity should facilitate an efficient crisis resolution. Liquidity support from the host central bank is unlikely, since the parent bank has equity, funding and reputation at stake. If the parent bank should fail to support its subsidiary, one would expect the bank to be insolvent and LLR support will not be an appropriate instrument. I consider this position to be in line with the recent drift towards a more leading role for the home supervisor, but recognize at the same time that the parent bank in an extreme situation may decide to abandon its subsidiary, see Tschoegl (2004).[10] Thus, the situation is quite confused today as to whom will actually assist a subsidiary in a crisis — if any.

Crisis resolution in a branch. Crisis resolution should be more straight-forward in a branch structure. The home supervisor is responsible for the whole group,[11] and the deposit insurance scheme covers all depositors, including foreign deposits.[12] A branch establishment is often used by cross-border banks dealing in wholesale markets, as the branch can then draw on the group's combined financial strength in its operations. Branches have so far been less common in other market segments and subsidiary structures continue to dominate cross-border banking.[13] However, recent EU legislation now paves the way for branch establishments and this has intensified the discussion about crisis resolution responsibilities in a branch structured cross-border bank, especially which role the host authorities will have if a systemic branch gets into difficulties?[14]

The host-country authorities have generally little influence over crisis management in a branch bank. They may therefore be interested in gaining more influence and responsibility for crisis solutions affecting their branches, especially if the branch is large. In New Zealand, the authorities responded to this situation by instructing all systemically important branches in the country with total assets in excess of NZ$10 billion to re-establish as subsidiaries. A similar solution is not feasible in Europe, where the system is based on freedom of establishment and home-country super-vision of banks. A home authority can therefore in theory decide to close a host bank, without considerations for financial stability in that country.

---

[10]Tschoegl (2004) describes the limited liability of the parent bank as "an option to abandon with the strike price being the loss of reputation if it walks away". Hüpkes (2005) also discusses the likelihood of parental support, p. 31.

[11]The host supervisor retains formally some responsibility for liquidity supervision, but this function is in practice often left to the home supervisor.

[12]With the well-known exceptions of US and Australia, where *depositor preferential* gives national depositors preferential treatment.

[13]For a discussion of why banks choose branch or subsidiary structure, see Dermine (2003) and Huizinga (2003).

[14]Freixas (2003) shows that the home-country authorities do not have the incentives to contribute to an optimal crisis solution if only host countries are affected. However, Calzolari and Loranth (2005) find, in another model, that the incentive to monitor are maximal with a branch structure, as the home bank is more affected by failures in the host branches than with a subsidiary structure.

In practice, such decisions will be taken after close consultations between home and host authorities.[15]

The Committee on European Banking Supervisors (2005) has recently issued a consultation document with guidelines for home–host coordination. The home supervisor should communicate *essential information* to the host supervisor, if that information "could materially influence another Member State's assessment of the financial soundness of a credit institution." The home supervisor should in addition communicate other *relevant information* on request. This is a pragmatic approach to cross-border cooperation that could give the host supervisors a more substantial role in crisis resolution and enable them to contribute to an efficient crisis resolution. But increased involvement by host authorities in supervision and crisis resolution could also weaken the key role of the home authorities in crisis resolution and increase investors' expectations of a host assisted bailout.

Nordea's planned move to a branch structure has highlighted the difficulties in reaching cross-border agreements among the affected authorities. Since Nordea has a large market share in most of the Nordic countries, the host authorities have requested assurances that they will be actively involved in supervision and crisis resolution in a new branch structure bank. So far no new agreements have been signed among the Nordic supervisors or central banks. Nordea's planned transition to a branch structure has also been postponed until at least 2007.

Are cross-border banks "too-large-to-save"? If the cross-border banking group is large in relation to its home country, the home country may be unwilling to support the foreign parts of the groups, should they require support. Dermine (2000) showed that the cost of a public bailout in some small countries (Belgium, the Netherlands, and Switzerland) would be spread over a smaller tax base, thus putting these countries at a competitive disadvantage. Table 2, from BankScope, shows that the cost of a bailout could be relatively large in relation to gross domestic product (GDP).

If these financial groups are organized in a subsidiary structure, limited liability reduces the potential exposure of the parent bank and/or the home authorities. But the reputation risk of non-intervention could be damaging for the group as a whole, thus forcing the authorities hand in a public bailout. The home responsibility is even more direct in a branch structure, but the

---

[15]Several new member states in EU have banking sectors that are dominated by foreign banks, often branches. These countries have been vocal in getting the home–host coordination issue on the agenda in Committee on European Banking Supervisors.

Table 2. Bank equity capital in relation to home country

	Equity (book value) € billion 2004	Equity/GDP
UBS	26.1	9.1
Credit Suisse	24.9	8.6
ABN	16.2	3.5
ING	15.7	3.4
Fortis	18.0	6.3
Dexia	11.5	4.0
Santander	40.9	4.9
Nordea	11.8	4.2

parent bank or the authorities would surely try to share the fiscal burden with the host authorities. Nyberg (2003) thus notes that:

> According to current EU legislation, prudential supervision and crisis management would in principle be an issue for Swedish authorities. But would the Finnish authorities accept that Sweden takes responsibility for the most important part of the Finnish financial system? And would we in Sweden be willing to resolve a banking crisis in Finland, with all that it would ask of the Swedish taxpayers, if Nordea were to run into difficulties? The answers to these questions are not straightforward.

The Swedish Deposit Guarantee Board (2003) has also noted that "... a possible solution (to the excessive burden on the home scheme) could be to revise the deposit guarantee directive and put more of the financing burden for host depositors on the host guarantee scheme." The European Deposit Guarantee Scheme is currently under review, partly to address some of these issues, but a change in responsibilities along the lines suggested above seems unlikely.

Where does this leave us with regard to crisis resolution responsibility? In my view, financial difficulties in a foreign-owned bank should be resolved by the parent bank and if required be supported by the home country authorities. The home authorities may not necessarily share this view,

Table 3. Home country's position on public support for a large cross border bank

STRUCTURE	
Branch	reluctant
Subsidiary	unwilling
Small home country	unable

as they may be reluctant or unwilling to support a rescue of the host bank, especially if the resolution costs are high (Table 3). If the bank is large in the home country, the authorities may even be unable to support the bank, should a crisis occur.

The roles and responsibilities for crisis resolution are therefore rather fluid at the moment. Is this bad for market discipline? Not necessarily so, if investors hold "true" forbearance expectations in the face of this uncertainty. But can we really expect them to see though this cloud of "resolution ambiguity" and price "correctly"? Not very likely, if they have adaptive expectations and recall how the last banking crises were resolved. Hanweck *et al.* (2002) indeed show that "lengthy forbearance expectations still seem to prevail, despite a legislative mandate to the contrary."

4. Who Will Provide LLR to a Cross-Border Bank?

Much of the "home–host" discussions have so far primarily dealt with the division of responsibilities between national supervisory authorities. There has been less discussion about the division of labor between central banks in liquidity provision to a cross-border bank in financial difficulties. This is strange, given that it is only central banks (or the national treasuries) that can provide funds to resolve a cross border banking crisis. However, this is a delicate field and the prospects of getting central banks to agree on *ex ante* principles for liquidity provision seem remote. Central bank lender-of-last-resort (LLR) policies vary so much, from those that have published their policies, like the Bank of Canada (2004), Norges Bank (2004) and Riksbanken (2003b), to those central banks that do not have an official LLR view or simply rely on "constructive ambiguity".

Johnston *et al.* (2003) observed that there were different views on LLR policies among the Nordic central banks, and they recommended that the authorities should "seek a greater cross-border harmonization of approaches to distinguishing between liquidity and solvency problems, as well as to the implementation of ELA."

This advice is in line with the classic policy for emergency liquidity assistance advocated by Bagehot, that central banks should provide unlimited liquidity against good collateral in a crisis. However, if the risk of liquidity provision is thus lowered, why cannot central banks agree on cross-border liquidity provision? The answer is obvious; the distinction between solvency and liquidity is hard to define, especially in a crisis, and as a consequence most LLR operations will be fraught with credit risk, see Clarke (2005). This is also why emergency liquidity provision to a large cross-border bank is unlikely without some involvement of the Treasury; see Goodhart (2005) and Huertas (2005). But negotiating burden sharing between national Treasuries in the midst of a banking crisis is not likely to be a quick process. The risk is that politicians could be faced with bailout as the only viable policy option to avoid a cross border systemic banking crisis.

On the other hand, the politicians or authorities may be reluctant (or prohibited) to risk taxpayers' money to guarantee stability for a failing bank in another country. A possible "solution" could be to limit assistance to those banks affected by the failed bank. This solution has actually been advocated by the Riksbank (2003a)[16]:

> One important consequence of the conclusion that not even one of the major banks is always important in itself for the functioning of the financial system is that one of these banks can be declared bankrupt if the potential contagion risks can be managed. On condition that a bankruptcy would only give rise to contagion effects in the form of liquidity problems, the Riksbank can manage these by providing ELA to other banks affected by the failing bank's payment default. In this way the functioning of the financial system can be maintained.

But if the home central bank were to follow such an LLR policy, would it not weaken the home supervisors leading role in crisis resolution?

---

[16]See also Rochet and Tirole (1996) for an early argument along these lines.

5. Can the Authorities Credibly Commit to a No-Bailout Policy?

Market discipline would clearly be strengthened if the home authorities could in fact commit to a no-bailout policy in cross border banks. But such a hard commitment is not credible if the banks can be struck by common macroeconomic shocks, like recessions, asset market crashes and the like. A fixed policy rules may then break down, even if the authorities would like to disengage. If the crisis erupts suddenly and spreads rapidly, a policy of no-bailout may even be less feasible.

Rochet (2004) suggests that the government's commitment problem could be resolved by an independent supervisor, in combination with a rule that would allocate liquidity loans only to banks with low exposure to systematic macro risk. However, the question remains what the authorities would do if a large cross-border bank with macro exposures actually failed.

The cost of non-intervention, that is, the impact on the real economy, will be a key variable when the government reviews various resolution options. But as policy makers are well aware, this is a difficult variable to quantify. Nevertheless, the decisions by deposit insurers and central banks should in principle be based on such calculations. In the recent review of Norges Bank's lender of last resort policies, our board thus stated that emergency liquidity assistance "should be restricted to situations where financial stability may be threatened if such support is not provided;" see Norges Bank (2004).

If estimates of the economic costs of a banking crisis are hard to compile during a crisis, they are no easier to calculate after the crisis. Estimates for the economic cost of the Norwegian banking crisis in the 1990s vary between 7 percent and 27 percent of GDP, depending on the methodology used; see Moe, Vale and Solheim (2004). We concluded that "it is necessary to explore different methods of output loss estimation in order to see how robust the estimates to changes in methodology are." In practice, the decision to intervene in a crisis will be taken on the basis of the best available data "there-and-then", with a potential bias in favor of intervention due to the fear of systemic contagion.

Kane (2005a) has been concerned about this bias in favor of public intervention and has suggested that standstills could be employed during a crisis "to allow government forensic analysts and private auditors to assess the depth and character of troubled bank's wounds." This would enable the government to sort out the good banks from the bad ("hopelessly insolvent zombie institutions") and eliminate the need for blanket guarantees. Others have pointed out that such standstills are unrealistic in today's electronic around-the-world trading environment, and that authorities can not even hope to get a week-end to sort out an acute banking crisis.

This is an empirical question. Experience from Argentine would suggest that the economic fallout of a prolonged banking holiday was indeed large, while experience from Sweden indicates that a developed economy could manage without banking services for some time.[17] However, many would hold the view that government intervention is almost inevitable if a banking crisis becomes systemic. But "systemic" is a vague term that can easily be used as an excuse for government intervention. The challenge is obviously to avoid the temptation of (too) early an intervention.

Pre-commitment to non-intervention will always be problematic in a world with intrinsic uncertainty, see Kohn (2005). Faced with a sudden crisis in a large cross-border bank, the authorities will have to improvise in uncharted territory. Somehow we need to take account of this "fact of life" in a more ruled-based approach to crisis management. At the same time, the authorities should be able to increase the credibility of a no-bailout policy by continuing their work on risk proofing of the financial infrastructure, see Huertas (2005). This would include reviews of concentration risk and outsourcing policies. The question is whether a policy of no-bailout can be a credible policy if only one or two large banks dominate the domestic banking market?

6. Preconditions for Market Discipline to Succeed

Shareholders have been exposed to losses in many recent banking crises. Uninsured creditors have not been so much exposed. Investors have high forbearance expectations based on past experience. Crisis resolution methods involving blanket guarantees have reinforced such expectations; see Kane (2005b). Ingves (2005) has argued that such guarantees may sometimes be required in a force majeure situation to prevent a "financial meltdown." The obvious response is to avoid situations where such policies have to be

---

[17]A labor dispute led to a week long bank holiday in the late 1990s. There were no reports of major difficulties, although it should be noted that the non-availability in banking services were known in advance.

considered. Thus, both Ingves and Kane agree that we should work harder to reduce the likelihood of a systemic crisis (PD) or reduce the cost of a crisis (LGD) — should it occur. Only by reducing the potential negative impact on the real economy can the authorities credibly adhere to a policy on non-intervention.

Recent policy initiatives have explored ways to involve all creditor groups in a bank resolution strategy. They should provide better incentives for investors and thereby lessen the fiscal burden of a bank restructuring operation. The bank creditor recapitalization (BCR) initiative by the Reserve Bank of New Zealand is an innovative scheme that aims for a rapid crisis solution with uniform haircuts; see White and Ledingham (2005). Mayes, Halme, and Liuksila (2001) have proposed something similar, with the authorities stepping in and distributing the losses across creditors in order to re-open the bank quickly for business without any material interruption in trading.

These initiatives are interesting and point in the right direction. However, if they were applied to large cross-border banks, issues of different bankruptcy laws and burden sharing between different jurisdictions could topple an otherwise efficient crisis resolution model. As Goodhart (2005) observes "... if it is difficult to allocate burden sharing when losses have been suffered internally within a country, it will be many times more difficult to do so internationally".

The development of a new crisis resolution model should therefore be supplemented by other measures that will both reduce the likelihood of a crisis or reduce the cost of a crisis:

- **Large cross-border banks should be required to hold ample capital**, reflecting the large perceived negative externalities associated with a failure in such a bank. The "Swiss finish" is an interesting example of this policy: The Swiss authorities hold that banks in Switzerland are not over-capitalized, even with a capital adequacy that is 20 percent to 50 percent above the Basel requirements (see Zuberbühler, 2004).

- **The parent bank's commitment and funding strategy for the rest of the cross-border group should be clearly spelled out,** as part of its disclosure policy, ref. pillar 3. This would reduce the scope for parent "constructive ambiguity", especially regarding its responsibility for liquidity to overseas subsidiaries in a crisis. The parent bank could also pre-commit lines-of-credit to alleviate the need for official emergency assistance.

- **Large cross-border banks could contribute to a joint ("insurance") fund** that would act as an international, private safety net in the event of a serious financial crisis. Such a fund could provide support to a cross-border systemically important bank, much like the pooling arrangements that have been established for the UK payment system, Bank of England (2003).
- **National deposit insurance schemes need to be realistically funded with risk-based premiums.** If home schemes cover large groups of overseas depositors, this needs to be officially acknowledged and the potential liabilities to the home taxpayers spelled out clearly. Then at least the country's taxpayers would be aware of the liabilities facing them (see Nyberg, 2005).
- **Deposit insurance coverage could be lowered for large cross-border banks** to reduce the scope for free riding on the official safety net. There is a widespread perception that large cross border banks pursue scale in order to become too big to fail (see Kane, 2000). To counter this incentive, a system of co-insurance could also be introduced. A more radical proposal would be to limit insured deposit taking in these banking groups to "narrow bank" affiliates (see Wilmarth, Jr., 2002).
- **National financial infrastructures should be further risk-proofed** to reduce the negative effects of a failure in a large cross-border bank. Great progress has already been made in reducing systemic risk in national and international payment systems (see Huertas, 2005). However, some large banks hold market shares that make them almost too big to fail. Hüpkes (2004) suggests that national authorities should adopt a functional approach and try to protect only the functions that are systemically important.

7. How to Harness Market Discipline in Cross-Border Banking

To sum up, market discipline can only work if stakeholders are exposed to losses if a bank fails. But investors seem to hold strong forbearance expectations, despite legislative mandates to the contrary. The expansion of cross border banks continues, even though the synergies are hard to detect (see Nicoló *et al.*, 2004). This has led to a concern that cross-border banks are reaching for size to qualify for safety net subsidies. However, many cross-border banks have outgrown their national jurisdictions and should rather be considered as "too big to save."

If crisis resolution in a large cross-border bank is too large to handle for the authorities in one country, the natural response would be to arrange a multi-country burden sharing. But, as Goodhart (2004) has observed: "There is no mechanism in place to devise a generally acceptable sharing of burdens from international (banking) crises ... Can we rely on voluntary co-operation and co-ordination between the countries involved under such crisis circumstances? Frankly I am doubtful."

A coordinated resolution could perhaps work if only a few countries were affected, but crisis resolution exercises have shown that even this can be hard to achieve. It is not obvious that taxpayers in one country will be happy to bail out the banks of other countries. Thus, as Gros (2003) observed "... the first step the authorities should discuss when a bank crisis arises is how to arrive at good private solutions."

If a crisis comes quickly, there will inevitably be strong pressure for official intervention and liquidity support by central banks. To avoid a "blackmail" situation, authorities need to strengthen their early-warning capabilities and take prompt corrective action to avoid such situations in the first place. But most importantly, they need to take steps to make a no-bailout policy credible. Only then can market discipline be relied upon to harness the expansion of cross-border banks.

References

Amihud, Yakov, Gayle L. DeLong, and Anthony Saunders, 2001, "The Geographic Location of Risk and Cross-Border Bank Mergers," draft paper.

Bank of Canada, 2004, "Bank of Canada Lender-of-Last-Resort Policies," *Financial System Review*, December 2004, pp. 49–55.

Bank of England, 2003, "Strengthening Financial Infrastructure," *Financial Stability Review*, 15.

Basel Committee, 1996, "The Supervision of Cross-Border Banking."

Basel Committee/Joint Forum, 1999, "Supervision of Financial Conglomerates."

Basel Committee/Group of Ten, 2001a, "Report on Consolidation in the Financial Sector."

Basel Committee, 2001b, "Consultative Document: Pillar 3 (Market Discipline)."

Borchgrevink, H., and Thorvald G. Moe, 2004, "Crisis Management in Cross-border Banking," *Norges Bank Economic Bulletin*, 3/04.

Calzolari, Giacomo, and Gyongyi Loranth, 2005, "Regulation of Multinational Banks — A Theoretical Inquiry," ECB Working Paper Series, no. 431.

Committee on European Banking Supervisors, 2005, "Guidelines for Cooperation between Consolidating Supervisors and Host Supervisors."

Clarke, Alastair, 2004, "Challenges for Financial Stability Policy," *Economic Affairs*, December, pp. 41–46.

De Nicolo, G., P. Bartholomew, J. Zaman, and M. Zephirin, 2004, "Bank Consolidation, Internationalization, and Conglomeration: Trends and Implications for Financial Risk," *Financial Markets, Institutions and Instruments*, pp. 173–217.

Dermine, Jean, 2000, "Bank Mergers in Europe, the Public Policy Issues," *Journal of Common Market Studies*, pp. 409–425.

Dermine, Jean, 2003, "Banking in Europe: Past, Present, and Future," in Gaspard, Hartmann, and Sleijpen (ed.): *The Transformation of the European Financial System*, ECB.

European Financial Services Roundtable, 2004, "Towards a Lead Supervisor for Cross-Border Financial Institutions in the European Union."

Economic and Financial Committee, 2000, "Report on Financial Stability" (Brouwer I report).

Economic and Financial Committee, 2001, "Report on Financial Crisis Management" (Brouwer II report).

Freixas, Xavier, 2003, "Crisis Management in Europe," in Jeroen Kremers, Dirk Schoenmaker, and Peter Wierts (ed.): *Financial Supervision in Europe*, Edward Elgar.

Goodhart, Charles A. E., 2004, "Some New Directions for Financial Stability?" Per Jacobsson lecture, BIS.

Goodhart, Charles, A. E., 2005, "How Far Can a Central Bank Act as a Lender of Last Resort Independently of Treasury (Ministry of Finance) Support?," draft paper for Norges Bank conference on Banking Crisis Resolution — Theory and Policy, June 2005.

Gros, Daniel, 2003, "Comments," Comments on Andrea Enria and Jukka Vesala: "Externalities in Supervision: The European Case". In Jeroen Kremers, Dirk Schoenmaker, and Peter Wierts (ed.): *Financial Supervision in Europe*, Edward Elgar.

Hanweck, Gerald A., and Lewis J. Spellman, 2002, "Forbearance Expectations and the Subordinated Debt Signal of Bank Insolvency," Paper presented at the fall 2004 Research Conference, FDIC.

Herring, Richard, 2004, "International financial conglomerates: Implications for bank insolvency regimes," Unpublished working paper presented in London Financial Regulation Seminar series, London School of Economics, 2004.

HM Treasury, FSA, and Bank of England, 2005, "Supervising Financial Services in an Integrated European Single Market: A Discussion Paper."

Hüpkes, Eva, 2005, "Insolvency — Why a Special Regime for Banks?" in *Current Developments in Monetary and Financial Law*, Volume 3, IMF (2005).

Hüpkes, Eva, 2004, "Protect Functions, Not Institutions," *Financial Regulator*, December 2004.

Huertas, Thomas F., 2005, "Dealing with Distress in Financial Conglomerates," Speech at the Fed/IMF/World Bank Conference in Washington, June 2005.

Huizinga, Harry, 2003, "Comment," Comment on Dermine (2003). In Gaspard, Hartmann, and Sleijpen (ed.): *The Transformation of the European Financial System*, ECB, pp. 97–116.

Ingves, Stefan, 2005, "Blanket Guarantees — A Necessary Resolution Tool? The IMF View," Presentation at Norges Bank conference on Banking Crisis Resolution — Theory and Policy, June 2005.

Joint Forum on Financial Conglomerates, 1999, "Supervision of Financial Conglomerates."

Johnston, R. Barry, Balázs Horváth, Luca Errico, and Jingqing Chai, "Large and Complex Financial Institutions: Challenges and Policy Responses — Lesson from Sweden," IMF Policy Discussion Paper, PDP/03/1.

IMF, 2004, *New Zealand: Financial Sector Assessment Program*, pp. 26–27.

Kahn, Charles M., and João A. C. Santos, 2004, "Allocating Bank Regulatory Powers: Lender of Last Resort, Deposit Insurance and Supervision," Unpublished paper.

Kane, Edward, 2000, "Incentives for Banking Mega Mergers: What Motives Might Regulators Infer from Event-Study Evidence?" *Journal of Money, Credit, and Banking*, 32(3), pp. 671–701.

Kane, Edward, 2005a, "Containing a Systemic Crisis: Relicensing vs. Blanket Guarantees," Presentation at RBNZ Conference on Banking Crisis Management.

Kane, Edward, 2005b, "Alternatives to Blanket Guarantees," Presentation at Norges Bank conference on Banking Crisis Resolution — Theory and Policy, June 2005.

Kohn, Donald L., 2005, "Crisis Management: The Known, the Unknown, and the Unknowable," Speech at the Wharton/Sloan/Mercer Oliver Wyman Institute Conference on Financial Risk Management in Practice.

Lastra, Rosa Maria, 2003, "Cross-Border Bank Insolvency: Legal Implications in the Case of Banks Operating in Different Jurisdictions in Latin America," *Journal of International Economic Law*, 6(1), pp. 79–110.

Llewellyn, David T., 2005, "Inside the 'Black Box' of Market Discipline," *Economic Affairs*, March.

Mayes, David G., and David T. Llewellyn, 2003, "The Role of Market Discipline in Handling Problem Banks," Bank of Finland Discussion Papers 21/2003.

Mayes, David G., Liisa Halme, and Aarno Liuksila, 2001, *Improving Banking Supervision*, Palgrave.

Moe, Thorvald Grung, Jon A. Solheim, and Bent Vale (eds.), 2004, "The Norwegian Banking Crisis," Norges Bank Occasional Paper No 33.

Moe, Thorvald Grung, 2004, "Norway's Banking Crisis: How Oslo Got it Right," *Financial Regulator*.

Norges Bank, 2004, "Norges Bank's Role in the Event of Liquidity Crises in the Financial Sector," *Financial Stability Report*, 2, pp. 36–37.

Nyberg, Lars, 2003, "Current Financial Stability Issues," Speech at The Riksdag Standing Committee on Finance.

Nyberg, Lars, 2005, "Financing of Deposit Insurance — A Central Banker's Perspective," Speech.

Riksbanken, 2003a, "Financial Integration and Responsibility for Financial System Stability in the EU," *Financial Stability Report*, 2, p. 86.

Riksbanken, 2003b, "The Riksbank's Role as Lender of Last Resort," *Financial Stability Report*, 2, p. 69.

Rochet, Jean-Charles, 2004, "Macroeconomic Shocks and Banking Supervision," *Journal of Financial Stability*, 1, pp. 93–110.

Rochet, Jean-Charles, and Jean Tirole, 1996, "Interbank Lending and Systemic Risk," *Journal of Money, Credit, and Banking*, pp. 733–762.

Swedish Deposit Guarantee Board, 2003, "Promemorian Europabolag" (Ds 2003:15).

Tschoegl, Adrian E., 2004, "Financial Crises and the Presence of Foreign Banks," Wharton Financial Institutions Center, Working Paper 03/35, p. 17.

Wilmarth, Arthur E. Jr., 2002, "Controlling Systemic Risk in an Era of Financial Consolidation," Paper at IMF Seminar on Current Developments in Monetary and Financial Law, Washington, D.C.

White, Bruce, and Peter Ledingham, 2005, "Resolving Systemically Important Banks," Presentation at RBNZ Conference on Banking Crisis Management.

Zuberbühler, Daniel, 2004, "Implementation of Basel II in Switzerland," Swiss Federal Banking Commission, Press Conference, 29 April 2004.

Thorvald Grung Moe is a Special Adviser in the Financial Stability Wing in Norges Bank (the Central Bank of Norway). The views expressed are those of the author and not necessarily the views of Norges Bank. This paper has benefited from useful comments by Bent Vale and Arild Lund.

Cross-Border Banking, Market Discipline and the Ability to Stand Alone

Juan Pablo Graf*
Banco de México

Pascual O'Dogherty
Banco de México

1. The Impact of Foreign Direct Investment on Host-Countries' Financial Systems

Over the course of the last decade, several countries have lifted their restrictions on foreign direct investment in their financial systems. As a result, foreign ownership of domestic institutions has been growing rapidly. Major international financial entities have acquired banks in many Latin American as well as Central and Eastern European countries. In places as diverse as Finland, Poland, New Zealand, and Mexico, foreign banks nowadays control more than 50 percent of the banking sector's assets (see Table 1). In many countries, foreign direct investment in the financial system is significant. In fact, as Table 1 demonstrates, foreign-owned banks rank among the top five banks in many of the host countries.

The entry of foreign direct investment brings several benefits to local financial systems and their respective economies. Some benefits are the result of efficiency gains stemming from new technologies, products, and management techniques. Others can be attributed to the increased resiliency of foreign-owned banks to local business cycles and their potential access to overseas resources. In some cases, foreign investment has been crucial to recapitalizing failing banking systems after major crises. The presence of foreign banks also benefits host-country economies as banks' credit gets allocated in more efficient and competitive ways. In countries where wealth is highly concentrated, bank owners and large entrepreneurs are usually

Table 1. Foreign bank's participation in emerging markets

Country	Market Share of all Foreign Banks*	Foreign Banks Among Top 5 Banks		
		Number	Market Share*	Market Share* of Listed Banks**
Argentina	27%	2	14%	8%
Bolivia	27%	2	25%	0%
Brasil	21%	0	0%	0%
Chile	39%	2	31%	31%
Mexico	82%	4	57%	0%
Peru	36%	2	33%	14%
Venezuela	27%	2	27%	13%
Bulgaria	73%	5	58%	0%
Croacia	92%	5	80%	70%
Czech Republic	96%	5	87%	24%
Estonia	98%	3	98%	63%
Hungary	92%	5	74%	12%
Latvia	47%	2	40%	0%
Lithuania	90%	4	90%	0%
Poland	75%	4	40%	32%
Romania	42%	3	33%	22%
Slovakia	96%	5	79%	23%
Slovenia	23%	1	7%	0%
Indonesia	42%	2	29%	29%
Malaysia	24%	0	0%	0%
Phillipines	17%	1	8%	0%
South Korea	20%	0	0%	0%
Memo:				
New Zealand	*99%*	*5*	*91%*	*0%*

*Percentage of each country's total bank assets.
**Criteria: Banks must not only be listed, but the majority stockholder must own less than 85% of stock.
Source: Authors' calculation with data from National Central Banks' Publications and Bankers' Almanac database.

closely related.[1] Banks are often owned by local entrepreneurs who are, in many cases, inclined to lend other people's money to themselves. This can become a relevant issue given that related credit portfolios generally have higher default rates, especially in times of crisis (La Porta *et al.*, 2002). Finally, the presence of foreign banks may contribute to fostering the stability of the local deposit base during periods of stress by allowing domestic depositors the option of moving their deposits to foreign-owned domestic banks, instead of shifting them abroad.

Despite the benefits, increased foreign participation creates new challenges for host-country financial authorities. These challenges may vary according to the size, characteristics, and diversity of the foreign investment. Thus, the challenges are not the same in countries like Mexico, where the largest four foreign-owned banks account for 71 percent of the domestic market, as in Poland, where they account for 40 percent of the local market. Likewise, the challenges are different in countries such as New Zealand, where the majority of the foreign investment comes from a single foreign country than they are in Mexico or Poland, a country that has a well-diversified investor base.

The challenges facing local authorities are particularly important when a large or systemically important local bank ends up in the hands of a single foreign financial entity. Global firms tend to centralize their major strategic business decisions, as well as their operational and risk management, at the parent level. As a result, this centralization gives way to decisions that, although they benefit the controlling shareholder, could hamper some subsidiaries.

2. The Operation of a Global Bank

The banking business is characterized by the existence of asymmetric information, which makes it very difficult, for example, for a French bank to lend

---

[1] In many emerging market economies the number of listed companies is rather small. Moreover, ownership concentration is high and reflects the significant concentration of wealth within these economies. For example, a recent study of publicly listed firms by the Institute for International Finance mentions Greece, Colombia, and Mexico as the countries with the highest ownership concentration levels in the world (Institute of International Finance, 2003).

to small entrepreneurs in Aruba. Global banks are able to overcome information asymmetries by establishing branches or acquiring subsidiaries abroad. After Markowitz's work, it has become widely understood that diversification yields better combinations of risk and return. Therefore, by investing abroad, global banks are able to gain access to a wider array of opportunities than are local banks, thereby diversifying their investments.

Global banks maximize their expected risk-adjusted profits by managing all of their resources as an investment portfolio. Therefore, they allocate their capital to countries where they expect to obtain a higher risk-adjusted return. They also take advantage of negative correlations among business lines and local economic cycles to improve their overall risk-adjusted returns. As a result, they are able to attain higher risk-adjusted rates of return than local banks, which do not have access to as many investment opportunities. However, in the process of maximizing their expected returns, global banks might choose a combination of business lines, and capital allocations that could hamper the soundness of some subsidiaries while at the same time benefiting others. While these policies make perfect sense from the point of view of a parent bank, they could have adverse effects on some host country economies, presumably the less profitable ones. In this sense, global banks have less vested local interest and thus, are more prone than domestically owned banks to reallocate their investments when they are not performing as expected.

As an example, assume that we have three different retail banks, each one located in a different country; Spain, Mexico, and the United Kingdom (UK). In a frictionless world, each of the three banks would be able to diversify their capital and business lines in the international market. However, in the presence of asymmetric information, each of the three banks will attempt to maximize its expected profits by investing the majority of its capital locally. The Spanish bank decides to become a global bank and therefore acquires both the Mexican and the UK banks. The aggregate risk level of an international conglomerate that comprises the three banks could be smaller than the sum of each bank's risk if there are negative correlations among the assets and liabilities of the three entities. Hence the Spanish global bank could easily reduce its new aggregated global risk level and achieve higher profits by reallocating its capital and business lines among Spain, Mexico, and the UK. Furthermore, the Spanish bank would benefit from registering some of its operations where it enjoys economies of scale or regulatory advantages. However, it is unlikely that the Mexican and UK bank portfolios would remain as they were prior to the acquisition. If the Mexican and UK banks were maximizing their risk-adjusted returns before they were acquired, then the new situation in which they find themselves would be less sound, unless they receive a capital injection from the parent bank.

Global banks also divide their products and services among different business lines, where matrix arrangements replace traditional vertical reporting lines. Hence, local banks' treasurers, risk units, and local comptrollers report directly to the head of the parent banks. These corporate arrangements weaken the responsibilities and control exercised by local boards and chief executive officers. In some ways, subsidiaries are often managed like branches. The extent to which a global bank centralizes its decision-making processes depends on the degree of control that it has over its subsidiaries, the relative size of the subsidiaries, and their own particular practices. The degree of control over a subsidiary is closely related to its ownership structure.

In general, the well being of a subsidiary should not be a matter of special concern for host-country authorities, provided that they are relatively small and their resolution in case of failure will not generate unreasonable costs for the host country economy. In fact, it is desirable to have markets where financial entities can enter and leave at reasonable costs. However, when banking services are highly concentrated and a local bank is relatively important to the host country, decisions by banks' shareholders could have important consequences for the host-country economy. Therefore, in this situation, the banks' ownership structure and corporate governance practices becomes relevant.

A controlling shareholder might make decisions that could hamper the soundness of a subsidiary for reasons other than maximizing its global risk-adjusted returns. For example, he or she may consider that the global exposure to a particular country's credit risk is excessive or that the subsidiary may need to obtain resources to cover losses at other subsidiaries or at the parent bank. Many authors have studied the importance of having publicly held corporations. The idea is that a widely held ownership structure could ensure that a corporation would not be subject to the pressures of a controlling shareholder (Fama *et al.*, 1983; Shleifer *et al.*, 1986; Holderness *et al.*, 1988). It is generally accepted that a widely held bank would make it more difficult for a controlling shareholder, for reasons of self-interest, to support investment decisions that are not necessarily in the best interest of the other bank's stakeholders. In fact, many countries have set limits that restrict the percentage of shares that a single shareholder could acquire without seeking the approval of local authorities.

3. Promoting Local Banks' Soundness

Credit institutions play a major role in a country's economic activity, as they facilitate the allocation of resources, reduce transaction costs, and transform and diversify risks and maturities profiles. They are also fundamental for the optimum functioning of the country's payment system. The important role of banks and the inevitable liquidity risks that they incur by the very nature of their operations lead governments to implement a series of measures to reduce the risks of bank failures and contagion. These measures include the establishment of deposit insurance programs and lender of last resort facilities. Governments also put regulations in place and create supervisory agencies to contain "moral hazards" that might result in the absence of these facilities.

The facilities and the ensuing regulations are generally directed at all banks licensed to operate in a particular country or jurisdiction. However, these regulations usually distinguish between subsidiaries (banks owned by another financial entity) and branches of foreign banks. The reason for this difference is simple; a branch is an office or window of another bank, while a subsidiary is a legally independent entity established in a different jurisdiction and subject to different laws and courts than its parent bank. As in any limited liability company, the legal responsibilities of the bank's shareholders are limited to their invested capital.

Nevertheless, there is a commonly held view that a foreign bank's subsidiary might offer greater protection to local depositors than it would to a locally owned bank, as the former will be supported by its parent bank's capital while the locally owned bank is dependent solely on its own resources. From a theoretical point of view, a parent bank's decision to support a subsidiary will be made by taking into account the balance of future profits and costs (including reputation costs). Hence, support from parent banks should not be taken for granted. Furthermore, in some countries, legislation and contracts set limits on the obligations of parent banks to support their overseas branches. This practice is widely known as "ring fencing." Additionally, parent companies, under special circumstances, may not even recognize the obligations undertaken by their branches (for example, war or insurrection in the host country). Therefore, financial authorities do have an interest in propping up and preserving the soundness of all banks — foreign or domestically owned — under their jurisdiction.

A bank's soundness depends on its capacity to sustain unexpected capital losses, its liquidity, proper management procedures, and its ability to generate profits on an ongoing basis. Any financial authority should, therefore, be concerned with the soundness of their banks and their ability to stand alone in the event that they are abandoned by their controlling shareholder. Hence, the challenge for the authorities of countries whose major banks are foreign-owned is to devise the right incentives to impede controlling shareholders and local managers from making decisions that could hamper their subsidiaries.

4. Market Discipline

The growing number of diverse financial institutions and the increasing volume and complexity of their operations make it difficult for economic agents to evaluate their risks and performance. These factors have also made the work of banking supervisors more difficult. Hence, the need to encourage "market discipline" to supplement the work of supervisors in order to ensure the safety and soundness of banking system is widely recognized at the international level.

The Basel Committee on Banking Supervision, as well as other multilateral organizations, has acknowledged the importance of market discipline. Pillar 3 of the new Capital Accord recognizes that the regulation and supervision by authorities has to be complemented with a set of incentives to stimulate market participants in order to generate relevant information which can then be used to evaluate the condition of financial institutions.[2] Market signals, such as share prices and interest rates on banks' liabilities, provide supervisors with the view that market participants have about the soundness of the regulated institutions. Therefore, market signals could help increase discipline and provide authorities with the information they need

---

[2]Basel II suggests that banks should reveal information regarding their structure and capital adequacy, exposure and risk measures, credit risk, methodologies to calculate credit risk, securities portfolio, techniques to reduce credit risk, securitizations, models to measure market risk, operative risk and interest rates risk. (Basel Committee on Banking Supervision, 2003a).

to act swiftly, if needed. In addition, market participants can discipline bank managers when they take excessive risks, by withdrawing funds or requiring higher yields on their investments.

It is commonly accepted that the market participants with the strongest incentives to discipline bank managers are depositors (especially uninsured depositors), general creditors (in the inter-bank market, for example), holders of long-term bank debt (especially if they are subordinated top other claimants in case of failure) and outside (minority) shareholders. Several studies have analyzed the different incentives that these participants need to have in order to monitor and influence how banks behave. In addition, there is an abundance of empirical literature that tests the existence and effectiveness of different market discipline channels in the case of developed countries and, increasingly, for emerging market economies.[3] However, to date there is not much literature that addresses how the entry of foreign banks affects the operation of the different market discipline channels in host countries.[4] We can distinguish three effects of foreign bank entry on the way in which market discipline works. The first effect is how market discipline of the parent bank may affect its subsidiary. A second effect, is enhancing the credibility of limited deposit insurance schemes as governments will be reluctant to rescue foreign banks and lastly, the de-listing and reduction of issuance of subordinated debt by subsidiaries (the "removal" of important channels of market discipline).

Global financial institutions that have a presence in emerging markets are usually subject to strong market discipline in their home countries. It has been argued that subsidiaries benefit from having a market disciplined parent bank.[5] However, this depends largely on the size of the subsidiary in question relative to its parent bank. If the subsidiary's earnings represent a large percentage of the group's profits, it is likely that the parent bank's share price will reflect the risk-taking behavior of the subsidiary. Nevertheless, if the subsidiary is relatively small, its behavior will not have a significant effect on the parent bank's share prices, even if the subsidiary is systemically

---

[3]For developed countries see, for example, Basel Committee (2003b). For emerging markets, see Caprio and Honohan (2004). Both papers present an extensive review of the literature. See also De Ceuster and Masschelein (2003).

[4]An exception is Inter-American Development Bank (2005), which shows, in the context of banks in Latin America, that the relationship between risk taking by banks and depositor behavior is the same for privately-owned and foreign-owned banks.

[5]See Caprio and Honohan (2004), p. 21.

important in the host country.[6] In addition, market participants monitoring the consolidated group will primarily be concerned with the risk-return profile of the group as a whole as opposed to its different parts. If a subsidiary is experiencing losses that are compensated by gains elsewhere, investors are less likely to care about the composition of their return. The entry of foreign banks is also likely to affect the operation of the local safety net. Host-country governments are likely to face considerable political opposition if they choose to support a foreign bank subsidiary that has problems that threaten the interests of its depositors, even if the subsidiary is considered systemically important to the host financial system. Therefore, the entry of foreign banks may increase the credibility of the limited deposit insurance scheme, thus enhancing the case for market discipline.

Finally, the third effect on local market discipline comes when subsidiaries are de-listed from stock markets when all of its shares are acquired by a foreign stockholder. For example, in Mexico five of the six largest banks were acquired by foreign banks and were, subsequently, de-listed from the stock market. This situation is similar to that of other countries (for example, Bulgaria, Latvia, and Lithuania) where the largest banks are closely held subsidiaries of foreign banks and are not listed in stock markets (see Table 1). Moreover, parent banks may decrease the outstanding amount of subordinated debt issued by subsidiaries. In this case, host countries will not benefit from the existence of these important market discipline channels.

When stocks are de-listed, the financial markets are deprived of information on that particular company. In the financial sector, the loss of information is particularly troublesome if the institutions are highly leveraged. As a result, the lack of information affects large, sophisticated investors and governments that protect small, unsophisticated depositors. However, requiring financial institutions to increase information disclosure will not in itself lead to a more stringent enforcement of market discipline. The lack of market-traded instruments, such as shares, will preclude the existence

---

[6]Parent banks subject to strict market discipline in their home countries will impose a certain level of discipline on the managers of local subsidiaries. Closely held subsidiaries will be subject to new risk assessments techniques, more transparent and rigorous business guidelines and accounting systems. Thus, in principle, subsidiaries' managers are likely to operate in a sounder and safer manner for the benefit of a single shareholder. Thus, although managers of local subsidiaries will not be subject directly to market discipline, the incentives created by belonging to a global bank subject to market discipline at home are likely to bring some of the effects of direct market discipline.

of market signals as well as the scrutiny of independent bank analysts, minority shareholders, and even their competitors, who are able to participate in shareholder's briefings and annual corporate meetings in order to obtain information regarding the listed financial institution's strengths, weaknesses, and future plans. Furthermore, independent bank analysts untangle and interpret otherwise not-so-easy-to-understand financial information. Since financial statements seldom reveal all that there is to know about a company, analysts do not rely solely on public information; they also talk to as many people as possible to get a more complete picture of what is going on inside the firm.[7]

5. Policy Options

As discussed in the previous sections, when a country's main (systemic) banks are wholly owned subsidiaries of foreign banks, host-country authorities should be conscious that parent banks will manage their subsidiaries as part of a global bank. In addition, they cannot assume that the parent bank will always support its subsidiary. Thus, host-country authorities must consider policy options that promote two objectives: to search for mechanisms that ensure that the subsidiaries will be managed prudently at all times in the best interests of all stakeholders including: shareholders, creditors, depositors, and the government (as the local safety net administrator); and to make sure that market participants can exert discipline mechanisms over the subsidiaries' managers. In the following section, we consider three complementary measures: strengthening the subsidiary's corporate governance, requiring them to list a certain percentage of their shares on the local stock exchange and, finally, to issue subordinated debt. To avoid any kind of distortions in the operation of institutions in the host countries and to keep the playing field level, locally owned systemic banks should be subject to the same requirements.[8]

---

[7]An analyst from Credit Suisse First Boston (CSFB) expressed his concerns regarding these problems by saying that "important banks, after de-listed, have not provided any information at all to analysts and investors. Mexican Banamex is the perfect example, after being acquired by Citibank it does not provide any quarterly press release and does not receive any investors or analysts for meetings anymore."

[8]These measures are in addition to the need to establish agreements between host and home supervisors and central banks in exchanging relevant information and co-ordinate actions, especially when the parent or the subsidiary (or any other part of the group) is experiencing problems.

6. Corporate Governance

Host-country authorities must be certain that incentives provided to the subsidiary's Board of Directors and its management are aligned with the subsidiary's interests, and that the bank can operate on a stand-alone basis. In order for this to occur, board members and management must have the legal obligation to act in the best interest of the subsidiary and to not act in the best interest of the parent when doing so would be detrimental to the subsidiary. The Reserve Bank of New Zealand has moved in this direction. The Company Act in New Zealand establishes that "... a director of a company that is a wholly owned subsidiary may, when exercising powers or performing duties as a director, if expressly permitted to do so by the constitution of the company, act in a manner which he or she believes is in the best interests of that company's holding company even though it may not be in the best interests of the company."[9] However, if the company is a bank, the Reserve Bank of New Zealand Act requires the company (as a condition of registration) "not to have a constitution which permits the directors to act in the interests of the holding company."[10] Additionally, it states that any change to the bank's constitution must be authorized by the Reserve Bank.[11]

Furthermore, the Basel Committee on Banking Supervision is revisiting its recommendations regarding corporate governance for banks and has recently stated that: "The corporate governance responsibilities of both the bank and its parent should be respected. The parent board or senior management — acting in the discharge of its own corporate governance responsibilities — is charged with setting the general strategy and policies of the group and its subsidiaries and for determining what governance structure for its subsidiaries would best contribute to an effective chain of oversight for the group as a whole. The board of a subsidiary bank retains its corporate governance responsibilities for the bank itself, including the soundness of the bank and the protection of the interests of its depositors ..." (Basel Committee on Banking Supervision, 2005).

The role of independent board members is particularly important when there are potential conflicts of interest between managers, the firm and shareholders. However, when firms have a single shareholder, the role of

[9]Companies Act Section 131(2).
[10]Reserve Bank of New Zealand Act, Section 73B.
[11]Reserve Bank of New Zealand Act Sections 74 and 78.

the independent board members becomes more complicated. The governance framework of the banking group should also take into account that the subsidiary must be able to operate on a stand-alone basis. For this to be possible, authorities must regulate outsourcing agreements and carefully review the management arrangements by making local boards and CEOs bear more responsibility for the operation of the subsidiary. This is especially important in cases where the host country authorities were obliged to intervene and take control of the bank.

6.1. *Requiring wholly owned subsidiaries to list a certain percentage of their capital*

Requiring de-listed banks in a host country to list shares yields important benefits by including the presence and decisions of minority shareholders. Minority shareholders ensure that managers increase the value of the firm through their votes in meetings, the nomination of the board's members and managers and with their decisions to keep or sell their shares. For this reason, they also play a major role in promoting market discipline. Moreover, signals extracted from shares prices offer information about the risk exposure of institutions. The existence of minority shareholders also represents an important element for market discipline as they help limit the control that majority shareholders can exert over managers in pursuit of their own interests.[12]

If a country were to adopt this rule successfully, it would first have to find a fairly deep and liquid equities market where these shares could be traded easily and, secondly, there could be no restrictions on the ownership of these shares, apart from the bank itself, the holding company and related parties. The experience of subsidiaries that have been listed for some time in other countries (for example, Chile and Poland) should be carefully studied. Apparently, if the proportion of the shares listed is very small or they are not listed in an internationally recognized market, the liquidity will be minimal and, thus, not very useful for providing authorities with reliable information as to the condition of the bank.[13]

---

[12]The Banking Law in Mexico establishes that shareholders owning more than 10 percent of the common shares of a company may designate a board member.

[13]One major investment bank (CSFB) mentioned, for example, that they do not give coverage to shares of some subsidiaries of foreign banks operating and listed in Argentina and Chile, since they are relatively illiquid and are restricted to trading in local markets, do not have corresponding American depositary receipts and do not attract the interest of foreign investors.

Nevertheless, this proposal has several problems. First, the regulatory cost of complying with the listing requirement would be substantial. Second, since the cost of equity is likely to be higher for the subsidiary than for the parent, this measure would increase the cost of capital for the subsidiary, which would then most likely be passed on to the consumer. Finally, at low levels of banks' capitalization, minority shareholders' interests are likely to be very similar to those of the controlling shareholder and, therefore, there will be few incentives to limit the risk appetite of managers (gambling for resurrection). However, in the event of failure, the presence of minority shareholders may make it more difficult for the controlling shareholder (the parent bank) to shift the subsidiary resources in order to benefit the rest of the parent bank.

6.2. *Requiring banks to issue subordinated debt*

Some of the arguments that support the proposal to require banks to issue subordinated debt are similar to the case of banks having to list their equity. The purpose is to increase market monitoring and to exert influence over banks' managers. Similarly, consideration should be given to the effect that requiring the subsidiary to raise funds at a higher cost than the parent bank could have on subsidiaries cost of funding. However, there are important differences between requiring them to issue debt and list a percentage of their shares. Subordinated debt yields have at least two determinants: the market view on the risk-taking position of the subsidiary and the probability of support by the parent bank. It would not be easy to distinguish which of these two factors drives market yields. If market participants believe that support from the parent is likely to come in the event of trouble, then the subordinated debt yield would not react to the risk-return profile of the subsidiary. Additionally, the liquidity of subordinated debt markets is likely to be even lower than it is in the equities market. Therefore, there is a need to carefully study the trade-offs between issuing size and frequency.

7. Conclusions

In this paper we argued that wholly owned subsidiaries of foreign banks will be managed on a global portfolio basis. This means that the risk–return profile of the subsidiary will be determined for the benefit of a single shareholder. A host country in which the main (systemic) banks are wholly owned subsidiaries is exposed to potential situations in which the parent banks may not act in the best interest of their subsidiaries. In addition, support for the subsidiary cannot be taken for granted in every situation.

We outlined three complementary policy measures to deal with these problems. The first, is to enhance the governance of subsidiaries; second, to require wholly owned subsidiaries to list certain percentage of their shares, and third, to require them to issue subordinated debt. Further analysis is needed to establish the extent to which these policy objectives can be achieved with the measures proposed, or whether there are more cost-efficient ways of attaining them. Policymakers should carefully consider the costs and benefits of these measures.

References

Basel Committee on Banking Supervision, 2003a, "Overview of the New Basel Capital Accord," April.

Basel Committee, 2003b, "Markets for Bank Subordinated Debt and Equity in Basel Committee Member Countries," August.

Basel Committee on Banking Supervision, 2005, "Enhancing Corporate Governance for Banking Organizations," July.

Caprio, G., and Honohan, P., 2004, "Can the Unsophisticated Market Provide Discipline?," The World Bank, Policy Research Working Paper Series 3364.

Cárdenas, J., P. Graf and P. O'Dogherty, 2003, "Foreign Bank Entry in Emerging Market Economies; A Host Country Perspective," Paper prepared for the CGFS Working Group on FDI in the Financial Sector.

De Ceuster, Marc, and Nancy Masschelein, 2003, "Regulating Banks Through Market Discipline: A Survey of the Issues," *Journal of Economic Surveys*, 17(5), pp. 749–766.

De Hass R., and I. Naaborg, 2005, "Foreign Banks in Transition Economies: Small Business Lending and Internal Capital Markets," Paper presented at the 3rd Halle Workshop on Monetary and Financial Economics.

Fama, Eugene F., and Jensen, Michael C., 1983, "Agency Problems and Residual Claims," *Journal of Law & Economics*, 26(2), pp. 327–349.

La Porta, R., Lopez-de-Silanes, F. and Zamarripa, G., 2002, "Related Lending," National Bureau of Economic Research, Inc., Working Papers 8848.

Holderness, Clifford G., and Denris P. Sheehan, 1988, "The Role of Majority Shareholders in Publicly held Corporations," *Journal of Financial Economics*, 20, pp. 317–346.

Institute of International Finance, 2003, "Corporate Governance in Mexico: An Investor Perspective," Institute of International Finance, Washington, DC.

Inter-American Development Bank, 2005, "Unlocking Credit: The Quest for Deep and Stable Bank Lending," Report on Economic and Social Development in Latin America, Washington.

Reserve Bank of New Zealand Act, 2004, "Statement of Principles: Bank Registration and Supervision," Section IV (d) paragraph 59, July 2004. Published under section 73B. Reserve Bank of New Zealand (2004) Act Sections 74 and 78.

Shleifer, Andrei, and Vishny, Robert W., 1986, "Large Shareholders and Corporate Control," *Journal of Political Economy*, 94, pp. 461–488.

Juan Pablo Graf and Pascual O'Dogherty work in the Financial System Analysis Division of Banco de México. The paper was prepared for the Cross-Border Banking Conference held at the Federal Reserve Bank of Chicago in October 2005. The views expressed in this paper are the authors' and do not necessarily reflect those of Banco de México.

Market Discipline Issues Associated with Cross-Border Banking

Federal Reserve Bank of Chicago

The purpose of his year's conference was to address the current landscape of cross-border bank activity, the resulting competitive implications, emerging challenges for prudential regulation, safety net concerns, failure resolution issues, and the potential future evolution of international banking. Papers on this session address how market discipline in financial markets may be affected by the proliferation of cross-border banking. Is market discipline enhanced or hampered as banks expand geographically? Does it depend on local market regulatory and/or institutional conditions? Can more reliance be placed on supervision by the marketplace for internationally active (cross-border) banks? Addressing these and related issues was the reason for including this topic on the conference agenda.

Let me briefly summarize some of the highlights of each paper on this session and then discuss a somewhat common theme detected in the papers. Moe discussed the challenges cross-border banking imposes on bank supervisors emphasizing home–host supervisory issues. This has been a common theme for almost every session of this conference. However, he also emphasized that just as important as the supervisory issues are the central banking issues. Thus, decisions concerning the means to address liquidity constraints, deposit insurance, and corporate governance issues are just as important as the supervisory issues. The Norges Bank has the view that if a branch of a subsidiary of a foreign bank encountered difficulties, the parent bank would be responsible for addressing the associated problems. If they were unable to resolve the problems, perhaps because they too were encountering difficulties, the home-country authorities would be expected to take responsibility for resolving the problem. However, Moe allowed that the home-country authorities may not agree with this stance and the actual responsibilities for resolution were quite "fluid." That is, decisions concerning which central bank (home or host country) would serve as lender of last resort, which bankruptcy laws would be adhered to, and which resolution procedures would be followed are still being decided. This fluidity is not encouraging and suggests that far too much uncertainty currently exists. The greater the uncertainty, the higher the probability that supervisors would resort to bailing out the troubled institution; a possibility that raises a magnitude of moral hazard issues.

Graf and O'Dogherty do a good job of describing the extent of cross-border banking in a number of countries, with a special emphasis on Mexico.[1] Mexico significantly revised its banking laws following the Mexican crisis of the mid-1990s to enable and encourage foreign banks to enter the market. Since that time they have seen foreign banks gain control of a significant share of bank assets — for example, controlling five of the largest seven banks and over 80 percent of total bank assets. While this brings benefits to the Mexican economy, it also creates issues of uncertainty and steps are currently being considered to help address these issues.[2]

Finally, Kane discussed the appropriate role of regulation and the elements that should be included in the objective functions of each regulator in a home-country, host-country environment. He emphasized the potential for inherent conflicts of interest between home- and host-country supervisors, supervisors and the citizenry, and citizens from the two countries. He explained that, over time, a country-specific 'regulatory culture' may evolve and discussed how this culture can affect the information flow available to supervisors and the market. He used the New Zealand-Australia situation as an example and emphasized the advantages of the role of accountability and disclosure requirements recently introduced in New Zealand. The current New Zealand situation is a welcomed movement away from the common regulatory model where regulatory avoidance is achieved via "loophole-supported" misrepresentation with the regulated firm practicing regulatory-avoidance behavior.

The theme of this session deals with market discipline in a cross-border banking environment. While we are fortunate to have three interesting papers, there appears to be a strong tendency by the authors to discuss

---

[1]See Dermine (2006), Cetorelli and Goldberg (2006), and Hohl, McGuire and Remolona (2006) for a discussion of the current situation in Europe, the Americas and Asia, respectively.
[2]Some of these issues are also discussed in Ortiz (2006).

auxiliary issues. For example, Kane discusses means to change the super-visory and regulatory environment in a manner that could directly affect the ability of market discipline to regulate bank behavior; although there is never an attempt to explicitly link these changes to the effectiveness of market discipline. While Moe and Graf and O'Dogherty discuss the role and mechanisms by which market discipline alters firm behavior, their emphasis is on the uncertainties associated with existing failure resolution plans and the current difficulties in making market discipline effective in the specific countries discussed.

This is somewhat discouraging to someone who for years has argued for increasing the role of market discipline in the regulation of financial institutions. It was a welcomed event when the Basel II proposal introduced a significant role for market discipline with the third pillar of capital reform.[3] If properly implemented, this could be very important as it would signal a willingness to increase reliance on market forces; forces thought by many to be the best regulator of firm behavior.

The effectiveness of market discipline, however, is predicated on the presence of certain fundamental principles or a basic infrastructure that allows it to function properly. That infrastructure includes:

- a credible legal system with well defined property rights;
- appropriate accounting procedures and standards;
- a high-quality auditing system;
- access to relevant and high-quality information (data);
- transparency, so data can be used; and
- the appropriate alignment of incentives.

There is a general understanding that these elements do not exist in many countries. The discussions of the Mexican and Nordic situations both questioned the presence of the last component, raising doubt about the credibility of a threat to impose losses on market participants. Given the recent history of creditor bailouts, market participants, at best, have reason to question the potential for suffering losses if the banks encounter solvency problems. So when evaluating the effectiveness of market discipline, it is imperative to bifurcate the banks into subsamples based on the status of their country's infrastructure: where the conditions exist verses where they do not. This is

---

[3]While it is definitely a step in the right direction, some, including myself, believe the role of market discipline should be further enhanced. For example, see Benink (2004a, 2004b).

a distinction that may be proxied by the level of development across countries or some other relatively easy to quantify measure. Whatever measure is used, it is obvious that the infrastructure conditions differ significantly across countries and any attempt to evaluate the effectiveness of market discipline in banking markets must take account of this difference.

It should come as no surprise that in countries that do not have the appropriate infrastructure, markets may not discipline firm behavior. But in countries where these conditions are not met, it is not a failure of market discipline to regulate firm behavior, rather it is a failure of the regulatory infrastructure. One can not expect discipline to "work" if you don't allow it to work. Nor, and most importantly for this session of the conference, should the effectiveness of market discipline in the presence of cross-border banking be questioned.[4] I will argue that there is ample evidence both in Europe and in the U.S. that market prices (debt spreads and equity price information embedded in distance to default measures) track closely with the financial condition of the bank. The market sends meaningful signals when the necessary infrastructure conditions exist. They also typically find evidence that the relationship between market information and bank risk weakens in the presence of implicit or explicit guarantees from the government. Studies generally aligning with this view include Evanoff and Wall (2000, 2001, 2002), Gropp, Vesala, and Vulpes (2004), Krainer and Lopez (2001, 2003a, 2003b), and Sironi (2003).[5]

In countries where the infrastructure is sufficient to allow for market discipline, and one is still concerned about the adequacy of that discipline, there are a number of things one might want to consider to improve oversight of financial institutions. First, the host-country regulators could require foreign-owned banks to hold additional capital (the "Swiss–Finnish" approach). Second, consideration could be given to implementing an early intervention approach similar to the prompt corrective action policy introduced in the U.S.[6] This would serve to address relatively minor problems before they have an opportunity to grow into major solvency concerns. To further insure against the growth of bank problems, consideration should probably be given to setting higher "triggers" (for example, capital levels) to initiate early intervention and consideration should be given to using

---

[4]One possible exception raised by Noe is that banks may delist equities when they are acquired by a nonlocal bank; that is, cross-border acquisitions.

[5]More generally, see, Borio, Hunter, Kaufman, and Tsatsaronis (2004).

[6]This was introduced in the FDIC Improvement Act of 1991.

market signals to trigger the action. The use of market signals would reduce the potential for supervisory forbearance and could even provide a more accurate signal (see Evanoff and Wall, 2001). A fourth option would be to consider mandating that financial institutions issue subordinated debt to satisfy a portion of their regulatory capital requirement. This would explicitly place a sophisticated group of investors in a junior priority position should the financial firm encounter difficulties. Thus, this group of creditors would have incentives to closely scrutinize and discipline the risk activities of the financial firms.[7] Finally, supervisors should put into place explicit procedures to follow during resolutions, for example, "haircut" rules for bank creditors. This would avoid having to create the procedures during the crisis and could be an initial step in establishing credibility. However, none of these are quick fixes and acquiring regulatory credibility takes time.

References

Benink, Harald, 2004a, "Are Basel II's Pillars Strong Enough?" *The Banker*, 1 July, page 162.

———, 2004b, "Will Supervisors Have Too Much Discretion under the New Regime?" *Global Risk Regulator*, July/August.

Borio, Claudio, William C. Hunter, George G. Kaufman, and Kostas Tsatsaronis, 2004, *Market Discipline: The Evidence Across Countries and Industries,* MIT Press, Cambridge.

Cetorelli, Nicola, and Linda Goldberg, 2006, "Risks in U.S. Bank International Exposures," *Cross-Border Banking: Regulatory Challenges*, New York and Singapore: World Scientific Publishing Company.

Dermine, Jean, 2006, "European Banking Integration: Don't Put the Cart before the Horse," *Cross-Border Banking: Regulatory Challenges*, New York and Singapore: World Scientific Publishing Company.

---

[7]This group of creditors has a number of favorable characteristics that could decrease the likelihood that they will be 'rescued' during a bank failure. There can be little merit in, nor sympathy to, arguments that the debt-holders are unsophisticated and unaware of their claimant status. Additionally, since banks are not subject to bankruptcy laws (at least in the U.S.), the debt-holders could not argue for a preferred position by refusing to accept the bankruptcy reorganization plan. Thus they are unable to block the resolution. So pressures to rescue debt-holders should not result from their status as unsophisticated investors, nor their bargaining power in the failure resolution process. For a more detailed discussion of these characteristics, see Evanoff (1993).

Evanoff, Douglas D., 1993, "Preferred Sources of Market Discipline," *Yale Journal on Regulation*, 10.

Evanoff, Douglas D., and Larry D. Wall, 2000, "Subordinated Debt and Bank Capital Reform," in *Research in Financial Services: Private and Public Policy*, George G. Kaufman (ed), Vol. 12, JAI Press.

———, 2001, "SND Yield Spreads as Bank Risk Measures," *Journal of Financial Services Research*, 20, pp.121–145.

———, 2002, "Measures of the Riskiness of Banking Organizations: Subordinated Debt Yields, Risk-Based Capital, and Examination Ratings," *Journal of Banking and Finance*, 26, pp. 989–1009.

Gropp, Reint, Jukka Vesala, and Giuseppe Vulpes, 2004, "Market Indicators, Bank Fragility, and Indirect Market Discipline," *Economic Policy Review*, Sep., pp. 53–62.

Hohl, Stefan, Patrick McGuire, and Eli M. Remolona, 2006, "Cross-Border Banking in Asia: Basel II and other Prudential Issues," *Cross-Border Banking: Regulatory Challenges*, New York and Singapore: World Scientific Publishing Company.

Krainer, John, and Jose A. Lopez, 2001, "Incorporating Equity Market Information into Supervisory Monitoring Models," Working Paper, Federal Reserve Bank of San Francisco, WP-01-14.

———, 2003a, "How Might Financial Market Information Be Used for Supervisory Purposes?," *Economic Review*, pp. 29–45.

———, 2003b, "Monitoring Debt Market Information for Bank Supervisory Purposes," *Economic Letter*, 35, November.

Ortiz, Guillermo, 2006, "Cross-Border Banking and the Challenges Faced by Host Country Authorities," *Cross-Border Banking: Regulatory Challenges*, New York and Singapore: World Scientific Publishing Company.

Sironi, Andrea, 2003, "Testing for Market Discipline in the European Banking Industry: Evidence from Subordinated Debt Issues," *Journal of Money, Credit, and Banking*, 35, pp. 443–472.

Douglas D. Evanoff is senior financial advisor and vice president in the Research Department of the Federal Reserve Bank of Chicago.

Safety Net Issues

Challenges for Deposit Insurance and Financial Stability in Cross-Border Banking Environments with Emphasis on the European Union

Robert A. Eisenbeis*

Federal Reserve Bank of Atlanta

George G. Kaufman

Loyola University Chicago and Federal Reserve Bank of Chicago

1. Introduction

Foreign ownership of banks increases competition and efficiency in the banking sector of the host country, reduces risk exposures through greater geographical and industrial diversification, and enlarges the aggregate quantity of capital invested in the banking sector. Indeed, foreign entry through direct investment is widely recommended by researchers and analysts as a means of strengthening weak and inefficient banking structures, particularly in emerging economies.[1] Despite the benefits that might accrue to foreign ownership, either in the form of branch offices or subsidiary banks, cross-border banking raises serious policy concerns with respect to the provision of deposit insurance, the effectiveness of prudential regulation, the strength of market discipline, the timing of placing an insolvent institution into receivership or conservatorship, and the procedures for resolving

---

[1]Reviews of the benefits appear in Barth *et al.* (2006), Committee on the Global Financial System (2004), Goldberg (2003), and Soussa (2004). Brief previous warnings about the unsettled state of affairs in cross-border banking appear in Goodhart (2005), Eisenbeis (2005), and Mayes (2005). See in particular the analysis of the Nordea Bank, which is headquartered in Sweden but operates in a number of other countries in the appendix to Mayes (2005).

insolvencies. If not designed properly, these activities may be subject so significant agency and moral hazard costs that could significantly impact regulatory responses to financial crises. This paper examines how alternative banking regulatory structures are likely to function within and across countries at times of financial strain. Our emphasis is on the European Union (EU), which is debating how to reform its regulatory structure.

In succeeding sections, we describe the EU cross-border banking regulatory structure and discuss agency problems that may arise. Of particular concern are the risks associated with providing deposit insurance for institutions operating in that environment and the process of resolving bank failures. Finally, we offer some incentive compatible alternative policies that can limit the costs that poorly designed system may entail.

2. Key Features of EU Financial Regulatory and Deposit Guarantee Systems

To achieve a single economic and financial market place, the European Union instituted the concept of a single banking license. Once a banking institution receives a charter from an EU member state, it can establish branches anywhere within the EU countries. Prudential supervision and regulation of the bank is the responsibility of the charter-granting country (home country), regardless of where it operates branch offices. Should entry into other countries take place through a separately chartered subsidiary, the host country is responsible for supervision and regulation of the subsidiary. It also retains responsibility for lender of last resort functions, regardless of the form in which entry takes place. Should supervisory efforts to head off the insolvency of a systemically important bank fail, the home country is to provide lender of last resort assistance, at least until it threatens to become a pan-European problem when it then becomes the responsibility of the European Central Bank (ECB).[2]

Although EU banking directives establish minimum prudential standards and provide common principles and coordinated approaches that would be followed when institutions experience financial difficulties, substantial differences exist in terms of how the safety net is structured across countries in terms such as the types of deposits and amounts that would

---

[2] See Gulde and Wolf (2005) for a review of the financial stability responsibilities in Europe.

be insured. These differences contain substantial incentives for institutions to engage in regulatory arbitrage, and create important differences in how nations might respond should substantial institutions get into financial difficulty.[3] These problems are detailed in the next sections.

3. Agency Problems and Conflicts

Cross-border banking can subject institutions to different, and potentially conflicting, banking laws and multiple regulators, making regulatory compliance uncertain and difficult.[4] Furthermore, bank supervisors and regulators in both home and host countries understandably operate in what they consider is the best interest of their country and its citizens and not necessarily that of host countries (Bollard, 2005).

These agency problems that have two dimensions: a home-country dimension and a cross-border dimension.[5] Home-country issues are the classical principle/agent type problems existing between the banking supervisors and taxpayers. Regulators have incentives both to pursue policies that preserve their agencies and to pursue their own private self-interest to ensure both their jobs and future employment in the banking industry (see Kane, 1991, 1989; Schüler, 2003; Lewis, 1997). These conflicts may lead to more accommodating regulatory policies, lower than appropriate capital requirements, and regulatory forbearance when institutions get in trouble, thereby shifting risk and any associated costs to others, including taxpayers.

Cross-border issues focus on conflicts among regulators in home and host countries and can become intensified when host-country regulators face a loss of constituents to supervise and regulate. For example, in areas like the EU, as foreign banking organizations begin to increase their market share and dominance through the establishment of branches, nationalistic concerns, may lead regulators to favor domestic over foreign institutions. They may attempt to limit the acquisitions of indigenous banks, or move

---

[3]In contrast, Mayes and Vesala (2005) argue that the sharing of responsibilities between home- and host-country regulators during the movement toward a single market objective is viable.
[4]See Eisenbeis and Kaufman (2005b) for a detailed discussion of these issues.
[5]Schüler (2003).

to create "national" champions which would be protected from outside takeover.[6]

Adding to the problem is that the quality of host-country monitoring and supervision of foreign institutions may be reduced. Host-country regulators are generally less able to obtain useful financial information from foreign-owned institutions than they are from domestically owned banks.[7] This concern is especially acute in the case of foreign branches that do not have meaningful balance sheets or income statements separate from the home office. Schüler (2003) argues that this information access issue can develop into a form of agency problem between the home- and host-country regulator. When monitoring and performance is weak, it may create an incentive for the home-country regulators to disguise poor performance or be less than diligent in supplying the host-country regulator with timely information. Without adequate and timely information, the host country may be in a poor position to assess the potential risks or externalities to which its citizens and economy may be exposed from foreign branches. These incentive conflicts may be especially acute in host countries with a large foreign banking presence.[8] The information problems are likely to become increasingly significant as banking organization expand and consolidate many of their managerial and record keeping functions to achieve cost efficiencies.

Finally, home-country regulators may take insufficient account of the externalities on how a failure may affect the host country, even when coordinating bodies or agreements and understandings exist, such as in the

---

[6]This problem has arisen both in France and the country's attempt to preserve Credit Lyonnais with injections of governmental funds in more than three separate instances in the past several years. More recently, an editorial in the *Wall Street Journal Europe* (2005), entitled "Spaghetti Banking," pointed out that the governor of the Bank of Italy had refused to approve the acquisition of a single Italian bank by a foreign institution for the last 12 years. The governor indicated his desire to "... preserve the banks' Italianness also in the future. ..." This protectionism is being challenged by the European Union's Internal Market Commission in connection with the proposed acquisitions of two Italian banks by ABN Amro and Banco Bilbao Vizcaya Argentina.

[7]Differences in quality can exist simply because countries fund their banking regulators differently, because they have had only limited experience in supervision market entities, as is the case with many countries from the former Soviet Union, or because of the sheer complexity of the operations involved (Committee on the Global Financial System, 2004).

[8]This characterizes many of the ten new EU entrants which have 70 percent of banking assets controlled by foreign banks. See Schoenmaker and Oosterloo (2005) and European Commission (2005).

European Union.[9] A home-country regulator may reasonably be expected to pay less attention to externalities and focus primarily on protecting its own residents from possible costs of failure.[10] At the same time, host-country regulators are likely to favor indigenous institutions and customers. These incentives problems may be especially significant with respect to the provision of deposit insurance, which in the EU case is primarily the responsibility of the home country. These issues are considered in the next section.

4. Deposit Insurance

The European Union's Deposit Guarantee Schemes Directive (DGD) (94/19/EC) endorses a decentralized approach to deposit insurance. The design leaves to the member home countries the responsibility of providing coverage to depositors. The DGD only specifies the general features that an acceptable deposit insurance system should have, such as deposit insurance coverage of 20,000 euros, no coverage for inter-bank deposits, and the discretion to exclude other liabilities. Co-insurance of liabilities is permitted but not required. Coverage of depositors in branches in countries other than the home country is the responsibility of the home country, but these can also be covered by the host country at its option. Additionally, should the host-country account coverage be greater than that available to a branch thorough its home-country deposit insurance scheme, the foreign branch may purchase top-off coverage to match that available to competing

---

[9]The Sveriges Riksbank (Bank of Sweden) recently raised the question " How much responsibility home countries are willing to take for financial stability in other countries where a bank operates? For example, the Nordea Group is a Swedish bank that has its largest market share in Finland. Would the Swedish authorities be willing and able to judge Noreda's impact on stability in Finland? And would the Finnish authorities be prepared to transfer responsibility for a considerable part of its financial system to Sweden? Similar problems exist in other countries." (Sveriges Riksbank, 2003, p. 2).

[10]A classic case of just such an externality occurred in the Herstatt Bank failure in which German authorities closed the institution at the end of the business day in Germany, but before all the bank's foreign exchange transactions had settled with counter parties in other time zones. While not affecting the total amount of loss, the timing of the legal closure did shift losses, either intentionally or not, from holders of mark claims on the bank, primarily German depositors, to those expecting to receive dollars from the bank later in the day, primarily U.S. and UK banks.

host-country-chartered institutions.[11] There may be more than one scheme for different types of institutions. But most terms of the deposit insurance structure are not prescribed and the details of the schemes are left to the discretion of the individual member countries.[12] These include funding of the plans, pricing of coverage, who should operate the plan (the private sector or public sector), how troubled institutions should be handled or how conflicts would be resolved where two deposit insurance funds might be affected by failure of an institution with top up coverage (see Dale, 2000). Additionally, it is the responsibility of the home country's central bank to serve as the lender of last resort in cases that do not involve EU-wide systemic risk issues (see Kane, 2003a). The European Central Bank is the lender of last resort only for large, systemically important banks in the EU.

In effect, the system design separates the responsibilities for controlling banking risk between the micro-risk associated with problems at relatively small institutions from the macro-risk associated with contagion risk at larger banks that may spread from one institution to others regardless of where the institutions are headquartered.[13] Although the EU's Council of Economic and Financial Affairs has recently promulgated a structure for coordination of financial stability efforts for banking supervisors and central banks within the EU, little attention has been paid to how the responsible agencies should decide whether a problem is a micro-risk or systemic risk problem.

Because of these differences, the structure of these systems may significantly impact the efficiency of resolving insolvent banks at minimum cost to the host country. When coupled with the bifurcated approach to controlling systemic risk, the heterogeneous set of deposit insurance schemes seems fraught with agency and conflicts of interest problems (see Kane, 2003b). These arise from several sources, including:

1. Uncertainties about the funding of the deposit insurance plans,
2. Differences in deposit insurance coverage and pricing of coverage,

---

[11]This also means that if home-country insurance is superior in other features to that provided generally in the host country, then the branch would have a competitive advantage relative to institutions chartered in the host country.

[12]For a brief review see European Commission (2005) and European Parliament (1994).

[13]Neito and Penalosa (2004) describe the proposed structure in great detail and discuss recent efforts to deal with the problems of coordination.

3. Reliance upon the home country, as opposed to host country, should institutions get into financial difficulties,
4. Differences in treatment with respect to the lender-of-last-resort function,
5. Differences in approaches to bankruptcy and priority of claims in troubled institutions, and
6. Differences within the EU between European Monetary Union versus non-European Monetary Union participants.

The EU countries differ in their insurance treatment of foreign branches and deposits. Most countries enable foreign branches to elect to be insured by their deposit insurance funds, and some countries also permit foreign operated branches to purchase additional insurance, over and above that provided by their home-country insurance scheme, if the host country's coverage is more generous.[14] Some provide insurance of foreign deposits, with most, but not all, being limited to foreign currency deposits of other EU member countries.[15]

When an EU country provides deposit insurance for its home banks, policies must be established for how foreign banks operating in the country will be treated. Unlike branches, host-country chartered or licensed subsidiary banks of foreign parents receive treatment equal to that accorded chartered domestic banks in the country, per EU directives. But host-country monitoring is not likely to be as effective as home-country monitoring, in part because less meaningful financial reporting information is available from domestic subsidiaries of cross-border banks. Even if information from the home country about the entire legal entity were available, host countries are unlikely to be able to take actions against banks outside their own jurisdiction. Finally, the potential losses to uninsured creditors and to the deposit guarantee fund depend as much upon the home country's closure and resolution policies as on the financial condition of the institution.

---

[14] Huizinga and Nicodeme (2002) demonstrate that within the guidelines established by the EU, the discretionary differences in insurance system design have affected international depositor decisions as to the placement of their funds.

[15] Several countries, including France, Italy, and Germany, are substantially more generous in their coverage than the minimum coverage of 20 thousand euro. Finally, many of the attributes that Huizinga and Nicodeme (2002) found to be important to international depositors, such as private administration and co-insurance, do vary substantially across EU countries.

Branches present a particular problem. The more insolvent an institution is before it is legally closed and the longer are accounts frozen during the resolution process so that depositors do not have access to them, the greater are the losses to the economy, including the home country's insurance funds and possibly its taxpayers. The larger the negative net worth, the greater also the losses are likely to be to guarantee schemes in host EU countries that offer supplemental deposit insurance coverage.

When a large number of foreign branches from different home countries coexist in a host country, bank customers in that country may encounter a wide variety of insurance plans that are likely to differ in terms of account coverage, premiums, insurance agency ownership (private versus government) and operation, ex ante funding, and credibility. This increases both confusion for depositors and potential confusion for regulators. Table 1 provides a general tabulation of the kinds of differences that can and do exist within the EU, despite attempts to ensure uniformity.

5. Insolvency Resolution Problems

Important practical issues arise if large cross-border institutions experience financial difficulties and have to be legally closed and resolved. These concern the timing of the official declaration of insolvency and the process by which insolvency is resolved, the relative supervisory roles of host- and home-country supervisors, the role of cooperation, the importance of externalities in the closure decision, and the importance of accounting rules in the closure process.

Cross-border coordination and decision-making would be extremely difficult, especially in the absence of explicit ex ante plans.[16] The EC Directive 2001/24/EC of April 4, sets forth EU policy for how failed banks are to be resolved and was intended to create a common approach to insolvency resolution, but even those involved are not fully aware of the differences in regimes that exist. Despite attempts to promote equal treatment for creditors, regardless of where they are located, the directive leaves the

---

[16]The European Commission is engaged in a review of its Deposit Insurance Directive 94/19 and surveys are still being conduced to provide an up to data compendium of the exact provisions of each country's scheme.

Table 1. **Variability of country policies towards deposit insurance and insolvency determination**

Account coverage

Less than 20,0000 Euro	IR, HU, LT, SL, LI
20,000 Euro	AU, BE, DE, GR, LX, NE, SW, CY, MA, ES, PO, SL R
More than 20,000 Euro	FI, FR, GE, LX, PT, UK, CZ, IT

Foreign Currency Deposits

Only for Euro Members	AU, FR, NE, SP, IT, LI (plus $)
Not Covered	CY, MA, FR
All Covered	BE, DE, GE, GR, IR, IT, LX, SW, UK, CZ, ES, HU, LA, PO, SL R, SL

Coinsurance

Yes	AU, BE, GE, IR, NE, SL, LI, UK, CY, CZ, ES, PO, SL R
No	DE, FI, FR, GR, IT, LX, PT, SP, HU, LT, MA, SL

Topping UP

Yes	LX, UK, LA, MA, PO, SL R, SL, SW, LI
No	AU, BE, DE, FI, FR, GE, GR, IR, IT, NE, PT,SP, CY, CZ, ES, HU

Ownership

Private	FI, FR, GE, IT, LX, UK
Public	AU, IR, NE, PT, SW, CZ, LA, SL
Joint	BE, DE, GR, SP, CY, ES, HU, LI, MA, SL R

Funding (Premiums)

Ex ante Payments	BE, DE, FI, GE, GR, IR, SP, CY, CZ, ES, HU, LA, PO, SL R, SL, LI
Ex post Payments	AU, FR, GE, IT, LX, NE, MA
Risk Based	IT, PT, SW

Reserve Fund

Permanent	BE, DE, FI, GE, GR, IR, IT, NE, PT, SP, SW, CY, CZ, ES, HU, LA, MA, PO, SL R, SL, LI
Not Permanent	AU, FR, LX, UK

Government Support

Explicit (Official)	AU, BE, DE, FI, IR, PT, SW, LA, SL
Implicit	IT, SP, UK, CY, ES, HU, MA, SL R, FR, NE, CZ
Prohibited	GE, LX

Austria (AU), Belgium (BE), Cyprus (CY), Czech Republic (CZ), Denmark (DE), Estonia (ES), Finland (FI), France (FR), Germany (GE), Greece (GR), Hungary (HU), Ireland (IR), Italy (IT), Latvia (LA), Lithuania (LI), Luxembourg (LX), Malta (MA), Poland (PO), Portugal (PT), Slovenia (SL), Spain (SP), Slovak Republic (SL R), Sweden (SW), United Kingdom (UK).

actual closure decision to each home country and its applicable bankruptcy procedures.[17]

With different deposit insurance coverage, sorting out who would be responsible for what claims at insolvent institutions would be a daunting task, especially when it comes to the top-off coverage claims for cross-border branches. In addition, because of different laws governing claims in bankruptcy across the different countries, there would be the added complication that depositors' claims might be treated differently if held in a branch than a subsidiary. Imagine the difficulty for a depositor, especially a corporate customer, who might have multiple accounts across countries, in choosing an account in his/her own country among say branches of banks headquartered in 23 other countries with different insurance and resolution systems. Any claims might be settled differently depending upon which bank or country the account was held and whether the account was in a branch or subsidiary. As cross-border bank expansion increases, even apparently small differences between deposit guarantee schemes may generate significant cost shifting when a troubled intuition needs to be closed or resolved.

The effectiveness of home-country prudential regulation of its foreign branches and subsidiaries in most countries depends on a number of factors, including the strength and credibility of the home country's deposit insurance scheme and the relative and absolute sizes of the banks in each country (Mayes, 2004; Eisenbeis, 2004). Host countries would prefer home-country prudential regulation of foreign branches particularly when the home country's deposit insurance scheme is strong and host country's branches are large. Home-country regulation is least satisfactory to host countries when its deposit insurance scheme is weak and branches in the host country large.

6. Possible Solutions to the Deposit Insurance Problems

Poorly designed deposit insurance, safety nets, and regulatory structures encourage both moral hazard behavior by banks and poor bank regulator performance that leads to excess forbearance on problem institutions. These

---

[17]Krimminger (2004) indicates that conflicts are supposed to be resolved through a mediation process that conveys that responsibility to the home country. Hüpkes (2003) indicates that in most countries in the EU bank insolvencies are covered under the general bankruptcy statutes, but several countries provide exceptions.

effects increase both the likelihood and costs of a banking crisis. Provisions to effectively reduce, if not eliminate, these adverse consequences directly by altering the structure of deposit insurance have proven difficult both to design and to implement. Risk-based insurance premiums, co-insurance, termination of coverage, and other schemes adopted from private insurance programs, have not proven very successful. Thus, it may be time to focus on alternative approaches to correcting the moral hazard and principal-agent problems.

One such solution involves a four point program for efficiently resolving insolvent banks so that both their credit losses and the widespread fear of bank failures are minimized and the adverse moral hazard incentives inherent in deposit insurance become benign. Indeed, with efficient insolvency resolution, deposit insurance provides desirable built-in redundancy in case specific resolutions turn out ex-post not to be efficient as hoped. The proposal is based on a fundamental understanding of the nature of bank failures and where the costs occur. Bank failures potentially involve not only credit losses when the market (recovery) value of the bank's assets decline below the market value of the bank's debt liabilities, but also liquidity losses, when depositors do not receive full and immediate access to the value of their deposits at the insolvent bank and qualified borrowers to their credit lines. Efficient resolution minimizes both types of costs. This can best be done when an institution is legally closed before their net worth goes to zero.[18] If this can be achieved, what remains is to reorganize and recapitalize the institution, either as an independent bank or through sale or merger with a solvent partner.

All four of the points in the program proposed focus on the term "prompt:"

1. Prompt legal closure when the bank's capital declines to some pre-specified and well-publicized minimum value greater than zero (legal closure rule),
2. Prompt estimates of the recovery value and assignment of any credit losses (haircuts) to de jure uninsured bank claimants,
3. Prompt reopening (for example, the next business day), particularly of larger banks, with full depositor access to their accounts on their due dates at par value for insured deposits and recovery value for

---

[18]To the extent that the timing of officially declaring a bank insolvent is under the control of bank regulators, the credit losses are also potentially under the control of the regulators.

uninsured deposits and borrower access to their pre-established credit lines, and

4. Prompt re-privatization and re-capitalization of the bank in whole or in parts at adequate capital levels.

Uniform adoption and application of these four principles by all countries, together with the development of the necessary infrastructure to make them work, would largely eliminate most of the agency problems, negative externalities, insurance fund losses, and coordination problems associated with the current EU system that has been identified. Legally closing institutions and placing them in receivership under new management while there is still the possibility of positive net worth, minimizes credit losses and means that differences in member country coverage and policies toward co-insurance, toping off, and netting become relatively irrelevant. It would also reduce the need and incentives to engage in ring-fencing of assets in branches, since equity holders (and perhaps some non-deposit debt holders) would be the only class of liability holders incurring losses.

Liquidity losses would be minimized since the institution would be reopened under different ownership and management in a day or so., instead of the three months or more waiting period that has often characterized past EU experience. This would go a long way towards reducing or eliminating the negative externalities, especially for smaller countries, of the failure of branches in host countries with large foreign presence. With minimum credit and liquidity losses, regulators would also be much more likely to legally close insolvent banks rather than engaging in forbearance. Finally, resolution would presumably be under the control and responsibility of the home country, whose regulators not only should have superior information, but also less need to coordinate the process across multiple countries and regulatory authorities. Policies would be both uniform and known, and this would reduce uncertainty on the part of all creditors and stakeholders.

To successfully apply an efficient resolution strategy to achieve an efficient deposit insurance structure requires some critical pre-conditions to be in place. Implementing these should be among the reforms instituted. First, it requires the political will of the regulators to use their available tools in a timely fashion to achieve least cost resolution for the insurance fund, the depositors, and the economy as a whole. Second, clear lines of authority and accountability for their actions are critical to establishing the right incentives. Third, regulators, who should have an information advantage over other possible responsible parties, should not only supervise banking organizations but also should be responsible for initiating closure, since this is the primary determinant of loss. Fourth, efficient resolution depends upon having the necessary legal tools in place and a means for quickly resolving conflicting claims. The necessary tools would include authority to legally close a bank before its capital is fully depleted. Finally, the law should that mandate mandatory speedy and irrevocable action to impose pro-rata haircuts on de jure claimants, minimize liquidity losses, and sell the bank's assets.

7. Conclusions

The focus of this study has been on the structure of deposit insurance systems in cross-border banking with particular emphasis on the EU and the related aspects of failure resolution and coordination when problems arise. We have identified a number of issues and concerns about the present system design that are likely to result in higher than necessary costs of insolvencies in cross-border banking. To date, little progress appears to have been made in the EU in dealing with them. Indeed, as cross-boarder branches and subsidiaries increase in importance in host EU countries, the resulting inefficiencies of the current structure, particularly for foreign branches, are likely to become large and may not only reduce aggregate welfare in the affected countries substantially when foreign-owned banks sink into insolvency, but also threaten financial stability. Serious doubts are cast about the longer-term viability of the single passport concept for cross-border branch banking under the existing institutional environment. To provide a more efficient arrangement, we propose four principles to ensure the efficient resolution of bank failures, should they occur, with minimum, if any, credit and other losses. These include: prompt legal closure of institutions before they become economically insolvent, prompt identification of claims and assignment of losses, prompt reopening of failed institutions and prompt recapitalizing and re-privatization of failed institutions. Implementing these proposals would go a long way towards mitigating or eliminating many of the potential agency and related problems inherent in the current confusing EU crisis resolution and deposit insurance regimes across countries.

References

Barth, James R., Gerard Caprio, Jr., and Daniel E. Nolle, 2004, "Comparative International Characteristics of Banking," Economic and Policy Analysis Working Paper 2004-1, Washington, D.C.: Comptroller of the Currency, January.

Barth, James R., Gerard Caprio, Jr. and Ross Levine, 2006, *Rethinking Bank Regulation and Supervision: Till Angels Govern*, Cambridge University Press, forthcoming.

Bollard, Alan, 2005, "Being a Responsible Host: Supervising Foreign-Owned Banks," in Douglas Evanoff and George Kaufman, eds., *Systemic Financial Crises: Resolving Large Bank Insolvencies*, Singapore: World Scientific.

Cardenas, Juan, Juan Pablo Graf, and Pascual O'Dogherty, 2003, "Foreign Bank Entry in Emerging Market Economies: A Host-Country Perspective," Committee on the Global Financial System (Basel, SW), working paper.

Citigroup, 2004, Form 10-Q for Citigroup Inc, Quarterly Report, November 4, 2004.

Committee on the Global Financial System, 2004, *Foreign Direct Investment in the Financial Sector of Emerging Market Economies*, Basel, Switzerland: Bank for International Settlements, March.

Dale, Richard, 2000, "Deposit Insurance in Theory and Practice," Societye Universitaire Europeenne de Recherches Financieres, Amsterdam.

Danmarks Nationalbank, *Financial Stability 2003*, Coppenhagen, DK.

Dell'Ariccia, Giovanni and Robert Marquez, 2001, "Competition Among Regulators," IMF Working Paper 01-73.

Dermine, Jean, 2003, "Banking in Europe: Past, Present and Future" in Vicor Gaspar *et al.*, eds., *The Transformation of the European Financial System*, Frankfurt: European Central Bank, May.

Di Giorgio, D. *et al.* 2000, "Financial Market Regulation: The Case of Italy and a Proposal for the Euro Area," Wharton Financial Institutions Center, working paper 00-24.

Eisenbeis, Robert A., 2004, "Agency Problems in Banking Supervision: The Case of the EMU," Federal Reserve Bank of Atlanta working paper, August.

Eisenbeis, Robert A. and George G. Kaufman, 2005a, "Cross-Border Banking: Challenges for the European Union," Federal Reserve Bank of Atlanta, Working Paper, 2005.

Eisenbeis, Robert A. and George G. Kaufman, 2005b, "Bank Crisis Resolution and Foreign-Owned Banks," prepared for a conference on "Banking Crisis

Resolution: Theory and Practice," Norges Bank, Oslo, Norway, June, forthcoming in the Federal Reserve Bank of Atlanta *Economic Review*, December 2005.

European Commission, 2005, "Financial Integration Monitor," Internal Market and Services working paper, background document, June.

European Financial Round Table, 2005, "On the Lead Supervisor Model and the Future of Financial Supervision in the EU: Follow-up Recommendations of the EFR," Position paper of the European Financial Round Table, June.

European Parliament, "Directive 94/19/EC of the European parliament and of the Council of 30 May 1994 on Deposit-Guarantee Schemes."

Garcia, Gillian G. H. Garcia and Maria J. Nieto, 2005, "Banking Crisis Management in the European Union: Multiple Regulators and Resolution Authorities, forthcoming.

Goldberg, Linda, 2003, "Financial FDI and Host Countries: New and Old Lessons," Committee on the Global Financial System (Basel, Switzerland), working paper, March.

Goodhart, Charles A. E., 2005, "Multiple Regulators and Resolutions" in *Systemic Financial Crisis: Resolving Large Bank Insolvencies*, Douglas Evanoff and George Kaufman, eds., Singapore: World Scientific.

Guilde, Anne-Marie and Holger C. Wolf, 2005, "Financial Stability Arrangements in Europe: A Review," Oesterreichische Nationalbank, Proceedings of OeNB Workshops No. 4.

Hall, Maximilian J. B., 2001, "How Good are EU Deposit Insurance Schemes in a Bubble Environment?," in *Asset Price bubbles: Implications for Monetary and Regulatory Policies*, Elsevier Science Ltd, Vol. 13.

Hüpkes, Eva, 2003, "Insolvency — Why a Special Regime for Banks?," *Current Developments In Monetary And Financial Law*, Vol. 3, International Monetary Fund, Washington, D.C., forthcoming.

Kahn, C. M. and J. A. C. Santos, "Allocating Lending of Last Resort and Supervision in the Euro Area," in V. Alexander, J. Melitz and G. M. von Furstenberg, eds., *Monetary Union: Why, How and What Follows?*, Oxford University Press: London.

Kane, Edward J., 1987, "Who Should Learn What From the Failure and Delayed Bailout of the ODGF?," *1987 Proceedings of Conference on Bank Structure and Competition*, Chicago: Federal Reserve Bank of Chicago, pp. 306–326.

Kane, Edward J., 1989, "Changing Incentives Facing Financial-Services Regulators," *Journal of Financial Services Research*, 2(3), pp. 265–274.

Kane, Edward J., 1991, "Financial Regulation and Market Forces," *Swiss Journal of Finance*, 127(3), pp. 325–342.

Kane, Edward J., 2003a, "How Country and Safety-Net Characteristics Affect Bank Risk-Shifting," with A. Hovakimian and Luc Laeven, *Journal of Financial Services Research*, June, pp. 21–30.

Kane, Edward J., 2003b, "What Kind of Multinational Deposit-Insurance Arrangements Might Best Enhance World Welfare?," *Pacific-Basin Finance Journal*, 11, pp. 413–428.

Kaufman, George G., 2004, "Bank Regulation and Foreign-Owned Banks," *Reserve Bank of New Zealand Bulletin*, June, pp. 65–74.

Kaufman, George G. and Steven Seelig, 2002, "Post-Resolution Treatment of Depositors in Failed Banks," *Economic Perspectives*, Second Quarter, pp. 27–41.

Kremers, Jeroen J. M., Dirk Schoenmaker and Peter J. Wierts, 2003, "Cross-Sector Supervision: Which Model?," eds. Robert E. Litan and Richard Herring, *Brookings-Wharton Papers on Financial Services*.

Krimminger, Michael H., 2004, "Deposit Insurance and Bank Insolvency in a Changing World: Synergies and Challenges," International Monetary Fund Conference, May.

Lewis, D., 1997, "Incongruent Incentives in Banking Supervision: The Agent's Problem," *The Journal of Economics*, 23(1), pp. 17–31.

Mayes, David, 2005, "The Role of the Safety-Net in Resolving Large Financial Institutions," in Douglas Evanoff and George Kaufman, eds., *Systemic Financial Crises: Resolving Large Bank Insolvencies*, Singapore: World Scientific.

Mayes, David and Jukka M. Vesala, 2005, "On the Problems of Home-Country Control," Bank of Finland, working paper.

Mayes, David G., 2004, "An Overview of the Issues," in David G. Mayes and Aarno Liuksila, eds., *Who Pays for Bank Insolvency?*, New York: Palgrave Macmillan.

Merton, Robert C. and Andre F. Perold, 1993, "Management of Risk Capital in Financial Firms," *Financial Services: Perspectives and Challenges*, Samuel L. Hayes III ed., Boston, MA: Harvard Business School Press.

Murton, Arthur J., 2005, "Resolving a Large Bank: The FDIC's Perspective," Douglas Evanoff and George Kaufman, eds., *Systemic Financial Crises: Resolving Large Bank Insolvencies*, Singapore: World Scientific.

Nieto, Maria J. and Juan Ma Penalosa, 2004, "The European Architecture of Regulation, Supervision and Financial Stability: A Central Bank Perspective," *Journal of International Banking Regulation*, 5(3), pp. 228–242.

Oosterloo, Sander and Jacob de Haan, 2005, "Arrangements for Financial Stability in OECD and EU Countries," in Douglas Evanoff and George Kaufman, eds., *Systemic Financial Crises: Resolution of Large Bank Insolvencies*, Singapore: World Scientific.

Peek, Joe and Eric S. Rosengren, 1997, "The International Transmission of Financial Stocks: The Case of Japan," *American Economic Review*, September, pp. 495–505.

Pulkkinen, Thomas E. and Eric S. Rosengren 1993, "Lessons from the Rhode Island Banking Crisis," *New England Economic Review*, May/June.

Schüler, Martin, 2003, "Incentive Problems in Banking Supervision-The European Case," Centre for European Economic Research, Mannheim, discussion paper, No. 03-62, November.

Schoenmaker, Dirk, and Sander Oosterloo, 2005, "Financial Supervision in an Integrating Europe: Measuring Cross-Border Externalities," *International Finance*, 8(1), pp. 1–27.

Soussa, Farouk, 2004, "A Note on Banking FDI in Emerging Markets: Literature Review and Evidence," Committee on the General Finance System (Basel, SW), working paper, March.

Strum, Jan-Egbert and Barry Williams, 2004, "Foreign Bank Entry, Deregulation, and Bank Efficiency," *Journal of Banking and Finance*, July, pp. 1775–1799.

Sveriges Riksbank, 2003, *Financial Stability Report*, 2/2003, Stockholm.

Thies, Clifford F. and Daniel A. Gerlowski 1998, "Deposit Insurance: A History of Failure," *Cato Journal*, 8(3), Winter.

Vives, Xavier, 2001, "Restructuring Financial Regulation in the European Monetary Union," *Journal of Financial Services Research*, February, pp. 57–82.

Wall, Larry D. and Robert A. Eisenbeis, 2002, "Reforming Deposit Insurance and FDICIA?," *Economic Review*, First Quarter, pp. 1–16.

Wall Street Journal Europe, 2005, "Spaghetti Banking," Friday/Saturday, April, pp. A8.

Walter, Norbert, 2001, "The Banking Supervision Issue in Europe," Briefing Paper for the Committee on Economic and Monetary Affairs (ECON) of the European Parliament, May.

Robert A. Eisenbeis is executive vice president and director of research at the Federal Reserve Bank of Atlanta and George G. Kaufman is the John Smith Professor of Banking at Loyola University Chicago and a consultant to the Federal Reserve Bank of Chicago. A longer version of this paper is a Federal Reserve Bank of Atlanta Working Paper, Eisenbeis and Kaufman (2005a).

The Lender of Last Resort in the European Single Financial Market

Garry J. Schinasi*
International Monetary Fund

Pedro Gustavo Teixeira
European Central Bank

1. Introduction

Financial crisis management in the single financial market of the European Union (EU) is a subject attracting increased attention. As one of the key objectives of the political, economic, monetary, and legal integration of the EU's 25 Member States, the single financial market is becoming a reality with the progressive expansion of cross-border financial services and the increased integration of national financial systems. While EU market liquidity and efficiency are no doubt improving, financial disturbances are now more likely to affect more than one Member State. Moreover, while European national financial systems are becoming systemically integrated, the EU's financial-stability architecture is still based primarily on the exercise of national responsibilities. The extent to which the EU architecture of purely national responsibilities and tasks is also capable of addressing cross-border (and perhaps pan-European) financial disturbances is often discussed and questioned, in part because it has not yet been tested.

In this context, the particular question addressed in this paper is how might the lender-of-last-resort function materialize during a systemic financial disturbance affecting more than one EU Member State. The paper is organized as follows. Section 2 sets out the key features of the European financial landscape that might have increased the likelihood that cross-border, if not systemic, financial disturbances would, if they occur, affect the EU. Section 3 very briefly describes the EU's architecture for financial crisis management. Section 4 runs through the fundamental issues that are likely to arise in implementing the lender-of-last-resort function in the EU context. Section 5 discusses the main challenges. Section 6 identifies ways forward for enhancing the effectiveness of the existing architecture.[1]

2. Systemic Risk in the Single Financial Market

The European financial landscape is in an increasing state of flux. The process of financial integration accelerated as a result of the efforts — particularly in the past five years — to remove barriers to cross-border business, of the resulting higher competition which is also leading to concentration, and the introduction of the euro in 1999. At the same time, integration is also leading to broader and deeper systemic inter-linkages across the EU, which increasingly represents in this respect the features of a single financial market. In particular, the following represent the transmission channels that may increase the scope for systemic risk in the EU.

2.1. *Integrated financial markets and market infrastructures*

Wholesale financial markets are closely and in some cases fully integrated in the EU. This applies in particular to euro-denominated unsecured money and government bond markets. Bank financing remains predominant in financial intermediation. Cross-border activity takes place mainly in high-volume markets for commonly tradable financial assets, including money market instruments, corporate bonds, or in the areas of investment banking and provision of financial services. Direct cross-border provision of financial services remains very limited in the retail sector; notably, traditional lending/deposit activities are very rarely conducted across borders. Market infrastructures are also becoming increasingly integrated. The TARGET payments system, operated by the Eurosystem, represents around 90 percent of large-value payments in euros. In securities and derivatives trading, regional and EU-wide mergers and alliances such as Euronext and the initiatives between the London Stock Exchange and Deutsche Börse, are moving toward reducing the existing fragmentation. In post-trading activities, there

---

[1] In this paper, "lender of last resort" and "emergency liquidity assistance" are used interchangeably.

are now established pan-European providers of clearing and settlement services, such as Euroclear and Clearstream.

2.2. *Banking concentration at the domestic level*

Mergers and acquisitions in the banking sector in the past decade, mostly domestic, reduced the number of credit institutions in the EU and led to high concentration ratios in many Member States, particularly the small- and medium-sized ones. For instance, in Belgium, Finland, and the Netherlands, the concentration ratio of the five largest banks exceeded 80 percent (European Central Bank, 2004). More generally, the stability of the financial system in most Member States is increasingly dependent on a small number of systemically important institutions whose size may range from half of gross domestic product (GDP) (France/Germany) to one-and-a-half of GDP (Belgium/Netherlands) (Praet, 2005). Cross-border mergers and acquisitions are less significant, but are increasing since 1999 vis-à-vis a slowdown in domestic operations. Financial integration, competition, and limits to domestic concentration, as well as the introduction of the euro are the possible explanations (European Central Bank, 2005).

2.3. *The emergence of pan-European banking groups with complex structures*

Pan-European banking groups are emerging through cross-border mergers and acquisitions and the increasing provision of wholesale services in other Member States. Although the direct provision of services across Member States is the most cost-efficient mode of market entry, the EU's single passport for banking services has been infrequently utilized. The indirect provision of services through the establishment of subsidiaries has been the preferred mode for several reasons, ranging from the need to adapt business activities to specific national features, taxation, insulation of liability, or legal and supervisory constraints (Dermine, 2003). The main implication is that the major banking groups have complex financial and institutional structures. There are around 40 major banking groups which on average are present in probably more than six of the 25 Member States, with some having establishments almost across the whole EU (Padoa-Schioppa, 2004). The expansion of complex banking structures presents a number of inconveniences, particularly in terms of structural, capital, and compliance costs.

2.4. *Centralization of business functions in banking groups*

Financial integration is also providing incentives for banking groups to re-organize and centralize certain key business functions at the group and EU levels. This allows banking groups to enhance operational efficiency and rationalize costs with regard to, for instance, back-office and strategic activities relating to financial markets. Liquidity and risk management are areas that are becoming increasingly centralized. One of the possibilities for re-organization is the merging of banks within a group into a single legal entity, which can then conduct cross-border business through the direct provision of services. As an example, the Nordea group has recently announced the adoption of the European Company Statute, which facilitates the merger of foreign entities into one. The re-organization of banking groups from complex structures into more simplified ones has a number of advantages linked to the unification of management and other internal systems, regulatory simplification, capital savings, and integrated risk management. At the same time, this will change the distribution of responsibilities between national authorities: while before all supervisors that licensed banks within a group were involved in its supervision, a unified group will be under the full jurisdiction and responsibility of a single national supervisor.

2.5. *The emergence of large and complex financial institutions*

Cross-sector financial activities are also intensifying in the single financial market. Major financial groups are engaging in a broad spectrum of financial services. These financial conglomerates, while in the most part combine banking and insurance services, are also involved in investment services and asset management. They are increasingly systemically significant within Europe. As a weighted average, financial conglomerates account for approximately 30 percent of the deposits and 20 percent of premium income in EU 15 Member States. In relation to assets, financial conglomerates have a considerably higher market share (European Commission, 2004).

2.6. *Increased foreign ownership of financial assets*

The accession in May 2004 of the ten new Member States in the EU accentuated another potential transmission channel: systemic linkages between countries through cross-border ownership of financial assets. While certain regions, such as the Benelux and the Nordic countries, already presented a

Table 1. Major transmission channels in the single financial market

Integrated money markets and other financial markets

Integrated financial market infrastructures:

- Payment systems
- Securities clearing and settlement systems and other market infrastructures (trading systems, OTC markets)

Major banks in concentrated domestic markets (direct and indirect losses)

Emergence of pan-European banking groups with systemic relevance in several Member States (contagion through intra-group linkages and exposures among network of counterparties)

Centralization of business functions in banking groups

Emergence of large and complex financial institutions with systemic relevance in several Member States

Increased foreign ownership of financial institutions and assets (as intensified by the recent EU enlargement)

---

high degree of interdependence, the integration of the new Member States gave rise to considerably higher levels of linkages between banking systems. This is due to the strong presence of EU-based foreign ownership of the capital and assets of the banking systems of the new Member States, in many cases in excess of 70 percent and in case of Slovakia and Estonia, around 90 percent of banks' share capital (European Commission, 2004). This compares with the previous EU average of 30 percent foreign ownership of banking assets/capital. Table 1 summarizes the key transmission channels that could increase the potential that a shock affecting a financial market or banking group would be transmitted and amplified across the EU.

3. The Architecture for Financial Crisis Management

The EU's institutional architecture for financial crisis management reflects three principles: decentralization, segmentation, and cooperation (see Table 3).[2]

---

[2]Lastra (2003) uses this triad to describe financial supervision in the EU.

Table 2. The committee-structures of the single financial market

Decision-making	ECOFIN Council	European Parliament	ECB's Governing Council (euro area of 12 Member States)
Finance Ministries (policy-making)	ECOFIN Council (Informal Eurogroup)	Economic and Financial Committee	Financial Services Committee
Commission and Finance Ministries (regulatory)	European Banking Committee	European Insurance and Occupational Pensions Committee	European Securities Committee — Financial Conglomerates Committee
Supervisors (operational)	Committee of European Banking Supervisors (London)	Committee of European Insurance and Occupational Pension Supervisors (Frankfurt)	Committee of European Securities Regulators (Paris)
Central banks (operational)	Committees of the Eurosystem — in euro area or EU-wide compositions (market operations, payment and settlement systems, banking supervision and financial stability)		

First, it is based on decentralization since the performance of financial stability functions relevant for crisis management is based in large part on the exercise of national responsibilities by banking supervisors, central banks, treasuries, and deposit insurance schemes. The European Central Bank (ECB) and the Eurosystem have financial-stability-related responsibilities, notably in the field of oversight of payment systems and contribution to national policies on financial stability and supervision. The performance of the lender of last resort function is likewise a national responsibility. This is also the case in the euro area, where the provision of emergency liquidity assistance (ELA) is under the responsibility and liability of national central banks. It is a unique circumstance in which a central bank may be providing ELA but has no monetary policy (as opposed to monetary operations) responsibilities. There are arrangements for an adequate flow of information within the Eurosystem in order that the potential liquidity impact of ELA operations can be managed in the context of the single monetary policy (European Central Bank, 2000).

Second, the financial stability functions are segmented across sectors and Member States. Banking supervision is exercised by cross-sectoral authorities and national central banks and, in some cases, is shared between the central bank and the supervisor.[3] The prudential framework followed by supervisors is largely harmonized by EU legislation, however, although its practical application may vary. Supervision of banking groups and financial conglomerates is conducted separately by each of the supervisors that licensed each entity of the group. Coordination between supervisors is achieved by "consolidating" and "coordinating" supervisors, which have limited powers to override decisions by individual authorities. In the single monetary jurisdiction of the euro governed by the ECB, banking supervision and ELA are under the responsibility and liability of the national authorities. Lastly, although some elements of deposit guarantee schemes are harmonized, they have broadly developed in different ways in each Member State.

Third, a number of cooperation structures are in place for bridging the potential gaps of coverage between national responsibilities and the several functions. These structures range from legal provisions (for example, consolidated supervision) to committees and memoranda of understanding.

---

[3]National central banks perform supervisory functions in 13 of the 25 Member States: Austria (in part), Cyprus, the Czech Republic, Germany (in part), Greece, Italy, Lithuania, the Netherlands, Poland, Portugal, Slovakia, Slovenia, and Spain.

Table 3. The institutional architecture of the single financial market

Levels	Functions	Decision-Makers	Cooperation Structures
EU (25 Member States)	• EU legislation (minimum harmonization) • Policy-coordination • Policy-shaping • State aid control	• ECOFIN Council • European Parliament • European Commission: (1) legislative Proposals/ (2) competition authority	• Economic and Financial Committee • Financial Services Committee • Regulatory committees
EMU (12 Member States)	• Single monetary policy • Payment systems' oversight • Contribution to financial stability and supervision	• ECB's Governing Council	• Eurosystem committees
National	• National legislation • Use of public funds • Banking supervision • Insurance supervision • Securities regulation	• 25 finance ministries • 25 national parliaments • 13 national central banks • 13 cross-sectoral agencies • 1 banking supervisor	• At the EU level • Home-/host-country relationships • Consolidated Supervision of banking groups

Table 3. (*Continued*)

Levels	Functions	Decision-Makers	Cooperation Structures
	• Supervision of financial conglomerates	• ca. 12 insurance and pensions supervisors • ca. 12 securities regulators	• Supplementary supervision of financial conglomerates • Supervisory committees • Bilateral, banking groups', regional and EU-wide MoU
	• Central banking functions (Member States outside euro area) • Lender of last resort (emergency liquidity assistance)	• 25 national central banks	• ECB's Governing Council (euro area) and General Council (EU) • Eurosystem committees (euro area or EU) • EU-wide and regional MoU
	• Deposit insurance	• Ca. 35 schemes (with diveirse features)	• Informal

Legal framework: EU Treaty + directly applicable national laws and regulation (minimum harmonization through EU legislation) enforced by national authorities and courts

3.1. *Cooperation between functions through committee-structures*

Given the decentralization and segmentation of financial stability functions, a number of committees organize cooperation at the EU level between authorities. These include supervisory, treasury, and central banking functions (Table 2). In the supervisory field, there are sectoral committees in the areas of banking, securities, and insurance. The role of these committees is to provide technical advice to the European Commission on regulation and pursue the convergence of supervisory practices. Cooperation between treasuries takes place at highest level through the Council of the EU consisting of the Economics and Finance Ministers (Ecofin Council), which decides the EU policy on financial markets. The Economic and Financial Committee (EFC) — comprising finance ministries and central banks — provides advice to the Ecofin, also on financial stability issues, including crisis management.[4] In central banking, the existing committees are established under the Eurosystem to advise the decision-making bodies of the ECB.

3.2. *Cooperation agreements*

The architecture also comprises EU-wide cooperation agreements between authorities — memoranda of understanding (MoU) — in crisis situations. The general aim of the MoU is to set out basic principles and procedures for disseminating information once disturbances are apparent and support the performance of financial stability tasks in the single financial market. This, however, is without prejudice to the discretionary exercise of responsibilities by national authorities, particularly since the MoU are non-legally binding and have thus a voluntary nature.

There are two MoUs currently in place on financial crisis management. The first MoU was adopted in 2003 between EU banking supervisors and central banks under the aegis of the Banking Supervision Committee of the Eurosystem. It should apply in crises with a possible cross-border impact involving individual banks or banking groups, or relating to disturbances in money and financial markets and/or market infrastructures with potential common implications for Member States. The MoU is designed to facilitate the interaction between central banking and supervisory functions in terms

---

[4]Economic Paper No. 156, European Commission, July 2001, (available at http://www.europa.eu.int / comm / economy_finance / publications / economic_papers / economicpapers 156_en.htm).

of assessing the systemic scope of a crisis and taking actions. Its provisions include principles and procedures on identifying the authorities responsible and on the cross-border flow of information.[5] The second MoU was adopted in May 2005 between the EU banking supervisors, central banks and finance ministries.[6] The explicit objective is to preserve the stability of the financial system of both individual Member States and of the EU as a whole, thus acknowledging the need to consider how to balance the different dimensions of systemic risk. The MoU aims in particular at providing initial conditions for policy coordination between all these authorities in the case of systemic crisis with spillovers in several countries.

3.3. *Conclusion*

The potential effectiveness of the lender of last resort function in the single financial market needs to be assessed in the context of the other components of the EU and national architecture for crisis management. In other words, the provision or not of ELA and the conditions under which it will be considered, might be determined to a large extent by the outcomes of the domestic, cross-border, and cross-functional interplay between the different authorities involved.

4. The Lender of Last Resort Function in Practice

What would happen if a pan-European banking group — with banks licensed and operating in several Member States — would suddenly experience a liquidity shock? Banking groups play an important role in European money markets, often acting as providers of liquidity in the inter-bank markets — acting thus as "money-centers" — to smaller banks (Cabral *et al.*, 2002). They are also counterparts to other large European and global financial institutions spanning a large set of markets. And they are key participants in the main payment systems as well as clearing and settlement systems. Therefore, a shock affecting such banking groups could potentially lead to systemic implications in both national markets and the European financial system as whole, notably in terms of impact on the liquidity distribution channels.

---

[5]Press release available at http://www.ecb.int/press/pr/date/2003/html/pr030310_3.en.html.
[6]Press release available at http://www.ecb.int/press/pr/date/2005/html/pr050518_1.en.html.

4.1. *Detection of a liquidity shock*

Central banks would likely be the first authorities to detect disturbances at the level of liquidity in money markets, payment systems, and common market infrastructures. Disturbances would be first detected at the national level, also in the euro area given the decentralized setting for the conduct of operational tasks by the central banks of the Eurosystem. Central banks could detect warning signs such as: intra-day or overnight liquidity shortages in individual banks; delays or failures to settle inter-bank transactions or collateral in monetary policy operations; settlement delays; or the failure of a central counterparty, clearing house, or securities-settlement systems to process securities transfers, which could spillover to payment systems.

Given the systemic inter-linkages described above, the local knowledge gathered by central banks would need to be considered at the EU level. In the case of the euro area, the existing infrastructure of the ECB/Eurosystem would certainly play a major role. In particular, the above Eurosystem committees would have an operational role in collecting local information and thus in detecting and assessing the extent of the disturbances for the euro money markets and market infrastructures. In the case of the central banks outside the euro area, more bilateral or regional cooperation could be expected, although the Eurosystem committees could also be involved.

4.2. *Assessment of systemic risk*

Central banks are also the authorities in an advantageous (and perhaps the best) position to assess the potential implications for systemic stability. They have a clear mandate for preserving financial stability and have the competencies required to assess the possible systemic implications of a financial problem or crisis both on the real economy and in terms of spillovers to other financial institutions and/or markets.

Understanding the potential systemic extent of disturbances affecting a banking group present in more than one Member State would involve a complex mapping of the relevant transmission channels. This may include intra-group (across jurisdictions) and inter-group relations (inter-bank/inter-country), market exposures, infrastructures, and any combination of these. In addition, central banks would have recourse to sources of information beyond their tasks, notably supervisors, foreign central banks, or market participants. Depending on the magnitude of the shock, this exercise could be quite challenging to coordinate.

Furthermore, the potential for systemic risk can be considered in different dimensions. It may be considered in terms of the impact on other banks, markets, and infrastructures wherever they are located in Europe or globally; or it may be considered in terms of the components of the national financial system. The national scope of systemic risk would likely diverge across countries, given for instance the importance of the banking group's activities in each national market, its counterparty relationships, or participation in payment or settlement systems. Some central banks could therefore have different perceptions on systemic risk, which may have a bearing on the process leading to the provision of ELA (if systemic risk is indeed a criterion for providing it).

4.3. *Jurisdiction of the lender of last resort*

With regard to the banking group affected directly by the liquidity shock, if it is not able to obtain collateralized funding from the markets — in spite of the central banks' supply of aggregate liquidity — it could warrant or expressly request ELA from a central bank.

The preliminary issue is jurisdiction. Which national central bank would be the lender of last resort vis-à-vis a banking group, and on what terms? There are several possibilities. The first is that the lender of last resort operates with regard to the group as a whole, thus meeting its total liquidity needs. Considering factors such as national brands, consolidated supervision, or the trend of centralization of liquidity management, the banking group could request ELA from the central bank of the jurisdiction of the parent or main bank. The liquidity provided could then be channeled intragroup to the banks in other countries. The other possibility is that each of the banks of the group requests separate ELA from the national central bank of the jurisdiction where they are licensed, on the basis of each bank's specific liquidity needs and assets.

These jurisdictional possibilities would represent different forms of credit risk-sharing among central banks. Centralized ELA without limiting the supply of liquidity to its jurisdiction would mean that one national central bank would bear the full credit risk with regard to a banking group that could be present in more than 6 countries and up to 19 countries (Schoenmaker and Oosterloo, 2005). The backing of cross-border externalities by a national central bank would correspond to a sort of exercise of "federal" responsibilities. In the decentralized option, there would be some degree of risk-sharing among the central banks. This would be not straightforward in case the group has centralized liquidity management: liquidity needs would relate to the group as a whole and not to individual banks, and collateral could be also centralized and not be easily transferable.

4.4. *Assessing the solvency position of a pan-European banking group*

A national central bank considering ELA would also need to assess the solvency position of the banking group and/or of the individual banks of the group. While central banks have direct access to information from their operational tasks, they would need to enhance their understanding of the banking group's problem, notably by requesting information from the group itself and more crucially from supervisors. How this would be organized in practice would probably very much depend on the specific features of the situation. Obtaining a comprehensive set of information on a pan-European banking group would however involve good coordination between the central banks and supervisors.

On the central banking side, the trend towards centralization of liquidity and risk management by banking groups suggests that the central bank of the jurisdiction where such centralization is made would have an informational and logistical advantage. On the supervisory side, as analyzed above, there are EU coordination rules that provide that relevant information should be gathered by the consolidating supervisor, normally at the level of the parent bank. In turn, this supervisor has the duty to disseminate such information in emergency situations to all the supervisors and the central banks concerned. Cooperation structures, such as committees or MoUs may facilitate the interaction between authorities, but they may also add a layer of complexity.

National central banks would therefore rely to a large extent on banking supervisory information and related assessments on the financial condition of the banks. This might be a challenge because pursuit of the respective mandates of central banks and supervisors might not be perfectly aligned, given the different nature of such mandates. In particular, central banks will be concerned about assessing rapidly the degree of credit risk that might be involved in providing liquidity to individual banks. Supervisors, on the other hand, might have constraints in terms of the supervisory process and timing in providing their assessment to central banks.

4.5. *Interaction with treasuries*

Credit to individual banks can only be provided against collateral and at market rates or higher penalty rates. A credit operation below market rates would represent an injection of public funds, which is not a function of central banks but rather of the state. Moreover, the EU Treaty provides that state aid may only be provided if it complies with certain conditions and after a process of approval by the European Commission; in addition, the treaty's prohibition of monetary financing also prevents central banks from incurring financial costs to be borne by the state.

As a lender of last resort, central banks may incur greater credit risk — on an exceptional basis in order to ease liquidity constraints — by accepting collateral below the standards required for monetary policy operations. The exact degree of credit risk incurred may be difficult to assess in practice given the nature of banks' assets (for example, loans which may not be disposed of swiftly enough without loosing value). If the ELA operation results in losses, national budgets will bear such losses either by the need to compensate central banks or via the lower return on dividends. This has an important bearing in justifying a lender of last resort as a national function, because there is no EU contingency budget for financial crisis.

Therefore, the provision of ELA in situations of significant credit risk may warrant some degree of interaction with treasuries, given that public funds might ultimately be put at risk. For instance, in the UK it is explicitly stated that the Chancellor would be given the option of refusing a financial-support operation proposed by the Bank of England or the Financial Services Authority.[7] In other countries with less explicit terms, this understanding is probably implicit. This interaction could potentially lead to national biases in assessing the degree of the threat to the financial system, given that national budgets will ultimately cover losses. In a cross-border systemic crisis, cooperation between treasuries — along the lines of the 2005 MoU — may thus be warranted to dispel such a bias.

4.6. *Conclusion: Pressure points of the lender of last resort*

Several pressure points (summarized in Table 4) can be identified in the performance of the lender of last resort function. The common denominator

---

[7]Memorandum of understanding (MoU) between HM Treasury, the Bank of England and the Financial Services Authority, available at http://www.bankofengland.co.uk.

Table 4. Pressure points of the lender of last resort function

---

Detection of disturbances at the European level (sharing of local knowledge)

Jurisdiction of the lender of last resort for banking groups: centralization vs. decentralization

Assessment of systemic risk at the European level:

- Complexity in mapping propagation channels
- Multiplicity of sources of information
- Uneven systemic implications across countries

Assessment of the solvency position of pan-European banking groups:

- Coordination in gathering information (from the banking group, market participants, supervisors)
- Access and reliance on supervisory information

Interaction between of central banking and supervisory functions — mandates may not be perfectly aligned

Interaction with treasuries

---

to these pressure points is that in stress situations the potential cross-border externalities will need to be adequately considered by all the authorities involved, in particular with regard to major players, such as pan-EU banking groups.

5. Challenges

Given that the expansion of cross-border banking activities is also observed in other regions and globally, what is distinct about the challenges to the EU's financial stability architecture? The answer is that the single financial market is a declared objective of the EU. A framework comprising rules, tools, and incentives (such as the single passport) is specifically set up for cross-border financial services. The pursuit of financial stability should be one of its basic components. In addition, there are supranational mechanisms available for dealing with coordination problems between authorities. Such mechanisms include EU legislation and, at the limit, may involve a single jurisdiction for the performance of financial stability functions. This section identifies the challenges that may arise in implementing the

EU lender of last resort function and also for the EU's financial stability architecture more generally. A final section concludes with a brief discussion of the possibilities for enhancing the effectiveness of the existing architecture.

5.1. *Institutional coordination issues*

Safeguarding financial stability generally, and an effective lender of last resort more specifically, require the assessment and containment of financial problems before they become systemic and have the potential to adversely affect the real economy.[8] Within the current EU architecture, this necessarily must be seen as a joint objective of the authorities responsible for financial stability, including central banks, supervisors, and treasuries to varying degrees. As elsewhere, within Europe a number of pre-conditions seem necessary to support this objective: (1) a clear assignment of responsibilities to the various authorities within the architecture; (2) the effective collection, dissemination, and sharing of information in crisis situations; and (3) the coordination of decisions by different authorities to the extent necessary and possible, so that the pursuit of their respective mandates can be aligned for safeguarding stability across the single financial market.

The credibility of the public policy architecture for assessing and containing systemic risk relates to its effectiveness in a real crisis. The pre-conditions mentioned above may be decisive, for instance, in terms of supporting private sector solutions, preventing the breakdown of liquidity distribution channels, avoiding bank runs, or facilitating the orderly winding down of institutions in difficulties. Moreover, transparency of the architecture is also linked to its credibility. Constructive ambiguity regarding the predisposition of authorities to intervene is not ambiguity about the allocation of responsibilities or the mechanisms in place for crisis situations; instead, it relates to the conditions in which public support may be given to institutions in difficulties.

Against this background, the pressure points identified above for the lender of last resort suggest three main challenges for institutional coordination among authorities.

First, the lender of last resort is a function performed at the national level by central banks. This means that central banks' decisions will be

---

[8] See Schinasi (2005), in particular Chapter VI.

guided by their national mandates (circumscribed to their jurisdiction) and institutional frameworks. In the case of the potential provision of ELA to a pan-European banking group, they may have to deal with significant cross-border externalities. In particular, the decision of one central bank to perform or not the function of the lender of last resort will necessarily affect the other central banks' jurisdictions. Coordination between the central banks involved may not be straightforward, however. More precisely, the assessments of the credit risk and systemic risk involved in the ELA may differ among central banks from their respective national perspectives. For instance, the systemic risk of the banking group in a certain Member State may not be deemed important, although it might be systemically relevant in the other countries involved. The potential contagion to national systems may be uneven, or there might be different macroeconomic considerations in each system. The credit risk may be considered too high. Or a central bank may not deem itself lender of last resort to the group. This balancing act of central banks as potential lenders of last resort will involve careful assessments of their responsibilities in the single financial market, which may require close coordination between them.

Second, there is the question of whether the responsible authorities — banking supervisors, central banks, and treasuries — would be able separately or collectively to effectively process the available information into a cohesive assessment of the systemic ramifications of a crisis situation throughout the EU. A formal mechanism for assessing systemic risk for the EU as a whole does not yet exist. The distribution of responsibilities is based on the home-country principle for supervisors, while central banks perform their tasks in their respective jurisdictions. In the case of a banking group, the consolidating supervisor is expected to gather and disseminate micro-prudential information, while macro-prudential information will be gathered by the central banks with jurisdiction over the markets and infrastructures in which the banking group is a key player. The mismatch between home-country control of supervision and host-country (central bank) operational conduct of financial market surveillance, may give rise to a gap between micro- and macro-prudential controls. Overcoming this mismatch would be essential for effectively dealing with a crisis since home- and host-country cooperation would be required for mapping and understanding the relevant transmission channels. Lastly, finance ministries would also need to obtain both national and EU-wide assessments of the systemic risk of a crisis situation.

Third, it follows that the actual decisions of central banks and supervisors (and eventually treasuries) involved vis-à-vis a European banking group or its components may need to be coordinated at the cross-border level in order to be aligned towards common objectives (or at least for facilitating instead of canceling each other's out). In particular, the macroeconomic responsibilities of central banks may need to be coordinated with the microeconomic responsibilities of supervisors. This may prove a challenge to the extent that responsibility for a bank or a particular market at the national level may not translate well to cross-border spillovers. The more diffuse the responsibility (with a number of different authorities in several countries) the harder it could be to achieve cross-border coordination of decisions.

5.2. *Coordination models*

Given the coordination issues identified above, there are alternative models of coordination for the performance of the lender-of-last-resort function vis-à-vis a banking group.

The first relies on detailed ex ante arrangements and may be designated as the Nordic model. It is set out in the MoU between the Nordic central banks[9] which will apply in the event of a crisis of a bank with operations in two or more Nordic countries.[10] It consists in the establishment, once a crisis is detected, of a coordination structure — a crisis management group — among the central banks involved. Under the leadership of the central bank where the management of the banking group is domiciled, this crisis management group centralizes the gathering and analysis of information regarding the financial condition of the banking group and the potential systemic implications. In addition, it centralizes the contacts with the banking group's management. It will also be responsible for briefing the decision-making bodies of each central bank. The briefing will include

---

[9]MoU available at http://www.riksbank.com/upload/Dokument_riksbank/Kat_AFS/samradsdok_kris_eng.pdf.

[10]The main example is Nordea, as the largest Nordic banking group with approximately EUR 250 billion in assets. Its market shares in domestic markets range between 15 percent and 40 percent. The holding company, established in Sweden, owns Nordea Bank in Finland, as well as Nordea's securities, asset management and insurance arms established in Sweden and Denmark. In turn, the Nordea Bank (Finland) owns banks in Sweden, Denmark, and Norway. Very recently, Nordea decided to move into a single company with a cross-border branching structure.

information on the systemic relevance of the crisis, the solvency position of the bank(s) affected, and — most importantly — clarify any differences of opinion between the central banks. The aim is that each central bank takes informed and possibly coordinated decisions. The main advantage of this model is that it attempts to minimize informational and analytical asymmetries among central banks and thus mitigate prisoners' dilemma type situations. On the other hand, the extent to which an effective coordination structure could be set-up for all EU banking groups can be questioned, if not disputed. The Nordic context is characterized by strong systemic (but also cultural and linguistic) inter-linkages. This is not applicable to other regional markets or the EU as a whole, where the systemic impact would probably differ considerably among countries.

The second model of coordination may be designated as the supervisory model. Because the EU implementation of Basel II will lead to a reinforcement of the coordination tasks of the consolidating supervisor (vis-à-vis the other supervisors of the group), it can be argued that the national central bank of the jurisdiction of the consolidating supervisor could also assume coordinating tasks vis-à-vis the other central banks concerned. A supporting argument is that this model would be consistent not only with the supervisory framework but also with the centralization of liquidity management in banking groups. However, this would imply that one central bank would take a higher degree of responsibility for the banking group with regard to the other central banks. It would for instance have to consider with greater intensity the group- and EU-wide — *vis-à-vis* the domestic — perspective in terms of solvency and systemic risk. It would attribute to the national central bank to some extent — as it does to the consolidating supervisor — limited EU "federal" tasks with regard the banking groups under its jurisdiction.

Lastly, there is the possibility of no ex ante coordination arrangements in terms of risk-sharing, but the commitment of the central banks involved to exchange information and coordinate their policy measures on the basis of the existing cooperation structures, as described above.

6. Ways Forward: Coordination versus Centralization of Policymaking

One of the conclusions of this paper is that the lender of last resort function in Europe cannot be disentangled from the overall architecture for financial stability. The efficient operation of the lender of last resort in a systemic crisis will crucially depend on the effectiveness of the other financial stability functions, notably supervision and potentially the treasuries. In an optimal setting, the authorities' mandates should be aligned in the pursuit of the stability of the single financial market. Thus, short of reforming the existing architecture, the overall challenge is its effective implementation. Two options are apparent for optimizing the current framework.

First, coordination between authorities — central banks, supervisors, and treasuries — could be ensured. The expansion of cross-border business increases the likelihood of conflicts of interest between the pursuit of national mandates and the need to consider the wider cross-border systemic implications in decision-making. It might be illusory to believe that conflicts of interest may be resolved ex ante or optimally during a crisis in view of the present architecture. Even if the authorities had the benefit of complete and perfect information, reliance on the pursuit of national mandates could still leave gaps in the consideration of the systemic impact of a crisis. A possible means to help manage conflicts is to make clear the possible cross-border systemic implications of the crisis to all authorities involved. This may help avoid the most serious and costly outcomes. Mechanisms may include — following the "Nordic" model — pooling of information on systemic risk, joint assessments of systemic implications associated with the failure of a large institution, procedures for consideration of EU-wide systemic threats, and regular stress-testing and simulation exercises. The implementation of Basel II is also an opportunity to enhance coordination, because a consolidating supervisor will be nominated for each banking group, and the supervisors involved will adopt written coordination agreements.

More generally, as markets become pan-European, the nature of systemic risk will continue to change, because markets can act as both vehicles of contagion as well as stabilizing forces. In the case of the near collapse of Long Term Capital Management, there was a simultaneous crisis of markets and institutions very much driven by the strong inter-linkages between participants in derivatives and other markets. Greater coordination at the EU level could also aim at providing an effective multilateral surveillance mechanism over pan-European markets as well as the institutions within them. Given their vital role in ensuring both financial and monetary stability, central banks would seem to have a natural, if not central role to play in this effort. This applies in particular to the ECB and the Eurosystem, which comprise a supranational network that is well placed to assess the systemic nature of a liquidity shock and generalized financial market disturbances.

All in all, a coordination model should make the most of the advantages of a decentralized approach to preserving financial stability, in particular the local knowledge on the features of the components of the financial system. Therefore, the wealth of knowledge associated with the EU decentralized approach can be seen as particularly valuable, as long as effective coordination procedures and mechanisms are in place to tackle the systemic implications of a crisis. Accordingly, banking supervisors, central banks, and finance ministries are working towards enhancing substantially their coordination arrangements, which include the 2005 MoU, a crisis simulation exercise to test the MoU and to assess how cooperation might work in practice,[11] and agreements on best practices in crisis management.

The second option for enhancement is the centralization, or rather the federalization, of financial stability functions. This option might emerge if coordination issues are not adequately resolved. As noted before, given the decentralized banking supervision and financial market surveillance, it would most likely be difficult to work out responsibilities in the midst of a crisis and on an ad hoc basis. This may be particularly valid with regard to the increasing number of European banking groups. In terms of business functions, banking groups are increasingly integrated — notably in terms of liquidity management — and may establish themselves under a single legal entity. Therefore, they operate already in a sort of federal business environment. The question is whether financial stability functions should mirror such an environment and be federalized. This could happen either at the national level, with the extension of the home-country control to all the components of a banking group, or at the EU level, with a transfer of competence to supranational authority(ies). The analysis in this paper suggests that such an institutional move, if ever required by potential coordination issues, would need to involve all financial stability functions. That is, if the option for federalization of the lender of last resort function — at the national or EU levels — would be elected, it should involve similar arrangements for supervision of banking groups, which, in turn, could involve some degree of mutualization among Member States of the contingency public funds to be potentially employed in a systemic crisis.

---

[11] See *Financial Times* news article, "EU agrees financial crisis plan", 16 May 2005, p.15.

References

Aglietta, Michel, 1999, "A Lender of Last Resort for Europe," Working Paper no. 12, CEPII.

Cabral, Inês, Frank Dierick, and Jukka Vesala, 2002, "Banking Integration in the Euro Area," Occasional Paper no. 6, European Central Bank.

Dermine, Jean, 2003, "Banking in Europe: Past, Present and Future," in *The Transformation of the European Financial System*, European Central Bank, pp. 31–95.

Enria, Andrea, and Jukka Vesala, 2003, "Externalities in Supervision: The European Case," in *Financial Supervision in Europe*, Kremers/Schoenmaker/Wierts, eds., Elgar, pp. 60–89.

European Central Bank, 2000, "Annual Report 1999."

European Central Bank, 2004, "Report on EU Banking Structures."

European Central Bank, 2005, "Report on EU Banking Structures."

European Commission, 2004, "Financial Integration Monitor," Commission Staff Working Document, available at http://www.europa.int.

Freixas, Xavier, Curzio Giannini, Glenn Hoggarth, and Farouk Soussa, 1999, "Lender of Last Resort: a Review of the Literature," *Financial Stability Review*, Issue 7, November 1999, Bank of England.

Garcia, Gillian G. H., 2005, "Preserving Financial Stability: A Dilemma for the EU," paper prepared for the Western Economic Association, July 2005, mimeo, October.

Goodhart, Charles, and Gerhard Illing, 2002, Introduction to *Financial Crises, Contagion, and the Lender of Last Resort, A Reader*, Goodhart/Illing, eds, Oxford.

International Monetary Fund, 2003, "Managing Systemic Banking Crises," Occasional Paper no. 224, Washington D.C.

Lastra, Rosa, 2003, "The Governance Structure for Financial Regulation and Supervision in Europe," *Columbia Journal of European Law*, 10, pp. 49–68.

Padoa-Schioppa, Tommaso, 2003, "Central Banks and Financial Stability: Exploring the Land in Between," in *The Transformation of the European Financial System*, eds. Vitor Gaspar, *et al.*, Frankfurt: European Central Bank, pp. 269–310.

Padoa-Schioppa, Tommaso, 2004, "How to Deal with Emerging Pan-European Financial Institutions?," speech at the Conference on Supervisory Convergence, organized by the Dutch Ministry of Finance, The Hague, 3 November 2004.

Padoa-Schioppa, Tommaso, 2004, *Regulating Finance*, Oxford.

Praet, Peter, 2005, "A Central Bank Perspective on Large Banks in Small Countries and Crisis Resolution," presentation at the Norges Bank, June 2005, available at www.norgesbank.no.

Prati, Alessandro, and Garry J. Schinasi, 1998, "Will the European Central Bank Be the Lender of Last Resort in EMU," in *The Euro: A Challenge and Opportunity for Financial Markets*, eds. Artis, Weber, and Hennessy, Frankfurt: Routledge and SUERF, pp. 227–256.

Prati, Alessandro, and Garry J. Schinasi, 1999, "Financial Stability in European Economic and Monetary Union," *Princeton Studies in International Finance*, No. 86, August 1999.

Rochet, Jean-Charles, and Xavier Vives, 2004, "Coordination Failures and the Lender of Last Resort: Was Bagehot Right After All?," IDEI Working Papers 294, Institut d'Économie Industrielle (IDEI), Toulouse.

Schinasi, Garry, 2003, "Responsibility of Central Banks for Stability in Financial Markets," IMF Working Paper 03/121 (Washington: International Monetary Fund, June).

Schinasi, Garry, 2005, "The Euro at Five: Ready for a Global Role?" Chapter 5 in *Euro at Five: Ready for a Global Role*, ed. Adam S. Posen, Washington, D.C.: Institute for International Economics, April.

Schinasi, Garry, 2005, *Safeguarding Financial Stability: Theory and Practice*, Washington D.C.: International Monetary Fund (December).

Schoenmaker, Dirk, and Sander Oosterloo, 2005, "Financial Supervision In an Integrating Europe: Measuring Cross-Border Externalities," *International Finance*, 8(1), pp. 1–27.

Sveriges Riksbank, 2003, "The Riksbank's Role as a Lender of Last Resort," *Financial Stability Review* no. 2, 2003, Riksbank.

Garry J. Schinasi is an advisor in the Finance Department of the International Monetary Fund. Pedro Gustavo Teixeira is principal expert in the Directorate Financial Stability and Supervision of the European Central Bank. The views expressed in this paper are those of the authors and should not be attributed to the International Monetary Fund, its Executive Board, or its management, or to the ECB or the Eurosystem. They are grateful for comments received from Peter Praet, Panagiotis Strouzas, and participants in the conference.

Payment Systems and the Safety Net: The Role of Central Bank Money and Oversight

Jeff Stehm*
Board of Governors of the Federal Reserve System

1. Introduction

The financial safety net in the United States is commonly defined to include components such as federal deposit insurance, Federal Reserve lender-of-last-resort (LLR) facilities, and access to Federal Reserve payment services (see Greenspan, 2001 and Meyer, 2001). Although the financial safety net provides important public benefits in the area of financial stability, it is recognized that these benefits may come at a cost. In particular, the safety net may create incentives that encourage greater risk taking and, as a result, greater moral hazard for the government (see Furlong, 1997). Although much has been written in the safety net literature on deposit insurance and the discount window, less systematic attention has been given to the safety net implications of the central bank's role in the payments system as a settlement institution and prudential overseer.

Two recent central bank reports issued by the Group of Ten (G10) Committee on Payment and Settlement Systems provide a good starting point for exploring the payments system aspects of the safety net by shedding light on how central banks view their monetary and financial stability roles in relation to the payments system. The purpose of this paper is to discuss some of the intriguing ideas in these reports and to highlight some particular areas where further research might prove fruitful in extending understanding of safety net issues.

The first report, *The Role of Central Bank Money in Payment Systems* (Central Bank Money Report) issued in August 2003, discusses the pivotal role of central banks in promoting safer and more efficient payment systems along three dimensions — (1) providing a safe and liquid settlement asset in the form of central bank money; (2) acting as a settlement institution; and (3) providing intraday credit to facilitate the safe and smooth settlement of payments. The report also points out some of the costs associated with such roles — issues of direct and indirect credit risk to the central bank and, more broadly, moral hazard and the potential need for central bank oversight of payment systems.

The second report — *Central Bank Oversight of Payment and Settlement Systems* (Central Bank Oversight Report) issued in May 2005 — discusses some of the risks and externalities that have led central banks to increase their oversight of payment systems in recent years. It also discusses the issues faced by central banks in determining the scope of their oversight responsibilities and activities, including the challenges of cooperating among central banks to oversee effectively cross-border and multi-currency systems.

2. Payment Systems and the Role of the Central Bank

The payments system plays a fundamental role in the economy by providing a mechanism to settle claims generated by various economic actors across both the real and financial sectors. In its simplest form, a payment system is a procedure for transferring money between a payer and payee. Such transfer procedures may range from simple models where a payer and payee exchange currency (a central bank liability) in a face-to-face transfer, to more complex models where a payer and payee interact through intermediaries, such as banks, that in turn exchange and settle payment orders using the settlement assets of a settlement institution(s). Settlement institutions are typically banks and the central bank, and the settlement asset, therefore, can be either commercial bank money (deposit liabilities) or central bank money (reserve balance liabilities), although other forms can exist.

Given the fundamental role of payment systems and the complexities of the inter-bank payment process, the ability to make payments safely and efficiently is critical to the functioning of banking and financial markets and the economy more generally. In making payments, banks and their customers face uncertainties concerning the timing of payment receipts and disbursements (see Bech and Garratt, 2003; Hancock and Wilcox, 1996). Managing such uncertainties is particularly challenging for banks, which must be ready at all times to honor the payment orders of their customers by converting their deposits into central bank deposits or deposits at another commercial bank at par. To manage these uncertainties, bridge the timing gaps between payment receipts and disbursements, and facilitate the smooth functioning of payments, a liquid settlement asset and credit is needed by payment system users.

Two key components in the ability to make payments safely are (1) a safe and liquid settlement asset; and (2) a sound settlement institution. The choice of a settlement institution, and hence a settlement asset, is an important one. When settlement institutions or assets carry with them credit or liquidity risk, banks and other payments system participants face potential losses and liquidity pressures.[1]

The *Central Bank Money Report* points out four broad factors that likely influence a payment system user's choice of a settlement institution and settlement asset — safety, liquidity and credit provision, payment services, and competitive neutrality. The first factor — the safety of the settlement asset — refers to the likelihood of the settlement asset retaining its value to the holder and hence its acceptability to others as a means of payment.[2] Central bank money is generally considered the safest settlement asset given the explicit or implicit state support for central banks, the risk-adverse tendencies of central banks, and the ability of central banks to cover their obligations by issuing additional central bank liabilities. Although the balance sheets of commercial banks are typically riskier than the central bank's, commercial bank money often plays a prominent role as a settlement asset in the payments system. In part, this reflects the role banks play in providing deposit and credit facilities and, in part, the ability of banks to provide a broader range of payment and settlement services under more flexible terms and conditions than is typically the case for central banks. The use of commercial bank money as a settlement asset also may benefit from depositor

---

[1]CPSS (2001) states that "... [settlement assets] should carry little or no credit or liquidity risk," and the CPSS-IOSCO (2001) says that "[system participants should be protected] from potential losses and liquidity pressures arising from the failure of the settlement institution whose assets are used."

[2]Although the acceptability of a settlement asset among potential counterparties depends in part on the creditworthiness of the settlement institution, it also depends, in part, on the attributes of the payment system used to transfer the settlement asset or convert it into another settlement asset, such as scope, speed, and cost.

protection schemes, prudential supervision, and the risk management controls of inter-bank payment and settlement systems.[3]

The second factor involves the liquidity of the settlement asset issued by a settlement institution and the ability and willingness of the settlement institution to provide routine credit under terms and conditions acceptable to accountholders.[4] The liquidity and credit aspects of a settlement asset depend on the settlement institution's ability to expand its balance sheet by issuing additional settlement assets at short notice and in sufficient quantity. As the monetary authority, central banks can expand their balance sheets rapidly and inject very large amounts of liquidity to facilitate the smooth settlement of payments. Banks, on the other hand, may be constrained by the dictates of private business judgments or by prudential or supervisory requirements from rapidly expanding their balance sheet liabilities, particularly in times of stress.[5]

Another factor is the price, terms and conditions under which credit is provided by a settlement institution. In providing credit to their customers,

---

[3] "Prudential supervision reduces the likelihood of default by supervised institutions, improving the safety of claims on these institutions. And the existence of investor/depositor protection schemes has the effect of maintaining at least partial convertibility of a failed bank's liabilities into other forms of money, and hence supporting their value as settlement assets. Utilities like clearing houses often go further in lowering default risk by fully collateralizing any exposure to their members and not engaging in any further financial activities which could expose them to risk." CPSS (2003), p. 13.

[4] Participants in the payments system generally find it valuable to have access to some form of credit in order to use the system efficiently. Alternatively, they can hold precautionary balances to settle payments. It is generally inefficient, however, to hold sufficient precautionary balances at banks or the central bank to meet payment obligations under all possible timing scenarios for payment inflows and outflows. Participants may also attempt to address mismatches between payment inflows and outflows through the design of payment mechanisms that more effectively match incoming and outgoing payments so as to reduce the liquidity needed for settlement.

[5] Private business judgments about a bank's liquidity and solvency impose limits (market discipline) on the bank's ability to raise new liabilities or capital. Flannery (1996), pp. 805–806, for example, states that "An illiquid bank may have trouble convincing private lenders of its solvency [because in part banks specialize in financing assets which are intrinsically hard to value]." He goes on to state that a financial crisis exacerbates this problem by making "...private lenders uncertain about the accuracy (appropriateness) of their traditional underwriting techniques and judgments. Just when some banks require credit from new sources on short notice, potential lenders become uncertain about how to identify borrower solvency."

banks generally have more flexibility with regard to pricing, collateralization, and repayment terms for credit than do central banks. Central banks, in lending to banks, may be limited by statute or policy to lending only on a secured basis, requiring repayment of intraday credit by the end of the day, and imposing penalty charges when intraday credit is not repaid. Such constraints stem, in part, from the safety net implications of central bank credit. First, such credit extensions expose the central bank to intraday credit risk (that is, puts central bank funds at risk) and may result in spillovers to the discount window (another element of the safety net). Second, if central banks provide intraday credit at below market prices, moral hazard incentives may be created.

The final two considerations in the choice of a settlement institution are the payment and related services provided by the settlement institution and the perceived competitive neutrality of the settlement institution. Payment services involve a complex mix of information services (account balances, progress of particular payments), single currency and multicurrency accounts, account access methods, payment instruction input, and availability factors. The range of choice, service cost and quality, and reliability of services relative to users' needs are key factors in the choice of a settlement institution. In a competitive environment, commercial banks will have significant incentives to provide efficient and innovative payment services that meet their customers' needs, including the settlement needs of other (respondent) banks or inter-bank payment arrangements. Commercial banks, however, can be placed at a disadvantage in providing payment and settlement services to other banks or inter-bank arrangements if central banks provide services as a settlement institution on a subsidized basis. Such subsidies may cause competitive and resource allocation distortions and inefficiencies in the payments system. One result may be an overuse of and over reliance on the central bank as a settlement institution, thus shifting additional operational risk and possibly direct or contingent credit risk to the central bank.

Competitive neutrality refers to the extent to which the use of a particular settlement asset makes the user reliant on, or requires the user to provide sensitive business information to, a settlement institution that is a competitor. In this regard, central banks are generally seen as competitively neutral by most financial market participants due to their public-sector nature, limitations on who can access their services, and the limited scope of their services. In some cases, however, a central bank may be perceived as a competitor in some respects, for example, by correspondent banks or private-sector operators of inter-bank payment and settlement arrangements.

Payment system users, including banks, make different choices regarding settlement institutions based on different assessments of their private costs and benefits. Overall, commercial bank money is the most available and frequently used settlement asset in the payments system. This largely reflects the important role played by banks as settlement institutions in providing deposit and credit facilities and the associated payment services required to transfer deposits. The central bank, however, also plays an important role in the payments system as a settlement institution, particularly in systemically-important inter-bank systems. The central bank is generally seen as a competitively neutral institution that can provide a safe and liquid settlement asset and access to intraday and overnight credit on a large scale at short notice. These factors are generally perceived to contribute to the smooth operation of the payments system and the reduction of systemic risk.[6] In holding accounts for a large portion of the banking system, the central bank also can settle different transactions among a broad set of accountholders at a single settlement institution (the central bank), which may help accountholders to economize on liquidity usage. Finally, the pricing of central bank services, by helping to reduce or eliminate public subsidies, can allow more efficient allocation of resources to payment services and level the playing field among service providers.

While one reading of these factors and benefits might point to a broader role for the central bank as a settlement institution, central banks typically limit their role on three policy grounds. First, in a market economy, significant reliance is placed on competitive forces to promote efficiency and innovation in payment and settlement services. In some circumstances, the provision of central bank settlement services could cause the disintermediation of commercial providers of settlement accounts and related services, and discourage the emergence of innovative, market-oriented solutions to payment and settlement needs. Second, when the central bank provides intraday credit to its accountholders and through them to the broader financial system, central bank funds are put at risk. And third, there may be

---

[6]"The widespread adoption of real-time gross settlement (RTGS) payment systems settling in central bank money has enhanced the safety of payment systems within countries. Similarly the development of CLS Bank, which uses central bank money for funding and defunding, addresses a major risk in the settlement of foreign exchange transactions across countries." CPSS (2003), p. 43.

a perception that access to an account at the central bank provides either explicit or implicit access to central bank liquidity on both a routine and emergency basis. These latter two reasons are classic safety net concerns. Most central banks, therefore, require clear public policy grounds to justify their provision of settlement accounts, settlement services, and intraday credit to private sector systems and institutions. As a result, central banks generally limit access to accounts and credit to financial institutions — primarily banks — that form a country's system for deposit transfers and that are a subject to prudential supervision and oversight.[7]

Central banks may also face certain practical limits on their role as a settlement institution. For instance, using the central bank as the settlement institution for a multicurrency system may be impractical because the supply of central bank money and central bank accounts and services is normally confined to the central bank's area of jurisdiction and currency of issue. Furthermore, central banks may have constraints, similar to those of commercial banks, in providing credit (that is, creating liquidity) in a currency other than their own. Finally, the payment services provided by a central bank as a settlement institution may be seen as competing with private-sector inter-bank systems, raising possible concerns about conflicts of interest and competitive "non-neutrality."

In summary, as an institution that holds accounts and reserves for a large share of the banking system, the central bank is in a unique position to act as a settlement institution and contribute to the safe, smooth, and efficient operation of the payments system. It can provide a safe settlement asset, serve as a competitively neutral and relatively default-free settlement institution, and, by granting intraday credit, provide settlement liquidity on short notice and in large quantities. These attributes are most potent for systemically important payment systems, where the values settled are very large in relation to participants' balance sheets and capital. The failure of a settlement institution for such a system could cause serious and widespread disruption to the financial system and place significant demands on the safety net. The *Central Bank Money Report* states that "the widespread choice of central bank money as a settlement asset reflects its overall qualities of safety ... and finality ... and the use of the central bank as a settlement institution minimizes the risk of settlement institution failure,"

---

[7]Few central banks, including the Federal Reserve, limit access to central bank accounts strictly to banks. Some provide accounts to a wide range of financial and non-financial institutions. See CPSS (2003), pp. 26–29.

(CPSS, 2003). But the benefits of access to central bank accounts, central bank money, and central bank intraday credit to facilitate the settlement of payments may come at a cost — possible competitive distortions and disintermediation, significant credit risk borne by the central bank, perceptions by accountholders of access to the broader safety net, and moral hazard.

3. Moral Hazard, Externalities, and Central Bank Oversight of Payment Systems

Although access to central bank accounts, services, and credit can contribute to financial stability goals, it also may create riskier behavior by central bank accountholders and reduce market discipline concerning risk management in payment systems. First, access to central bank accounts, per se, may create the perception that the accountholder has access to the central bank as the lender of last resort, especially if an accountholder is allowed, either routinely or inadvertently, to use intraday credit or overdraw its account. Second, the provision of central bank intraday credit, if subsidized and provided largely without constraints, may provide incentives for banks to hold lower liquidity reserves (that is, riskier, less liquid balance sheets) while at the same time to not economize on intraday credit, making banks more dependent on liquidity-intensive payment practices. Third, the use of a relatively default-free settlement institution (the central bank), particularly if payment and settlement services are subsidized, may provide incentives for banks to overuse central bank settlement services and reduce the monitoring of their counterparties in the payment process. Fourth, payment system participants may under invest in risk management if they assume that the central bank, as the lender of last resort and as the "settlement institution of last resort," will in all cases provide liquidity and services when a private-sector system has difficulties in order to avoid the possibility of systemic problems (see Godeffroy, 2004, and Lacker, 2005). These assumptions may be reinforced if the central bank is viewed as having a direct incentive to avoid a disruption either because a disruption might affect directly the central bank's ability to implement monetary policy, or because a disruption might directly or indirectly affect a central bank's core mission for macro-economic and financial stability. Finally, externalities, coordination problems, economies of scale, and non-contestable monopolies in private-sector payment and settlement systems may lead to underinvestment in risk management and risk reduction (for example, security, resilience, risk controls, or liquidity), or impede the establishment of or migration to safer systems. The result may be higher levels of risk, including systemic risk, than is socially optimal (see CPSS, 2005a; Godeffroy, 2004; Tumpel-Gugerell, 2005).

Central banks can and do mitigate these incentives and perceptions through the terms and conditions on which they provide settlement services to accountholders, including other systems that use their settlement services. First, policy clarity regarding access to accounts, intraday credit, and lender-of-last-resort facilities help to remove ambiguities and manage perceptions regarding such access.

Second, central banks can reduce or eliminate any subsidies associated with the provision of central bank settlement services and intraday and overnight credit. In the case of the Federal Reserve, the Monetary Control Act of 1980 requires that fees for Federal Reserve payment services recover, over the long run, all direct and indirect costs actually incurred by the Federal Reserve as well as certain imputed costs that would have been incurred and profits that would have been earned if Federal Reserve payment services had been provided by a private firm.[8] The Federal Reserve also charges fees for intraday credit and, in addition, places constraints on the provision of intraday credit, including caps and, in certain cases, collateral.[9] Such fees for services and intraday credit mitigate any subsidy element. The Federal Reserve also charges for discount window borrowings at rates above the target federal funds rate, and a penalty rate significantly above the target federal funds rate for any overnight overdrafts.

Finally, where warranted, central banks and other regulators can seek to strengthen payment and settlement systems, thus reducing the likelihood of systemic disruptions and pressures. One approach central banks have taken to strengthen payment and settlement systems is the oversight of public and private-sector payment and settlement systems. Through an oversight process, central banks seek to establish reasonable standards for risk management, monitor and assess systems' compliance with such standards and, through dialogue, moral suasion, and supervisory processes, induce changes

---

[8]Imputed costs include financing costs, return on equity (also referred to as profit), taxes, and certain other expenses that would be incurred if a private business firm provided the services. The imputed costs and imputed profit are collectively referred to as the private-sector adjustment factor (PSAF). For further background on the PSAF, see www.federalreserve.gov/boarddocs/press/boardacts/2000/200012212/researchpaper.pdf.

[9]The Federal Reserve charges 36 basis points for intraday credit. Most central banks require intraday credit to be collateralized, but they do not charge a fee.

in risk management where warranted to reduce risk and the potential for systemic disruptions.[10]

As discussed in the *Central Bank Oversight Report*, there are at least three conditions that may indicate a need for public sector oversight of payment and settlement systems (see CPSS, 2005a). The first condition is where negative externalities exist that may cause systemic risk. As a result of these externalities, payment system users and operators may have insufficient regard for the potential costs or loss that others would incur in the event of their failure to meet their obligations, and thus under invest in security, resilience, risk controls, or liquidity. The second condition is where network externalities and coordination problems may impede the establishment of or migration to safer or more efficient systems. And the third condition is where the existence of market concentration or non-contestable monopolies may result, among other things, in lower investment in risk reduction than is socially optimal.

The *Central Bank Oversight Report*, however, goes on to acknowledge that these conditions may not be sufficient for justifying the oversight of payment and settlement systems. In addition to these conditions, the costs of oversight must be weighed carefully against the benefits, and a level of confidence established that oversight produces a net social benefit. For example, determining whether a system is systemically important and therefore subject to higher standards of risk management and oversight is a complex task involving qualitative and quantitative factors. The Federal Reserve's payments system risk policy considers, among other things, such factors as

- Whether the system has the potential to create significant liquidity disruptions or dislocations should it fail to perform or settle as expected;
- Whether the system has the potential to create large credit or liquidity exposures relative to participants' financial capacity;
- Whether the system settles a high proportion of large-value transactions;
- Whether the system settles transactions for critical financial markets;
- Whether the system provides settlement for other systems; and

---

[10]"... the aim of oversight is the safety and efficiency of a [payment or settlement] system as a whole, focusing on the interconnections between participating institutions inherent in systems. The concept of payment and settlement oversight is therefore distinct from [albeit complementary with] prudential supervision and regulation, which focuses on the soundness of individual financial institutions." CPSS (2005a), p. 11.

- Whether the system is the only system or one of a very few systems for settlement of a given financial instrument.

Assessing the costs and benefits of oversight, however, is complex and not clear cut. Central banks, therefore, should carefully guard against any presumption that oversight will, in all cases, improve public welfare. Furthermore, even where oversight is deemed useful, a "one-size-fits-all" approach to oversight may not be the optimal approach, particularly for systems that are not systemically important. Smaller systems, for example, may not need to comply with the full panoply of standards intended for systemically important systems, or may not present significant enough risks to the broader financial system to warrant any oversight.

4. Challenges of Oversight

In addition to carefully considering if oversight is warranted, central banks also face several challenges in conducting oversight where it is warranted. One challenge is translating broad policy concerns about macro-economic and financial stability and safety and efficiency into appropriate risk management standards for payment and settlement systems. The CPSS central banks have spent considerable effort in the last five years developing a set of international standards for systemically-important payment systems and, in conjunction with the International Organization of Securities Commissions (IOSCO), recommendations for securities settlement systems and central counterparties (see CPSS, 2001; CPSS-IOSCO, 2001; CPSS-IOSCO, 2004).

A second challenge is determining the object and scope of oversight. Based on legal mandates or policy considerations, the objects of a central bank's oversight may encompass systems, instruments, or participants, and the scope of oversight may cover risk management, security, or efficiency issues to greater or less degrees. For example, the Federal Reserve Board's policy on payments system risk focuses largely on the risk management aspects of "inter-bank" payment and securities settlement systems. Other central banks have arrived at different objects and scope of their oversight.

A third challenge is applying standards to specific systems, where inevitably some level of judgment will be necessary in assessing particular system designs and circumstances against recommended minimum standards. A fourth challenge is determining the frequency and depth of oversight activities in order to achieve effective oversight. In part, this is determined by the potential effects disruptions in a particular system may have for the financial system, the significance and complexity of the system, and the degree of change the system may be undergoing. The greater the potential disruptive effects, more complex and significant the system, and the more change it is undergoing, the more frequent and deep the oversight attention may need to be.

There is one final oversight challenge that I would like to briefly discuss — the challenge of effective cooperation among relevant authorities, especially in a cross-border context. In a domestic context, several national authorities may have an interest in the operation of payment and settlement systems. Central banks and banking supervisors, for example, have an interest in the mechanisms used by banks for the payment of inter-bank obligations and for the provision of payment services to customers. Similarly, the clearance and settlement of securities transactions relies on and is relied upon by payment systems and hence is of interest to both central banks and securities regulators. Competition authorities too often have an interest in certain aspects of the payments system, such as access to and competition among payment services. Likewise, in a trans-national context, several central banks may have an interest in a cross-border or multicurrency system involving their currencies or financial institutions.

The benefits of cooperation are readily apparent — more effective discharge of each authority's responsibilities, avoidance of unnecessary, duplicative oversight activities, reductions in the cost of oversight (both for the overseen system and for the relevant authorities), promotion of consistent oversight approaches, minimizing conflicting requirements on a system, and avoidance of "gaps" in oversight. The magnitude of these benefits, of course, will vary depending on the risk and efficiency considerations posed by various systems.

Some of the costs of cooperation are also fairly apparent — additional staff time and effort to work with other authorities, development of mutually agreed upon procedures for sharing of information, agreed upon standards for evaluating a system, and coordination of actions to be taken with regard to identified weaknesses in a system. These costs are often non-trivial and in some cases can be very substantial. This is especially true in the context of a cross-border system where material differences among the various authorities in oversight responsibilities, objectives, policy weights, and available resources, can affect both the level and distribution of costs.

In a cross-border context, another challenge is reconciling the potentially different perceptions that central banks may have of the systemic relevance that a particular cross-border or multicurrency system may have in the context of their national financial systems. For example, one central bank may consider a particular cross-border system to be systemically important for its markets and subject to oversight, but another central bank may not consider it systemically important for its markets. Such different views may be particularly difficult to address in a cooperative oversight venue when the cross-border system in question is located in the jurisdiction of the central bank that does not consider it systemically important.

The *Central Bank Oversight Report* articulates a set of principles intended to help manage these challenges by establishing a general understanding and framework for how central banks should cooperate in overseeing cross-border or multicurrency systems. The CPSS also believes that these principles, with appropriate adaptation for particular circumstances, may provide a useful basis for cooperation between central banks and other authorities. The principles cover such issues as informing other relevant central banks of cross-border or multicurrency systems of interest, determining primary responsibility for oversight of the system, assessing the system as a whole and determining the adequacy of its risk controls, and addressing unsafe systems (see CPSS, 2005a). Although these principles provide a useful and flexible framework for oversight cooperation, the effectiveness of cooperation depends first on whether the concerned central banks believe oversight of a particular system is warranted and, if so, on the existence of a certain minimum level of shared understanding, objectives, views, and approaches among the central banks regarding the system.

An important axiom underlying these cooperative oversight principles is that central banks and other authorities cannot delegate their statutory and legal responsibilities and accountability for oversight to another authority, particularly in a cross-border context. In other words, cooperation is not a case of designating a single, comprehensive overseer and delegating responsibility and accountability to it. Rather, the organizing framework is one of collective information gathering and sharing coupled with dialogue and consensus building on assessment of the system and follow-up actions. The *Central Bank Oversight Report* states that "The principles in no way prejudice the statutory or other responsibilities of central banks or other authorities participating in a cooperative arrangement. Rather, they are intended to provide a mechanism for mutual assistance ... in carrying out ... individual responsibilities in pursuit of ... shared public policy objectives for the efficiency and stability of payment and settlement arrangements" (see CPSS, 2005a). Within such a process, central banks may agree to defer, in some degree, to the central bank in a better position to oversee a particular system effectively (for example, because of jurisdiction, legal powers, or resource reasons), but it is understood that each central bank in a cooperative oversight arrangement remains accountable for fulfilling its own oversight responsibilities, and ultimately may choose to act independently of other authorities in the arrangement if the need arises.

5. Conclusion

Access to Federal Reserve payment services is often seen as one element of the financial safety net in the United States. This element involves a complex set of issues, costs, and benefits regarding access to central bank accounts, intraday credit, and settlement services. On the benefit side, the role of central bank as a default-free settlement institution that holds accounts for a large portion of the banking system and that provides a relatively risk-free and liquid settlement asset contributes in important ways to the safe and smooth functioning of the payments system. These benefits, however, may be difficult to quantify and do not come without a cost. On the cost side, access to central bank accounts, intraday credit, and settlement services may put central bank funds at risk and create perceptions of access to lender of last resort facilities.

Central banks face a number of challenges in understanding and balancing these costs and benefits. As with other elements of the safety net, the optimal balance is not clear-cut and must be carefully considered. Although much has been written on the safety net, especially the elements of deposit insurance and lender of last resort, less systematic attention has been given to the safety net implications of the central bank's role in the payments system as a settlement institution and prudential overseer. The *Central Bank Money Report* and the *Central Bank Oversight Report* raise a number of interesting perspectives and provide one starting point for further thinking and research in this important area.

One set of further research topics involves the relationship between (1) access to central bank accounts, intraday credit, and payment services, on the one hand, and 2) classic safety net concerns about financial system stability and incentives for risk taking and moral hazard, on the other hand. What social benefits are produced when the central bank acts as a settlement institution? Do these benefits vary depending on the potential for systemic risk in a particular system? What private benefits do central bank accountholders receive and how do those benefits influence their perception and management of risks? To what extent does access to central bank accounts, credit, and related services entail significant public subsidies that may contribute to misperceptions of risk-adjusted returns, particularly for central banks that do not charge for credit or services? To what extent are any subsidies eliminated by the pricing of a central bank's settlement services and intraday credit or by other policies? And, is there a "public goods" argument for such subsidies, if they occur? (see Bolt and Humphrey, 2005; Holthausen and Rochet, 2005; Pages and Humphrey, 2005)

The *Central Bank Money Report* raises a second set of related research topics regarding the demand for and effects of access to central bank accounts and settlement services. In particular, the demand for "… accounts and credit from particular classes of institutions, and whether that demand reflects (for example) the desire to avoid risk, to reduce costs, to avoid reliance on a commercial competitor, to receive equal treatment, or simply to obtain the (perceived) imprimatur of the central bank" (see CPSS, 2003).

When serving as a settlement institution, the central bank is likely to have important effects on the structure of the payment system, the role of payment intermediaries, the patterns and concentrations of payment flows, and the risk and efficiency in the financial system, with commensurate implications for the safety net. Further research may help to understand better these effects on and implications for the financial safety net.

References

Bech, Morton L. and Rod Garratt, 2003, "The Intraday Liquidity Management Game," *Journal of Economic Theory*, 109, pp. 198–219.

Bolt, Wilko and David Humphrey, 2005, "Public Good Issues in TARGET: Natural Monopoly, Scale Economies, Network Effects and Cost Allocation," European Central Bank, Working Paper No. 505, July.

Committee on Payments and Settlement Systems (CPSS), 2001, *Core Principles for Systemically Important Payment Systems*, Basle: Bank for International Settlements, January.

Committee on Payments and Settlement Systems (CPSS), 2003, *The Role of Central Bank Money in Payment Systems*, Basle: Bank for International Settlements, August.

Committee on Payments and Settlement Systems (CPSS), 2005a, *Central Bank Oversight of Payment and Settlement Systems*, Basle: Bank for International Settlements, May.

Committee on Payments and Settlement Systems and the International Organization of Securities Commissions (CPSS-IOSCO), 2001, *Recommendations for Securities Settlement Systems*, Basle: Bank for International Settlements, November.

Committee on Payments and Settlement Systems and the International Organization of Securities Commissions (CPSS-IOSCO), 2004, *Recommendations for Central Counterparties*, Basle: Bank for International Settlements, November.

Flannery, Mark, 1996, "Financial Crises, Payment System Problems, and Discount Window Lending," *Journal of Money, Credit and Banking*, 28(4), November.

Furlong, Frederick, 1997, "The Federal Subsidies in Banking: The Link to Financial Modernization," *FRB San Francisco Economic Letter*, No. 97–31, October 24.

Godeffroy, Jean-Michel, 2004, "Payment Systems and Financial Stability," European Central Bank, Remarks to the Technical Assistance to the Commonwealth of Independent States (TACIS) Seminar, Central Bank of Russia, September 29.

Greenspan, Alan, 2001, "The Financial Safety Net," Remarks at the 37th Annual Conference on Bank Structure and Competition, FRB Chicago, May 10.

Hancock, Diana and James A. Wilcox, 1996, "Intraday Management of Bank Reserves: The Effects of Caps and Fees on Daylight Overdrafts," *Journal of Money, Credit and Banking*, 28(4), pp. 870–908.

Holthausen, Cornelia and Jean-Charles Rochet, 2005, "Incorporating a Public Good Factor into the Pricing of Large-Value Payment Systems," European Central Bank, Working Paper No. 507, July.

Lacker, Jeffrey M., 2005, "Payment Economics and the Role of Central Banks," Remarks to the Bank of England Payments Conference, May 20.

Meyer, Laurence H., 2001, "Controlling the Safety Net," Remarks at the 37th Annual Conference on Bank Structure and Competition, FRB Chicago, May 10.

Pages, Henri and David Humphrey, 2005, "Settlement Finality as a Public Good in Large-Value Payment Systems," European Central Bank, Working Paper No. 506, July.

Tumpel-Gugerell, Gertrude (Member of the Executive Board, European Central Bank), 2005, "The Need for Regulatory Involvement in the Evolution of Payment Systems," Speech, International Payments Conference, London, April 25.

*Jeff Stehm is an assistant director at the Board of Governors of the Federal Reserve System. The views, remarks, and conclusions set forth in this paper are those of the author and do not indicate concurrence by the Board of Governors, the Federal Reserve Banks, or their staffs.

Designing a Bank Safety Net: Regulatory Challenges for Cross-Border Banking

Asli Demirgüç-Kunt*
World Bank

1. Introduction

Designing and managing a proper bank safety net is a very challenging task. A bank safety net can be defined as a set of policies designed to prevent or reverse widespread disintermediation from banks, losses in bank capital, and bank failures. These policies include insurance of bank deposits, lending to banks through lender of last resort facilities, resolution of insolvencies that occur, and regulation and supervision of institutions.

Bank safety nets are difficult to design and operate because they strive to achieve conflicting objectives of protecting against financial crises that can magnify economic shocks while also avoiding moral hazard problems that give rise to imprudent banking practices. Ironically, in many countries the very safety nets that were meant to limit the vulnerability of the financial system have had quite the opposite result, and were indeed identified as the greatest single source of financial fragility.[1] Finding the right balance between crisis prevention and market discipline is the most important challenge facing the policymakers.

Clearly designing and operating a bank safety net well is challenging for regulators. But these challenges are even greater in an integrated international market like the European Union where there are complex set of rules and shared responsibilities between national and international authorities.

---

[1]For example, Kane (1989), discusses the role of the safety net in leading to the U.S. savings and loan crisis. Demirgüç-Kunt and Detragiache (1998, 2002) show that existence of an explicit deposit insurance scheme increases banking system fragility.

In the remainder of my remarks, I will first discuss the need for a safety net, its components, and how these components should be designed to minimize the costs and maximize benefits of a safety net. Next, I will apply these concepts to the European single financial market and conclude with a discussion of the three papers presented in this session.

2. Why is There a Need for a Bank Safety Net?

Why do policymakers feel the need to protect banks with a safety net? First, banks provide credit to other firms and manage the flow of payments throughout the economy. Thus, disruptions in bank credit supply and a breakdown of the payments system may have large spillover effects for the rest of the economy. When a bank fails, valuable firm-bank relationships are destroyed, negatively impacting the firms that depended on that bank for credit. Bank failures or losses in capital lead to contractions in aggregate bank credit with large social costs to bank borrowers outside the banking system.

Second, banks are especially prone to failures because the value of their assets is difficult to observe and their debt is often very short term. Since bank loans are not marked to market and bank debt is demandable, small shocks to bank solvency may lead to widespread disintermediation from banks, contraction in credit and a decline in economic activity. The difficulties in observing the true value of banks, or asymmetric-information problems, may lead to costly systemic runs, where depositors overreact to information and possibly lead to closure of solvent institutions.

Clearly, safety nets provide benefits in that they limit the cost to banks and firms that would result from runs. More importantly they make runs less likely by insulating banks from runs and reducing depositors' incentives to withdraw their funds.

There are also costs, however. The benefits of a safety net come from preventing systemic banking problems, *not* individual failures. Overly generous protection of banks insulates them from market discipline and encourages them to increase their asset risk. Banks are willing to increase their risk because potential losses will be borne by taxpayers through government bailouts of the banking system while they get to keep the gains.

This excessive risk taking by banks — moral hazard — becomes worst at the time of adverse economic shocks since these shocks erode bank capital and increase incentives to take on more risk. Thus, badly designed safety nets may exacerbate problems in the wake of adverse economic shocks, introducing greater fragility into the system. The costs of these safety nets may end up exceeding their potential benefits.

3. Components of the Safety Net

Bank safety nets are made up of various components. These are deposit insurance, lender of last resort, insolvency resolution, and prudential regulations and supervision. Each component needs to be designed and operated with equal care, since a weakness in any one component would undermine the whole safety net. Whether market discipline is undermined through blanket coverage of deposit insurance, or by providing continuous liquidity through the lender of last resort facility to keep insolvent institutions afloat, or even through relaxation of prudential regulations to avoid facing insolvencies, sooner or later, it will aggravate problems of imprudent banking. Therefore, to make sure the safety net captures the benefits of crisis prevention without suffering the costs of moral hazard, each component of the safety net should be designed to impose a margin of private loss on bank claimants. This private loss is the margin of safety that limits the exposure of taxpayers to bailout costs ex post, and also banks' willingness to undertake risks ex ante.

A well-designed bank safety net. The key challenge in designing a well functioning safety net is to retain market discipline in banking while preventing systemic runs. One way of avoiding moral hazard is to design each component of the safety net such that there is a group of private claimants that would have to absorb a certain amount of loss in the event of an adverse outcome. The emphasis is on private loss, because government protection does not have a good record around the world. Regulators and politicians tend to have little incentive to enforce market discipline, indeed rigorous monitoring often conflicts with their own personal interests. Bankers have strong incentives to exploit this lack of market discipline and abuse the safety net at the taxpayers' expense. In the remainder of this section, I discuss design options for each element of the safety net such that moral hazard costs are minimized and the benefits of the safety net are retained.

Deposit Insurance.[2] Since governments tend to be incapable of credibly committing not to provide insurance ex post, every country has an

---

[2]This section draws on Demirgüç-Kunt and Kane (2002).

explicit or implicit deposit insurance scheme. Moral hazard problems are most commonly associated with the deposit insurance element of the safety net. Even in favorable circumstances, with well-developed supporting institutions, deposit insurance can have an impact on financial fragility by reducing the degree of private market discipline that banks experience. Appropriate design features are important to control and offset these effects.

A first step in the design of deposit insurance is to set enforceable and low coverage limits to ensure that large depositors, and other sophisticated parties such as subordinated debt holders and other banks understand that their funds are truly at risk. Exposure to loss carries an incentive to monitor and police the risk-taking behavior of banks and their financial regulators. Providing strong incentives for private parties to remain vigilant is critically important in weak contracting environments where private monitoring must overcome weaknesses in official supervision.

Another method of introducing market discipline to deposit insurance design is to incorporate the concept of co-insurance. This is done by insuring only a certain proportion of deposits up to the coverage limit. In this way, each depositor still has incentives to monitor the institutions given that they would be experiencing a loss in the event of failure. Coinsurance and related private loss-sharing arrangements such as subordinated debt and extended stockholder liability sharpen these incentives to monitor.

Requiring compulsory membership in the deposit insurance system for financial institutions increases the size of the insurance pool and prevents low-risk institutions from selecting out of the system, that is, adverse selection. This also encourages solvent and well-managed banks to help officials to monitor and police riskier institutions.

While taking the government out of insuring deposits is not feasible especially during periods of systemic failure, a deposit insurance system that is entirely publicly run can be dangerously flawed. There is an extensive literature that describes how in a government-run deposit insurance system, the cost and quality of insurance examinations can be compromised by political influences. This literature discusses how government officials are slow to take prompt corrective action and how they often have proven to be more concerned with minimizing the number of failures recorded on their watch than they have been with minimizing the aggregate value of the insurance losses their policies accrued. Also, economic theory and practical experience suggest that because they operate under a different set of incentives, private-sector employees more efficiently perform monitoring and loss-resolution functions than government employees.[3]

Finally, it must be made clear that funds that ultimately cover bank losses will come principally from surviving banks. Taxpayer assistance should be expected only in the special case of a verifiable systemic crisis. Convincing the banking industry that it cannot routinely dump insurance losses on taxpayers will encourage healthy banks to support high-quality regulation and to monitor other banks. Conversely, to the extent that emergency funding is expected to be provided from government revenues, market discipline is compromised and financial fragility increased.

Lender of last resort. It is important that no component of the safety net undermines market discipline. Lender of last resort function is no exception. Lender of last resort function should be used only to alleviate short-term liquidity problems by lending at a penalty rate on good collateral.[4] Unfortunately, many countries use their lender of last resort facility to implicitly bail out their insolvent institutions. An immediate supply of liquidity is essential to an effectively structured lender of last resort, only if collateral requirements and penalty interest rates are applied. These are rules that discourage the abuse of the safety net.

Insolvency resolution. Effective and timely resolution of insolvencies is probably one of the most important elements of a well-designed safety net. Often regulators keep insolvent institutions in operation with the hope that they will recover their solvency. Quite to the contrary, insolvent institutions that are allowed to operate have greater incentives to take risk since they no longer have their own capital in the line. Indeed after that point, the losses only accrue to the taxpayers while the banks reap the gains and the fragility of the system increases by undermining market discipline.

As with the other components of the safety net, the crucial issue in designing insolvency resolution mechanisms is to refrain from undermining market discipline. To establish accountability for the insolvency-resolution process, objective procedures must be developed to clarify how firms are to be targeted for takeover, liquidation or merger. Failure resolution method used in each case should be the most efficient and least costly one.

In many countries the weakness of the insolvency process has been in the lack of transparency in restructuring and poor asset recovery in the

---

[3]See for example Calomiris (1990), and Kane (1992).
[4]This is a classic policy prescription. See Bagehot (1873).

liquidation process. For the success of the insolvency resolution it is important to improve the transparency of the process and to eliminate or at least minimize the capacity of the shareholders to interfere with it through legal means. As with any bankruptcy process, bank insolvency resolution requires clear and enforceable priority of claim rules. This would establish seniority of various classes of claimants, generally starting with depositors' claims and ending with those of the shareholders'. Finally, it is essential for the legal and regulatory framework to specify the exact criteria and the point the resolution process is activated such that this is not left to regulatory discretion and political influences.

Prudential regulation and supervision. Prudential regulation and supervision of banks is the most important defense against the abuse of the safety net by the bankers. Through appropriate regulation and supervision, it is possible to limit the risk taking activities of the banks and most importantly, to ensure that there will be a credible first layer of private loss when banks suffer adverse consequences. In most countries, capital regulations attempt to provide this assurance, since a well capitalized bank will have a cushion of protection (private loss) before the insurer needs to step in. However, true capital is not observable, so additional regulations, such as reserve or liquidity requirements are often used. Basel II bank capital regulations attempt to measure risk-based capital requirements more accurately by adding two new pillars, with pillar 2, supervisory review, and pillar 3, market discipline.

Another proposal to limit the erosion of bank capital before it is too late is "the early intervention/closure" approach.[5] The idea here is to create a capital buffer that insulates the safety net from loss by forcing the bank to recapitalize or close if a certain threshold is crossed. The advocates of this method argue that credible enforcement of accounting standards and minimal capital requirements would lessen regulatory discretion and political influence. However, this method still depends on regulators to identify undercapitalized banks without explicit help from market signals. The central banks should continue the reassessment of point of intervention to further reduce discretion and to incorporate market signals to bolster the justification of this intervention.

The important point of this discussion is to remember the purpose of prudential regulation and supervision is to retain an adequate capital cushion

---

[5]Benston and Kaufman (1988).

in the banks that would act as a credible margin of private loss on bank shareholders and uninsured creditors. Bank owners should be the first line of defense against abuse of the safety net. Only if they are motivated to limit excess risk-taking, could bailout costs in the event of crises be contained.

4. Ideal Design Versus Practice

Assuming there is broad consensus on how to best design and operate safety nets, why do we see so many cases of poor design and application around the world? Earlier work has established that in weak institutional settings only good design would limit the costs of lower market discipline and prevent instability. But recent research is starting to discover that adopting good design is also very difficult in poor institutional settings. For example, Demirgüç-Kunt, Kane, and Laeven (2005) show that developed countries with good institutions are more likely adopt deposit insurance and design it better. Furthermore, political considerations and external pressures play an important role in the adoption decision and adoption during distressed periods is associated with poor design. Thus, while "good design" is particularly important in poor institutional settings, it may not be possible to adopt good design precisely because of institutional weaknesses. These findings confirm the importance of taking into account individual country circumstances in safety net design.

These findings also have important implications when a large number of countries with different levels of institutional development are expected to adopt a uniform safety net, as was required by the EU deposit insurance directive. Huizinga (2000) shows that the minimum coverage of E2000 required by the directive imposes costs on some European countries, particularly for accession countries, as it leads to over-insurance and greater risk of moral hazard.

The three papers in this session address different components of the safety net and challenges for the European Union. Eisenbeis and Kaufman (2006) discuss the structure of deposit insurance systems in the EU. They argue that poorly designed deposit insurance and safety nets lead to moral hazard and increase fragility, and that improving deposit insurance design to minimize these adverse consequences has proven difficult. As an alternative, they suggest a focus on efficient insolvency resolution, which should make weaknesses in deposit insurance design and their adverse consequences benign. They propose four principles to ensure efficient resolution of bank failures. These are (1) prompt legal closure of institutions before they become economically insolvent; (2) prompt identification of claims and assignment of losses; (3) prompt reopening of failed institutions; and (4) prompt recapitalization and re-privatization of failed institutions.

There is significant merit to this proposal, since efficient insolvency resolution is indeed a very important component of the safety net. If the authorities were able to adopt and implement such an early closure process, it would certainly go a long way towards mitigating the weaknesses in the rest of the safety net. However, in practice, there are two problems with this argument. First, different components of the safety net are not likely to be designed independently. The same institutional and political weaknesses that lead to poor design of deposit insurance, generally also undermine efficient insolvency resolution. Thus, if deposit insurance design leaves much to be desired, it is highly likely that the insolvency resolution system will also be less than perfect. That is why in poor institutional settings we often see weaknesses in all components of the safety net, characterized by generous, mispriced deposit insurance, inefficient insolvency resolution, regulatory forbearance and lax lender of last resort practices. Second, even if it were possible to design and operate an efficient system of insolvency resolution despite the weaknesses in other components of the safety net, it would be difficult to sustain this over the long term. Weaknesses in deposit insurance, lender of last resort or regulation would lead to increased moral hazard, increase the number of institutions that need to be closed and hence put pressure on the insolvency resolution system, eventually making it less prompt. Thus, in practice it is less likely that authorities can focus on one component of the safety net and de-emphasize the others. Safety nets, like chains, are as strong as their weakest links.

Schinasi and Teixeira (2006) discuss the lender of last resort function in EU. They identify challenges in effectively implementing emergency liquidity assistance, namely, jurisdiction of the lender of last resort, assessing the solvency of European banking groups, and potential for coordination failures among national central banks. Information issues emerge as one of the most important challenges facing the authorities. Both generating reliable information, and processing and sharing this information, by different responsible authorities to distinguish liquidity from solvency problems and to assess systemic risk for the EU as a whole is likely to be quite challenging. An important point that deserves more emphasis in the discussion is the implication of differing institutional capacities of the national authorities involved, particularly those of the accession countries. Such differences in capacity and implementation ability are likely to affect the success of coordination efforts and the pace with which coordination can proceed.

Related to lender of last resort, Stehm (2006) focuses on the payments system, providing an overview of the Federal Reserve settlement services. He emphasizes the role of the payments system as part of lender of last resort and the safety net, and discusses the important role of central banks in providing a safe settlement asset in the form of central bank money, acting as a settlement institution, and providing intraday credit to facilitate the safe and smooth settlement of payments. He also discusses implications for the safety net, and the tendency for central banks to limit their role as a settlement agency, to prevent giving the perception of easy access to central bank liquidity. He argues that although access to central bank as a settlement institution is one of the classic components of the financial safety net in the United States, it has not received much systematic attention compared to deposit insurance and lender of last resort services.

In conclusion, good safety net design, which is very challenging in a domestic context, is likely to become even more complicated with greater integration and internationalization of financial services. While we have learned much from studies to date, much more work remains. Some potential areas for future analysis are the determinants of design of insolvency resolution processes, interactions between design of different components of the safety net, impact of different scope of central bank activities on bank stability and performance; as well as how greater consolidation and globalization are likely to affect these relationships.

References

Bagehot, W., 1873, *Lombard Street*, London: Henry S. King.

Benston, G., and G. Kaufman, 1988, *Risk and Solvency Regulation of Depository Institutions: Past Policies and Current Options*, New York: Salomon Brothers Center, Graduate School of Business, New York University.

Calomiris, C., 1990, "Is Deposit Insurance Necessary? A Historical Perspective," *Journal of Economic History*, June, pp. 283–295.

Demirgüç-Kunt, A. and E. Detragiache, 1998, "The Determinants of Banking Crises in Developing and Developed Countries," *IMF Staff Papers*, (45)1, pp. 81–109.

Demirgüç-Kunt, Asli, and Enrica Detragiache, 2002, "Does Deposit Insurance Increase Banking System Stability? An Empirical Investigation," *Journal of Monetary Economics*, 49, pp. 1373–1406.

Demirgüç-Kunt, Asli, and Edward Kane, 2002, "Deposit Insurance Around the Globe: Where Does it Work?" *Journal of Economic Perspectives*, 16, pp. 175–196.

Demirgüç-Kunt, A., Edward Kane, and Luc Laeven, 2005, "Determinants of Deposit Insurance Adoption and Design," World Bank mimeo.

Eisenbeis, Robert A. and George G. Kaufman, 2006, "Cross Border Banking: Challenges for Deposit Insurance and Financial Stability in the European Union, *Cross-Border Banking: Regulatory Challenges*, New York and Singapore: World Scientific Publishing.

Huizinga, Harry, 2005, "The EU Deposit Insurance Directive: Does One Size Fit All?" Tilberg University and CEPR, mimeo.

Kane, E., 1989, *The S&L Insurance Mess: How Did It Happen?*, Urban Institute Press.

Kane E., 1992, "The Incentive Incompatibility of Government-Sponsored Deposit-Insurance Funds," in *The Reform of Federal Deposit Insurance*, Harper Business, pp. 144–166.

Schinasi, Garry J. and Pedro Gustavo Teixeira, 2006, "The Lender of Last Resort in the European Single Financial Market, *Cross-Border Banking: Regulatory Challenges*, New York and Singapore: World Scientific Publishing.

Stehm, Jeff, 2006, "Payment Systems and the Safety Net: The Role of Central Bank Money and Oversight, *Cross-Border Banking: Regulatory Challenges*, New York and Singapore: World Scientific Publishing.

Asli Demirgüç-Kunt is the senior research manager in finance in the Development Research Group of the World Bank's Development Economics Vice Presidency and senior adviser in the Operations and Policy Department of the Financial Sector Vice Presidency. The findings, interpretations, and conclusions of this paper are entirely those of the author and do not necessarily represent the views of the World Bank, its Executive Directors, or the countries they represent.

Insolvency Resolution Issues

Banking in a Changing World: Issues and Questions in the Resolution of Cross-Border Banks

Michael Krimminger*

Federal Deposit Insurance Corporation

The globalization of finance has led to the development of more integrated global exchange networks among countries and deeper interrelationships between their economies. Many financial institutions and activities that once were local are now international. While business and finance are global most regulatory systems and laws are not. Many of the regulatory and legal norms that govern these networks and interrelationships have not kept pace with these innovations. There are few international rules and norms to govern the linkages between financial institutions, payments systems, and markets. National laws almost exclusively define the relationships between internationally active banks and other financial institutions. The real task of the future is to develop regulatory and legal norms that allow the benefits of increased global interaction to blossom while mitigating the more troubling consequences of global finance.

This paper focuses on the challenges faced by national authorities in responding to financial instability in a cross-border bank. In the absence of a common international insolvency system for cross-border banks, national authorities must improve their understanding of the options available and improve coordination with other regulators if they are to be successful in limiting the consequences of a potential cross-border failure. This paper seeks to describe some of the key difficulties and to identify some of those practical steps.

1. Background — Insolvency Principles

The ultimate insolvency of any individual or company is not an event but a process of continuing efforts over a longer or shorter period of time to stem the slide into the financial abyss of bankruptcy. For highly regulated banks, and many other financial companies, this process will entail extensive efforts by bankers and supervisors to restructure, revitalize, and recapitalize the bank. If the crisis intervention efforts are unsuccessful, then the supervisors face the question of whether the bank must be placed into a formal insolvency legal process or whether some form of supervisory forbearance should be exercised.

If banks truly are "different" from other companies, then a flexible insolvency system triggered by clear, mandatory standards that require action before the bank's capital is exhausted should be applied. At this point, the bank has demonstrated that it is unlikely to survive, delay will only increase losses, and intervention is necessary to ensure protection of the public interest. A well-developed insolvency system must balance the need to avoid increasing moral hazard in the financial system by imposing losses on those creditors, obviously starting with equity holders, who could have averted the failure, while allowing a prompt protection of smaller depositors and facilitating the continued availability of credit in the economy. Once clear and mandatory criteria for intervention have been triggered, the insolvency authorities must have the power to implement a flexible resolution of the failed bank to strike this balance.

Some common components of effective insolvency systems for banks have been identified.[1] First, the laws should have clear criteria for initiating insolvency proceedings to avoid allowing unsalvageable institutions to operate indefinitely by raising funds from depositors and acting as a drag on or diversion of economic capital. Next, this process should be designed to reimburse depositors up to the insured maximum as soon as possible, while minimizing the cost to the deposit insurance fund. While depositor confidence in the guarantee is based on the certainty of repayment, it is equally based on the speed of repayment. A more limited deposit guarantee, combined with explicit requirements to minimize losses in the resolution, promotes a well-funded insurance system as well as limits the moral hazard that can be engendered by deposit insurance. A third component is that the insolvency laws should give the resolution authority the immediate power to control, manage, marshal, and dispose of the bank's assets and liabilities

---

[1]See Group of Ten, 2002, "Insolvency Arrangements and Contract Enforceability," Sept.; Financial Stability Forum, 2001, "Guidance for Developing Effective Deposit Insurance Systems" at 8–11, Sept.; IMF Legal Dept., 1999, "Orderly and Effective Insolvency Procedures."

once it is appointed. Many difficulties in resolving individual insolvencies, and in addressing broader instability, have been exacerbated by the inability of trustees or receivers to take prompt action. Finally, the insolvency laws should confer adequate legal powers on the resolution authority that are sufficient to permit flexible and decisive action to maximize recoveries on assets and minimize delays in providing money back to depositors.

2. International Complications

The difficulties in balancing the competing interests in bank insolvencies are made even more complex when the supervisory and insolvency laws of two or more nations are involved. The few international rules that exist tend to address insolvency rules within defined geographical or economic relationships, such as the European Union's winding up directives.[2] Even these few rules address primarily judicial and regulatory cooperation and not the substance of the law governing an insolvency.

The absence of a common international approach affects both the home country of the cross-border bank and the host country of the bank's branches or subsidiaries. Some home countries must supervise large global banks with their principal operations located outside the home country. Switzerland is the home to two banks — United Bank of Switzerland and Credit Suisse — whose domestic Swiss operations are only a small part of their total business. Their global operations, however, could spread turbulence to Switzerland through their many market, inter-bank, and settlement linkages with financial institutions around the globe.[3]

Other countries are the hosts of foreign banks which hold a large or even predominant share of the host banking market. In some cases, those foreign banks are far less systemically significant in their home country. For

[2]See Group of Ten, 2002, "Insolvency Arrangements and Contract Enforceability" at Appendix A, A16–17, Sept.; Krimminger, Michael, 2004, "Deposit Insurance and Bank Insolvency in a Changing World: Synergies and Challenges," *Current Developments in Monetary and Financial Law*, IMF, at 10–16; Nierop, Erwin and Stenstrom, Mikael, 2002, "Cross-Border Aspects of Insolvency Proceedings for Credit Institutions — A Legal Perspective," paper delivered at the International Seminar on Legal and Regulatory Aspects of Financial Stability, Basel, Switzerland, Jan., at 11.
[3]For further information see Hüpkes, Eva, 2004, "Bank Insolvency Resolution in Switzerland," in David Mayes and Aarno Liuksila, eds., *Who Pays for Bank Insolvency?*, at 262–64, Helsinki: Bank of Finland.

example, in New Zealand, approximately 85 percent of the banking assets are Australian-owned.[4] Some European countries have even higher levels of foreign-owned banking assets — in Luxembourg 95 percent of the banking assets are foreign-owned, while in Estonia three foreign banks control over 97 percent of the banking assets.[5]

These host jurisdictions can face a daunting task. Where a foreign bank occupies a dominant position in the host banking market, the host country may find itself without the information or tools to act effectively.

3. The Division of Labor between Home and Host Countries

When a bank has operations in more than one country, fundamental choices must be made about which jurisdiction will have primary responsibility for supervision, crisis intervention, and any insolvency, and what will be the role of other affected supervisors. The commonly used principle to determine primary supervisory responsibility is "home-country control."[6] Under this principle, the home supervisor is the consolidated supervisor for the worldwide activities of international banks chartered in that country, including its branches, subsidiaries, and other operations. The host supervisor is responsible for ensuring that foreign subsidiaries operating within its borders are effectively supervised.

While the principle of home-country control could logically extend to determine primary responsibility for crisis intervention and insolvency, it has not commonly been extended to those issues. Today, most countries will seek to exercise authority for the resolution of a failing bank subsidiary or branch operating within their borders under their national insolvency law. For subsidiaries, the host country is the home country since the entity was

---

[4]See Bollard, Alan, Governor of Reserve Bank of New Zealand, speech to Trans-Tasman Business Circle in Sydney, Australia on Aug. 11, 2004, RBNZ Bulletin, Vol. 67, No. 3.
[5]See European Central Bank, "Banking Structures in the New EU Member States" at 17, Table 4 (Jan. 2005); Ralph de Haas and Iman van Lelyveld, "Foreign Bank Penetration and Private Sector Credit in Central and Eastern Europe," DNB Staff Reports No. 91 (July 2002).
[6]See Basel Committee on Banking Supervision, "Core Principles for Effective Banking Supervision" at Section VI: Cross-Border Banking (1997); Basel Committee on Banking Supervision, "Minimum Standards for the Supervision of International Banking Groups and Their Cross-border Establishments" (1992), both available at http://www.bis.org/publ/index.htm.

incorporated under its laws. For branches, most nations permit cooperation with foreign insolvency authorities within constraints imposed by the
national insolvency policies, while reserving the right to conduct wholly
separate insolvency proceedings to protect creditors of the branches' local
operations.[7]

To the extent that national insolvency laws directly address how to deal
with debtors, creditors, assets, and liabilities outside the national boundaries, these laws adopt one of two basic positions: territorialism or uni-
versalism. Under a territorial approach each country adjudicates claims
against the assets within its borders for the benefit of creditors of the insolvent local firm. This approach focuses on the primacy of national law
within the territory of the country although courts or administrators may
cooperate with foreign proceedings. In general, the law where the assets
are found thus controls their distribution. A universal approach, on the
other hand, allows a single jurisdiction to adjudicate the worldwide claims
against the debtor and its worldwide assets with the cooperation of courts or
other authorities in each affected country. This approach effectively applies
national law to all worldwide assets and claims. Most nations currently
apply a territorial approach to cross-border insolvencies. Ultimately, cooperation between different national authorities remains based on principles
of comity.

The European Union has taken significant steps to break down the barriers to cross-border banking. In October 2004, the EU adopted the "European
Company Statute" that allows cross-border companies, including banks, to
operate more easily through a European-wide branch structure under a unified set of rules and reporting systems.[8] The EU also has adopted a common
approach to cross-border crisis management and crisis resolution for EU

---

[7]See Hüpkes, Eva, 2000, *The Legal Aspects of Bank Insolvency: A Comparative Analysis
of Western Europe, the United States, and Canada* at 141–42, The Hague: Kluwer Law
International; Baxter, Thomas C., Jr., Hansen, Joyce, and Sommer, Joseph, 2004, "Two
Cheers for Territoriality: An Essay on International Bank Insolvency Law," 78 *Am. Bankr.
L. J.* 57, 73–76.
[8]EU Council Regulation (EC) No 2157/2001 of 8 October 2001 on the Statute for a European
company; see Schoenmaker, Dirk and Oosterloo, Sander, 2004, "Cross-Border Issues in
European Financial Supervision" at 11, prepared for Bank of Finland conference "The
Structure of Financial Regulation," Helsinki, Finland, Sept. 2–3, 2004. As of October 2004,
only Belgium, Austria, Denmark, Sweden, Finland and Iceland had taken the necessary
measures to allow European Companies to be founded on their territory. EU Press Release,
Oct. 8, 2004.

banks. Under this approach, the home country's authorities will have primary responsibility for crisis management as the home-country supervisor and, if appropriate, as provider of liquidity to the bank.[9] Even within the EU many issues remain to be resolved and the actual roles of home and host supervisors and insolvency authorities in a crisis have yet to be tested.

Within these complexities, a useful way of identifying the key questions for home and host countries is to look at the issues in two phases: pre-failure crisis management and post-collapse crisis resolution.

4. Pre-Failure Crisis Management

Effective crisis management is an extension of effective supervision, but also may involve other tools such as central bank liquidity lending or public recapitalization. In defining the respective responsibilities of the home and host countries during crisis management the key questions include:

- Does the home or host country have primary responsibility for supervision?
- What role is assigned to the supervisor without primary responsibility?
- How readily is information available to home and host supervisors and crisis managers?
- What is the effect of different regulatory and supervisory infrastructures?
- Is the bank systemically significant in the home or host country? If so, what will be the response of the supervisors or of the central bank as the lender of last resort?
- How will different corporate structures for cross-border banking — such as branches or subsidiaries — affect crisis management?

The answers to these questions and additional related issues will have a significant effect upon the effectiveness of crisis management.

---

[9]See EU Winding Up Directive for credit institutions 2001/24/EC of April 4, 2001, Articles 2, 3, and 9; Brouwer, Henk, Hebbink, Gerbert and Wesseling, Sandra, 2004, "A European Approach to Banking Crises," in David Mayes and Aarno Liuksila, eds., *Who Pays for Bank Insolvency?* at 211, Helsinki: Bank of Finland.

4.1. *Primary supervisory responsibility*

Crisis management may include both supervisory and non-supervisory steps. The home-country supervisor can be expected to take the lead on corrective actions for branches, while the host country can take appropriate action for subsidiaries. Within the European Union, it is anticipated that the home-country supervisor will be coordinating policymaker for a distressed international bank with branches, while the host country supervisor will coordinate responses to a subsidiary in crisis. It is fair to say that the U.S. supervisors take a more direct role in crisis management as host supervisors both for branches and subsidiaries.[10]

One way for the host country to address its secondary role for cross-border branches is to require that all cross-border operations be conducted through subsidiaries. For example, New Zealand has opted to require all foreign banks operating in the country — which dominate the New Zealand banking market — to be locally incorporated as subsidiaries able to operate independently of the parent bank. In this way, the Reserve Bank of New Zealand strengthens its ability to respond to the slide toward insolvency of a cross-border bank with a potentially systemically important New Zealand subsidiary. For example, the Reserve Bank conditioned its approval of the acquisition of the National Bank of New Zealand by Australian-owned ANZ Banking Group (New Zealand) Ltd. in 2003 on capital adequacy for the New Zealand subsidiary and on the subsidiary maintaining local systems to enable it to operate independently.[11]

4.2. *Availability of information*

A critical element in successful crisis management is access to timely and complete information about the troubled bank. With branch operations, the home country of the parent can directly access information, while the

---

[10]See Baxter, Thomas C., Jr., Hansen, Joyce, and Sommer, Joseph, 2004, "Two Cheers for Territoriality: An Essay on International Bank Insolvency Law," 78 *Am. Bankr. L. J.* 57, 70–77.

[11]See RBNZ Consent to ANZ Purchase of National Bank (Oct. 24, 2003), available at www.rbnz.govt.nz/news/2003/0141629.html; see also Bollard, Alan, 2004, Governor, Reserve Bank of New Zealand, in address to Trans-Tasman Business Circle in Sydney, Australia, Res. Bank of New Zealand Bulletin, Vol. 67, No. 3 at 33.

host nation must gain this information through cooperation with the home country authorities. Even with cross-border subsidiary operations, the host supervisor needs access to information about the overall risk characteristics of the home bank as well as developments that may affect its stability in the home country, other host countries, or the specific host country from the home supervisor of the larger bank. The host supervisor can contribute a view of the trends and risks in its national market that may not be otherwise evident to the home country supervisors. It is crucial that the home country supervisors have the ability to assess the aggregate effect upon the cross-border bank.[12]

Supervisory information exchanges are normally arranged through bilateral memoranda of understanding. Under the memoranda of understanding the banking regulators of each country typically agree to share information about developments or supervisory concerns, administrative penalties, and other information. The agreements usually recognize that concerns about sovereignty, security or other public policy questions are grounds to refuse to exchange information. However, these supervisory memoranda of understanding usually do not address the special information needs in a crisis.[13] Some steps are now being taken to address crisis management. In May 2005, the EU member states entered into an memorandum of understanding (MoU) on cooperation during financial and banking crises. While the MoU is not public, it has been described as a set of principles and procedures for sharing information, analyses, and views during crises along with calls for the development of contingency plans for the management of cross-border crises. Similarly, in June 2003, the Nordic countries (Finland, Denmark, Iceland, Norway, and Sweden) agreed to crisis management procedures, which included setting up a crisis

[12]See Mayes, David and Vesala, Jukka, 1998, "On the Problems of Home Country Control," Bank of Finland, *Studies in Economics and Finance* 20/98, at 12; see also Basel Concordat (1983); The Supervision of Cross-Border Banking (1996); and Supervision of Financial Conglomerates (1999).

[13]See Brouwer, Henk, Hebbink, Gerbert and Wesseling, Sandra, 2004, "A European Approach to Banking Crises," in David Mayes and Aarno Liuksila, eds., *Who Pays for Bank Insolvency?* at 211, Helsinki: Bank of Finland. It is important to note, as well, that coordination issues are discussed internationally within the Basel Committee structure and within a variety of other coordinating bodies. See Gulde, Anne-Marie and Wolf, Holger C., 2004, "Financial Stability Arrangements in Europe: A Review," proceedings of Oestereichische Nationalbank conference, Nov., at 56–7.

contact group, the sharing of key information, and steps to address liquidity funding.[14]

In a crisis, however, national supervisors may perceive a benefit from delaying or avoiding the sharing of confidential information if the information may cause regulatory action in another jurisdiction. In addition, if either the home or host supervisor has no financial stake in the losses that may be caused by delays in governmental intervention, that supervisor is more likely to delay intervention.

In fact, the incentives inherent in a universal resolution process focused on home country supervisory authority — such as that in the EU — may create additional challenges. Since the host supervisor has little ability to protect the branch creditors by initiating formal intervention, the host supervisor may be less likely to take any available supervisory steps. The home supervisor may delay intervention for reasons other than the solvency of the bank.[15] In such a system, some constraints on the home country supervisor's ability to delay needed supervisory action or intervention may be needed to better balance the home-host relationship.

The host country of a large cross-border bank operating through a branch structure is faced with a difficult dilemma — it lacks the means to independently gain key information and take direct supervisory control over the larger bank, but it must remain responsible for and bear the burden of the potential effect on its national economy. As a cross-border bank deteriorates, the gaps between available information and legal power to act will become increasingly crucial. The host country will likely demand detailed information about host-country operations and reviews of the larger bank and on-site examinations. In addition, the host country can be expected to require the branch to confirm independent functionality of key banking services. The host country also may require maintenance of additional assets and collateral for obligations within the host country. While the home country may accede to the information requests of the host country, it is unlikely to respond positively to the efforts to separate functions, capital and assets for the host country. At this stage of the crisis, the home country can be

---

[14]See Text of Memorandum of Understanding available at www.norges-bank.no; Borchgrevink, Henrik and Moe, Thorvald, 2004, "Management of Financial Crises in Cross-Border Banks," *Norges Bank Economic Bulletin*, 4th Quarter at 161.

[15]See Baxter, Thomas C., Jr., Hansen, Joyce, and Sommer, Joseph, 2004, "Two Cheers for Territoriality: An Essay on International Bank Insolvency Law," 78 *Am. Bankr. L. J.* 57, 78–79.

expected to pursue supervisory action to ensure the survival of the cross-border bank without expenditure of public money — including disposing of certain operations, strengthening the bank's internal controls, and perhaps withdrawal from some host countries.

4.3. *Regulatory and supervisory infrastructure*

Cross-border coordination in supervision and in crisis management can be affected as well by differences in national regulatory and supervisory infrastructures. For example, the United States has four primary federal regulators of banks and thrifts, 50 state banking regulators, and a national deposit insurer with direct responsibility for administrative proceedings to resolve failing insured banks and thrifts. European banks are supervised by national banks or by separate supervisory entities, or by a combination of both.

National differences in who regulates different activities and how this regulation is implemented will give rise to divergent policy choices, incentives, and mandates.[16] The array of possible policy alternatives raises a number of questions. The questions include whether the laws in the home country provide for a system such as prompt corrective action or whether action is at the discretion of the supervisor? What has been the home supervisor's historical pattern — strong action or inaction? Are there contextual incentives that will affect the home supervisor's response — such as past successes or failures with intervention, political considerations, inadequate staffing or training, and policy perspectives? Are coordination problems created by supervisory jurisdictional issues arising from a multiplicity of regulators either in the home or host country or as a result of the complexity of the bank's internal organization and business lines? Are the home or host authorities sufficiently creative, or legally empowered, to foster a privately organized recapitalization or rescue?[17]

---

[16] See Gulde and Wolf, "Financial Stability Arrangements in Europe: A Review" at 54–55 and Table 1; Eisenbeis, Robert A., "Agency Problems in Banking Supervision: The Case of the EMU" at 15, paper presented at a conference on The Structure of Regulation, Sept. 2–3, 2004, Helsinki, Finland; Bliss, Robert, "Resolving Large Complex Financial Organizations" at 25–26, Federal Reserve Bank of Chicago Working Papers 2003–2007 (2003).

[17] See Mayes, David, "The Role of the Safety Net in Resolving Large Financial Institutions" at 14–16; Bliss, Robert, "Resolving Large Complex Financial Organizations" at 28–29.

4.4. *Systemically significant banks*

If the bank is systemically significant the normal division of labor between the home and host countries may be called into question. Under the principle of home country responsibility, the home country of the international bank would have primary responsibility to provide liquidity lending to support its operations, including branches in other countries. If the bank is not systemically significant in the home country, but its branches are systemically significant in the host country the dilemma becomes whether the home country will continue to provide liquidity resources or other support. While other considerations, such as political concerns, international relationships, and governmental desires to prevent cross-border contagion from the home country, may lead to liquidity funding by the home country, it is apparent that the initial incentives militate against such funding. Conversely, while the host country may have more at stake, it may be reluctant to lend to a "foreign" bank.

Differing structures and protections for depositors also may become a key issue for the home and host countries. If the home country's deposit insurance system covers the host country's branch depositors — as it must under the applicable EU directive — the home country may be reluctant to take action that could lead to a payoff of those foreign depositors. These incentive questions will loom ever larger if the bank continues its slide to insolvency.

If the cross-border bank is systemically significant in the host, but not the home, country it is unlikely that the home country will take broader steps to prop up the institution to reduce the impact on host country creditors or its economy. Both with subsidiaries and branches, the host country may have to take responsibility for protecting its creditors and economy through supervisory efforts or, if unsuccessful, through a territorial or "ring fencing" approach. The difficulty is that the host country likely will not have complete supervisory information if the home country is the primary supervisor under a branch structure. A ring fencing approach may allow the host country to control its exposures and localize the resolution process, but its prospect will complicate the efforts to resolve the crisis short of liquidation.

These issues are increasingly significant. Finland and other Nordic countries are hosts for Nordea Bank, which holds a predominant position in Finland but not in Sweden, its home country. While the Nordic crisis management MoU seeks to address some of these difficult issues, the actual response to a crisis remains untested. As a home country to two very large global banks, Switzerland faces the dilemma of supervising banks whose resolution could swamp the available Swiss resources. Switzerland has responded to this reality by placing a cap on the outstanding expenditures from the Swiss deposit insurance system for bank failures.[18] Naturally, the cap itself raises a number of questions.

4.5. *Crisis management by the bank*

Crisis management planning must take into consideration the reaction of bank management to the crisis and to supervisory initiatives. A key issue in countries in which foreign banks occupy a predominant market position is that foreign banks are likely to respond to financial crises differently than host country domestic institutions. While a large foreign bank can be a stabilizing influence through its diversified business operations and greater capital resources, it may be less likely to support flagging operations in the host country in a crisis and may reallocate liquidity and capital to other operations. Even in the absence of a crisis, such cross-border banks will reallocate capital to more promising investments if host country operations lag behind.[19]

4.6. *Corporate structures*

Clearly, these difficulties are at their most extreme for systemically significant banks operating through foreign branches. However, the issues do not go away entirely for banks operating through the more common subsidiary structure. The host's greater access to information about the subsidiary bank will not provide a full understanding of the overall risks unless there is active sharing of information and analyses with the home-country supervisor about the home bank and, perhaps, other third country operations of that bank.[20]

---

[18]See Hüpkes, Eva H.G., "Bank Insolvency Resolution in Switzerland," in David Mayes and Aarno Liuksila, eds., *Who Pays for Bank Insolvency?* at 262–264 (2004).

[19]See European Central Bank, "Banking Structures in the New EU Member States" at 26 (Jan. 2005); Cárdenas, Juan, Graf, Juan Pablo, and O'Dogherty, Paschal, "Foreign banks entry in emerging market economies: a host country perspective," Bank for International Settlements (2003).

[20]See Calzolari, Giacomo and Loranth, Gyongyi, "Regulation of Multinational Banks: A Theoretical Inquiry" at 13–14, ECB Occasional Papers (July 2004).

In effect, the host country does not fully control crisis management of the larger bank — whether it operates through branches or subsidiaries — while the home country will naturally be focused on its domestic concerns and will be less concerned about the effects upon host countries.

To be sure, if the bank operates through subsidiaries, the host country can take decisive action on the subsidiary itself.[21] Nonetheless, the host country will continue to suffer from an information deficit that may impede its ability to act in a timely manner unless coordination remains effective with the home country authorities throughout the crisis. If the crisis requires formal intervention or resolution proceedings, a ring-fencing response — both with branches (for banks outside the EU) and subsidiaries — is the likely result in any event because it allows the host country to initiate the process and define the terms of the resolution.

Today, most international banks conduct their foreign operations through subsidiaries in each country. Indeed, while the EU goal has been to encourage European-wide integration of credit and financial markets through a single charter recognized throughout the EU with free branching into all EU countries, European banks have continued to rely on subsidiary banking. Over time, however, and particularly in long-integrated regional financial markets, it could well make business sense for even a systemically significant bank to operate in other countries through branches. For example, the largest Nordic bank, Nordea Bank, currently conducts its foreign business through subsidiaries, but is restructuring into a European company operating through branches.[22] While there may be practical difficulties that inhibit the changes, such as variable taxation regimes for cross-border transactions and the differences in deposit insurance between countries, the EU rules may make it difficult for small host countries to object. Smaller countries will then be faced with the necessity of protecting their economy from the systemic consequences of foreign bank failure while, under the principle of home country supervision, lacking the full panoply of tools to control the risks.

---

[21] See Jon Sigurdsson, "Small Countries, Large Multi-Country Banks: A Challenge to Supervisors — the Example of the Nordic-Baltic Area," in David Mayes and Aarno Liuksila, eds., *Who Pays for Bank Insolvency?* at 151–154 (2004).

[22] See Nordea Press Release, dated June 19, 2003, available at www.nordea.com

5. Crisis Resolution

Once events pass from crisis management to the need for formal crisis resolution, the difficulties in dealing with cross-border banks continue and intensify on a number of questions. Among the key questions are the following:

- What laws govern the initiation of government intervention or insolvency proceedings?
- Under the applicable laws, what are the "triggers" for regulatory or judicial intervention, such as prompt corrective action?
- What law applies — both to govern initiation and conduct of insolvency proceedings and to govern key banking issues, such as collateral, payment finality, and financial markets transactions?
- What deposit insurance laws apply and how do they affect different claimants?
- Which governmental entities, if any, will provide funding for any resolution?
- How will the applicable insolvency laws interact with the regulatory, legal, and financial systems of other affected countries?
- Do responsible authorities have the legal powers, incentives, and resources to facilitate a prompt resolution and availability of depositor funds and credit to the public?

The resolution of a cross-border bank should proceed under laws and policies consistent with recognized components of an effective insolvency system. As discussed earlier in this paper, among the key components of an effective insolvency system are (1) clear criteria for initiating insolvency proceedings; (2) prompt reimbursement of depositors within controls to minimize costs; (3) immediate authority to control and sell assets and liabilities; and (4) adequate legal powers to permit flexible and decisive action to mitigate the effects of the failure. Measured against these criteria, it is apparent that the current processes for dealing with the resolution of cross-border banks falls short.

5.1. *The law governing initiation of proceedings*

While the principle of home country control will often provide the home country of an international bank operating through a branch structure with the first opportunity to initiate formal intervention or insolvency proceedings, nothing prevents a host country of a branch from starting such proceedings under local law.[23] The uncertainty about what law applies and which nation's authorities will take action is increased by the absence of any common international standard for *when* a banking institution should be subject to formal intervention or insolvency proceedings.

While the European Union has defined what law and which nation's authorities will control reorganization or insolvency proceedings, it has not created a common substantive standard. Under the EU's Winding Up Directive for credit institutions, the home country's authorities have exclusive jurisdiction to decide to open "reorganization measures" and "winding-up proceedings." The home country's substantive law also governs critical legal issues, such as determination of claims, assets covered by the proceedings, conditions for set-off, and effects of the proceedings on current contracts. The decisions of the "home Member State" on these and other issues are recognized and fully effective in other EU states.[24] Under the EU directive, if the bank operates through foreign subsidiaries — as is currently the norm — then the host country will have plenary power to initiate formal intervention or insolvency proceedings against that separately chartered subsidiary.[25] The rules are unresolved for international banks outside the EU and even for those non-EU banks operating within the EU. Since the home country's substantive law governs these issues, the variations between different EU countries on the standards for intervention as well as the substantive rights after intervention can give rise to significant differences for cross-border banks operating in the same host country.

5.2. *Grounds for intervention*

To be effective, the triggers for intervention and resolution should be clear and mandatory. The prompt corrective action process codified in

---

[23] See Baxter, Thomas C., Jr., Hansen, Joyce, and Sommer, Joseph, 2004, "Two Cheers for Territoriality: An Essay on International Bank Insolvency Law," 78 *Am. Bankr. L. J.* 57, 78–79; U.S. law explicitly allows the U.S. as a host country to institute insolvency proceedings for branches. 12 U.S.C. § 3100–3102.

[24] EU Directive 2001/24/EC of April 4, 2001, Articles 3, 9, 10, and 21.

[25] See Mayes, David and Vesala, Jukka, "On the Problems of Home Country Control" at 20, Bank of Finland, *Studies in Economics and Finance* 20/98 (1998); see also Gulde and Wolf, "Financial Stability Arrangements in Europe: A Review" at 58–59, 2004, proceedings of Oestereichische Nationalbank conference, Nov. 5.

the United States provides a calibrated system of increasingly stringent supervisory controls and, once capital reaches a defined threshold, mandatory appointment of a receiver within a brief timeframe.[26] The benefit of a system of required action in response to specified trigger points is to provide clear notice of the consequences of declining capital to banks and to mitigate the pressures on the supervisor which, in some countries, have contributed to delayed intervention and higher resolution costs. Since prompt corrective action begins before the bank must be closed it provides an effective array of supervisory powers to rehabilitate institutions that can be salvaged, while providing the prod necessary to spur the bank's management to seek a privately developed solution. In fact, in the U.S., most banks which receive a "critically undercapitalized" notice do achieve a private solution through a merger or new capital even at that late date.

A well-designed system of mandatory triggers for action also provides an opportunity for insolvency authorities to get the information necessary to plan and implement a closing strategy. In the U.S., the Federal Deposit Insurance Corporation's (FDIC) resolution staff typically gains direct access to a failing bank's asset, liability, and operational information once a notice of "critically undercapitalized" is sent to the bank. At this point, the supervisory efforts continue to salvage the institution, but the resolution staff must begin to focus on how to resolve this bank if it cannot be salvaged.

Unfortunately, the law in many countries does not include a clear trigger for intervention or insolvency proceedings. While differing trigger points are subject to debate, a definite trigger mechanism allows intervention before capital is completely exhausted and limits opportunities for unproductive forbearance. If properly designed, such a triggering mechanism provides resolution authorities with a better opportunity to fashion a resolution transaction that will allow the continuation of critical banking functions.[27]

---

[26] 12 U.S.C. § 1831o.

[27] See Mayes, David, "An Overview of the Issues," Hupkes, Eva, "Bank Insolvency in Switzerland," and Hadjiemmanuil, Christos, "Bank Resolution Policy and the Organization of Bank Insolvency Proceedings: Critical Dilemmas" in David Mayes and Aarno Liuksila, eds., *Who Pays for Bank Insolvency?* at 33–35, 251–252, and 279, respectively, Helsinki: Bank of Finland.

5.3. *Deposit insurance*

A limited deposit guarantee, combined with explicit requirements to minimize losses in the resolution, promotes a well-funded insurance system as well as limits the moral hazard that can be engendered by deposit insurance. The goal of prompt reimbursement of depositors may be achieved under applicable national laws, but even here the inconsistencies between national deposit insurance rules may create disincentives for effective action by the home or host country and differential coverage for depositors in the same country. The rules for deposit insurance vary widely from country to country. Differences often exist on the types of accounts covered, the maximum limits to coverage, the funding mechanisms for the deposit insurance system, the extent of government backing for coverage, the speed of payment to insured depositors, the availability of other supplementary insurance, and how the insolvency process is administered.[28]

The differences between different national deposit insurance systems introduce additional complications. Under EU directives, the principle of home country control extends to the protection of branch depositors in an EU host country. Alternatively, the branches of the cross-border bank can opt to seek coverage under the host country's laws. If a cross-border bank's branches have opted for such host country coverage, it could balance some incentive issues for the home and host supervisors.[29]

In the EU scenario, the host country will be able to take comfort in protection of its depositors, while the home country will be required to consider the potential liability for those foreign depositors in making decisions about the resolution. Within the European Union, the home country authorities will have to judge the costs and chances of success of supervisory forbearance through injections of public money or central bank liquidity funding against the costs of insolvency proceedings and outlays for deposit insurance payments. The host country will lack the authority to impose a solution. Even if the host country desired to threaten or impose a ring fencing solution, the EU's Winding up Directive denies it this option.

---

[28] See Eisenbeis, Robert E. and Kaufman, George G, "Bank Crisis Resolution and Foreign-Owned Banks," presentation at Norges Bank Conference on Banking Crisis Resolution — Theory and Policy, Friday, June 17, 2005.

[29] See Directive 94/19/EC of the European Parliament and of the Council of 30 May 1994 on deposit guarantee schemes, OJ 1994 L 135/5, Article 4; Gulde and Wolf, "Financial Stability Arrangements in Europe: A Review" at 54–55 and Table 1, proceedings of Oestereichische Nationalbank conference (Nov. 5, 2004).

The situation, however, is quite different if the failing bank is American. Under U.S. law, depositors in foreign branches of a U.S. bank are not insured under the FDIC's deposit insurance and are subordinated to uninsured depositors of the U.S. branches in the distribution of the proceeds from the sale of the bank's assets. Depositors in foreign branches of U.S. banks are covered by FDIC deposit insurance only if the deposit is payable in the U.S. in addition to the foreign branch.[30] If the cross-border bank is American, the host country will have to rely on its deposit insurance coverage system to protect depositors (if foreign branch depositors are covered under the host country's laws) and bear those costs or aggressively seek collateral or other protection from the American bank or its regulators. Certainly the absence of coverage for the host country's depositors under U.S. law makes a ring fencing response by the host country more likely.

5.4. *Legal powers of controlling authorities*

An effective resolution process also must give the insolvency authority clear legal power to take flexible and decisive action to maximize recoveries on assets and minimize delays in providing money back to depositors. These legal powers should include independence from undue interference by other governmental bodies, the ability to terminate contracts, the power to enforce contracts, the authority to sell assets, the right to avoid fraudulent or unauthorized transfers, and broad flexibility to design resolution and asset sales structures to achieve the goals of the resolution. Many difficulties in resolving individual insolvencies, and in addressing broader instability, have been exacerbated by the inability of trustees or liquidators to take prompt action.

The ability to take prompt and decisive action is critical if the bank is systemically significant. One solution is simply to prop up the bank through government funding or guarantees. However, this response — particularly if undertaken without a stringent restructuring of operations, management, and ownership — can create a drag on the economy, distort banking competition, and dramatically increase the costs to the public. The use of a bridge bank or other temporary institution to continue critical banking functions through an insolvency process allows termination of shareholder and management control as well as the restructuring of operations to focus on profitable businesses and impose losses on appropriate parties. While an open bank solution may make continuation of operations easier, it does not

---

[30]12 U.S.C. § 1813(l) and (m).

eliminate the need for restructuring, close oversight, valuation of assets to support write downs of shareholder and other claims, and imposition of appropriate capital or other mechanisms to require repayment of any governmental funding.

Under U.S. law, the FDIC as deposit insurer is delegated broad authority to operate or liquidate the business, sell the assets and resolve the liabilities of a failed insured bank immediately after its appointment as receiver or conservator. This authority enables the FDIC to immediately sell many of the assets of a failing institution to an open bank or to an FDIC-created bridge bank — and, in effect, maintain critical banking functions. A crucial component of the ability to immediately transfer banking operations is the availability of detailed information about the failing institution, its operations, assets, and liabilities. If the ultimate resolution authority gains access to this information only after intervention proceedings begin, a prompt sale and transfer of functioning banking operations is very unlikely.

Will this authority to act quickly and decisively be available in a cross-border resolution? This appears unlikely. First, as discussed above, the relevant countries may lack clear, mandatory triggers to start the insolvency process. Without such triggers, there is a strong likelihood that necessary action will be delayed until it is more costly and ineffective. Second, many countries do not provide a strong and immediate power to an insolvency administrator to control and sell assets and resolve liabilities. Among the impediments are legal structures that require court approval for sales of assets and provide for extensive rights of appeal by shareholders and other interested parties before sales can be completed. In addition, some laws simply do not include authorization for flexible transactions, such as a bridge bank or a similar temporary "bank."[31] If a bank is systemically significant, the traditional bankruptcy stay that halts or, at least, calls into question the validity of new claims is not a viable option. Third, even if the home or host country's administrators possess such authority, the potential for ring-fencing and the uncertainties about the applicable law for different issues will impede a prompt and effective resolution. The alternatives of government recapitalization or other bailouts serve only to increase moral hazard and to impair the efficient functioning of the banking market.[32]

---

[31] See Hupkes, Eva, "Protect Functions, Not Institutions," *The Financial Regulator*, Vol. 9, No. 3 at 46–49 (Dec. 2004).

[32] See Mayes, David, "The Role of the Safety Net in Resolving Large Financial Institutions" at 4–6, paper initially prepared for Federal Reserve Bank of Chicago Conference on "Systemic Financial Crises: Resolving Large Bank Insolvencies," Sept. 30–Oct. 1, 2004.

Under U.S. and some other national laws, the power to act decisively is provided directly to the central bank or to deposit insurer. Under other systems, the resolution power is provided to the judiciary. The locus of power may not be crucial, but the ability to act promptly and decisively to stem the effects of the failure is. While there are clear advantages to creating a wholly administrative process by conferring this power on a single actor, such as the deposit insurer, other considerations may militate towards a more judicially based approach.[33] Irrespective of the ultimate decision-maker, the opportunities for delay and challenges to asset and function transfers must be limited and clearly defined.

6. Future Directions?

Where a deteriorating bank operates in multiple countries the affected parties' divergent interests and incentives may be difficult to discern or resolve. The parties' interests and incentives are complicated by the interaction and conflict between different national supervisory, deposit insurance, central bank, and insolvency rules and cultures. As our discussion has illustrated, the home and host country authorities may face a mismatch between supervisory control, access to information, and responsibility for protecting the local economy. The law in one or more countries may preclude effective cooperation, as where there are legal limitations on sharing of confidential information, or the law may mandate certain crisis management tools or require particular resolution strategies, such as ring fencing.

While this mismatch most often affects the host country, the home country of the cross-border bank faces uncertainty about how the host country's laws and authorities will respond. These uncertainties, and the potential for ring fencing by the host country, make successful crisis management and crisis resolution much more difficult for the home country as well. The uncertainties increase the likelihood that affected parties — the bank, customers, and other private sector participants as well as national authorities — will take steps to define their exposures in a way that may destroy any

---

[33] See Hadjiemmanuil, Christos, "Bank Resolution Policy and the Organization of Bank Insolvency Proceedings: Critical Dilemmas" in David Mayes and Aarno Liuksila, eds., *Who Pays for Bank Insolvency?* at 291–300, Helsinki: Bank of Finland; Hupkes, Eva, *The Legal Aspects of Bank Insolvency: A Comparative Analysis of Western Europe, the United States, and Canada* at 63–81 (2000).

opportunity for continued banking operations. The understandable desire to avoid continued uncertainty and "limit" exposures may lead to a collapse of communication and coordination.

How can the national authorities respond to these risks? As a first step, the key participants in the management and resolution of a crisis need to recognize and understand the considerations that will affect their and other parties' responses to a potential crisis. More specific and practical contingency planning by affected participants — including national regulators, insolvency authorities, and bankers — is a crucial step.

In recognition of the different interests and incentives, contingency planning should focus on the critical goals of crisis management and resolution. If the bank is not systemically significant, then the focus should be on an orderly private restructuring of the bank or a timely closing. Where the failing cross-border bank is systemically significant either to the home country or the host country the management and, if necessary, the formal resolution of the crisis should focus on maintaining the critical functions performed by that bank. This does not necessarily require a bailout of the bank or even the overall bank's continued operation. It does require a skeptical appraisal of precisely which operations of the bank are truly systemically significant. Once such operations are identified, then pre-resolution planning and resolution implementation should focus on maintaining those functions.

The use of a bridge bank or even a privately-developed entity to maintain these functions are workable solutions that do not necessarily require continuation of the complete banking enterprise. The practical details for implementation of these approaches are many and complex, but these approaches may offer significant advantages to propping up the entire failed bank.

If a resolution is necessary, it is imperative that the responsible authorities continue to share key information about the failing bank. While the incentive issues described in this paper will undoubtedly complicate cooperation, pre-crisis agreements and cross-border contingency planning will help create the environment for better coordination. As we have discussed, much of the difficulty lies in the diversity of national laws, standards, and cultures affecting crisis management and resolution. Memoranda of understanding should reflect realistic cooperation protocols and be expanded to include crisis management. An agreement, however, is insufficient unless adherence to it can be stress tested by realistic appraisals of the conflicting incentives, legal requirements and the limits of cooperation in an actual crisis.

A helpful precursor to such agreements may be legal changes to ensure some degree of harmonization in key elements of the crisis management and crisis resolution processes. A common legal infrastructure for the resolution of insolvencies is very unlikely and is not required. However, greater harmonization of key elements of effective resolutions would be an important step forward. For example, greater harmonization and clarity about the triggers for action, the tools to return insured funds quickly to depositors, the authority to implement a quick resolution, and the legal powers to restructure and continue key banking functions would allow more effective crisis planning.

If those legal changes prove impossible, a more modest goal for legal changes could focus on insuring the continuation of systemically significant banking functions, such as payments linkages and the capital markets. An important way to prevent instability from spreading is to harmonize the cross-border or national insolvency rules governing the key linkages between systemically significant cross-border banks. Over the past twenty years, vast improvements have been made toward standardized laws that protect the settlement of transactions and the reduction of inter-bank and cross-border credit risk in the capital markets and payments processing.

Further improvements can be achieved through national legal reforms and international protocols that allow authorities to take prompt and decisive action to continue systemically significant functions. As Eva Hüpkes has pointed out, preservation of the systemically significant functions does not require preservation of the entire failing bank. Combined with practical contingency planning, harmonization of these national standards may serve to reduce moral hazard by providing more realistic alternatives to a broad government bailout.

Michael Krimminger is senior policy advisor to the Director of the Federal Deposit Insurance Corporation's Division of Resolutions and Receiverships. The views expressed in this paper are solely those of the author and do not necessarily represent the policies or views of the FDIC. © 2005 Michael Krimminger.

Bank Insolvency Procedures as Foundation for Market Discipline

Apanard Angkinand*
University of Illinois at Springfield

Clas Wihlborg
Copenhagen Business School and University of California at Riverside

1. Introduction

Formal and informal insolvency procedures for dealing with distressed firms constitute an essential part of a competitive market mechanism by allowing exit of inefficient firms and the reallocation of resources to new ventures, or by contributing to rehabilitation and reorganization of firms. Efficient procedures provide contractual predictability for stakeholders in the sense that they can value their claims contingent on a firm's economic condition. The contractual predictability contributes to the ex ante incentives of investors, lenders and other stakeholders to commit resources.

Predetermined, operational procedures for dealing with banks in distress are conspicuously absent across the world with very few exceptions. Instead governments and regulatory authorities intervene when banks approach failure for reasons that will be discussed. Bailouts of important creditors, sometimes including shareholders, and blanket guarantees for creditors become the norm rather than the exception. Incentives of stakeholders in banks become distorted and the competitive mechanism dysfunctional.

In this paper we argue that efficient incentives of banks' creditors, as well as of shareholders and managers, require predetermined rules for dealing with banks in distress, and a group of creditors that are credibly non-insured. Predetermined bank insolvency procedures — if appropriately designed — contribute to the credibility of non-insurance of creditor groups.

This credibility requires that distress resolution for banks can be implemented without the issuance of ad hoc guarantees at the time of distress.

Cross-border banking increases the need for pre-determined bank insolvency procedures. Herring (2003) coined the phrase "too complex to fail" to describe the international financial conglomerates supplying financial services in a number of countries in an often opaque subsidiary structure. Following Goldberg, Sweeney and Wihlborg (2005) we argue here that appropriate, credible bank insolvency procedures make it possible to integrate banks' cross-border activities across home-and host countries in branches supervised by home-country authorities. Thus, the seemingly distant European Union (EU) vision of competition between international banks with mutual recognition of supervisors and regulation could be realized.

In the empirical part of this paper we provide evidence based on Angkinand and Wihlborg (2005) that market discipline on banks is enhanced by credibility of non-insurance. We show how our proxies for lack of market discipline — the probability of banking crisis and non-performing loans in a sample of developed and emerging market countries — depend on the coverage of explicit deposit insurance schemes in these countries. The analysis of Angkinand and Wihlborg (2005) is then extended to capture effects of rule-based insolvency procedures in the U.S. in particular.

2. Insolvency Procedures for Banks

Efficient insolvency procedures allow appropriate restructuring, debt-reduction, management change, liquidity infusion or other actions to take place.[1] The difficulty of designing efficient insolvency procedures is to a large extent caused by information problems and asymmetries of information about the cause of distress and asset values. Collateralized loans and priority rules discourage "runs" on the available resources of a distressed firm. A run can force a firm into bankruptcy prematurely. In banking this "run problem" is particularly acute. Guarantees of creditor groups, such as deposit insurance for banks' creditors, can discourage runs but they make creditors insensitive to risk and, thereby, they cause misallocation of resources.

---

[1]The discussion of insolvency procedures for nonbanks is based on Wihlborg, Gangopadhyay with Hussain (2001).

In countries with explicit restructuring law such as Chapter 11 in the U.S. bankruptcy code, an independent body with enforcement powers, such as a court, is required to determine the value of the firm and the value-maximizing course of action. Contracts are abrogated when firms enter restructuring proceedings. Therefore, the predictability of the outcome for various stakeholders is low and the outcome is generally more favorable to the shareholders and management than the outcomes in countries with a more liquidation oriented approach to insolvency. Predictability and, therefore, *ex ante* efficiency is also influenced by arbitrariness of court procedures, corruption of judges, and political influences on procedures.

Although the role of insolvency procedures for banks in principle is the same as for non-financial firms and nonbank financial firms, there are important differences between banks and other firms. First, banks supply liquidity. A large part of their liabilities are very short term and they play an important role in the payment mechanism. These liabilities may be subject to bank runs if creditors fear non-repayment. Second, there are generally substantial amounts of very short-term inter-bank liabilities that may contribute to contagion among banks if one bank fails. Third, creditors of banks in particular are diverse and many. Thus, banks do not generally have one or a few large creditors with a strong interest in resolution of distress. The risk of runs on a bank in distress and contagion implies that speed of action in distress resolution is of the essence. Conventional liquidation and restructuring procedures are too time-consuming to be applied to banks without modification.

For the reasons mentioned regular bankruptcy-and restructuring laws are not often applied in cases when banks face distress. One could argue that in countries with extensive deposit insurance, the insuring authority could take the coordinating role that large creditors often have in nonbank restructurings. However, in many countries the insuring authority may be the government and, even if there is a specific authority, there are in most countries neither pre-established procedures for settling claims against non-insured creditors, nor the expertise in the authority to manage the insolvency. Most countries simply do not allow banks to fail. The main exception is the U.S. that has implemented bank-specific insolvency procedures through the FDIC. We return to practices in different countries in the next section.

Although many economists have argued that the fear of contagion from one bank's failure is exaggerated, few governments are willing to test this belief. A regulatory authority facing an actual or perceived threat to the banking system is compelled to respond in order to eliminate the risk of bank runs. The authority or its government may bail out banks fully or partially — even nationalize the banking sector, as in Norway in the late 1980s. Other solutions include (1) debt restructuring; (2) a mix of government and more or less voluntary private recapitalization; and (3) the creation of specialized agencies to take over bad loans, such as the Resolution Trust Corporation in the U.S.

The mentioned solutions may assist in restoring a functioning market, but they tend to be assembled by regulators, central banks and governments in time of crises. Therefore, they fail to provide the sector with transparent, predictable consequences in cases of mismanagement or excessive risk-taking. When the crisis occurs the political pressures to resolve it by protecting strong interest groups are high. *Ex ante* knowledge of these political pressures lead to expectations of bailouts and comprehensive liability guarantees.

Transparent, pre- and well-specified insolvency procedures for banks could increase the credibility of no bailout policies, enhance market discipline and thereby reduce the probability of banks facing distress, and where distress occurs, prevent one bank's failure from having contagion effects.

Given the specific characteristics of banks, liquidation and restructuring procedures for nonbanks are not practical in the banking sector. One alternative, prompt corrective action (PCA), has been implemented in the U.S. It offers a degree of predictability of actions for shareholders and management although substantial discretion remains. Insolvency rules should allow both liquidation and restructuring. They would complement PCA by being more complete and predictable with respect to the claims of different stakeholders.

The European Shadow Financial Regulatory Committee (1998) proposed the following characteristics of special bank insolvency procedures:

1. Pre-specified trigger capital levels for pre-specified regulatory or legal action (PCA).
2. A pre-determined trigger initiating liquidation. This trigger point may actually be set at a positive capital ratio given uncertainty about asset values (part of PCA).
3. Priority among creditors must be contractually pre-specified in such a way that claims with high liquidity value are given high priority.
4. Valuation procedures should be made transparent.

5. In liquidation other banks or the central bank need to be organized to honor claims with high liquidity value including inter-bank claims on behalf of the distressed bank. Banks may have incentives to organize such arrangements themselves, if clear liquidation procedures exist, but if they do not, then regulators must make sure that arrangements exist.
6. The lender of last resort function should not be extended to insolvent banks.
7. The authorities managing a crisis must be made independent of ad hoc political pressures in order to enhance the credibility of the process.

The implementation of insolvency law for banks with these characteristics should achieve an acceptable, low risk of runs and low risk of contagion while inefficient owners and managers exit. The contractual predictability of claims and the predictability of bankruptcy and PCA costs should provide efficient ex ante incentives. By achieving these objectives the government's and the regulator's fear of a system crash should be alleviated. Thereby, non-insurance of groups of creditors and shareholders would be credible.

3. Current Distress Resolution Practices in Banking

The U.S. with its high coverage deposit insurance system has been leading in the creation and implementation of pre-specified rules.[2] The Federal Deposit Insurance Corporation Improvement Act (FDICIA) of 1991 sets trigger capital ratios for specific prompt corrective actions by banks and regulatory authorities. There are four trigger points at which the FDIC in particular must take action or order the bank to take certain actions. The Fed's ability to act as lender of last resort has been strongly restricted unless there is substantial systemic risk. Questions remain, however, about the ability and willingness of the Fed and the FDIC to follow the PCA-procedures if a bank in distress is considered "too big to fail." Nevertheless, PCA increases the predictability of distress costs for shareholders at different levels of capital providing incentives for shareholders and management to have a sufficient capital buffer corresponding to risk taking.[3]

Norway is another country with pre-specified distress resolution procedures for banks. Already before the Norwegian banking crisis in the late

---

[2]This section is based on Angkinand and Wihlborg (2006).
[3]See Wihlborg (2005).

1980s, there were rules for public administration of banks in distress. The procedures are more similar to liquidation procedures than to restructuring procedures and the distressed bank is not expected to remain under public administration for long. The Norwegian case illustrates that it is not merely the existence of pre-determined insolvency procedures that matter. Banking in Norway is dominated by a few banks. Each one tends to be too big to fail. Therefore, liquidation is not a politically acceptable alternative and liquidation procedures will not be enforced. Thereby, they lose credibility.

The vast majority of countries lack formal distress resolution procedures for banks. Regular bankruptcy laws apply in principle on banks. In some countries insolvency law may include procedures that are particularly suitable for banks. In particular, the UK insolvency law includes a procedure called "administration" designed to enable reconstruction of a firm. An "administrator" can be appointed by a group of creditors or a court to lead a distressed firm. The administration procedures are similar to Chapter 11 in several ways except that the administrator takes over management functions. In administration, firms are protected from actions by creditors while negotiations with creditors are ongoing. The intention of administration is to be short lived and the administrator can enter new agreements with the purpose of avoiding liquidation. Existing contracts remain valid, however.

After 1997 the British Financial Services Authority (FSA) has been given strong authority to issue rules for banks with the purpose of ensuring financial stability. The FSA can force a bank to enter bankruptcy or administration proceedings. It has the right to issue opinions about the result of administration proceedings. The division of responsibility between the FSA, the Bank of England, and the Ministry of Finance has been specified in a memorandum of understanding.

As a country experiencing a severe banking crisis in the early 1990s, Sweden has had a debate about distress resolution procedures during the 1990s. The Swedish banking crisis was essentially resolved by the issuance of a blanket guarantee for all bank creditors. Even shareholders were indirectly bailed out by this guarantee. In 2000, a government committee proposed specific legislation for a separate insolvency law for banks, much in the spirit of the European Shadow Committee proposal described above. Specifically, the proposal for public administration contained a mixture of the American and the Norwegian rules. Like the American FDICIA the purpose of the proposed procedures was primarily to make restructuring possible. Liquidation procedures were also clearly specified. For example, the liquidity problem was addressed directly. The proposal is resting after being positively received although some reservations on specifics were expressed by, for example, the Swedish FSA.

Crisis management for banks is an issue addressed in Europe as well on the EU level. In particular, the coordination problem arising when an international bank faces distress has led to some activity with respect to development of principles for crisis resolution. Since most major banks within the EU have some international activity, these principles are the closest the EU comes to insolvency procedures for banks.

In a Report on Financial Crisis Management, the Economic and Financial Committee[4] states that *"there is no blueprint for crisis management"* and as a general principle *"private institutions should be involved as much as possible in both crisis prevention and, if this fails, in crisis management ... If financial losses occur, the firm's shareholders should bear the costs and its management should suffer the consequences. For this reason, the winding down of the institution may be a sensible strategy."* EU crisis management procedures do not become more specific than this.

Other sections of the report refer to alternative solutions in a bank crisis. Private sector solutions are "preferred" but *"Liquidity support might have to be granted in order to stabilize the troubled institution or the market as a whole in order 'to buy time.' In a less volatile environment, public measures may then be considered, if the winding-down of the institution is not a viable option."* Competitive implications of crisis management measures are also discussed in a separate section.

The implication for crisis management of these very general principles is that central banks, financial supervisors, and responsible ministries will become involved when a bank faces distress. The lack of clear procedures in combination with the need to act quickly and the political incentives to protect depositor groups creates a system where the authorities are obliged to support the distressed bank.

4. Market Discipline in Cross-Border Banking; Too Complex to Fail Versus Too Big to Save?

Cross-border banking can occur through subsidiaries or branches in the host countries. In this section, we discuss distress resolution procedures

---

[4]Economic Paper No. 156, July 2001 from The Economic and Financial Committee.

for the subsidiary organization before turning to the branch organization. Subsidiaries are by far the most common form of host-country establishment in retail banking. Branches are, with few exceptions not accepted by host-country regulators.

Subsidiaries are independent legal entities subject to host-country law, regulation, and supervision. Their assets are more or less controlled by the parent, however. Cross-border banks can therefore engage in opportunistic risk-shifting, possibly with the consent of the home-country supervisor, who may approve of more risk being placed in host countries with weaker supervision.

As noted by Herring (2003) financial conglomerates operating with subsidiaries in several countries tend to become too complex to fail. Crisis resolution must involve authorities in all countries the bank is operating and the asset-liability structure may be very opaque. Only under the rare circumstances that the parent bank is not committed to the subsidiary's survival and allows it to operate as an entirely separate entity, can a crisis be resolved by host-country authorities alone.

In general where banks operate across borders there are memoranda of understanding about cooperation between home- and host-country supervisors. These memoranda are typically very general. For example, in the EU report from The Economic and Financial Committee quoted above, stating that "there is no blue print for crisis resolution," the following statement covers coordination and the assignment of responsibility for decision making with respect to crisis management:

"The presumption in international banking supervision is that the home-country authorities are responsible for decisions on crisis management." However, "The principle of home-country control is not directly applicable to foreign subsidiaries, as the host-country authorities are obliged to treat these as domestic institutions with their own legal identity. In the event of a crisis at a foreign subsidiary, the host-country supervisor — which is in fact the subsidiary's home-country supervisor — can take any preventive measure envisaged in this context." Since most international activity takes place in subsidiaries there is very little guidance in these statements. Thus, if a crisis occurs in an international EU bank, *ad hoc* solutions must be developed quickly in committees including central banks, financial supervisors and ministries in the countries concerned. Politics of fiscal burden sharing and other national concerns easily become the major issues in negotiations rather than long-term consequences for incentives of stakeholders in banks.

The Banking Directives of the EU state the principles of Home Country Control, Mutual Recognition (of law, regulation and supervision), home-country deposit insurance coverage, and the free establishment of banks across borders. These principles seem to be designed for banks operating cross borders through branches rather than subsidiaries. Current EU practices in banking stand in stark contrast to these principles. Many EU countries' attitude to foreign banks and their home-country supervisors is characterized by discrimination and distrust rather than mutual recognition.

An EU test case of branch banking is under way. Nordea is a Nordic bank created in 2000 by the mergers of four systemically important banks in four countries. Its strategy is to operate across the four countries in a unified functional organization although its legal organization consists of subsidiaries in the different countries. The response of the supervisors in Denmark, Finland, Norway and Sweden has been to form a joint Nordea committee with a number of joint sub-committees to be able to supervise the bank by function across the legal entities.

Nordea has recently proposed to re-organize to form an EU-company headquartered in Sweden with branches in the other three countries. The supervisors have not yet approved the organization but if the reorganization of Nordea turns out to be successful for the bank and the supervisors it can pave the way for expanded cross-border banking in the EU in particular.

On the face of it, the branch structure, if implemented, simplifies both the bank's organization and the supervisory responsibility. Clearly, greater correspondence between legal and functional organizations is an advantage from an internal efficiency point of view.

Based on the Nordea case Goldberg, Sweeney and Wihlborg (2005) discuss alternative approaches for supervision of cross-country banking through branches. They list five possible models for supervision of a bank with headquarters in Sweden and branches in the other three countries. *First,* the supervisors can continue with the current inter-supervisory committee approach, while depositors are covered by systems of deposit insurance in the host countries. Although this solution is contrary to EU principles, it is the solution that is closest to the current approach to host-country subsidiaries. *Second,* the inter-supervisory committee approach could continue while depositors in all branches become covered by the Swedish deposit insurance scheme. *Third,* there is the formal home-country EU-model wherein both supervisory responsibility and deposit insurance for all branches become entirely Swedish in the Nordea case. A *fourth* model would place supervisory responsibility in Sweden and deposit insurance in the host countries. *Last*, a Nordic or European supervisory authority and deposit insurance system could be established.

The last model is ruled out as politically unrealistic, as well as contrary to the EU principle of institutional competition by means of mutual recognition.[5] We have to consider national supervisory authorities as the realistic institutional structure for the foreseeable future. The lender-of-last-resort (LOLR) function is similarly a national responsibility for the central banks.[6]

An efficient supervisory structure should be incentive compatible in the sense that supervisory responsibility coincides with risk taking through deposit insurance responsibility. In addition to the one supervisor-one deposit insurance scheme, the two approaches that satisfy this condition are the first and the third. Under the first approach supervisors role remain similar to their role with the subsidiary organization. It is questionable whether the bank will be able fully implement the branch organization under this approach. Thus we are left with the third home-country approach as envisioned in the EU Directives.

The advantages with the home-country approach are that the organization of regulation and supervision, as well as the organization of the bank can become relatively transparent with clear assignment of responsibility. Market discipline of the bank's behavior may also be enhanced because, from the home-country perspective, the bank may become too big to save. Statements to the effect that depositors and other creditors are not protected beyond the explicit, partial insurance scheme become credible. Therefore, market discipline is likely to have a strong effect on the bank's behavior with respect to risk-taking and capital structure. In this way, so-called moral hazard problems in the bank's risk-taking are reduced substantially.

The mentioned advantages do not come automatically, however. As noted, mutual recognition of foreign supervisors' responsibility for large parts of the domestic banking systems requires trust in the effectiveness and fairness of the foreign supervisors. This trust requires institutional support in the form of supervisory organization and distress resolution procedures.[7]

---

[5]It must also be noted that Norway is not a member of the EU, while only Finland has joined the Euro.

[6]In the Euro-zone, national central banks are formally the LOLR, but the ECB must become involved if liquidity is to be increased.

[7]The Swedish FSA seems to favor a structure between the first and fourth approaches while Denmark, Finland and Norway are likely to prefer either the first or second models. Thus, a prediction for the Nordea case is that the first approach will be implemented.

Host country supervisors must rely on the home-country supervisor to treat all branches fairly in a crisis situation, and they must have trust in the home-country supervisor as head crisis manager. If this trust and acceptance does not exist, the host-country supervisors may intervene in a crisis to take over and bailout the branches in their countries. If markets expect this to happen, then the market discipline is going to be weak. Thus, rules for resolution of a crisis in a bank need to be clear and credible *ex ante*. These rules need to include binding measures for prompt corrective action.[8]

The rules for prompt corrective action must assure all countries involved that the intervention will be fair in relation to all branches and creditors independent of country. For the home-country supervisor to obtain credibility as the supervisor of branches in all countries, the supervisors in the host countries need to be informed about all supervisory activities and the results of these activities. The responsible supervisor must be able to obtain local expertise from the other supervisors upon request. Responsibility must not thereby be shifted towards the host countries, however. One solution for the home-country supervisor is to set up local branches with local employees.

The supervisors in the host countries must contribute to the credibility of the regulatory regime by making it clear that they take no regulatory, supervisory, or crisis resolution responsibility, but they accept the *ex ante* determined rules for structured intervention and partial deposit insurance.

If these principles were implemented, distress resolution procedures would become the subject of institutional competition. The government that wants to support the competitiveness of its banking industry can do this by implementing strong rule based bank insolvency procedures.

There is also concern that the potential differences in deposit insurance coverage between domestic and foreign banks operating in the same country could lead to politically unacceptable consequences in case a foreign bank with relatively low coverage fails. In the U.S., branches of foreign banks must join the U.S. deposit insurance system and, therefore, U.S. regulators also restrict the operations of foreign branches. The benefits of branch banking cannot be realized under these conditions.

If differences in deposit insurance coverage can be accepted, the coverage becomes the subject of institutional competition as well. Relatively low coverage reduces the international competitiveness of banks. Thus, the government that fears the potential costs associated with the failure of domestic

---

[8] See also Mayes (2004).

bank with large international branch operations would keep the insurance coverage relatively low.

Finally, the institutional support for cross-border banking through branches must include mutual recognition of insolvency procedures in the sense that host countries accept the home country's jurisdiction over bank assets located in the host country. International agreements of this kind with respect to general bankruptcy law exist among some countries.

5. Empirical Evidence on Determinants of Credibility of Non-Insurance as Disciplinary Device

In this section we use data from 56 developed and emerging market countries to test our propositions with respect to the relation between credibility of non-insurance of banks' creditors and market discipline, as well as with respect to institutional determinants of this relation. In particular, we want to estimate the impact of bank insolvency procedures, such as PCA. The analysis follows Angkinand and Wihlborg (AW) (2005), wherein *lack of market discipline* is captured by two proxies. One is *the occurrence of banking crisis*, which is identified by a banking crisis dummy.[9] This dummy is given a value of one in years when a country experienced a banking crisis during 1985–2003. The estimation methodology is a logit regression.

The second proxy for market discipline is *the share of non-performing loans relative to total loans* in the banking industry in each country and year. The data is taken from International Monetary Fund's Financial Stability Reports and covers the years 1998–2003. Table 1 presents descriptive statistics for the variables used in the estimations.

The main hypothesis tested in AW (2005) is that market discipline is increasing with the extent of credible non-insurance of banks' creditors.[10] Lacking a direct proxy for the extent of credible non-insurance AW argue that there is an inverse U-shaped relationship between the extent of credible non-insurance and explicit deposit insurance coverage. In other words, we expect U-shaped relationships between the lack of market discipline (degree of moral hazard) and explicit deposit insurance coverage, and between

[9]The banking crisis data is taken from Caprio and Klingebiel (2003).
[10]There is a large literature on deposit insurance and banking crisis. We do not review it here, since an extensive review can be found in AW (2005).

Table 1. Descriptive statistics

Variable	Obs	Mean	Std. Dev.	Min	Max
Banking Crisis Dummy	856	0.23	0.42	0	1
NPLs (% Total Loans)	291	8.45	7.95	0.4	42.9
Real GDP Per Capita	856	118.97	107.22	1.95	405.27
Real GDP Growth$_{t-1}$	856	3.19	3.8	−22.93	18.83
Domestic Credit$_{t-1}$	856	84.05	50.03	11.03	321.75
M2 to Reserve$_{t-1}$	856	9.27	9.26	0.78	63.95
Inflation$_{t-1}$	856	19.89	170.79	−3.96	410.24
Real Interest Rate$_{t-1}$	856	8.2	17.68	-91.72	112.12
Developed and Emerging Market Countries					
Covdep	853	1.05	1.02	0	3
Comprehensive DI	851	1.2	1.07	0	4
PCA	853	4.19	1.86	1	8
CA1	853	18.02	10.21	0	42
CA2	853	14.23	8.27	0	36
Developed Countries					
Covdep	380	1.13	0.95	0	3
CAEI	380	3.59	2.09	1	8
CA1	380	19.6	11.71	3.17	42
CA2	380	16.2	9.61	2.5	36
Emerging Market Countries					
Covdep	473	0.98	1.07	0	3
CAEI	473	4.67	1.5	1	6
CA1	473	16.75	8.63	0	36
CA2	473	12.65	6.61	0	30

the probability of banking crisis and explicit deposit insurance coverage. Figure 1 from AW (2005) illustrates the hypothesized relationships.

The U-shaped curve in the figure depends on an upward sloping relation between explicit deposit insurance and (lack of) market discipline (moral hazard) at a given level of implicit guarantees, and a downward sloping relation showing how the credibility of non-insurance increases with higher explicit coverage. Extensive non-insurance has no credibility because authorities are compelled to intervene rapidly to guarantee depositors' funds in a crisis. As the explicit coverage increases the credibility of non-insurance increases enhancing market discipline while the increasing

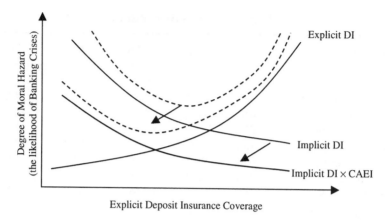

Figure 1. The relationship between (lack of) market discipline and explicit deposit insurance coverage
(Source: Angkinand and Wihlborg, 2005).

explicit coverage also reduces market discipline. The U-shaped relation is not a mathematical necessity but based on the conjecture that there is a degree of partial explicit deposit insurance that maximizes the extent of credible non-insurance.

AW (2005) find that the positive quadratic relationship between (lack of) market discipline and explicit deposit insurance coverage is significant in a panel data analysis of banking crises in 140 countries, as well as in sub-samples for emerging market economies and developed economies, for the period 1985–2003 when the banking crisis dummy is the dependent variable, and for the period of 1998–2003 when the non-performing loans variable is the dependent variable. The results for 59 emerging and developed market economies combined are reproduced in columns 1 (banking crisis dummy) and 5 (non-performing loans) in Table 2. Explicit coverage is the maximum coverage per deposit relative to total deposits per capita.[11] The U-shaped curves in Figure 2 show the relation between each (lack of) market discipline proxy and explicit coverage under the assumption that all control variables take on their average values for the period. The Appendix shows the definitions of all variables including the control variables used in the logit analysis and the ordinary least squares regressions.

---

[11]The deposit insurance variable is based on data gathered by the World Bank and presented in Demirgüç-Kunt, Karacaovali and Laeven (2005). Other proxies for coverage are also developed there and used in AW (2005).

Table 2. The credibility of non-insurance, deposit insurance coverage (proxied by covdep), and corrective action

Method/Dependent variable	(1)	(2)	(3)	(4)	(5)	(6)	(7)	(8)
	Logit Estimation/Crisis Dummy				OLS/NPLs			
Constant	-0.8798***	-1.7679***	-0.5196***	-0.6270*	13.2332***	7.2992***	10.7746***	11.2417***
	(0.2621)	(0.4709)	(0.3990)	(0.3703)	(1.0220)	(1.4402)	(1.1978)	(1.2365)
Real GDP Per Capita	-0.0061***	-0.0060***	-0.0057***	-0.0058***	-0.0528***	-0.0450***	-0.0470***	-0.0470***
	(0.0011)	(0.0013)	(0.0012)	(0.0012)	(0.0047)	(0.0040)	(0.0042)	(0.0042)
Real GDP Growth$_{t-1}$	-0.1357***	-0.1299***	-0.1428***	-0.1321***	-0.3940***	-0.4691***	-0.4931***	-0.4361***
	(0.0235)	(0.0245)	(0.0249)	(0.0245)	(0.1441)	(0.1366)	(0.1491)	(0.1418)
Domestic Credit$_{t-1}$	0.0084***	0.0089***	0.0067**	0.0078***	0.0409**	0.0344***	0.0347***	0.0399***
	(0.0025)	(0.0027)	(0.0029)	(0.0028)	(0.0092)	(0.0088)	(0.0097)	(0.0106)
M2 to Reserve$_{t-1}$	0	0	0	0	-0.0650***	-0.0800***	-0.0882***	-0.0710***
	(0.0110)	(0.0109)	(0.0117)	(0.0111)	(0.0274)	(0.0238)	(0.0266)	(0.0254)
Inflation$_{t-1}$	-0.0050***	-0.0040*	-0.0060***	-0.0053***	0	-0.03	0	0.0041*
	(0.0016)	(0.0023)	(0.0019)	(0.0018)	(0.0022)	(0.0411)	(0.0023)	(0.0023)
Real Interest Rate$_{t-1}$	0	0	-0.01	-0.01	0.03	0.03	0.0327**	0.0406**
	(0.0052)	(0.0052)	(0.0059)	(0.0062)	(0.0196)	(0.0182)	(0.0186)	(0.0190)
Covdep$_{t-1}$	-1.1669***	-1.0697***	-1.3432***	-1.2623***	-0.6	1.9717*	1.56	1.19
	(0.2761)	(0.3002)	(0.2982)	(0.2922)	(1.2024)	(1.1463)	(1.2062)	(1.1303)

Table 2. (*Continued*)

Method/Dependent variable	(1)	(2)	(3)	(4)	(5)	(6)	(7)	(8)
	Logit Estimation/Crisis Dummy				OLS/NPLs			
(Covdep × Covdep)$_{t-1}$	0.5852***	0.6181***	0.5022***	0.5426***	0.4	0.79	−0.13	0.16
	(0.0962)	(0.1037)	(0.1031)	(0.1024)	(0.4239)	(0.5175)	(0.4449)	(0.4861)
(CAEI$_{t-1}$ × (Covdep × Covdep))$_{t-1}$		−0.01				−0.2849***		
		(0.0168)				(0.0737)		
CAEI$_{t-1}$		0.1703**				1.0381***		
		(0.0713)				(0.2511)		
(CA1$_{t-1}$ × (Covdep × Covdep))$_{t-1}$			0.0106***				−0.01	
			(0.0037)				(0.0110)	
CA1$_{t-1}$			−0.01				0.0768*	
			(0.0113)				(0.0468)	
(CA2$_{t-1}$ × (Covdep × Covdep))$_{t-1}$				0.01				−0.0353[13%]
				(0.0048)				(0.0231)
CA2$_{t-1}$				−0.01				0.02
				(0.0142)				(0.0598)
No. of observations	889	853	853	853	302	290	291	291
% correctly predicted	79.19%	79.37%	78.74%	87.97%	—	—	—	—
Wald Chi-Square (F-statistics)†	116.94	109.54	120.84	113.92	53.76	27.96	45.63	46.66
Prob > Chi-Square (Prob > F)	0.0000	0.0000	0.0000	0.0000	0.0000	0.0000	0.0000	0.0000
Pseudo R2 (R2)	0.13	0.13	0.14	0.13	0.43	0.47	0.44	0.44
Log-Likelihood (Root MSE)	−419.64	−400.56	−399.89	−403.74	6.7	5.92	6.07	6.06

*, **, *** indicate the significance level of 10%, 5%, and 1% respectively. The numbers in parentheses are robust standard errors of estimated coefficients. †Statistics in parenthesis is for the OLS regressions.

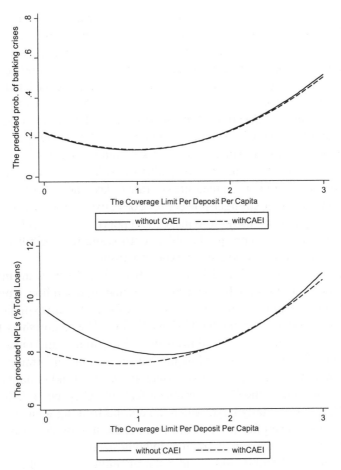

Figure 2. The predicted probability of banking crises and NPLs (% total loans)

Next we turn to the impact of bank insolvency procedures on the credibility of non-insurance and market discipline. Figure 1 shows how we expect insolvency procedures to affect (lack of) market discipline. Strengthened rule based procedures should increase the credibility of non-insurance, increase market discipline and, therefore shift the curve describing the relation between implicit insurance and explicit coverage down. As a consequence, the U-shaped curve should shift down and the minimum probability of banking crisis should occur at a lower level of explicit deposit insurance coverage.

As noted, there is little variation across the countries with respect to formal insolvency procedures. In Section 3 we identified the U.S. and UK as countries with explicit rule based procedures. Other countries differ with respect to the supervisors' powers to apply corrective action procedures as shown in data analyzed in Barth *et al.* (2004). We combine the latter data for Power of Corrective Action (scores 1–6) and the observations for the two countries in one variable (CAEI) by adding one to the UK score beginning in 1998 and two to the U.S. score beginning in 1992. Thereby we want to capture the benefits of explicit distress resolution procedures.[12]

Countries also differ in terms of quality of institutions more generally as reflected in commonly used measures of rule of law and lack of corruption. We hypothesize that stronger powers for corrective action in combination with higher quality of institutions make the supervisors' approach to distress resolution for banks more predictable, contributing to credibility of non-insurance of creditors who are not explicitly insured.

Table 2, columns 2, 3, and 4, and columns 6, 7, and 8 show the impact of institutional variables on the two proxies for market discipline. Columns 2 and 6 show the results when the CAEI-variable interacts with explicit deposit insurance coverage allowing the U-shape to shift. The results show that the CAEI variable shifts the curve downwards with a significant impact on the probability of banking crisis, while the impact on non-performing loans is significant both with respect to shape (interactive term) and minimum level. Figure 2 shows how the CAEI variable affects the U-shaped relationships. The shift is substantially larger when the non-performing loans variable is used as market discipline proxy. Furthermore, the shift downwards is larger when the explicit coverage is small as hypothesized.

In columns 3 and 4, and 7 and 8 the institutional variables CA1 and CA2 combines the CAEI variable for corrective action and two proxies for institutional quality. CA1 is CAEI multiplied by a rule of law score for each country. In CA2 a (lack of) corruption index is used. Column 4 in Table 2 shows a substantial improvement in banking crisis prediction when the corruption variable interacts with both CAEI and deposit insurance coverage.

---

[12]Barth, Caprio and Levine multiply their score for power with the existence of a formal capital ratio triggering intervention. We do not use this multiplicative term that makes the score for, for example, the UK zero. The existence of a formal trigger capital ratio for intervention by supervisors may only reflect how Basel capital requirements have been expressed in formal rules. Many countries have accepted the Basel rules without explicit reference to them in formal rules for supervisors.

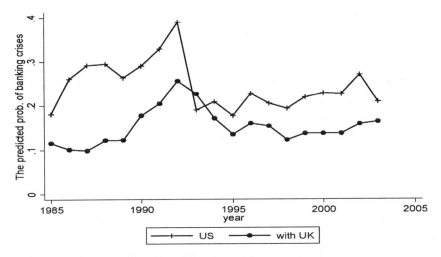

Figure 3. The predicted probability of banking crises for US and UK

In column 7, where market discipline is captured by non-performing loans, rule of law interacting with CAEI has a significant impact.

We do not want to push the interpretation of these results too far here, since so few countries have explicit distress resolution procedures for banks. We can say that corrective action procedures and other institutional factors are relevant for market discipline, although there is not one proxy for quality of institutions that demonstrates a consistent impact on the credibility of non-insurance and market discipline.

Finally in Figure 3 we plot the predicted probability of banking crisis in the U.S. and the UK each year. Changes in the probability depend on shifts in macroeconomic variables as well as shifts in the CAEI variable capturing U.S. and UK distress resolution procedures. There was a shift in the CAEI-score for the U.S. in 1992 when the FDICIA took effect and in 1998 for the UK. Clearly there is a dramatic shift for the U.S. in 1992 but it could depend on macro variables as well.

6. Conclusions

We have argued that efficient incentives of banks' creditors, as well as of shareholders and managers, require predetermined rules for dealing with banks in distress, and a group of creditors that are credibly non-insured.

Insolvency procedures for banks need to be designed taking the special characteristics of banks and their liquidity role into consideration.

An international overview of distress resolution procedures for banks reveal that only the U.S. has implemented a set of predetermined rules for dealing with banks before they reach insolvency while the UK has insolvency law that can be applied to banks. These procedures and rules enhance the predictability with respect to distress-related costs and potential losses for shareholders, managers, and creditors of banks. In the EU on the other hand distress resolution procedures seem to be based on the principle that "there is no blue-print for distress resolution."

To realize the full advantages of cross-border branch organizations, supervisors, central banks and governments must come to accept the principles of home-country control of banks, mutual recognition, and competition between different degrees of deposit insurance coverage depending on a bank's home country. This acceptance does not come easy and requires important institutional reforms of distress resolution procedures in particular. Prompt corrective action procedures could be the minimum requirement that enables host-country supervisors to trust home-country supervision of local branches.

In the last section we provided empirical evidence that market discipline linked to the extent of credible non-insurance of creditors tends to be low when the explicit deposit insurance coverage is very high as well as low. Thus, there is an intermediate degree of coverage that maximizes market discipline. We also tested and found support for the hypothesis that Prompt Corrective Action procedures enhance market discipline and lower the level of explicit deposit insurance coverage that maximizes market discipline. Thus, it could be argued that after the implementation of FDICIA in 1992, there is scope for lowering the deposit insurance coverage in the U.S.

References

Angkinand, Apanard, 2005, "Deposit Insurance and Financial Crises: Investigation of the Cost-Benefit Tradeoff," Claremont Center for Economic Policy Studies, Claremont Graduate University, Working Paper.

Angkinand, Apanard and Clas Wihlborg, 2005, "Deposit Insurance Coverage, Credibility of Non-Insurance and Banking Crisis," Center for Law, Economics and Financial Institutions at CBS (LEFIC), Copenhagen Business School, Working Paper No. 2005–010.

————, 2006, "Bank Insolvency Procedures and Market Discipline in European Banking," in L. Oxelheim (ed.), *Corporate and Institutional Transparency for Economic Growth in Europe*, Elsevier.

Barth, James R., Gerard Caprio Jr. and Ross Levine, 2004, "The Regulation and Supervision: What Works Best?," *Journal of Financial Intermediation*, 13, pp. 205–248.

Caprio, Gerard, Jr. and Daniela Klingebiel, 2003, "Episodes of Systemic and Borderline Financial Crises," The World Bank, Working Paper.

Demirgüç-Kunt, Asli, B. Karacaovali and L. Laeven, 2005, "Deposit Insurance around the World: A Comprehensive Database," World Bank Policy Research Working Paper, Washington, DC.

Economic and Financial Committee of the EU, 2000, "Report on Financial Crisis Management," *Economic Papers*, No. 156.

European Shadow Financial Regulatory Committee, 1998, "Resolving Problem Banks in Europe," Statement No. 1, London.

Goldberg, Lawrence, Richard. J. Sweeney and Clas Wihlborg, 2005, "Can Nordea Show Europe the Way?" *The Financial Regulator*, 10(2), Sept.

Herring, Richard, 2003, "International Financial Conglomerates; Implications for Bank Insolvency Regimes," in G. Kaufman (ed.), *Market Discipline in Banking: Theory and Evidence*, Vol. 1, London and New York: Elsevier, pp. 99–129.

Mayes, David. G., 2004, "The Role of the Safety Net in Resolving Large Cross-Border Financial Institutions," Bank of Finland, Research Paper.

Wihlborg, Clas, (2005), "Basel II and the Need for Bank Insolvency Procedures," *Financial Markets, Institutions and Instruments*, forthcoming.

Wihlborg, Clas and Shubhashis Gangopadhyay with Qaizar Hussain, 2001, "Infrastructure Requirements in the Area of Bankruptcy," *Brookings-Wharton Papers on Financial Services*.

Appendix A: Data Description

Variable	Description	Source
Banking Crisis	The banking crisis dummy, which is equal to 1 in a banking crisis year (both systemic and nonsystemic banking crises), and 0 otherwise	Caprio and Klingebiel (2003)
NPLs	The non-performing loan (% total assets)	IMF
Real GDP Per Capita	GDP per capita (constant 2000 US$. The data is in 100 U.S.$	WDI
Real GDP Growth Rate	GDP growth (annual %)	WDI
CA to GDP	Current account balance (% of GDP)	WDI

Appendix A: (*Continued*)

Variable	Description	Source
Domestic Credit	Domestic credit provided by banking sector (% of GDP)	WDI
M2 to Reserve	Money and quasi money (M2) to gross international reserves ratio	WDI
Inflation	Inflation, consumer prices (annual %)	WDI
Real Interest Rate	Real interest rate (%)	WDI
Explicit Deposit Insurance	The explicit deposit insurance dummy, which is equal to 1 in a year that a country has an formal deposit insurance system, and 0 otherwise.	Demirgüç-Kunt *et al.* (2005)
The Ratio of Coverage Limit to Deposits per Capita (Covdep)	The ordinal data of the ratio of deposit insurance coverage per deposits per capita. The value of this variable is assigned based on a value of the coverage to deposits per capita. This variable is =0 if there is no explicit deposit insurance coverage =1 if the coverage to GDP per capita ratio is between (0, 5) =1.5 if the coverage to GDP per capita ratio is between [5, 10) =2 if the coverage to GDP per capita ratio is between [10, 15) =2.5 if the coverage to GDP per capita ratio is greater than or equal 15 =3 if there is blanket deposit guarantee	Authors' construction Coverage to GDP per capita ratio is from Demirgüç-Kunt *et al.* (2005)
Corrective Action an Early Intervention (CAEI)	CAEI is the aggregated index of 6 survey questions capturing the extent of supervisors' prompt corrective action and intervention power. However, this variable does not consider the existence of a written law on pre-determined level of bank solvency deterioration (see Angkinand and Wihlborg, 2005). This variable is scaled 1–6. The scale is adjusted to 7 for the UK after the 1997 strengthen insolvency procedure, and to 8 for the US during the post-FDICIA (1992-present).	Authors' construction (six survey questions are from Barth *et al.*, 2004)
CA1	CA1 = CAEI × the rule of law index. The rule of law and order index with the scale of 1–6; high values indicate better quality of law and order.	Rule of Law Index is from International Country Risk Guide
CA2	CA2 = CAEI × the corruption index. The corruption index with the scale of 1–6; high values indicate less corruption.	Corruption Index is from International Country Risk Guide

Apanard Angkinand is an assistant professor of economics at the University of Illinois at Springfield. Clas Wihlborg is a professor of finance at Copenhagen Business School and a visiting professor at University of California at Riverside.

Policy Panel: Where to from Here?

Comments on Cross-Border Banking: Regulatory Challenges

Cesare Calari*
The World Bank

Good afternoon. I would like to thank the Chicago Fed and Michael Moscow and George Kaufman for their hospitality. Being from the World Bank, I would like to confine my comments to the implications of cross-border banking for developing countries. And I would like to make three points.

First, it is critical that regulators continue to open up their banking systems to international competition. This applies to all countries, industrialized as well as developing. Research is relatively clear that foreign entry in banking helps improve stability, access to credit, and the efficiency of the financial system (Barth, Caprio, and Levine, 2006). To be sure, the impact depends very much on the domestic environment. For example, Martinez-Peria and Garcia-Herrero find that foreign banks' local claims (through branches and subsidiaries) tend to be smaller, relative to their cross-border claims, in countries that limited banking freedom, such as through regulatory barriers. On the other hand, foreign banks tend to be more active in countries with better business opportunities, and where entry requirements, information, and startup costs are lower. And countries with a greater share of local claims by foreign banks tend to enjoy more stable foreign financing compared with countries that depend on cross-border flows. Thus authorities interested in increased entry and competition need to focus on regulatory costs and barriers, as well as on business opportunities, or what is often referred to as the investment climate. If non-financial sector firms can not find profitable opportunities, banks likely will not find attractive opportunities for themselves.

Foreign bank entry is particularly important for developing and transition economies where access to finance is typically limited to the well-connected elite. The political economy of financial reform in this environment is brilliantly presented in a book that you are probably familiar with, being by two economists from the University of Chicago: Ragurham Rajan, currently chief economist at the International Monetary Fund, and Luigi Zingales (*Saving Capitalism from the Capitalists*). The message from the book should resonate in this city as well as with everybody that has ever tried to do financial sector development work in developing countries. In that kind of contest, reform cannot be only a matter of economics, but it is very much a matter of breaking up excessive concentrations of power and of fostering open, inclusive, and democratic societies. Foreign entry and the competition and know-how that go with it are critical to achieving this goal. Thus, Clark, Cull, and Martinez (2005), using firm-level survey data for 79 countries, in addition to the Barth *et al.* database find that enterprises in countries with more foreign banks rated high interest rates and access to long-term loans as *lesser* obstacles to enterprise operations and growth. And the effect is highly statistically significant. True, larger enterprises are more likely to report improvements, but smaller enterprises also seem happier in countries with more foreign banks, and this effect appears to be robust.[1] As noted above, contestability, including through lower barriers to foreign entry, also improves banking stability (Barth, Caprio, and Levine, 2006), which then benefits smaller and newer firms.

The second point I would like to make is that, in addition to bringing in foreign banks, it is important, particularly for developing countries, to diversify entry across all countries. Countries in East Asia that relied heavily on Japanese banks experienced a severe shock that contributed greatly to the Asian crisis when these banks retreated due to problems at home. Similar shocks could be expected in those Latin American countries that are heavily exposed to Spanish banks if problems were to arise in the latter banking market. Our recommendation to our client countries, therefore, is not only to bring in foreign banks, but also to make efforts to diversify their presence across the country of origin.

---

[1]Of course one might get such results if foreign banks tend to be attracted to countries where the financial market works well anyway. To control for this, the authors also looked at enterprises' opinions about access to nonbank finance. It turns out that the presence of foreign banks has no significant impact on the responses to the control question, encouraging us to take the main results seriously.

However, this raises a real concern, namely that this recommendation may compound the coordination demands on developing country supervisors at a time when so many other demands arise due to, among other things, Basel II. In fact, one could imagine even with three to four home-country authorities that needed to be consulted, that these demands could actually overwhelm the limited supervisory capacity. Supervisors in countries adopting the more advanced variance of Basel II will have to acquire advanced technical skills in order to be able to apply the complex formula in pillar 1 and to use the supervisory discretion in pillar 2. Yet, their ability to retain qualified staff would be stretched severely due to the increased market value to the private sector of this staff and to the structures imposed by public sector pay. We think that for many countries Basel II is far too complex, and would note that no industrial country relied on a heavy hand of regulation when it was in its "industrializing" phase. In addition to differences in views as to the role of government, this may well have been because at that time scarce human capital at that stage were at a high premium.

This leads me to my conclusions and basically to a call for simplification, which would be possible with greater reliance on market discipline. Alan Blinder once called for a reform of the U.S. Income Tax Code that would make it simple enough for a Ph.D economist to understand and one that could fit on a postcard. Avinash Persaud, a noted financial economist, later argued that this test perhaps could be applied to bank regulation. Yet Basel II is enormously complicated in large part because it tries to have supervisors take the place of markets which, as the Soviets discovered decades ago, takes continuously more complicated planning manuals. Perhaps more ominously, even before Basel II is in force, recent surveys of international bankers showed that their chief concern nowadays is the complexity and cost of regulatory compliance. As this was discussed by Nick Le Pan recently, I shall not go into much detail, except to say that perhaps there is a need for a new model and one in which the supervision supports market discipline, rather than trying to second guess it. Here in Chicago two years ago, a conference on market discipline reminded us that the third pillar of Basel II should actually be the first pillar and the first line of defense against unsafe banking. The shadow regulatory committee has come to a singular conclusion and made a singular recommendation. Thus, Barth, Caprio, and Levine (2006) make a similar point, except based on a large cross-country sample. After reviewing evidence on bank regulation supervision in 152 countries, both industrialized and developing, they find the support for a system based on market discipline, but little or no evidence in favor of capital requirements or supervision at least in countries with weak institutional environments. And their bad news is that all but ten countries in the world have such weak environments! Besides the theoretical and empirical underpinnings, a model for regulation based on market discipline has the advantage of not stretching supervisory capacity at the time of increased cost border banking.

An approach to regulation grounded, but not relying entirely, on market discipline, is particularly important for nascent democracies, where institutional development lags in a number of areas: the functioning of checks and balances, the independence and skill of the media, and the development of the judiciary. Without these elements in place, abuses of supervisory discretion should be a top concern. In one low-income country, supervisors do everything from setting bankers' bonuses to conducting feasibility studies for bank entry. Imagine the scope for corruption with these powers! Where it is recognized that market discipline is important, supervision then can be crafted to support this process. At present, the Basel Core Principles are all about the information that banks need to disclose to supervisory authorities so that they can determine the health of a bank. If supervision were to be more concerned about supporting market discipline, the attention would be more devoted to compelling and verifying the disclosure of information by banks and meting out penalties for false or deliberately misleading compliance. True, there is always scope here too for corruption, but when more information is put out to the public, its availability can serve as a check on corruption. Supervisors' hands are often checked by political authorities, who may be defending a variety of vested interests, including their own positions, rather than maximizing social welfare. But where private funds are at risk, market monitoring will not be so shy about exerting pressure on risky banks to behave more prudently.

Where banks operate on a cross-border basis, it is entirely possible that local markets will become to be dominated by foreign institutions, raising the concern that market discipline is impractical. Of course, there will be market discipline operating in home markets, as for say Citibank in U.S. and world capital markets. This may, however, provide little comfort to local authorities who are concerned that a local subsidiary could fail without support by the parent. As we heard earlier at this conference, in Mexico the authorities are considering compelling the issuance of some debt or equity on local markets. This proposal merits serious consideration. We would point out that supervisory authorities' focuses should be on new licenses (the quality of new entrants), supporting disclosure, as just described, and the closure of failing institutions, with the market being the main monitor after entry and before closure. This New Zealand model is one that we would urge on small developing countries — understanding that in world financial markets, the vast majority of developing countries are tiny.

So I would close urging developing country authorities to take stock of whether they have the infrastructure and meet the preconditions — in terms of market foundations and availability of information — to consider moving towards the adoption of Basel II. If the answer is no, their attention and scarce resources should be focused on addressing these priority areas, rather than rushing into a flawed — and dangerous — implementation of the new capital standard.

References

Barth, James R, Gerard Caprio, Jr. and Ross Levine, 2006, *Rethinking Bank Regulation: Till Angels Govern*, Cambridge and New York: Cambridge University Press.

Garcia-Herrero, Alicia, and Soledad Martinez-Peria, 2005, "The Mix of International Banks' Foreign Claims: Determinants and Implications for Financial Stability," Banco Espana, Documentos de Trabajo, No. 0525.

Peek, Joseph, and Eric Rosengren, 2000, "Collateral Damage: Effects of the Japanese Bank Crisis on Real Activity in the United States," *American Economic Review*, 90(1), pp. 30–45.

Rajan, Raghuram and Luigi Zingales, 2003, *Saving Capitalism from the Capitalists: Unleashing the Power of Financial Markets to Create Wealth and Spread Opportunity*, New York: Crown.

*Cesare Calari is vice president of the financial sector at the World Bank.

Where to from Here?: Comments

Christine Cumming*
Federal Reserve Bank of New York

This conference has explored the challenges in supervising global financial firms, challenges that have preoccupied the Group of Ten (G10) supervisors since the mid-1970s. Starting with the early work of the Basel Committee and the Basel Concordat, banking regulators and central banks have long sought to ensure that all internationally active banks are subject to effective global supervision.

In the 1990s, as a global management model replaced a loosely affiliated regional structure at most large banks, clarifying the division of supervisory responsibilities between home and host countries took on added urgency. Host banking supervisors in the major financial centers found that key decision-making and risk monitoring were frequently centralized in the home country. The emergence of cross-sector financial conglomerates and the shared nature of capital and funding posed questions about how management would set priorities across sectors, especially in times of financial distress, and about how supervisors might detect problems and coordinate their activities.

The need for greater clarity motivated the initial work of the Joint Forum.[1] The Joint Forum observed the dilemma that global financial institutions were managing themselves along global business lines while supervisors focused on legal entities. To advance supervisory practice, the Joint

---

[1]The Joint Forum is sponsored by the three major international regulatory committees and consists of banking, securities and insurance supervisors. Its first major published work was Joint Forum, 1999, *Supervision of Financial Conglomerates*, Basel: Bank for International Settlements. Of particular interest are Section D, "Framework for Supervisory Information Sharing", and Section E, "Principles for Supervisory Information Sharing".

Forum advocated a series of cross-sector principles in areas such as capital and information sharing. Contemporary supervisory practice has incorporated much of the information-sharing principle. U.S. banking supervisors, for example, have developed much closer relationships with banking supervisors in the home countries of banks operating in the U.S. and in the major financial centers where U.S. banks operate. More, of course, remains to be done.

This conference has placed special emphasis on the supervision of banks and other institutions active in the emerging markets. The wave of foreign direct investment in financial institutions in the late 1990s, discussed in the first panel of this conference, has in many countries raised the share of direct foreign ownership of the banking system substantially, in some to over 50 percent. Consequently, financial authorities in emerging market countries have a substantial stake in the supervision of global financial institutions.

A study produced by G10 and emerging markets' central banks in 2004 underscored the considerable benefits of foreign direct investment while pointing out some key issues.[2] Of particular interest to this audience, central banks and supervisors of countries with the highest share of foreign ownership were concerned with the quality of the operation of their banking and capital markets, that is, the availability of credit to the national economy and the liquidity of national markets.

The interest of host-country central banks and supervisors in domestic credit and liquidity conditions reflects the central role that disruptions to credit and liquidity play in causing subpar economic performance and even financial crisis. Credit and liquidity in this context are inextricably linked. Credit quality, especially of financial firms, underpins financial market liquidity and an institution's access to liquidity. Credit availability reflects the ability of credit-granting institutions to bridge the maturity and other intermediation gaps with liquidity.

In recent times, the availability of both liquidity and credit in the global markets has expanded, with emerging market countries among the beneficiaries. Markets today are frequently described as "awash with liquidity," except in periods of recession or financial disturbance. Borrowers,

---

[2]Committee on the Global Financial System, 2004, *Foreign direct investment in the financial sector of emerging market economies*, Basel: Bank for International Settlements, as well as *Ibid.*, 2005, *Foreign direct investment in the financial sector — experiences in Asia, central and eastern Europe and Latin America*, Basel: Bank for International Settlements.

especially those at the more uncertain end of the credit spectrum, have seen credit constraints relaxed. The reasons are not controversial. Many factors have contributed to the expansion of liquidity and credit, including the diversity of risk-management strategies or market "views," a result of the large and shifting number of market participants; the use of active credit, liquidity and market risk management by market participants, aided by communication and technology advances; the growth of risk-bearing capacity with the profitability and capital strength of the financial sector and the growth of income and wealth more generally; and the progressive strengthening of market infrastructure by central banks, regulators, and the private sector.

Fostering capital markets alongside banking markets is one way to limit the overall risk to the credit and liquidity availability within an economy. One benefit of the wave of foreign direct investment in financial institutions is the development of domestic securities and other capital markets in many emerging market countries. Capital markets matter because they can continue to function even when banking markets are suffering distress, helping to mitigate potential credit and liquidity crunches. That was certainly true in the United States when, for example, the capital markets provided continued credit to large, high-quality borrowers even as the severe banking problems in the early 1990s constricted bank credit.

Why worry then about the impact of foreign ownership of financial firms on the credit and liquidity conditions in host countries? One reason is that the financial system has economized on both in the last twenty years. The large buffers to systemic shocks in the financial system once took the form of top credit ratings and high liquid asset ratios at the major financial institutions. These buffers have been replaced by much bolstered capital levels and more active risk management, including management of credit ratings and liquidity. Nonetheless, management — or external events — can alter the risk profiles of large financial firms rapidly and even dramatically.

A second reason is that a high degree of foreign ownership of banks makes both credit availability and liquidity dependent on the behavior of foreign institutions. While these institutions may be a source of financial innovation, technical know-how, market liquidity, and stability in domestic crises, domestic markets in the host country are vulnerable to changes in the business strategy of foreign banks in the host country. Changes in strategy can reflect changes in the financial health of the firm and developments in other parts of its business. Microeconomic decisions within the firm can have macroeconomic repercussions in the emerging market economy. That impact can be exacerbated when foreign ownership is concentrated in a small numbers of banks, or when foreign owners hail from one country.

A third reason is that credit and liquidity may be correlated with other risk factors at the macroeconomic level. The mature economies are only occasionally reminded of this — during major recessions or at the end of asset bubbles, for example. For emerging market countries, however, the risk of the "perfect storm" — the confluence of adverse outcomes that generates severe financial stress — has been significant in the post-war era.

Thus, the global financial system is highly dependent on the quality of supervision of financial strength and liquidity by the home country supervisor, but the host-country supervisor needs mechanisms for reliance. Supervisory information sharing and harmonized standards such as the Basel Capital Accord have helped to strengthen the oversight of global institutions. But supervisory information sharing across borders poses issues of efficient coordination. As global financial institutions expand their activities in emerging market countries, the coordination needed between home-country and host-country supervisors has become more complex and resource-intensive.

Transparency is an important supplement to supervisory information sharing, and one that has the potential to reduce both regulatory burden for financial institutions and coordination problems among supervisors, as discussed in the fourth panel. We have not really innovated and invested enough to make financial institutions more transparent and easier to benchmark against their peers. For example, we still seem tied heavily to the conventional paper-based financial statement. Spreadsheet software, for example, would provide the ability to "drill down" from a simple balance sheet or income statement to see details that would illuminate business line results or geographic exposures, presumably without reaching the point of revealing proprietary or vital competitive information.

Coordination especially matters in the supervision of troubled financial institutions, an issue covered by the last two panels. The ultimate test of private corporate governance, even in the presence of regulatory oversight, is how the firm responds to a failed business strategy and the attendant financial distress. In virtually all jurisdictions, the board of directors has a fiduciary duty to maximize the value of the firm. Making strategic decisions when the firm is troubled requires a hard-headed assessment of the competitiveness of the firm and its strategy. It requires consideration of the conditions and strategy necessary to turn around the financial institution or even contemplation of the potential obsolescence of the firm's services in light of substitute products or delivery methods. Cross-border mergers of firms help to deepen markets for emerging market financial institutions and their businesses, providing greater opportunity for the board of directors to arrange for the disposition of the firm's assets when it no longer makes sense to shoulder on.

In that vein, in 2002 an *ad hoc* group of central bank economists and lawyers studied the issues of legal uncertainty and complexity related to the resolution of cross-border financial institutions.[3] They found that the time from onset of financial distress to entry into resolution has shortened dramatically. As their report notes, it is widely agreed that resolution by the firm's management and board of directors through a sale, if necessary, is preferable to a court-supervised or regulator-administered insolvency process. Given the need for active financial management to preserve value, getting assets into the hands of new financial managers quickly is a priority, especially because the value of assets decays as the insolvency process drags on.

As a corollary, that paper argues, insolvency should be seen as a last resort, and therefore should be fast and efficient. The group noted the important role played by international comity, the deference of one court to another, and the substantial progress made in international forums to clarify the applicable law to many securities and derivatives matters. One such forum has been the work of the Hague Convention that has recently sought to clarify the applicable law applying to securities held in depositories.

These issues have prompted many global firms to revisit their liquidity strategy and approach to raising and deploying capital. In doing so, risk managers and attorneys are identifying areas for further progress in the legal arena. Events in Argentina earlier in this decade and the ongoing Yugobank case have revealed new issues and uncertainties associated with the choice of legal entity, subsidiary or branch, in operating outside the home country. Issues such as the appropriate insolvency regime, universal (or single entity) versus territorial insolvency continue to be debated. And uncertainties still exist about establishing priorities, approaches to administration

---

[3]Contact Group on the Legal and Institutional Underpinnings of the International Financial System, 2002, *Insolvency Arrangements and Contract Enforceability*, Basel: Bank for International Settlements.

and the treatment of intercompany exposures in the case of failing financial conglomerates.

As this conference indicates, we have had a well-defined, well-studied set of cross-border financial issues for at least a decade. The issues merit further study because the environment is evolving and the accumulation of new experience illuminates the underlying issues. Moreover, as financial markets continue to develop and deepen, such as the markets for financial businesses, the potential increases for private sector resolutions of failing financial firms in lieu of official intervention.

How might the agenda of cross-border regulatory issues evolve over the next decade? To enrich the menu of possibilities, consider an approach based in the decision sciences. The approach evaluates issues at the periphery — a look for developments on the horizon.[4] Using this technique, admittedly an exercise of imagination, let me conclude with three areas for possible attention by researchers and policymakers.

The integration of the large, rapidly growing economies of Asia, particularly China and India, into the global trading system is one such issue. While hardly a peripheral development as a macroeconomic phenomenon, the impact of Asia's expansion on the nature of cross-border financial activity and intermediaries remains a distant concern. It's worth recalling that the emergence of the United States as a financial power coincided with its rise as an industrial power in the late 1800s and early 1900s. In that example, the needs of a large industrializing power with scarce labor and large infrastructure need required innovation, such as the extensive development of capital markets and the creation of the modern business corporation to raise capital while limiting liability. In contrast, Asia's large and growing workforce but other managerial and technical needs may drive a different set of financial innovations.

A second issue is the impact of changing demographics in the United States and many other counties on financial activity. Until fairly recently, the financial system was characterized by the scarcity of capital and liquidity. Could we return to that scarcity as baby boomers age and spend down their savings while countries such as China and India develop a middle class with comparable needs for borrowing in order to bring forward the consumption of housing, automobiles, and other long-lived assets? Much economic literature suggests very weak links between demographic structure and asset

---

[4]George S. Day and Paul J.H. Schoemaker, 2005, "Scanning the Periphery," *Harvard Business Review*, November, pp. 135–148.

values.[5] But even if financial markets smooth demographic influences on saving and investment patterns globally, how they do so may raise new issues in the supervision of cross-border activities, especially if credit needs are growing elsewhere in the global economy.

A third issue is the potential for technology to further reshape the payments system. Rapid technology change is creating a demand for immediate payments. That demand is currently small, but the potential can be seen in the burgeoning technology for tracking physical goods. The ability to link payment directly to the delivery of goods or services with certainty is something that only cash today can deliver. Still, it is not hard to imagine that some combination of handheld devices and a debit instrument might achieve a borderless "virtual" service and that some nontraditional provider might introduce it. How would we supervise or handle financial problems in such a service? In another portion of the payments universe, the desire by financial firms and corporations to economize on liquidity and collateral are increasing pressures to integrate and simplify the global payments system. How could more harmonization and integration of payment systems affect the number of such systems operating globally today, especially in light of the economies of scale in payments systems?

Christine Cumming is first vice president at the Federal Reserve Bank of New York. The views expressed in these comments are the author's and not those of the Federal Reserve Bank of New York or the Federal Reserve System. The author has benefited from discussions and suggestions from Chris Calabia, Linda Goldberg, Joyce Hansen, Marc Saidenberg, and Joe Sommers.

[5] James M. Poterba, 2001, "Demographic Structure and Asset Returns," *Review of Economics and Statistics*, 83, November, pp. 565–584.

Designing the Home–Host Relationship to Support in Good Times and Bad: Trans-Tasman Developments

Adrian Orr*

Reserve Bank of New Zealand

The high degree of foreign ownership of banks operating in New Zealand puts the Reserve Bank of New Zealand (RBNZ) at one extreme of the "home-host" prudential regulation spectrum. The RBNZ has been working actively to make its important and necessary host role both welcoming and effective.

New Zealand has a vibrant economy that has an open capital market and floating exchange rate. However, New Zealand is heavily reliant on foreign capital (private sector net external liabilities are some 80 percent of GDP) with nearly half of this intermediated through New Zealand's banking system. The soundness of the financial system — and banks operating within it — is very important for economic welfare.

Only two of the 16 banks registered in New Zealand are domestically owned, accounting for just 2 percent of financial system assets. Four Australian-owned banks account for around 85 percent of New Zealand's financial system assets, with just one of these banks accounting for around one-third.

1. The Trans-Tasman Home–Host Perspective

For the RBNZ, a strong relationship with home country regulators — especially Australian — is critical given the very high level of bank foreign ownership.

The Australian Prudential Regulation Authority (APRA) is an integrated regulator of Australia's financial services industry. The APRA operates primarily under a statutory requirement to protect Australian depositors. By contrast, the RBNZ Act requires it to promote the maintenance of a sound and efficient financial system, or to avoid significant damage to the system from the failure of a registered bank.

The Reserve Bank's systemic focus comes in part from its other duties such as monetary policy implementation, liquidity and foreign reserves management, payments systems oversight, and lender of last resort. These activities provide the RBNZ considerable insight into the health of the economy and its institutions, as well as economies of scale and scope in undertaking prudential regulatory activities.

The systemic focus also stems from a preference for self-discipline (for example, director attestation) and market discipline (for example, disclosure) in the financial sector — rather than a reliance on regulatory discipline. The RBNZ remains wary of introducing moral hazard into the risk-management responsibilities of banks.

The RBNZ's approach thus allows banks operating in New Zealand to adopt their parent bank's rules and avoid compliance duplication in many areas. Foreign regulator or parent bank risk-management rules can be utilized, so long as the New Zealand bank board attest to their suitability and disclose this decision.

The difference in the breadth of tasks, regulatory objectives, and style of regulation has thus allowed APRA and the RBNZ to develop strong synergies in meeting their regulatory obligations, while also avoiding significant duplication and unnecessary cost from cross border regulation. The APRA-specific rules are utilized by all of New Zealand's large banks.

2. Managing Crises

It is important to recognize that the high level of foreign ownership of banks in New Zealand does not translate into foreign ownership of the financial system. The financial system is defined by the payment and settlement systems, financial markets (currency, debt, equity, and foreign exchange), as well as the financial institutions that operate within it — banks and nonbanks. The regulator's responsibilities, and the legal and tax system, are important defining factors also.

Shocks to the financial system can and do happen. The nature and source of the shock will also have different implications for the home and host regulator and the optimal national response. This places limits on the extent to which home and host regulators incentives remain the same.

Divergence in national interests can arise for several reasons, irrespective of how good the home–host relationship may be. These differences include: statutory objectives; the cross-country allocation of capital, risk, and funding; perceptions of whether a specific bank crisis is systemic; and techniques for responding to bank distress.

Country-specific crisis management tools, policies, and frameworks are thus necessary, especially in the case of New Zealand where the banking sector is both very important and had such a high level of foreign ownership. The requirement for Australian regulators to act in the best interests of Australian depositors also raises the chance of national interests diverging in the event of a financial crisis.

Over recent years, the RBNZ has worked hard on enhancing its relationship with APRA, with some outputs including a *Terms of Engagement* for coordinated implementation of Basel II, and the recently established *Trans-Tasman Council on Banking Supervision*.[1] There are other enhancements including staff secondments and shared training between regulators and joint regulator visits to Australian-owned banks operating in both countries.

The Terms of Engagement for Basel II implementation sets out a shared intent to implement Basel II in a way that preserves each supervisor's right to set its own minimum levels of capital, while at the same time seeking to reduce compliance costs where possible. It also lays out the home–host supervisory requirements in an effort to utilize each other's comparative advantage to and share information and supervisory reviews.

The Trans-Tasman Council on Banking Supervision comprises the chief executives of both countries' central banks and treasuries and of APRA. Its main goal is to promote the maximum coordination, cooperation, and harmonization of trans-Tasman bank regulation where sensible. The existence of the council does not derogate from national obligations and responsibilities.

The first order of business for the *Council* has been to identify any legislative changes to ensure that the RBNZ and APRA assist each other in the performance of their regulatory responsibilities at least regulatory cost.

---

[1] See http://www.rbnz.govt.nz/finstab/banking/supervision/index.html for details.

This legal approach recognizes that while national interests can diverge, it is possible to improve the ability of each regulator to support the other in times of crisis.

Amongst other things, such legislative change provides the RBNZ more confidence that the NZ board of a bank, and/or statutory manager, can maintain the appropriate legal and operational control over necessary banking functions in times of a crisis. Ministers are currently considering these proposed legal changes to the relevant Australian and New Zealand laws.

It is early days for the Council and Basel II engagement, however, some of the early lessons for the RBNZ have been:

- *Recognize that there are two separate financial systems.* This implies a limit to the home–host relationship.
- *Recognize that national interests, purposes, and incentives can differ in a crisis.* Working to identify and reduce the areas of potential divergent interests ahead of a crisis is extremely useful.
- *Utilize the benefits that come from prudentially regulating from the perspective of a central bank.* The focus on the financial system as a whole better enables us to dovetail with the home regulator's focus on the individual bank and banking group.
- *Agreeing on resolution procedures in advance.* There is a potential difficulty of a small country negotiating with a larger one in the heat of a crisis, and so pre-positioning is important.

Adrian Orr is deputy governor and head of financial stability at the Reserve Bank of New Zealand.

An Overview of Cross-Border Bank Policy Issues

Eric Rosengren*
Federal Reserve Bank of Boston

Cross-border issues are generated by a fundamental problem, national borders are a political not an economic construct. In fact, politicians are well aware that the construction of nation borders which may make political sense may nonetheless have negative economic consequences. For example, one of the major features of economic history in the United States was that the founding founders realized that borders were a significant impediment to economic growth and did not allow states to impede interstate trade. Similarly, the cost of borders has become more generally appreciated as Europe has moved to a more integrated economic model and countries around the world have sought to form alliances that would reduce the economic costs of borders. Because of the economic costs of borders, not surprisingly, borders have created cottage industries designed to avoid some of the costs of borders as they apply to financial institutions. The emergence of tax and bank havens are the natural response of countries competing for jobs and tax dollars by offering financial institutions legal ways to avoid some of the most onerous features of borders.

When borders are created, financial institutions that frequently consider themselves borderless in terms of their corporate governance and risk management are confronted by competing political pressures to adapt to the customs and social goals within the national border. Financial institutions are often considered critical industries because of their role in the transmission of monetary policy and their role in providing financing to domestic industries. Recognizing this, politicians often use borders to push local social goals on financial institutions. This can result in incentives to loan to particular industries, help finance economically disadvantaged groups, or comply with a myriad of regulations that may alter the terms of financial transactions. Thus, the goals of a financial institution to seek the highest risk-adjusted rate of return, may conflict with the priorities of the government. This is particularly true during times of economic distress. During such times, the financial institution and the home-country regulator tend to be primarily concerned with maintaining the equity invested in the country without impairing the financial condition of the parent, while the host-country regulator often is confronted with government goals of protecting depositors and borrowers from economic dislocation.

This paper is going to examine the incentives created by borders. Before analyzing appropriate public policies, it is important to understand the incentives that borders create for financial institutions. The next section will review the incentives to financial institutions and financial regulators created by borders. The second section will examine the implications for bank regulatory and supervisory policies. The final sections will focus on some of the broad public policy issues that remain unresolved.

1. Incentives Created by Borders

Global financial institutions are increasingly complex, creating the need for sophisticated management information systems as they span across increasing number of countries and business lines. This complexity generates a need for more centralization of corporate governance and risk management, and encourages senior management to have a more global perspective.

At the top of the organization, shareholders and the board of directors focus on performance of the entire company. This has created the need for enterprise-wide corporate governance. Information provided to shareholders and analysts generally focus on the entire organization, and it rarely provides any significant data by legal entity or by nation. Instead, most information is provided based on how management utilizes it, which tends to be by business line. Similarly, review of confidential board of directors' packets at several global financial institutions indicates relatively little information by legal entity or by country of origin except on an exception basis.

Risk-management has become increasingly focused on measuring and monitoring enterprise-wide risk. This is primarily designed to service the board of directors and senior managers, but it is also driven by regulatory necessity, such as the new Basel II proposal where risk exposures and capital for the entire organization need to be calculated. While there are centralized risk management structures set up at most global financial institutions, it is important for risk managers to also be present in the business line or in legal entities. While in some companies risk managers report to business line heads, increasingly they are reporting through the centralized risk structure to prevent potential conflicts of interest.

With managerial focus and risk calculated for the entire enterprise, most firms think of capital as being freely transferable across the company. By being part of a global financial firm, a business line or legal entity can derive significant diversification benefits. In essence, major decisions made by firms are often made as if they are borderless and firms focus on the capital needed for the portfolio of risks over the entire firm. This enterprise-wide focus can generate significant issues when regulations require managing operations within a particular national border. First, borders generate inefficient use of capital. If each subsidiary needs to be capitalized as if it is a stand-alone firm, the diversification benefits are lost, resulting in overcapitalized firms based on the sum of capital from the subsidiaries.

Second, politicians tend to focus on legal entities within their jurisdiction. As a result, most regulators are required to generate rules and reporting based on domestic legal entities. In addition, politics often requires financial institutions to abide by a variety of consumer protection, depositor protection, and investor protection rules that are often intended to fulfill social goals through the financial intermediary. As rules and regulations across countries diverge, firms are conflicted between the national focus of most of their compliance system, and the company focus of most of their management systems.

While in general, borders are undesirable for global firms, they do provide some advantages in terms of the ability to arbitrage across national jurisdictions. Particularly if the home country has onerous taxes and regulations, the presence of national borders can provide opportunities for firms to arbitrage. The more complex the differences across borders, the more incentives for firms to manipulate internal transfer pricing to minimize tax and regulatory differences across borders. In addition, when experiencing duress, a subsidiary structure certainly allows the parent to decide whether to recapitalize. However, most firms faced with this problem are conflicted whether to abandon, support, or partially support their subsidiary.

2. Regulator Incentives Generated by Borders

Regulators only have the ability to enforce regulations within their national borders. As a host regulator of a large legal entity, they have little power to impose requirements that extend to the global parent. The host regulator cannot influence the extraterritorial activities of the parent and receive only limited financial information and internal information that is potentially available to the home supervisor. These impediments make it quite difficult to persuade the parent to recapitalize the bank during duress. As the Argentine experience has highlighted, well-capitalized parents may indeed decide to abandon branches or subsidiaries if the financial difficulties become acute. In addition, during times of acute problems, politicians often seek to use financial institutions to mitigate the impact of the crisis on depositors, borrowers, or investors. This results in the host supervisor having different incentives from the parent, and often from the home supervisor. The primary concern of the home supervisor is to prevent problems from the subsidiary causing solvency problems for the entire firm. The primary concern in the host country is finding ways to mitigate problems and possibly encourage additional capital and lending in their country.

These differences in incentives can create significant supervisory issues. Differences across borders can encourage countries to compete in laxity. Borders have created tax and regulatory havens in countries such as Monaco, Luxembourg, and the Cayman Islands. These countries use borders to raise employment and taxes in their countries so firms can avoid taxes or regulations in other countries. However, competition in laxity makes it much more difficult for other countries to meet the broader objectives they seek in taxing and regulating financial institutions. In addition, appropriate regulatory/supervisory policies may be trumped by the desire to promote employment and taxes. This competition could potentially occur where firms outside Europe may seek to find a favorable environment to serve as their home country in Europe.

Borders have also provided politicians an opportunity to indirectly use bank regulation and supervision to promote domestic financial institutions. This has been particularly true in Asia where foreign competitors are often explicitly restricted or encounter numerous regulatory and supervisory impediments not faced by their domestic competitors.

Border issues become most problematic when banks start to experience financial difficulties. Actions by domestic regulators to secure sufficient collateral to protect domestic depositors and encourage continued domestic lending can often be at the expense of the parent company. In the extreme, actions taken by individual country regulators to protect domestic stakeholders may ultimately move the parent from an illiquid to an insolvent situation. This "beggar thy neighbor" potential in a crisis will become increasingly important as global banks further penetrate markets outside their home country.

3. Policy Issues

Currently, many cross-border policy issues are not being addressed because the number of truly global banks is relatively limited. However, the ability of banks to expand domestically in countries such as the United States, Canada, and the UK, are restricted due to competitive concerns, more globally focused acquisitions will be a necessity. One issue that has arisen is the potential conflict between macroeconomic issues and safety and soundness issues. A good example is provided by the Japanese experience in the 1990s. (For a more academic discussion of the cross-border implications of Japanese banking problems see Peek and Rosengren, 1997, 2000; Klein, Peek, and Rosengren, 2002.) Japanese banks had expanded internationally during the 1980s and became major financial participants in global financial markets. When they experienced problems in their domestic economy as a result of declines in stock and real estate markets, they had to shrink their balance sheet to maintain their capital ratios. Concerns with credit availability at home caused implicit and explicit restrictions on these banks that led them to slowly address their nonperforming loan problems. This fear of depressing asset values caused them to dramatically shrink their operations outside of Japan. While the global economy was fortunately performing well at the time, the Japanese pull-back did have consequences in other markets such as the United States real estate market. This is a classic example of a home country exporting macroeconomic problems abroad, an issue that is likely to be even more relevant in the future as more banks become global entities.

A second area that receives growing public policy attention is the potential conflict between domestic safety nets in addressing financial concerns of global financial institutions. Most countries have adopted deposit insurance, but it is intended to protect depositors within their country. At present, the obligations of home and host insurers to meet deposit insurance claims have yet to be fully tested. However, if each deposit insurer's primary concern is to minimize taxpayer exposure in their own country, then protecting depositors can quickly lead to runs on global organizations. Similarly, the lender of last resort role in most countries is focused on maintaining financial stability within national borders. Since the discount window in most countries operates by lending on collateral that receives significant haircuts by the lender of last resort, invoking lender of last resort facilities can lead to pledgeable assets no longer being available and potentially causing spillover problems in other countries.

A third major public policy issue is the desire to create a more level playing field. The new Basel proposal has taken significant strides in creating a more coordinated regulatory environment. However, despite the detailed proposal, the proposal relies on models, and any model based regulation is based on as much art as science. While pillar 2 implementation of Basel may cause differences across nations, the significant discretion available in pillar 1 can cause large regulatory differences across countries. For example, differences in stress calculations of loss given default and choices on through the cycle versus point in time calculations of probabilities of default can lead to vastly different required capital. This is particularly problematic since it involves estimating the tail of the distribution where most financial institutions will not have much historical data. The presence of fat tailed distributions for both credit and operational risk results in difficulty in standardizing capital for areas where many institutions have no recent experience, making it difficult for supervisors to validate and for institutions to do any reasonable backtesting.

While regulations are becoming more standardized across countries, there will be a need for greater coordination in the supervision of institutions. Enterprise risk management at most institutions is focused on risk over the entire organization. For the risk management to be coordinated with the supervisory process there will need to be much more harmonization of supervisory policies across national borders. While some of this activity has begun through the efforts of the Accord Implementation Group of the Basel Committee, as well as formal and informal bilateral coordination, much more will need to be done in the future.

4. Future Issues

Significant cross-border coordination will need to occur as financial institutions are increasingly constrained in growth in their home markets and seek to play a bigger role in global financial markets. However, as an increasing number of institutions span national borders, a conflict is likely to occur where financial institutions are global, but supervision and regulation remain national. While the Basel Accord is a very good first step in understanding how to supervise and regulate global banks, much remains to be done.

Financial institutions play a critical role in transmitting monetary policy, allocating critical bank credit, and often fulfilling other social goals of the countries in which they are active. However, the supervisory and regulatory efforts tend to be focused on the micro-economic issue of solvency and its impact on domestic deposit insurance programs. While these are critically important issues, countries in distress tend to focus on important macroeconomic implications of troubled financial institutions. This conflict between macroeconomic concerns, particularly in host countries with global banks, and microeconomic concerns for safety and soundness, particularly in home countries, will likely be even more important in the future. While it was fortuitous that the withdrawal of Japanese banks from Europe and the United States in the early 1990s did not coincide with problems in those regions, it is likely that in the future home and host countries may experience coincident problems. In such instances, the concerns of macroeconomic stability in the host country are likely to receive far more attention. This problem is complicated by the institutional responsibilities that have evolved in many countries (see Peek, Rosengren, and Tootell, 1999). In many countries, the central bank is primarily responsible for financial stability and macroeconomic policies while a financial supervisory authority is concerned with the safety and soundness of financial institutions. These distinct institutional powers are likely to further complicate disparate national interests. There is also a dynamic angle to this issue. Should future problems be addressed in favor of home country concerns, global banks may be restricted, leading to less substantial roles in host countries.

A second area for future work is whether the deposit insurer and the lender of last resort role can continue to be focused domestically. As the concentration of assets and deposits moves from home to host countries for many global entities, it will become increasingly complicated for policymakers to react to potential solvency issues. Future work should try to develop protocols for addressing illiquidity and insolvency issues in truly global organizations.

A third area that will require much more coordination in a global economy is improving the interaction of bank supervisors. While information flows have improved dramatically with the Basel process, global institutions are still not truly operating on a level playing field.

While progress is being made in obtaining greater cross-border coordination between countries, much more work needs to be done. The speed of consolidation leading to much larger global banks exceeds that of policy makers developing plans for how best to address the issues raised by these institutions.

References

Klein, Michael, Joe Peek, and Eric Rosengren, 2002, "Troubled Banks, Impaired Foreign Direct Investment: The Role of Relative Access to Credit," *The American Economic Review*, 92(3), pp. 664–682.

Peek, Joe and Eric Rosengren, 1997, "Collateral Damage: Effects of the Japanese Bank Crisis on Real Activity in the United States," *The American Economic Review*, 90(1), pp. 30–45.

Peek, Joe and Eric Rosengren, 1997, "The International Transmission of Financial Shocks: The Case of Japan," *The American Economic Review*, 87(4), pp. 495–505.

Peek, Joe, Eric Rosengren, and Geoffrey Tootell, 1999, "Is Bank Supervision Central to Central Banking?" *The Quarterly Journal of Economics*, 114, pp. 629–653.

Eric Rosengren is a senior vice president in charge of the Supervision, Regulation, and Credit Department of the Federal Reserve Bank of Boston.

Index

473